Is The Bible African History

Is The Bible African History

NEIL M.C. SINCLAIR

IS THE BIBLE AFRICAN HISTORY

ISBN 1518737390
ISBN 13: 9781518737398

Published & Distributed by
Dragon & Tiger Enterprises
Cover image: The Neteru: Amon-Ra & Anubis
Photograph of Author: Johno McKernan

Other Books By NEIL M. C. SINCLAIR, M.A.

The Tiger Bay Story

Cardiff Bay Experience

Endangered Tiger – *A Community Under Threat*

Nightmare In Yemen

Tiger Bay Moonshadows – A Play

Online Videos

A Stroll Through Tiger Bay

Tiger Bay Nation

For

WALTER M. SINCLAIR
(1910-1977)

An Afro-Celtic Gentleman

Acknowledgements

As the recipient of a duly appreciated gift from the Muse, I cannot put my hand on my heart and say that *I* began this book alone. Indeed, with ideas wanting to be recorded arriving at such a rapid pace, it apparently started itself as reams of pages began appearing in the autumn of 2014.

Carrying me through the trials and tribulations of this black life however, I owe a debt of gratitude to the classical African musical heritage of Miles Davis, John Coltrane, Milt Jackson, Ben Webster and Coleman Hawkins, among many, many other African-American jazz musicians and amazing vocalists whose innovative melodies and riffs formed the soundtrack of my formative years. For soothing my adolescent angst, The Platters, The Falcons, The Heartbeats, The Chantels and an entire musical catalogue of Rhythm & Blues and Rock & Roll vocalists whose plaintiff calls stretched thousands of miles across the Atlantic Ocean to Tiger Bay on the South Wales coastline also deserve my unfaltering appreciation. Through them the specific black key musical chords of an ancient Africa, though somewhat disguised in the refrains of popular music, served to inspire and validate the person I was meant to be.

And from the continent itself, I recall the African polyrhythmic inspiration of Fela Ransome Kuti and the many hours of Pan-Africanist discussion held at the Kalakuti Republic whilst imbibing the inspirational and hypnotic Juju rhythms of the Afro-beat sound.

Closer to home, my dear friend Olwen Blackman-Watkins was and still is a great lifetime inspiration as is Tiger Bay poet and prophet Leon Charles who saw this book coming.

Of course, there is a multitude of people I should like to thank but to name them all would only do injustice to those omitted. That said however, a special thank you must go to one whose operatic ear was essential to the tone of this work, Frank Andrus Morris, a gracious New York City host who organized the first and well received public reading of this manuscript at his Harlem home on the 16th of September 2015 and another at the Afro-Japanese *Nabe Harlem Restaurant* shortly thereafter.

Ultimately, my profound appreciation also goes to all those who sought out truth, in particular to Aaron Swartz (1986-2013), a courageous young man who fought to make the world a better place but for all his efforts was hounded out of this precious life by the pernicious, overzealous and avaricious pettiness of certain forces lurking within of our globalized patriarchal neo-liberal economic system.

Table of Contents

Preface

All religion is more or less false, but Christianity is all false.

ANONYMOUS

O n the morning of September 20, 2014, while pouring over various notes strewn across my kitchen table, a hand written non-return address letter arrived in the post. Containing a flyer from a Manchester based group identifying itself as a *Gathering Of Christ*, according to the handbill found inside that provenance unknown envelope, this gathering's unique interpretation of the Bible claimed among other things that: *the real Jews were black; the real children of Israel are in the ghettos, inner cities and slums across the four corners of the earth and are the ones suffering on this earth.*

Given that I was already in the process of researching that same topic, indeed in the very throes of compiling a manuscript with the tentative title of *Is The Bible African History*, the mysterious simultaneous arrival of that poignant, controversial and rather radical message on such a pleasant but gloomy Saturday morning came as quite an amazing coincidence.

Seeking answers to this controversially sensitive yet nevertheless intriguing subject had been a long-term obsession of mine, one indeed more recently catalyzed by the research of two French brothers who quite successfully drew similar conclusions in *Did The Pharaohs Write The Bible?* Written by the rabbis Messod and Roger Sabbah, this remarkable work that digs deeply into the intertwining seams of biblical and Egyptian history receives valuable support found in the writings of a wide variety of researchers, including Sigmund Freud. Their erudite work, which also includes the literary output of Immanuel Velikovsky, Ahmed Osman, Ralph Ellis and many other scholars, has helped to further the progress of the thesis being made herein. Besides the latter, many other authors have also come to similar findings after taking a similar route to that proposed here. Thus, given the foregoing there can be no doubt with regard to this subject that a biblical connection to the historical events that took place in the Nile valley is already standing on solid foundations.

Of course, nothing is perfect in this imperfect world, yet nevertheless the truth *is* the Truth and that being so there must have been hundreds if not thousands of researchers throughout the many past centuries who knew instinctively or simply expressed the genetic memory that ancient Egypt really was an African society and indeed the birthplace of what is generally perceived as Greek philosophy.

Suffering much persecution however, over the centuries many of those radical and intrepid truth seekers were severely ridiculed or worse yet forced to endure the drastic misfortune of some unspeakable torture before being burnt at the stake for attempting to uncover truths their current governing classes would have deemed subversive to their vested interests. With much gratitude therefore, and moreover with the hope of doing justice to those who fostered such countervailing beliefs, particularly the belief in a black African origin of the Nile valley civilization, we honour the courageous acts of those who paid the ultimate sacrifice for attempting to rectify contrary elite governed misperceptions or indeed deliberate deceptions. Clearly someone in the establishment has a vested interest in the alternative historical truth not being so.

That situation notwithstanding, although the aforementioned research of the brothers Sabbah strongly supports the conclusion that the Bible's origin is to be found in the land of Egypt, overriding indeed established belief in some mythical Semitic culture that emerged out of the mysterious depths of Mesopotamia, this still leaves open the question of the ethnic origin of the people who lived in the Nile valley.

Geographically speaking of course, Egypt is located on the African continent, but does that mean its history belongs to black Africa? Indeed, connecting Egypt with biblical tradition is one thing, for the purposes of identifying the black African origin of the people of Egypt however and determining moreover that they are the source for what is written in the Bible, it is therefore imperative that the Africanist must also be an Egyptologist, as well as a biblical scholar. Indeed, perhaps even a physicist!

Recent television programmes adding "a little colour" to history in their representations of Ancient Egypt notwithstanding, within the academic subject of Egypt however many references describing who the ancient Egyptians were *not* abound. Never or rarely do such citations state with clarity who they really *were*, a circumstance that leaves the general public in the dark, no pun intended, to decode a purposely camouflaged and vague assumption that conceals an inherent anti-black African bias.

Indeed, since British exploration of Egypt began in earnest after the defeat of Napoleon, over time there has been a quite discernible geographical separation, indeed a surgical excision, if you will, of the very idea that Egypt even belonged to Africa. Though not all British Egyptologists held this view, it has nevertheless become established dogma in the field. Indeed, according to Robert Bauval and Thomas Brophy, the authors of *Imhotep The African*, even the internationally renowned ex-Minister of Egyptian Antiquities, Zahi Hawass proclaimed "in all seriousness, that "Egyptians are not Africans!""[1]

Given such racially chaotic circumstances, such a state of affairs therefore has been a rallying call for those of an Afrocentric persuasion, who of course take the exact opposite view. Thus at the outset, I confess that I gravitate toward that compass position. That said however, this current document is not a pretext for an uncritical, politically correct, Afrocentric navel-gazing glorification of the black African past either. Nor is it an unwarranted regression to the late nineteenth century's discredited pseudoscience experiment in eugenics with its continuing biological warfare offshoot or its now defunct but still functioning pseudoscientific Race Theory of the 19th and 20th centuries that in blatant or reverse forms disgracefully continues in the current 21st century.

Though there is an attempt here to look at history from an African perspective, let us be more enlightened and keep our distance from such aforesaid anti-humanist matters. Rather the purpose of this investigation is intended as a truthful clarification and historical rectification of what lies at the beginning of modern civilization for therein we may find the root cause of the social and militaristic conflicts, particularly those in the so-called Middle East, occurring in the world today.

Granted Egyptologists as well as archaeologists and historians have done a remarkable job of bringing ancient Egypt back to life they do not however own this information, particularly those academic professionals of a white Western bent who are apparently unable to see that the ancient land was literally teeming with black folk and thus as a consequence of their myopia paint a false picture of the state of black life in ancient times.

Therefore, as a consequence of the foregoing myopic academic position on ancient Egypt, no apology is extended to those Egyptologists who continue to maintain the view that Egypt's heritage owes nothing to black Africa. On the other hand, no offence is intended and no intention is made here to disparage the people of modern day Egypt, or the people of Israel for that matter, with regard to the exploration of this investigation. However when it comes to interpreting events that took place long before those current societies were created, it has to be realized that the names *Egypt* and *Egyptian* are linguistic terms derived from the Greek language that have been wittingly or unwittingly used as euphemisms.

Such lexical substitutions however serve only to distort or otherwise deflect attention away from the apparently not so obvious fact that historical events that actually took place on the continent of Africa were events in which black African peoples played a most significant role not only in the development of modern civilization but more pertinently even in the formation of what has become known as the biblical text. Therefore, this intentional misunderstanding and continuous deliberate historical obfuscation cannot be allowed to persist in deafening silence nor subsist without comment or rebuttal.

For African history therefore such a precarious situation is made all the more difficult since it has been thoroughly transposed, concealed and reinterpreted as unassailable biblical legend as a result of its calculated transference into the sanctified pages of the so-called Holy Bible.

Cutting through the sanctity and sacredness that for centuries has surrounded this cherished book to arrive at its African root is therefore not an easy task to accomplish. Nevertheless, for black people to find their rightful place in the history of the family of man, the resurrection and reincarnation of the African soul at the root of Egyptian civilization is the essential hypothetical intention this work intends to substantiate. Therefore and moreover, it is further hoped that the retrieval of this history from the pages of the Bible will be well researched, proved and accomplished by the end of this book.

But however, if *the real Jews were black*, as the Manchester based *Gathering of Christ* propose, who then were the Hebrew people? There were no Jews in ancient times only the followers of the rebellious 18th Dynasty pharaoh Akhenaten and, as this work will demonstrate, these indeed were the devotees of the Yahuds, a native African priesthood. Thus theoretically the Old Testament account of the life of the Jewish people could be interpreted as an historical fiction based on events that did occur but not however in the so-called Middle East but rather on the soil of the African continent and in the realm of African consciousness and African history.

Thus without question, for the reconstitution of Africa's unrecognized past and the restitution of its people in diaspora, a substantive answer to this conundrum is exceedingly essential. For not only does the civilization of ancient Egypt come from black Africa but many other firsts also originated there. The fantasy conical tower of Disneyland fame for example or even the ubiquitous gabled roof seen in cities throughout the modern world are not European at all but in fact Sudanese architectural firsts, as are the chair you sit on, the bed you lie in, and, as will be shown, the Bible you read.

That said however, the humanities constitute the last bastion of prejudice! Nothing more demonstrates this than the fact that in the second decade of the new millennium, after a time when more people in the West have received so-called higher education than at any other time in human history, black people in the major cities of the United States of America are protesting against militarized police brutality carrying placards that say "Black Life Matters!"

And indeed it does, but until it is recognized that the Bible is a falsification of African history most scholastic debate will however be as mere blowing in the wind of highly contentious findings and inconclusive results while the political and social standing of black people in the world today will remain unchanged.

Therefore, it has now become imperative that the racist root of this officially sanctioned and judicially condoned homicidal behaviour be exposed to the light of day. For though at first it may appear controversial to pronounce, the heinous doctrinal source of this pathologically vicious sacrificial practice is nevertheless to be found, as this text will soon demonstrate, in the sacred pages of the Holy Bible.

Conjuring up an unexpected reaction to the subject of this work however was the response I received from a Congolese acquaintance. After previously stating that Africa would only receive respect in the global political sphere if it developed nuclear power, his alarming objection to the biblical project I was conducting was that black Africans, *men* in particular, do not read! This unexpected and indeed unanticipated anti-intellectual response momentarily caused me to reexamine the reason why I was writing this book. Notwithstanding the fact that South Africa, like Israel, does covertly possess such nuclear weapons, this disconcerting feedback however did not dissuade me from continuing for, in any event, I wanted to set the record straight but more importantly my protagonist's own statement provided the solution that determined my resolve. Indeed, if Africa were to acquire nuclear technology for the protection of its children, then Africans, *men* in particular, would have to do *a lot of reading* on the subject of quantum physics! So read they must!

Fortunately for those unfortunate peoples of black African descent who, as a direct consequential result of this multigenerational historical rift, are currently bereft of their souls intact, the movement against the tide of Egyptological opposition toward recognition of Ancient Egypt as a black African reality had its literary foundation laid in the 1950s when Senegalese author Chiekh Anta Diop published *The African Origin of Civilization*. Previously much disparaged and worse ignored, this theory has been somewhat vindicated and furthered by the indefatigable efforts of Robert Bauval & Thomas Brophy whose current unabashed works include, *Black Genesis* and *Imhotep – The African*.

The irony of course is that the Bible falsely asserts that man's inhumanity to man began in the Nile valley with the enslavement of the Hebrews whereas verifiable history however recounts a different truth, tracing the origins of this scourge to the decline of the culture of Sumer into that of an unscrupulous and decadent Babylon which cultivated ambitious long-term intentions of taking over the then known world through imperial conquest.

Creating the Yahwist traditions that continue to instil 'perpetual war for perpetual peace' to this very day, as Gore Vidal describes the current situation, the bullion brokers of Babylon, who sought imperial power by means of the infiltration of the Nile valley civilization through their insidious imposition of monotheism, have metamorphosed and metastasized into their current global manifestation as the dominant Anglo-American and European corporate power structure along with their secret service intelligence agencies.

Therefore, given that the basis for the enslavement and eventual colonization of otherwise innocent African peoples was founded on the Babylonian derived Venetian Convention that they – unlike Renaissance Man – were subhuman and subject to capture, herding like human cattle, and culling, for Africans living near to the end of direct European colonization of the world in the mid 20th century and black people of today living *in the ghettos, inner cities and slums across the four corners of the earth* it was and is still necessary to know if the ancient Egyptians were black Africans or not. For the continent of Africa not only possesses the original people found at the root of humanity's first Post Flood civilization but, equally as important, gold, uranium, diamonds, copper, cobalt, among many other precious metals and raw materials, including petroleum, required by the Western world for the maintenance of its continuing dominance of the planet through control of the global infrastructure necessary for the efficient function of its information technological society. Commodities, of course, acquired at the very detriment to and subsequent disadvantage of the various peoples who currently suffer across the length and breadth of Africa despite their living on one of the world's richest continents.

Moreover, the biological warfare and starvation we witness in Africa on a daily basis is of course the continuing consequence of an historical exploitation. Indeed, the suppression of the freedom of the African commoner is only made possible out of the barrel of a gun. There is no doubt that Ken Sarawiwa, defender of Nigeria's Ogoni people, died at the behest of Western transnational oil companies.

Nevertheless, many theorize that the cause of Africa's lack of development is the result of various African governments' administrative inability to govern but the reality is most African governments are in fact corrupt military operations, subordinate to the International Monetary Fund and the World Bank, designed solely for the benefit of the global corporate greed of massive transnational oil and other companies rather than the need of the people of Africa.

Thus the question to ask is why do modern African governments do what they do? Why do they betray their own people? What powerful aphrodisiac overwhelms their better judgment? Can it be that the reinterpretation of ancient African history as presented in the Bible, as that book has come down to modern society from the Council of Nicea, has weakened their mental resolve and encouraged them under its influence to behave this way because they have a misguided respect, reverence and faith in its veracity?

Indeed, long before the anti-colonial movements brought political, that is to say, as Kwame Nkrumah was eager to point out, *not economic* independence, to many of the countries on the continent, "Missionary-trained Africans were capturing the attention of the colonial administration,"[2] as John Henrik Clarke astutely observed in the *Forward* to Chiekh Anta Diop's *Civilization and Barbarism*. Through the actions of certain Western secret intelligence services, Patrice Lumumba of the Congo, and many other Pan Africanist leaders, indeed one might include the UN's Dag Hammarskjold, were murderously replaced with the aforementioned "Missionary-trained Africans." Even the arrest and incarceration of Nelson Mandela appears to be the result of certain actions taken by the American Deputy Ambassador and United States intelligence services.

Thus, we despair at the current myopia of the narrow-minded African leadership schooled in the economic techniques of the London School of Economics who, influenced by the reinterpretation of ancient African history as presented in the Bible, are only doing their job of weaning their peoples away from the elements of their otherwise so-called animist religions, the Yoruba population of Nigeria for example away from the Orisha, the Bantu peoples from the Muzimu, etc. Therefore, it is not surprising that an indoctrinated leadership would be unaware of what Joseph P. Farrell uncovered in *Yahweh: The Two Faced God*: that the Bible relates the story of its own establishment as "a history of violence punctuated by a series of massacres,"[3] and thus in such a format is therefore dangerous to Africa. And speaking of dangers, this raises the question of whether Africom, created and activated three years prior to the US condoned NATO bombing of Libya, the most advanced country on the continent at the time, and which also orchestrated the most brutal and vicious murder of the champion of Africa, Colonel Muammar Gaddafi, is indeed the prelude to a future African genocide?

Historically speaking, the institutionalized genocidal policy of Roman emperor Diocletian became theoretically formalized by degenerate Venetian economist Giammaria Ortes, plagiarized by Thomas Malthus, exercised by the British empire, and expanded by the American Empire, not only reflected in its massacre of native indigenous populations on the American continent but also in the United States military's 19th century genocide of the Muslim population of the Philippines (no 9/11 required); while in 1915 US Marines gunned down thousands of blacks in Haiti, at about the same time the Germans killed 100,000 of the Herero and Namaqua peoples during the Herero Wars of 1904 to 1907; as Belgium's King Leopold II killed 15 million souls in the Congo during the first and forgotten major holocaust of the 20th century; and finally as the British built the first concentrations camps ever in South Africa. All those souls so mercilessly wiped out. Who are and what indeed motivates these fiendish perpetrators?

Given that the aforementioned is the intolerable consequence of 500 years of an unconscionably brutal Euro-colonization of the planet that began in 1492, clearly there is a hidden agenda for we truly do not know the history of this planet Earth at all. Thus we despair at the myopia of a narrow-minded African leadership and at its current subordination to the strictures and conditionalities of the International Monetary Fund.

Indeed, we are dealing with an IMF ravaged Africa. Thus, under the continuing Anglo-American and World Bank threat of a new land grab and re-colonization or neo-colonization of the entire continent of Africa, to say nothing of the rest of the world, by means of the currently failing, thermonuclear war mongering and destabilizing neo-classical model of the Babylon derived monetarist economic system of corporate globalization today, a truthful answer to this investigation concerning the validation of Africa's vital contribution to the development of modern society, that derived from the philosophical basis of its "Sacred Science," is now all the more necessary and important to Africa's and, for that matter, the world's future survival.

That said however, with regard to such onerous concerns, some may wonder what makes a practicing Taoist, a Welshman of multigenerational Afro-Anglo-Celtic heritage no less, qualified to tackle the historical, biblical, religious and geopolitical issues that the subject of this book proposes to investigate. Although in possession of a certain degree of academic knowledge concerning the subject of the topical issues raised within, it is nevertheless incumbent upon me to admit that I am not a professional Egyptologist, political scientist, physicist or a theologian. As far as the latter category is concerned nevertheless I was raised in Christian belief and born in the Parish of St. Mary the Virgin.

Though slowly slipping into the realm of myth itself, at the beginning of the 20th century old Tiger Bay where St. Mary's church is located was, as described in *The Tiger Bay Story* and *Endangered Tiger – A Community Under Threat*, already a multi-ethnic community that provided a refuge from the racial torment that still afflicts the world today. Indeed, at that time in history, the largest concentration of Africans in the whole of Wales was located in and around Loudoun Square at the heart of the Tiger Bay community.

Therefore, as a result of my 'multicultural' birthplace, it appears that I have nurtured a lifetime of abiding concern for the well-being of the people of the continent of Africa, and as a consequence ultimately studied African history at university.

Nevertheless, separate cultures existing side by side but not integrating, the modern definition of multiculturalism, does not however apply to my place of birth. On the contrary, I grew up in a fully integrated multi-ethnic society with a healthy dose of suspicion that people of colour had played a much greater role in historical affairs than is publicly acknowledged. Indeed, at a time when blatant and *de facto* segregation was widespread in the USA and a covert and sometimes not so subtle "colour bar" was in place in the UK, my youthful imagination was sparked by my Afro-Celtic aunt, Christian Sinclair-Kennard, who told me with such definitive confidence and certitude that Cleopatra was black! Moreover, in an unpublished manuscript of more recent times, Patti Flynn, another Welsh-born Afro-Celtic resident of old Tiger Bay, one who was offered a place at Ruskin College in Oxford, speaks in her research project about *bringing women of colour out of the shadows of history and putting the black back into history*.

In spite of the fact that the protective cocoon of the Tiger Bay community brought some shelter from the harsher realities of racism, the subtle and pernicious imposition of a sense of being a *de facto* second-class individual nevertheless still filtered through. Therefore, it could be assumed that seeing black people in principle roles of human history, to say nothing of them being the authors of the Bible, could be described as some form of psychological overcompensation resulting from an earlier sense of personal and historical inadequacy. Be that as it may, and despite any human frailty or mental debilitation I may personally possess, such a problematic factor on my part does not invalidate the truth of the hidden role black people played throughout the entire length of human history.

Given the racial tension and anxiety that modern Western society inexorably and thus inevitably engenders, the issue of colour therefore, and what it signifies, never veered too far from my perception. Despite this, life goes on and in living it such racially sensitive concerns ebb and flow and you just get on with it. As time moves on however, those earlier, incipient thoughts continue smouldering in the background and by the time one has become a postgraduate student factual backing that supports the idea of black participation in crucially important historical affairs surges to the forefront.

Yet despite my not being a fully paid up member of white Western society, and my consequent self-internalized *de facto* second-class status, a consequential result indeed of the hidden assumption that to be European, or for that matter Welsh, one must be white, cosmically speaking nevertheless, like everyone else,

I am still a citizen of the universe and in my case a seeker after truth. However, as Franz Fanon has so poignantly asserted, the racially oppressed are also *the wretched of the earth*. Therefore, since intolerance continues in human society, even in the case of European Jewry who, having repossessed territory in the Levant, and despite Fanon's warning against the desire of the oppressed to become the oppressor, now mistreat Palestinian people in the same way they themselves were, and continue to be, mistreated in the Europe they left behind, where does the answer to such a persistent and omnipresent divisive dilemma lie? Where indeed? Indeed, I believe that the sorry seed of this continuing human conflict and struggle was sown thousands of years ago in Babylon but, as will be revealed in chapter four, the resultant poisonous root of this scourge is to be found on the banks of the Nile in the ancient short lived city of Akhetaten.

Of course from the biographical background picture I have painted, one could assume at the outset that the conclusion has been decided beforehand, the outcome predetermined. Nothing however could be more distant from the truth. In fact, at the beginning of this project I was not sure where the facts I might uncover would lead. Socio-politically speaking of course, I am a black Afro-Celt but for a person such as I, born into an integrated multi-ethnic environment which has been, like Africa itself, slighted and blighted, it is however important that this matter should be plainly understood as a Truth issue, not a Black one. Indeed, the preceding assumption of predetermination would not be well founded for the Muse itself has provoked the issue by providing many of the ideas, if not a third of them so far, for this particular work. They came at will, if you will, and strange though it be, at moments this book seemed to be writing itself and forming its own conclusions. Therefore, I *feel* that the "Neteru," the higher powers, more of which will be discussed within the pages of this book, want this information to finally see the light of day as a subject proved.

Thus this indeed is all I can truly offer as an answer to the above-framed concerns regarding the requisite qualifications I may possess to "tackle the historical, biblical, religious and geopolitical issues that the subject of this book proposes to investigate."

To conclude however, one final sensitive concern is proffered here. For those who may have objections or feel outraged that this work is an assault on their treasured spiritual and religious beliefs I beg your forgiveness and indulgence in advance for that is not the designed purpose. To the contrary, there is herein an attempt at the decoding of the fabricated aspects of the so-called Holy Bible. This investigation therefore does not dishonour as such the underlying veracity of this much *reinterpreted* biblical text for the narrative found therein does indeed contain a hidden historical truth, one however that has been buried for the better part of 2,000 or more years. The revelation of that hidden history therefore is what I hope will be revealed in the following pages of this book.

One

---✦---

BLACK AFRICAN OR WHAT?

*A look toward the Egypt of antiquity is the best way to
conceive and build our cultural future. In reconceived and
renewed African culture, Egypt will play the same role that
Greco-Latin antiquity plays in Western cultures.*

CHEIKH ANTA DIOP

I am Black but comely, O ye daughters of Jerusalem.

SONG OF SOLOMON

The fact of a civilization as influential as Ancient Egypt was in the formation
of European civilization contradicts and thereby critically refutes the prior
Venetian and later Victorian notion that the Greco-Roman world was the pin-
nacle and epitome of human civilization. Given the Western world's philosophy of
superiority prevalent in former times, indeed a dangerous misanthropic sophistry
which has inevitably induced our current worldwide racially malfunctioning social environment, this refutation is even more astonishing if one recognizes that
those latter classical civilizations' immediate predecessor was, in ethnic terms, a
black one. Indeed, the manner in which black people are currently treated and

1

depreciated throughout the world today would be very much different if the information about to unfold herein was common knowledge. In fact the fundamental
psychological basis for racial discrimination would vanish over night.

For mainstream Egyptologists however the jury is still out on the highly
contentious issue of what was the race of the ancient Nile Dwellers. Since from
a Western perspective they are not axiomatically considered black African the
hidden assumption therefore must be that they were either white or at least
olive-skinned Asiatics.

Notwithstanding the vagueness surrounding this ethnic issue, in ancient times
prior to the rise of Alexander the Great however, Egypt was known as *Khem*, a
word semantically similar to the Greek term *Ethiopia*. Indeed, both Egyptian and
Greek lexical terms have the similar meaning of "to burn something," as in the alchemical process of "burning metals," or makes reference to "burnt faces," an apt
description, of course, for people with dark skins, to say nothing of the fact that it
may also be the etymological source of the biblical reference to the name of Ham.

Interestingly, as comparative cosmologist and independent software designer Laird Scranton points out, "The word *khem* held such significance to the
Egyptians themselves that ancient Egypt was referred to as the Land of Khem."[1]

Although Scranton demonstrates in his ideophonic system that the word
khem also means "source of completion," in a more sacrosanct manner, British
Egyptologist, E. A. Wallis Budge however authoritatively defines the word *khem*
as "God; he whose name is unknown, he who is not known,"[2] an interpretation
therefore that unequivocally identifies ancient Egypt as the original "Land of God."

This potent identification of Egypt as the most ancient Holy Land raises
therefore some rather astonishing and quite dramatic implications, the most important of which, as this book will soon demonstrate, is that the fundamental
principles contained in the so-called Holy Bible, a book from which the Western
world has drawn its inspiration, have been surreptitiously expropriated with
quite underhanded conscious intention from the sacred annals of the ancient
continent of Africa, the true location of the "Land of God."

Placing that controversial issue aside for the moment however, that this ancient land has been portrayed in more recent times as a multiethnic society, a
smelting pot of peoples, if you will, is somewhat of a vindication by omission

of the research of the Senegalese pan-Africanist scholar and author Chiekh Anta Diop, whose 1953 Ph.D thesis was entitled: *The African Origin of Civilization*.

Given said racial diversity, and assuming that black Africans were part of that multi-ethnicity, it would appear that the Egyptians were not entirely Caucasian, if such a pejorative term is still permissible. However what proof is there to the foregoing assumption?

According to the ancient papyri and other records, the Egyptians (*rmt̲ w*) distinguished themselves from Asiatics [the *Amu*] and believed it was their god Horus who had created the human race and its many differences. "Thou makes the colour of the skin of one race to be different from that of another, but, however many may be the varieties of mankind, it is thou that makes them all,"[3] as so proclaimed the people of the Land of Khem with regard to the Creator.

Thus the ancients were clearly aware of racial distinction. However, olive-skinned Asiatics they were not. But, if not Asiatics, what then were they?

Until more recent times, descriptions of what the ancient Egyptians were *not* were often found in scholastic texts but rarely, on the other hand, a mention of what they actually *were*. In fact, contemporary Egypt is currently described as a Middle Eastern country, despite the fact that the latter definition applies only to those countries that lay east of the Mediterranean. Egypt however is not located in that direction. To the contrary, Egypt is in the south.

Moreover, though linguistic evidence shows that Arabic was a dialect of and essentially influenced by the Ancient Egyptian language, in truth it was only since the fall of Roman Egypt to the Muslims in the 7th century AD that Arabic has been the emergent national language of Egypt. Evidently Egypt was not therefore always a country under Arabic influence and since its geographic location is in the south on the continent of Africa, the question arises: Was Ancient Egypt therefore before the arrival of Arab hegemony, a black African country still speaking its native tongue while under Roman dominance?

To arrive anywhere near to an answer to that question, it is necessary to take a broader chronological view of history and reach much further back in time to the Persian invasion of Egypt in the 6th century BC. Indeed Palestine was invaded simultaneously in 576 BC when Jerusalem fell to the Babylonians. Close to 300 years later Alexander the Great liberated Egypt from the abuses the Persian

Empire imposed upon the ancient land. This he did by reopening the desecrated temples and reestablishing ancient Egyptian customs and culture which he ultimately validated by making himself a pharaoh after declaring himself to be the son of Zeus, the Greek name for the African god Amun.

Approximately 300 years after the Greek liberation came the Romans, whose empire guaranteed Egypt's permanent loss of autonomy, hastening thereby its total collapse and tragic demise from the world stage. That event occurred sometime during the 5th century AD. Thus by this stage, these historic facts irrefutably demonstrate that a Persian, Greek, Roman and Arabic element had evidently already entered the veins of Egyptian blood.

A proviso should be added here however as to the ethnic make up of the population of Roman Italy at the time of its invasion. The Hollywood movie industry's epic films, *The Robe*, *Demetrius And The Gladiators*, *Salome* and *Spartacus*, etc. made rather romantic representations of Roman culture giving the impression that they were of 'pure' white European stock, which incidentally it is about to do for ancient Egypt with the release of its new blockbuster 2014 version of *The Exodus – Gods And Kings*, as will be further discussed in chapter four. Yet despite the uncritical interpretation those aforementioned enjoyable films gave, that however is not the way many Roman writers described themselves.

During the span of time between the Republic and the Empire, the majority Italian population had become almost completely oriental, a fact which provoked Juvenal to go so far as to remark that "the Tiber had captured the waters of the Syrian Orantes."[4] Thus ethnically speaking, the Roman army was, as such, a Babylonian one. Other Roman chroniclers, Claudius, Pliny, Tacitus, and many more even described ancient Britons as "'Nimble-footed Blackamoors', 'Ethiopians', 'Cum Nigris Gentibus', 'Niger', 'Black,'"[5] etc. at the northern end of the Roman Empire. Clearly, there is much more "colour" to European history than we are accustomed to imagine. But we digress from Egypt.

Further back in time indeed, shortly before the biblical era, Siegried Morenz, the German Egyptologist who unearthed the previously mentioned ethnic distinction between Egyptians and Asiatics, discovered that the "Admonitions of Ipuwer contain a lament that foreigners are pouring into northern Egypt and gaining power there."[6] Stating further that the "tribes of the desert [?] (*hsstyw*) have become Egyptians [?] (*rmt̲ w*) everywhere."[7]

Morenz' first question mark in the above quote clearly indicates there is no determining whether the desert region from which these foreigners were invading refers to the Asian or Libyan deserts. Nevertheless, it is clearly apparent that *these foreigners were visibly distinguishable from the people of Egypt.*

Quoting from the *Book of the Gates*, Morenz revealingly highlights that the Egyptian deity is portrayed, "'as the protector as well as the creator of the souls' (*nd̲ bsw*) of Asiatics, Negroes and Libyans,"[8] a statement that draws attention not only to the term Negro, but to the fact that the Egyptians themselves are not mentioned. What are we to make of this? Given that the term *Asiatic* irrefutably implies people from Asia and *Libyans* people from Libya, where then exactly was Negro land? Are not the alleged Negroes and Egypt both progeny of the continent of Africa?

Meanwhile, with reference to the times of the biblical narrative which appear to coincide with Egypt's 18th Dynasty, Ghanaian author Nana Banchie Darkwah in *The Africans Who Wrote The Bible* gives prominence to an interesting observation concerning the "lack of any linguistic problems in the travels of Abraham, Joseph, and Jacob and his family to Ancient Egypt [which] simply and clearly reveals that the so-called people of the Bible were of the same racial, ethnic linguistic, and cultural heritage as the Ancient Egyptians to whom they supposedly went."[9] In fact, it will be demonstrated later that the area from which the Hebrews are said to have originated was a land already under the jurisdiction of Egypt making it the region, neo-geopolitically speaking, of northeast Africa! Today, since the Sykes-Pico Treaty, this region is generally known geo-strategically as the Middle East.

Be that as it may for the time being, all these external invaders of the land of Egypt and the continent of Africa mixed with the original population who were descended from the original Ancient Egyptians. Consequently we see a contemporary Egyptian populous ranging from the almost European in appearance to the darkest sub-Saharan African found anywhere on that continent.

Of course, the original name that the Nile valley dwellers bestowed on their country was not Egypt but Kem or Khem, the land of the people with burnt faces, as mentioned above. Its Arabic invaders however also knew it as Mizraim while at the same time they called it "Al Khem" from which the words "alchemy" and subsequently "chemistry" are derived.

Thus, the name Egypt is a Greek word and therefore obviously not the original name the civilization carried for multiple millennia prior to the Grecian arrival. Nevertheless, despite the Greek lexical replacement of its original name, a debt of gratitude is owed to the ancient Greeks who disseminated knowledge and interest of Khem into European society to such a lasting effect.

Sourcing the origin of the name Egypt however, the author of *The Moses Mystery*, Gary Greenberg, reveals that Menes, the first king of the unified monarchy, "established his capital in the city of Hikuptah, a name meaning "Soul of the House of Ptah" (and which the later Greeks pronounced as Aigyptus, giving rise to the modern name of Egypt)."[10] Indeed, for the ancient Greeks, Aigyptus was twin brother to the legendary Danaos who, "according to tradition, colonized Argos in Greece from Egypt,"[11] as Martin Bernal documented in his seminal work *Black Athena*. Ptah, from which the Greek name of Egypt is a corruption, was one of the principle divinities, a member of the Neteru, a concept that will be more fully discussed later.

By calling the land of Khem Egypt however, modern Egyptology, on the other hand, originating in imperial Victorian Britain and bolstered by biblical scholarship, has entirely dislodged Khem from its African root. Thus to rediscover Khem in the image of modern day black people living *in the ghettos, inner cities and slums across the four corners of the earth* or wherever in diaspora they may find themselves throughout the current geopolitical global arrangement, and reveal, as a consequence thereby, the hands of the true authors of the Bible, one is obliged to dispense with Greek nomenclature in order to uncover the securely hidden Africanisms that will undoubtedly unearth the ethnic truth of the paleo-ancient Nile valley civilization.

As such, and furthermore to no benefit for modern day Greeks, the "Indo-European" derived Greek language has been utilized as a linguistic encryption device of Egyptology, solely for the academic continuation of this cultural camouflaging for the purposes of deconstructing and reconstructing the civilization of Khem as a non-black African event.

As was stated in the *Preface, it has to be realized that the names Egypt and Egyptian are linguistic terms derived from the Greek language that have been wittingly or unwittingly used as euphemisms. Such lexical substitutions however serve only to distort or otherwise deflect attention away from the apparently not so obvious fact that historical events that actually took place on the continent of Africa were events in which black African people played a most significant role ... in the development of modern civilization.* Indeed, as the Nile flows from the heart of Africa and out into the Mediterranean it is not inappropriate to refer to the words Egypt and Egyptian as Africa and African.

As American professor of linguistics Joseph Greenberg had already demonstrated in 1966, in linguistic terminology the language of Khem belongs to the "Afro-Asiatic" language family, a branch of the world family of languages that includes Berber, Chadic, Cushitic (Somali) and Semitic (Arabic and Hebrew) subgroups, the latter being African languages spoken on the Asian continent. Furthermore, there are even sound-meaning correspondences evident in portions of the Nilo-Saharan, Niger-Kordofanian vocabulary lists as well as the more southern Khoisan linguistic groups still spoken on the African continent to this day.

Note that "Semitic" is a linguistic and thus not an ethnic term. Indeed, given that the present day black-skinned Dogon, Falasha, and the Massai peoples, as well as the Lemba of Zimbabwe, still maintain so-called Semitic traditions normally associated with Judaism one has to wonder why the Jews of the European and North American diaspora ultimately became Caucasian in appearance?

In *The Thirteenth Tribe*, Hungarian author Arthur Koestler proposes that an answer to that conundrum be found in the "country of the Khazars, a people of Turkish stock [that] occupied a strategic key position at the vital gateway between the Black Sea and the Caspian, where the great powers of the period confronted each other [providing] a buffer protecting Byzantium against invasions by the lusty barbarian tribesmen of the northern steppes – Bulgars, Magyars, Pechenegs, etc. – and later the Vikings and the Russians."[12]

Of the country of Khazar, located in the region of the great mountain barrier of the Caucasus, all that can be safely said about the Khazar nation, "is that the Khazars were a "Turkic" tribe, who erupted from the Asian steppes, probably in the fifth century of our era,"[13] that converted to the Jewish faith sometime around 740 AD, ostensibly for reasons of remaining neutral during the Crusades against Islam. After its adoption of the Jewish faith, the peak of power of the Khazar Empire occurred during the seventh to tenth centuries AD.

From his research, Koestler ultimately concludes that "the large majority of surviving Jews in the world is of Eastern European – and thus perhaps mainly of Khazar – origin. If so, this would mean that their ancestors came not from the Jordan but from the Volga, not from Canaan but from the Caucasus, once believed to be the cradle of the Aryan race; and that genetically they are more closely related to the Hun, Uigur and Magyar tribes than to the seed of Abraham, Isaac and Jacob. Should this turn out to be the case, then the term "anti-Semitism" would become void of meaning, based on a misapprehension shared by both the killers and their victims. The story of the Khazar Empire, as it slowly emerges from the past, begins to look like the most cruel hoax which history has ever perpetrated."[14]

Indeed, the black African descendants of ancient Khem, living *in the ghettos, inner cities and slums across the four corners of the earth,* labour under a similar hoax of misidentification and consequent loss of prestige. Clearly, history has played many a cruel trick on many a people. Thus from this explanation it can be seen that the majority of modern day Jews were never black to begin with and therefore it can be ascertained from Koestler's analysis of the conversion to Judaism of this European state that what truly makes a person Jewish, Christian or Muslim is not their ethnicity but a religious state of mind, and it is that cognitive mental state of consciousness whose source of origin will ultimately be identified with the monotheistic revolution that took place on African soil during Khem's turbulent 18th Dynasty.

Of course, time takes its toll and many historical facts are misplaced, as has been demonstrated. Sometimes however, it receives a helping hand. For example, the writings of Berrosso and Manetho, which unearthed the secret knowledge of an ancient Africa that includes the current political fiction referred to as the Middle East, were destroyed by Romanized Christians whose religion to a fundamental degree was nevertheless evidently founded upon the ancient myths and legends of the African God, Osiris, supporting proof of which will be momentarily discussed.

Despite the West's persistent navel-gazing for answers to Khemite or biblical riddles, which for more than a century has been steadily focused on the Middle East, the above linguistic analysis clearly implies that Egyptologists should at least be looking at African peoples much more closely for comparative linguistic traits and traditional customs to gain a truer picture of who the ancient Nile dwellers really were. As Laird Scranton does for example by relying on E. A. Wallis Budge's two-volume work *An Egyptian Hieroglyphic Dictionary* because "it has the advantage of leaning toward the African roots of Egyptian words than later dictionaries that rely more on later Greek sources…"[15]

Nana Banchie Darkwah, also indicated as much when he noticed a linguistic similarity to his native Ghanaian language in the "transposed Akan and other African tribal names of the authors of the Books of the Old Testament."[16]

Darkwah's and Scranton's research however will be examined later on but before deeper analysis of the biblical text and its potential origin in Khemite history is appraised, an example of the denial that black Africans played a part in the origin of this remarkable civilization would not go amiss here.

To his credit, the prolific outpourings of British author Ralph Ellis have done an excellent job in re-categorizing many a biblical legend as a major factual figure of Egyptian or, as we now prefer, Khemite history. Though regrettably his adamant insistence that black African people played no role whatsoever in the development of humanities' earliest civilization has marred his otherwise amazing scholastic achievement.

Nevertheless, I greatly respect, admire and highly recommend his meticulous works so I hope no one regards any of the following comments here as an attack on this incredible author. I merely wish to highlight a critical failing found within his copious and otherwise thorough output.

For example, in *Solomon − Falcon Of Sheba*, Ralph Ellis quotes selectively from the works of E. A. Wallis Budge, Herodotus, and Strabo, and in other works Diodorus Siculus, to make his case for his otherwise intellectually solid onslaught on the conventional interpretation of the biblical text. According to Ellis in fact, the accounts that Strabo "gave were largely first hand and for the most part they were thought to be reliable, but of Jerusalem and the province of Galilee he says:

This region lies towards the north; and it is inhabited … by mixed stocks of people from Egyptian and Arabian and Phoenician tribes … But though the inhabitants are mixed up thus, the most prevalent of the accredited reports in regard to the Temple at Jerusalem, represents the ancestors of the present Judaeans as Egyptians.

Thus, there was a consistent and unmistakable opinion abroad, in the centuries before the Christian era, that the Israelites were not simply emigrants who had escaped Egypt, but that they were actually of Egyptian stock themselves."[17]

From the preceding, Strabo unmistakably identifies the Judaeans as direct actual descendants of Egyptians. Without evidently regarding Egyptians as black African people however, it is nevertheless clear that Ellis is on a similar path to us in identifying the possibility of biblical legend as African history. Sadly however he betrays an ethnographic weakness that appears to be the major flaw in his otherwise humanistic approach to the alternative ancient history that forms the basis of Western civilization.

Evidently, Ralph Ellis has a Caucasian bias or perhaps a Eurocentric passion for a non-black African Egypt even though Budge demonstrated on page 17 of his major work *Osiris & The Egyptian Resurrection* that: "In the divinity and immortality of the god-man Osiris lay the strength of the power with which he appealed to the minds and hopes of the Egyptians for thousands of years, and we shall see in the course of the following pages that both these conceptions of Osiris are of *purely African origin*, and that they were in existence long before the Dynastic Period in Egypt." (Emphasis added). Indeed, Osiris is the African God *par excellence*. When you enter the realm of Osiris you enter the realm of African consciousness and witness the mythological archetypes of the African mind.

Now, given Ralph Ellis' point of view, are we to conclude that Wallis Budge perceived this "purely African origin" as manifestly Caucasian, that is to say white in some way, or is it the case that Ellis failed to observe the evidence of this relevant passage from such an important work? Indeed, are we to suspect that Budge is being politically incorrect? As both Strabo and Herodotus assert the

Egyptians were blacks, it has to be assumed so did Budge. Moreover, the former astute observers were veritable eyewitnesses!

In fact, in his life's effort Chiekh Anta Diop had already made this evidence axiomatic during the 1950s. In Chapter 1 of *The African Origin Of Civilization* for example, he clarifies this ancient fact by emphasizing that "In his *Geography*, Strabo mentioned the importance of migrations in history and, believing that this particular migration had proceeded from Egypt to Ethiopia, remarks: "Egyptians settled Ethiopia and Colchis. Once again, it is a Greek … who informs us that the Egyptians, Ethiopians, and Colchians belong to the same race, thereby confirming what Herodotus had said about the Colchians."[18] And of the Colchians, located in modern day Georgia, Herodotus said: "The Egyptians said that they believed the Colchians to be descended from the army of Sesostris. My own conjectures were founded, first, on the fact that they are black-skinned and have woolly hair…"[19]

Thus at the time of Herodotus, almost a thousand years since the beginning of the biblical age, the Nile valley dwellers of Khem were still visibly black in appearance. *They are black-skinned and have woolly hair*, according to Herodotus. As for the Ethiopia Strabo referred to, "Ethiopia" is as previously said another Greek word from the Indo-European language family one that merely describes people with naturally sun burnt faces. In essence it is no different from the terms black or Negro, which are in their turn Anglo Saxon and Latin words, respectively. Indeed, as Pan Africanist and African American scholar W. E. B. Du Bois so eloquently pointed out, "The Spanish word "Negro," from being a descriptive adjective, was raised to the substantive name of a race and then deprived of its capital letter."[20] These words and the terminologies that underpin them describe nevertheless only one thing: the blackness of the people in question.

To corroborate this and to gain an idea of what the ancient people of Khem thought of themselves, in his book, *Civilization Or Barbarism*, Diop demonstrates in photographic form a "painting from the tomb of Ramses III (1200 B. C.) [that] shows that the Egyptians perceived themselves as Black, and represented themselves as such without possible confusion with the Indo-Europeans or the Semites. This is a representation of the races in minute detail, which guarantees the realism of the colors. Throughout their entire history, the Egyptians never dreamed of representing themselves by types B or D,"[21] the latter being Indo-Europeans or the Semites, respectively, while types A and C are irrefutably black Africans.

Indeed, with new evidence emerging of the prehistoric migrations of black Africans travelling from the Sahara up through the Nile valley corridor into and through Nubia, Chiekh Anta Diop's racial assumptions are beginning to bear fruit. In corroboration of such contentions, in *Imhotep – The African*, Robert Bauval and Thomas Brophy believe that, "it seems logical to conclude that the earliest migration into Egypt was from the southwest by a black-skinned African population, followed by another wave, also black-skinned, from the Sahara carrying the rudiments and ingredients of civilization – domesticated cattle, sophisticated religious ceremonies, astronomy, and even perhaps an early primitive form of stone building and large-stone sculpting. These newcomers entered the Nile Valley in the 4th millennium BC and, as the evidence strongly suggests, kick-started what modern scholars call Egyptian civilization."[22]

Nevertheless, the ingenuity of these people cannot be seen in isolation to what happened on the banks of the Nile, for not only did they create the Nile valley civilization, but their creative impulse continued on within the heart of Africa itself bringing about the ancient realms of Ghana, Songhay, Timbuktu in Mali and Benin, among many other lesser known kingdoms, as well as the southern European kingdom of Moorish Spain where black African, Asian and Afro-Asiatic Moslem peoples ruled for over 800 years.

Having overlooked certain pertinent ethnic references by ancient scholars, one of whom gave accounts that "were largely first hand and for the most part … were thought to be reliable," Ellis then turns his attention to the Holy Book of the Ethiopians, *The Glory Of Kings*, and observes that, "It was probably at this same time that the Kebra Nagast also had all its references to 'Egypt' changed to 'Ethiopia', and a few very out-of-place comments about 'black faces' were inserted to try and substantiate this otherwise untenable claim to an Ethiopian heritage. That this is a complete falsehood is given away by the paragraph that says the father of the Queen of Sheba and the father of the pharaoh's daughter (who married King Solomon) were exactly the same person. Although the twenty-fifth dynasty Egyptian pharaohs were *said* to be kings of Nubia (Kush) and were given a darker skin pigmentation in their artistic representations, *there were no black pharaohs of Egypt* and so the likelihood of the Queen of Sheba being both a pharaoh's daughter and black is extremely unlikely."[23] (Italics added)

Bearing in mind that the Greek term 'Ethiopian' is also a euphemism for black people, the unbiased position of Herodotus, who communed with the actual priests of Khem, is far different from that of Ellis who is adamant that there were *no black pharaohs*. For example, after learning of Mên [Menes], the first king of the united monarchy, Herodotus unambiguously said that, "they read me from a papyrus the names of 330 monarchs who were his successors upon the throne. In this number of successors there were *eighteen Ethiopian kings*, and one queen who was a native; all the rest were kings and Egyptians."[24] (Emphasis added.)

It should be noted at this point, that on the outside wall of the Egyptian Museum in Cairo is a list of all the dynasties of Ancient Egypt, with the prominent exception of the 25th Dynasty, a factor that would indicate that even modern day Egyptian academics are leery at being associated with black Africa! But if Sheba is not black, as Ellis would contend, then indeed what was she? It is after all an ancient assumption that she was either from the Nile valley, Ethiopia or Arabia.

Indeed, as Chiekh Anta Diop had so meticulously demonstrated, until "the birth of Mohammed, Southern Arabia was inseparable from Ethiopia, their historical destiny was the same and the sovereignty of Ethiopia over Arabia was scarcely interrupted except from time to time; this can be affirmed by a verse of the Koran entitled "The Elephants". Mohammed related how the Ethiopian army, which was sent from Africa to suppress a revolt by the Yemenite Arabs against the Ethiopian Governor Abraha, was destroyed by the "Messengers of Heaven", though it was 40,000 men strong. Each soldier was hit at the top of his helmet by a miraculous missile which went through and through him and his mount. It is commonly supposed that the Ethiopian army must have been destroyed by a sandstorm or an epidemic of plague which had broken out en route. It thus appears according to the limited historical records we possess that the Queen of Sheba was connected more with Ethiopia than with "Sheban Arabia". [25]

Nevertheless, whatever her ethnic origin, Ralph Ellis indeed is emphatic that "there were no black pharaohs in Egypt!" Thus, even the 25th Dynasty kings of Khem were not black as they were only *said* to be, according to Ellis. But, one wonders, what about the biblical "Song of Solomon?" Particularly the lines associated with that famous queen where Shulemite (Palestinian) Sheba states, "I am black but comely O ye daughters of Jerusalem." Is this particular line of the poem not an example of what Ellis meant by *very out-of-place comments about 'black faces?'*

Modern day racial conundrums aside however, the people of Khem them-selves referred to their country as the Black land and the Red land or alterna-tively the "Two Lands." While the Red land represented the Sinai and the desert regions beyond, indeed, it represents what modern geo-strategists call the "Middle East," the Black land was all the fertile land on either side of the banks of the Nile. As will be shown later, this is a very important distinction.

For Rene A. Schwaller de Lubicz and the many other scholars who, reject-ing official Egyptological standards of chronology, recognize an older age for the Nile valley civilization, this designation of the "Two Lands," was representative of the Age of Gemini (c. 7,500 BC), the Zodiac sign of The Twins, hence the idea of the dual lands. The foundation of support for such a view, of course, would be a consequence of the stargazing knowledge the ancients possessed that will be discussed later. In any event, the term has caused some consternation about what it actually refers to.

In *The Lost City Of The Exodus*, Egyptian author Ahmed Osman questioned the meaning of this title by noting that, "While ancient Egyptian texts speak of the unification of the Two Lands in one political state, there has been some misun-derstanding in modern times regarding what those two lands represent. When they refer to the unification of Egypt, scholars usually talk about the North and the South, Lower Egypt and Upper Egypt. This, however, seems to be a mislead-ing statement, as *the Egyptians themselves didn't explain their Two Lands in this way*. Instead, Egyptian texts referring to the unification always talk about the Black land and the Red land. While the Egyptians called the Nile valley "black earth" (*kemet*), they referred to the desert as the "red earth" (*ta desharet*), so the union must have taken place between the Nile valley and the desert, represented by the only inhabited desert of Sinai. The unification of the two lands allowed for a centralization of authority which, as a result, became able to undertake massive administrative and building projects."[26] (Emphasis added.)

Although Ahmed Osman's analysis appears to give as such a reasonably exact interpretation of the ancient geography that the people of Khem would truly have recognized, his acute probing insight however does not challenge the belief of the Egyptologists that it is the soil that gives the name to the Black land. Since he was only trying to clarify how the ancients saw the division of their two lands however, the racial aspect of the people was not his uppermost concern. Such a result would not have been satisfactory or acceptable to the Senegalese academician Cheikh Anta Diop who adamantly proclaimed, "The interpretation according to which Kemit designates the black soil of Egypt, rather than the black man and, by extension, the black race of the country of the Blacks, stems from a gratuitous distortion by minds aware of what an exact interpretation of this word would imply."[27] Indeed, when Muslim Arabs moved further south in their Islamic conquest of Africa, they came to a land of the Nuba, the Dinka and other dark skinned people of the traditional land of Kush they would eventually call *Bilad as Sudan*, the Land of the Blacks! No historian worth his or her merit today would dare to suggest that this term designated any reference to the soil.

Nevertheless, Osman's observations are still useful for clarifying events alleged to have occurred in the delta region of so-called Lower Egypt since these could not realistically have occurred there at the time in question as this area was marshland, not yet reclaimed from the sea. Hence, they must have occurred in the Red land but not however in the designated region modern Egyptologists refer to as Lower Egypt.

Of that truly desert region, the Palermo Stone has "preserved at least nine archaic names of kings who wore only the Red Crown of Lower Egypt and who ruled before Menes."[28] Among them were "Scorpion," Ka, Zeser, Narmer, and Sma, the names of kings that Sir Flinders Petrie believed corresponded "to names given by Manetho in the list of ten human rulers who reigned at Tanis during the chaotic centuries."[29] Tanis, of course, is the Greek name of This. Thus, this was a place of definite pre-historic activity but where exactly was the boundary between these two lands?

According to Zecharia Sitchin, the Sumerian record for example indicates that Asia was the domain of Enlil while Africa the domain of Enki. But where was the specific boundary between Africa and Asia then? Or as Osman himself commented, "As the delta had not yet been inhabited at the time when Narmer unified Egypt about 3200 BCE, what does the expression "Two Lands" represent?

"We know that the Sinai Peninsula, located in western Asia, became part of unified Egypt from the very beginning, at the time of Narmer. We also know that Sinai had been inhabited in prehistory for a long time before the time of Narmer. For Sinai was not completely a barren desert; streams of fresh water, springing from clefts in the rock, are found at about 25-kilometer (about 15 miles) intervals. It also has small oases, where date palms grow along the banks of running water. Wheat, barley, and all sorts of trees are cultivated, and there are many trees and rare flowers. Archeological evidence shows that Upper Egyptians were using the Sinaitic turquoise mines at Serabit el-Khadim, even before the time of Narmer."[30]

Indeed, a BBC 4 television broadcast of 17 September 2014 reported the discovery of a Red Sea port called Wadi Al Jarf that was the entry point for huge amounts of copper that came from the Sinai Peninsular used for the making of the tools alleged to be employed in the construction of the Great Pyramid. With reference to the latter, Welsh engineer Peter James remarked that its impressive scale is on the order of magnitude of putting a man on the moon! Also discovered was a 4,500 year-old papyrus that was in fact the diary of a literate worker who "allegedly" participated in the construction of Khufu's pyramid 2,500 years before Christ. "Alleged" because the conventional age of the pyramids is also questionable. The possibility being, that the ancient 'literate worker' and his crew were merely refurbishing not building the Great Pyramid. In conflict with this idea however, and moreover based on the flimsiest of evidence, mainstream Egyptologists are convinced that the pyramids were built as tombs for the pharaohs.

Despite this conviction on the part of the establishment however, controversially many scholars dismiss the tomb theory and therefore question the true age of the Great Pyramid. As Ralph Ellis points out, "One of the questions that is probably most central to this enigma must be the purpose of these great monuments. The normal explanation – that the pyramids of Egypt were tombs – was looking increasingly untenable, yet there did not appear to be a reasonable theory with which we could replace this concept. But this is wrong: there has always been an alternative explanation, one that is provided by the legends of Egypt herself. The myths and legends that have filtered down to us from the distant past can tell us a different tale, and the myth that could be thought of as being central to this quest is that of Thoth...

"The legends of the god, Thoth, indicate that – apart from educating mankind in maths, physics and astronomy – he left some repositories of knowledge around the world so that his knowledge would be preserved. These repositories were supposedly hidden in such a fashion that only the dedicated or initiated could find them. Since many people have assumed that the Great Pyramid was one of those repositories, a veritable army of explorers have attempted, over the years, to drill and excavate every crevice at this site. It does not even matter too much at this stage if these myths are based on ancient facts of not. What seems to be apparent is that the pyramid builders themselves thought it was true and put considerable efforts into passing this information on."[31]

That the people of Khem indeed did believe such things is not in dispute but who the pyramid builders may have been is another matter. In any event, the Neter Thoth will be more closely examined in chapter five but in the meantime we return to the issue of the age of the Great Pyramid.

Referring to the two-sided victory tablet of the very first King, Menes, which depicts the forceful unification of the Land of Khem, Zecharia Sitchin for example, after giving a vivid description of the monarch in the midst of the conquering battle wearing the white crown of Upper Egypt on one side and on the other the red crown of Lower Egypt, states that found on the red side "To the right of his head the artist spelled out the epithet "Nar-Mer" acquired by the king; to the left the tablet depicts the most important structure in the newly acquired districts – the pyramid!"[32]

Representing the first major conflict in recorded history, the "forceful unification" of the Land of Khem was a major battle that has in fact determined the future course of human history and from the fortunate depiction of that triumph on the victory tablet we have discovered not only the Great Pyramid in existence prior to the accepted date of its construction as maintained by mainstream chronology but as an additional consequence the answer to the previously asked question of "where exactly was the boundary between these two lands."

As stated above, Ahmed Osman's "reasonably exact interpretation" of Sinai as "the only inhabited desert" gives the false impression however that the Sinai desert was the entire extent of the Red land when in fact it was only the beginning. Indeed, as the Great Pyramid unequivocally stood at the edge of the desert region known as the Red land, the Giza plateau marked the start of a boundary that potentially extended as far as the Euphrates in the east, a fact that will be demonstrated later, making that entire region exclusive to Africa, it being one of the dual lands of Khem, beyond which lay Asia.

Therefore, since the Red land was the land of the pyramid historians are now confronted with a major problem as the builder of this "Seventh Wonder of the World" is alleged to be the monarch Khufu. Zecharia Sitchin however has presented ancient graphic evidence of the preexistence of the Great Pyramid already standing on the banks of the Nile for more than six centuries prior to its alleged construction by the 4th Dynasty king Khufu who ruled during the 26th century BC.

Moreover, and particularly given the fact that no inscriptions whatsoever otherwise exist inside this remarkable monument, the red paint graffiti markings found in the Great Pyramid, alleging that it was built by the Shemsu Khufu, that is the workforce of Khufu, are probably fakes from the hand of the illustrious British Colonel Howard Vyse (1835) or his assistant John Perring as Sitchin exposed in *The Stairway To Heaven*, despite Zahi Hawass' contention to the contrary.

Indeed, in *Return Of The Golden Age*, Edward E. Malkowski states, "… there are no records left by Old Kingdom pharaohs chronicling their construction of pyramids or other monuments assigned by Egyptologists to the third millennium BCE.

"Given the evidence, one is compelled to accept the notion that what we see as the history of dynastic Egypt actually is a re-creation, a reestablishing of a preexisting civilization I call "Civilization X." Because the technology to build precise megalithic structures did not exist during the third millennium BCE and did not exist up to modern times, civilization must have existed prior to the catastrophe we refer to as the end of the Ice Age.

"So, when were these magnificent ancient structures of Egypt built, and by whom?

"There is but a single reference to these concerns in ancient Egyptian texts, the Edfu Building Texts, inscribed on the wall of the temple at Edfu, located sixty miles south of Luxor. These texts contain a wealth of information concerning ancient Egypt's religion, politics, and history from the oldest epochs of pharaonic history. According to the texts, the words of the "Seven Sages" were recorded by the god Thoth — the Egyptian principle of writing and wisdom — in a book entitled *Specifications of the Mounds of the Early Primordial Age.* This book listed the locations of sacred mounds along the Nile River as well as all the lesser mounds, or temples, along with the place where time began, the Great Primeval Mound. Furthermore, these sages were the only divine beings who understood how the temples were to be created. They were also the ones who began work on the **Great Primeval Mound**, planning out and erecting the mythical temple of the "First Time." (Bold added.)

"In the ancient Egyptian language, the First Time was Zep Tepi, and in their mythology Zep Tepi was a remote age when the gods established their kingdom on Earth, in Egypt."[33]

Thus, it is plain to see that Egyptology merely insists, without any established proof whatsoever, that the pyramids were built as tombs beginning in the 26th century BC. Only their academic insistence however constitutes proof!

Be that as it may for the moment, on a visit to Sinai in 1904, Sir W. M. Flinders Petrie made a monumental discovery there in the Red land. What he found, according to Laurence Gardner was "the alchemical workshop of Akhenaten and the generations of pharaohs before him."[34] This was the discovery of a temple of Khem on the very mount that Moses is said to have taken the Children of Israel after their departure from the Delta region in 1330 BC.

Known in the Old Testament as Mount Horeb, "the holy mountain of Moses is found soaring to over 2,600 feet within a high sandstone plateau above the Plain of Paran. Today it is known as Serâbit el-Khâdim."[35]

Dedicated to the goddess, or rather Neter, Hathor throughout its operative life of more than a 1,000 years, Gardiner asks appropriately, "why would there have been such an important Egyptian temple hundreds of miles away from the pharaonic centers, across the Red Sea gulfs at the top of a desolate mountain?"[36]

Built around 2613 BC in the Old Kingdom time of Sneferu the founder of the 4th Dynasty, and located in the Red land, this temple facility was clearly placed out of reach of the common people, like any modern military base, but was nevertheless still part of the unified state of Khem. Incidentally, the term "hundreds of miles away," pales into insignificance once it is realized that the name Khem also implied the world or the universe not the mere geographical regions along the river.

Serâbit el-Khâdim, of course, is the place where Moses is said to have seen the burning bush, spoken with God, and received the Ten Commandments. As Edward F. Malkowski mentions in *The Spiritual Technology of Ancient Egypt*, "The Hebrew name for God was Jehovah-Nissi, which, according to the Greek historian Diodorus Siculus (first century BCE), was derived from the name of the Greek god Dionysus. Furthermore, only the Egyptian god Osiris was allotted a place of birth and burial. In Egypt, his birthplace was called Nissa, the Hebrew equivalent of Mount Sinai. In other words, Osiris was born on Mount Sinai – Moses went to Mount Sinai to receive the Ten Commandments. Moses went to Mount Sinai because he knew from his Egyptian upbringing that it was the Mountain of God. So, there is an Egyptian tradition that becomes Hebrew."[37]

Indeed, "The fact that the original tablets (said to have been written with the finger of God) had nothing to do with what might have been placed in the Ark, has caused much consternation over the centuries. In religious terms, the whole lore of the Ark has been based on this ideal, but it is known by Judaic scholars to be an historical fallacy. In an attempt to reconcile the matter and appease clerical teaching, a compromise concept was born in the Middle Ages, when it was determined by theologians that there must have been two Arks! The one built by Bezaleel housed the Testimony stone, as explained in Exodus 40:20, while the other (a copy) contained the tables [sic] which had been broken by Moses! It was stressed, however, that it was the real Bazaleel Ark which found its eventual residence in King Solomon's Temple. As to the fate or fortune of the supposed duplicate with the Commandments, this was never discussed – at least not by Jewish historians.

"The notion of a "second" Ark was grasped with enthusiasm by the Christian fraternity in Ethiopia. If the Jews were not inclined to capitalize on the fable, then the Christians could surely build a new tradition around it. So it was that, in the 1300s, an anonymous Ethiopic book appeared, entitled *Kebra Nagast* (Glory of the Kings.) During this era of European infiltration into African countries, the object of the book was to establish *the pretence* of a long-standing Judaeo-Christian culture in old Abyssinia."[38] (Italics added.)

Doubting, as did Ralph Ellis, the authenticity of Ethiopia's claim to a Judeo-Christian heritage, from this point on, Laurence Gardner goes on to describe how Ethiopian Christian kings claimed to be descendants of Menelek, the alleged son of Solomon and Sheba and how the Ark of the Covenant came to reside in Ethiopia. Whether the Ethiopians actually maintained the remains of the original Ark of the Covenant however is not an issue at this moment in time, but "a long-standing Judaeo-Christian culture in old Abyssinia" most assuredly is.

Indeed, since, as will be proven in the text of this work, the religion of Christianity is undoubtedly the continuation of the ancient religion of the Nile valley, which itself originated from an inner African domain and therefore from the deepest recesses of African consciousness, and, moreover, since, as will be examined in detail in chapter four, the riverbank city of Akhetaten is the true birthplace of the Jewish phenomenon from which not only the Yahuds but the Medzay, the modern day Massai, who also left the Nile valley during the Exodus and still continue to practice the ancient traditions normally associated with Judaism, to say nothing of the Falashas of Ethiopia, whose very name itself means 'exile,' why would the Ethiopians of the Middle Ages have needed to 'pretend' any relationship to these religions since their relation to these practices is indelibly connected to their formative birth on the very sacred soil of Africa itself? Indeed, it is as much their religion, if not more so, as any of the descendants of Europe's converted Middle Age State of Khazar in the Caucasus!

Thus, the Diaspora from Akhetaten shows multiple so-called Semitic groups spreading across or out of Africa like the Falashas, Massai and Lemba, etc, in addition to their more famous cousins the Yahuds.

Notwithstanding the foregoing, six years after Ellis' *Solomon — Falcon of Sheba* was published, the February 2008 edition of *National Geographic*, reported an article by Robert Draper, entitled *The Black Pharaohs*, which referred to "an honoured chapter of history [that] tells of a time when kings from deep in Africa conquered ancient Egypt."

Another undated source by Charles Bonnet & Dominique Valbelle from The American University in Cairo Press discusses, *The Nubian Pharaohs, Black Kings on the Nile*, making a similar claim. Indeed, granted that these black Pharaohs existed, that is to say that there *were* black pharaohs, despite Ellis' contrary belief, one is compelled to shout out, or at least politely ask: What indeed were the others?

It was during 1976, while still a student at UCLA in the department of African Area Studies located in Ralph Bunch Hall, that I personally became aware of the Nubian pharaohs. Yet even though mainstream Egyptology acknowledged this fact, it seemed to me there was a certain amount of glee in identifying these so-called black pharaohs as belonging to the 25th Dynasty, a dynasty incidentally famous for the Shabaka Stone currently housed in the British Museum, the text of which is *a mere emulation* of the ancient style of the Old Kingdom pharaohs. As the Shabaka Stone itself so states, the creation story carved into it was originally written on a worm-eaten scroll that had been buried "in the great temple of Ptah at Memphis."[39] Thus, though acknowledged as black, Shabaka and the other pharaohs of his dynasty were not so great after all since they only copied but did not originate.

That covert message surreptitiously smouldered and niggled at my conscience for years until the day I read an article in the March 4, 1979 edition of the *Los Angeles Herald Examiner* entitled: *Called Oldest Monarchy. Ancient Nubia — Where Kings Began*, which detailed the research of archaeologist Keith C. Seele, a professor at the University of Chicago.

This interesting and informative report declared that evidence "of *the oldest recognizable monarchy in human history*, preceding the rise of the earliest Egyptian kings by several generations has been discovered in artifacts from ancient Nubia in Africa." Indeed, could these remnant artefacts be evidential traces of the convergence of the two waves of black-skinned peoples who journeyed from the Sahara to the Nile valley, according to Bauval and Brophy, in the 4th millennia BC? Whatever the case, we now find two Nubian Dynasties, thousands of years apart, forming "bookends" that enclose the entire conventional history, as maintained by mainstream Egyptology, of ancient Egypt. The earlier of the two however was the kingdom of Ta Seti, also known as the "Land of the Bow." (Emphasis added.)

In ancient times of course, Nubia was so designated because of copious amounts of gold that existed there. Indeed, on the question of the ancient gold mines of Nubia, in *Babylon's Banksters*, Joseph P. Farrell, quoting extensively from the late 19ᵗʰ century historian, Alexander Del Mar, who mistakenly believed that the people of the Nile valley originated in India, observes that, "Egypt was probably the largest gold-mining and producing state in the ancient world. The reason is simple: the Nile. As Alexander Del Mar puts it, "Gold has been found in nearly every region tributary to the Nile, from the Equator to the First Cataract." But no region was more connected to gold mining than was the region of Nubia, bordering modern-day southern Egypt and the Sudan. The term Nubia itself "appears to have originated in Egypt, where *Nob* or *Nub* signified gold, hence Nubia, the land of gold." Beneath the foothills of Nubia lies a vast gravel-and-sand expanse of desert, washed during the flood season by numerous streams and gullies. This region is known as the Bisharee or Bishara, the Great Nubian Desert. Del Mar notes that:

> Next to the mines of the Altai mountains of India, the Bisharee mines of Egypt are probably the oldest in the world; and in view of *the Indian origin of the Egyptians*, and the distant researches and conquests which have been made by the leading nations for the acquisition of gold, it seems not at all improbable that there existed a close connection between the discovery of the Egyptian mines and the original settlement of the country by Asiatic races."[40] (Italics added.)

During the British imperial era of course, it was impossible to imagine, and moreover was furthest from any rational thinking of those days, that black Africa had anything at all to do with the miracle that occurred along banks of the Nile.

Nevertheless, in his book *Babylon's Banskters*, Farrell's purpose however is to trace the origin of the bullion brokers back to Asiatic Babylon, making a connection between the banking and bullion trust and the temple and the consequent rise of an international trading class.

Using Del Mar as a source however makes some of his findings somewhat dubious though not incorrect in broad outline. Because the Indian Code of Manou had been determined to an age somewhere in the region of the fifteenth to the thirty-first century BC, Del Mar assumed the ancient gold mines of Nubia were being mined "by the hand labour of slaves"[41] during the reign of Menes, the first monarch of the Old Kingdom. The implication is that Menes was in fact the Manou of India who, like the British, would logically have only used black Africans as slaves. Nevertheless, from the foregoing assumption, Farrell observes that, "it is the presence of slaves at the Bisharee mines that affords us our first significant clue into the minds of the mentality of the ancient bullion brokers."[42]

Once again however, Del Mar's imperially tainted analysis is relied upon as Farrell quotes from the writings of Diodorus Siculus, the Greek historian who, after visiting the Bisharee mines in 50 BC, reported that:

> with the costs and pains of many labourers, much gold is dug. This soil is naturally black, but in the body of the earth there are many veins of shining white quartz, glittering will [sic] all sorts of bright metals, out of which those appointed to be overseers cause the gold to be dug by the labour of a vast multitude of people. For the kings of Egypt condemn to these mines not only notorious criminals, captives taken in war, persons accused of false dealings, and those with whom the kind is offended, but also all the kindred and relatives of the latter. These are sent to this work, either as a punishment, or that the profit and gain of the king may be increased by their labours.
>
> There are thus infinite numbers thrown into these mines, all bound in fetters, kept at work night and day, and so strictly surrounded that there is no possibility of their effecting an escape. *They are guarded by mercenary soldiers of various barbarous nations, whose language is foreign to them and to each other, so that there are no means either of forming conspiracies or of corrupting those who are set to watch them.* They are kept to incessant work by the rod of the overseer, who often lashes them severely. Not the least care is taken of the bodies of these poor creatures; they have not a rag to cover their nakedness; and whoever sees them must compassionate their melancholy and deplorable

condition, for though they may be sick or maimed or lame, no rest nor any intermission of labour is allowed them. Neither the weakness of old age, nor the infirmities of females, excuse any from the work, to which all are driven by blows and cudgels; until, borne down by the intolerable weight of their misery, many fall dead in the midst of their insufferable labours. Deprived of all hope, these miserable creatures expect each day to be worse than the last, and long for death to end their griefs."[43] (Emphasis added.)

Evidently, the brutality of the Middle Passage and subsequent slavery that made the wealth of Britain and the rise of America possible had this earlier barbarous model to draw its methods from. Though Farrell does point out that Diodorus Siculus' above quoted paragraph would "move any decent human being to compassion and pity for the poor wretches condemned to work the mines," he mistakenly grants however that "given the antiquity of the mines of Bisharee and the stability of Egyptian society and culture, it is reasonable to assume that the conditions at the mines had not changed throughout the several centuries that they were worked."[44]

Notwithstanding that assumption, he does make the astute observation that the presence of mercenaries might signal that there existed "a certain collusion between Egyptian kings and those able to supply such a large and disparate group of mercenaries. To put it succinctly, the mercenary guard contingent subtly implies the existence of an international money-power."[45]

Although Joseph P. Farrell's major contributions to this debate is most invaluable with regard to tracing the financial string pulling of non-African exploiters, the issues described above have to be addressed because the land of Khem is not centuries old but millennia and extrapolating from the abuses imposed on the Nubian and other African peoples by foreign kings who were ruling the land from the time of the Babylonian inspired Persian, and subsequent centuries long Greek and Roman invasions has no justification in claiming that such abuses existed in far more ancient times. Though the evidence does affirm that gold mining in the region of Nubia definitely took place at the time of Menes that such inhuman conditions existed in the Old Kingdom however has yet to be verified by any historical or archaeological measuring stick.

As even the Bible indicated, more than a thousand years before Diodorus Siculus' visit to the Bisharee mines of Nubia, "the Israelites parted with their earrings and small items to provide the gold with which Aaron made the calf (Exodus 32:2-3, 24). But Moses subsequently transmuted this to powder and fed it to the Israelites. Later, we are informed that they supplied bracelets, rings, armlets, and other personal items to aid the Ark and Tabernacle projects (Exodus 35:22), but these trinkets would have comprised a fraction of the total requirement. So, how did they acquire such a quantity in the midst of the Sinai plateau? There were no gold mines in the region – only copper and turquoise. The answer must be that it came from the Horeb mountain temple, where the white-powder *mfkzt* was already being made with Egyptian gold."[46]

According to Laurence Gardner, "In those times Egypt had what amounted to a monopoly of gold, with the most important mines located in the Eastern Desert between the Nile and the Red Sea. There was also extensive mining in the Nubian Desert east of Wadi Halfa, and south towards the Third Cataract. A 20th-dynasty papyrus map (c. 1200 BC) of the ancient gold mines of Wadi Hammamat is presently held by the Museo Egizio, Turin. Administration and overall control of gold mining was in the hands of high-ranking court officials, and the king received all resultant income, being the outright owner of the land."[47]

From the foregoing, it would therefore appear that at that time an "international money-power" of alien bullion brokers had not gained control in Africa prior to Akhenaten's betrayal. Thus, the horrific treatment of the miners at Bisharee that occurred in 50 BC may not have been the way they were treated during the self-governing times of Africa's Old Kingdom of almost 3,000 years earlier.

Indeed, the point in the history of Khem when outside Asiatic influences gained a destructive grip on the Black land of the Nile valley civilization surely occurred during the turmoil of the 18th Dynasty, the subject of which will be discussed in chapter three. At this point however, one has to consider what was the name of the land of the blacks before the Greeks called it Ethiopia?

As Zecharia Sitchin pointed out in *The Wars Of Gods And Men*, "More recent studies, such as *Egypt in Nubia* by Walter B. Emory, agree that Ta-Khenn was Nubia and that Ua-Ua was the name of its northern part, the area between the Nile's first and second cataracts. (The southern part of Nubia was called Kush.)"[48]

Though generally speaking referred to as Kush, in ancient times Nubia was also thus known as Khenn, a strategic location indeed in the battles between Horus and Seth which will also be discussed a little later in chapter two.

With its name and location thus determined, the remarkable and intriguing findings displayed in Keith C. Seele's article dramatically assert that this "discovery is expected to stimulate a new appraisal of the origins of civilization in Africa, raising the question of what extent later Egyptian culture may have derived its advanced political structure from the Nubians. The various symbols of Nubian royalty that have been found are the same as those associated, in later times, with Egyptian kings."

As these facts did not confirm his belief in a non-black African Egypt, either Ellis was unaware of these findings, which is entirely possible, or he chose to disregard them.

Either way, another curious racial camouflage tactic is also found in his *Scota – Egyptian Queen Of The Scots*. As was mentioned earlier the Roman invasion of Britain was confronted with "'Nimble-footed Blackamoors', 'Ethiopians', 'Cum Nigris Gentibus', 'Niger', 'Black,'" etc. at the northern end of the Roman Empire," raising the issue of an Afro-Celtic heritage in the British Isles, not that Ellis by any means regarded Scota as a black woman. Nevertheless, as I stated in *The Tiger Bay Story*, even in the Middle Ages Geoffrey of Monmouth "believed that the original Welsh came from Troy – which, of course is in the east. Troy was a city much affected by the declining Ancient Egyptian civilisation long before its legendary contact with Ancient Greece. According to Geoffrey, the ancient Welsh were led by the mythical Brutus, whose son Camber was bequeathed the territory west of the Severn then known as Cambria. The people were called Cymry and spoke a language called Cymric."[49] In point of linguistic fact, the Welsh language has a verb initial word order syntax structure, as does the ancient language that was spoken on the banks of the Nile.

As for the Scottish branch of the Celtic family, in *The Secret Chamber of Osiris*, Scottish author Scott Creighton "had read many of the ancient legends of how the Scottish (and Irish) people were believed to have originally descended from the land of the pharaohs."[50] According to such legends, "Princess Scota, an ancient Egyptian princess who ... had to flee Egypt with her husband and many of her followers, whereupon she traversed through Greece and the lands of the Mediterranean until, eventually, she reached Spain. From there Scota and her small band crossed over into Ireland, where they fought a bloody pitched battle, and finally, after a number of years, her people, the Scoti or Scots, finally crossed the Irish Sea and arrived in Scotland, which was so named in honor of the princess."[51]

The Afro-Celtic ethnicity issue aside however, on page 99 of *Scota - Egyptian Queen Of The Scots*, Ellis also analyzes the close relationship of the Kaphtor, Philistines and Canaanites. A summary of his observations follows:

> Kaphtor was Crete, the Egyptian Kefiu; the Philistines came from Crete; the Minoans came from Crete; the Canaanites were the Phoenicians; The Phoenicians came from Canaan; ... both *the Canaanites and the Philistines were immediate descendants of Ham*; and the Philistines were the descendants of Mizraim. However, in the Bible, Mizraim means Egypt, and so the Philistines were descendants of Egypt. Whew! (Italics, added)

Now have not all Christians been taught in Sunday school, at least as a justification for slavery in the United States, that black people were the legitimate targets for slavery because the Bible alleges that the children of **Ham**, the progenitor of the black people, should be the servants of others.

Indeed, what does the Bible actually say about the black African past? According to Genesis 10:6-10: the sons of Ham *were* Cush, Mizraim, Put, and Canaan. [7] The sons of Cush *were* Seba, Havilah, Sabtah, Raamah, and Sabtechah; and the sons of Ramaah *were* Sheba and Dedan. [8] Cush begat Nimrod; he began to be a mighty one on the earth. [9] He was a hunter before the Lord; therefore it is said, "Like Nimrod the mighty hunter before the Lord." [10] And the beginning of his kingdom was Babel, Erech, Accad, and Calneh, in the land of Shinar.

Thus from this biblical text we find substantiation of the black African presence and influence in the Fertile Crescent during ancient times. Clearly, such circumstance was the inevitable consequence of "the earliest migration . . . from the southwest by a black-skinned African population, followed by another wave, also black-skinned, from the Sahara," that Bauval and Brophy mentioned earlier in this text. Nimrod after all cannot be other than a black king.

Indeed, according to Zecharia Sitchin, as the waters of the flood receded the post-flood "descendants of Ham ("He Who is Hot" and also "The Dark-Hued One"), first "Cush and Mizra'im and Put and Canaan" and thereafter a host of other nation-states, correspond to the African nation-lands of Nubia, Ethiopia, Egypt and Libya as the core nations of African resettlement, again beginning with the topographically higher areas, then spreading to the lowlands."[52]

For whatever the reason that sparked the African migration from the southwestern region of the Sahara, a logical consequence of that migration would also be therefore the peopling of the near east. After all is said and done, why surmise that the river Nile was the only goal of these ancient migrants when the rivers of the Fertile Crescent also awaited them. Indeed the Australian Aborigines had already made that journey from their ancient African homeland many thousands of years previously.

With Cush, geographically speaking, being the area of Africa called the Sudan which in former times was a far greater portion of the continent than modern day Sudan currently represents, this textual evidence more than implies that Babylon and its predecessors, the Akkadian (Accad) civilization and even Sumer (the land of Shinar) were black civilizations from the start, if the Bible is to be taken at face value. Moreover, according to the Bible indeed, the children of Ham should be the servants of others? Doesn't the logic of Ellis' analysis therefore make Egyptians (Mizraim) black!

Earlier in the same book, we move from one extreme to the other as Ellis refers to the existence of blondes in Egypt and says: "it is entirely possible that some of those people could have been related to the (possibly) lighter-skinned Minoans (living in Egypt)."[53] No doubt there were blondes in Egypt at that particular era, but who were the implied darker-skinned people they were being compared with? This book proposes to find the answer.

Perhaps an excusable element exists for otherwise honest historians in the fact that the ethnic origin confusion that abounds these days may be attributable to the ancients themselves. For example, even though modern day Ethiopians are unarguably black in skin pigmentation their iconography does not reflect this fact but depicts light or white skinned Greek Byzantine type holy personages on murals found at their religious places of worship. If therefore no present day Ethiopians were in existence to state otherwise one could imagine from these representations that the ancient Ethiopians weren't black either!

Thus, in similar fashion to the Ethiopians however, neither would ancient Africans have been obsessed with their skin pigmentation as we are today. Therefore it is easy to see why contemporary culture, which is, would find it difficult to notice the true ethnicity of an ancient people more concerned with their spiritual representation and non-physical evolution and development in the Afterlife.

For them, the physical body, black though it be, was a culmination of seven non-physical entities and thus they lived their lives with the intention of perfecting their "light" body's transformation into a "glorified spirit" known as the Akhu that had earned the right to live like the greater Neteru, the cosmic elementals such as Osiris, Isis, Nut and Geb, in eternity in the Duat, as described in the *Pyramid Texts* out of which comes *The Book Of The Dead*.

The Christian Bible of course reflects similar concerns but the ancients, as will be discussed in chapter eight, had more clarification about the Afterlife than today's believers, for they followed a different Holy Writ that preceded the Bible by millennia.

Was there thus a Bible before the rise of Christianity? Indeed there was! In fact, the very name Bible itself is derived from paper scrolls made from a hardy reed plant that grew abundantly in the Nile called 'papyrus' that were used by the scribes of Khem for their writings.

Extracted from *The Pyramid Texts*, the oldest known writing hand carved in granite and laced with gold, was *The Book Of The Day Of Coming Forth Into The Light*, more commonly known as *The Book Of The Dead*. Or, as Gerald Massey so eloquently described it from a functional perspective: "The Book of the Dead in life became the book of life in death."[54]

This was Holy Scripture that the people of the true Holy Land had known since time immemorial. The sacred scriptures contained in the pages of this Holy Book however, emphasized the subject of eternal life by detailing the ritual practices necessary in this life for the continuation of the individual soul in the Afterlife. As Budge stated earlier, "In the divinity and immortality of the god-man Osiris lay the strength of the power with which he appealed to the minds and hopes of the Egyptians for thousands of years."

At this point a proviso is necessary to assuage any possible confusion between the written text of the Sacred Science of ancient Khem and modern religion. As Siegried Morenz said of this distinction, the religion of the ancient people and priesthood of Khem "with its sacrifice and its priesthood is distinguished by a predominance of cult. It may be classified among the pagan cult religions which stand in contrast to Judaism, Christianity and Islam, since the latter were *par excellence* scriptural creeds in which God speaks and demands."[55]

Though the words henotheistic or polytheistic however come closer to an understanding of their "cult" practice than does the term "pagan," which tends to carry a derogative slur, it is nevertheless quite clear that the Sacred Science was not a scriptural religion. Indeed, as Kenyan Christian religious philosopher John Samuel Mbiti stated with reference to the African concept of religion in general, and as a contrast to the aforementioned religions "par excellence," the ways in which African peoples worship God are such that, "they have no creeds to recite: their creeds are within them, in their blood and in their hearts. Their beliefs about God are expressed through concrete concepts, attitudes and acts of worship. The individual believes what others in his community believe: it is a corporate "Faith." And this faith is utilitarian, not purely spiritual, it is practical and not mystical."[56] With that distinction made clear, we now return to the soul's ultimate destination in the Afterlife, as revealed in the *Pyramid Texts* out of which comes *The Book Of The Day Of Coming Forth Into The Light*.

Describing the land through which the soul sojourns on its way to eternal life, or rather the "first floor level" of the Duat, Gerald Massey uses the term Amenta. Presumably, he took this term from the glyphs of its symbolic representation but no deeper explanation for its meaning can be found for this rarely used term. We know from the name Ta Seti, for example, that "ta" means land. Thus combining the term Amun or Amen, a God known to the ancients as "the Hidden One," with "ta" we get the appropriate term, "The Land of the Hidden

One" or the "Hidden Dwelling." As has previously been stated however, the subject of the Afterlife will be discussed in greater detail in chapter eight.

Nevertheless, with such prominent spiritual and transcendental concerns, it is self-evident that the modern psychological or rather pathological disease we call racism had yet to come into existence in those ancient days. Though the root of today's geopolitical conflicts can be found on the banks of the Nile, the ancients could not have foreseen the problems that would result from their political decision to 'excommunicate' and exile its troublemakers by means of the Exodus.

And speaking of the books of the Bible, for a book entitled: *Is The Bible African History* I suppose this title should be qualified as predominantly referring to the *Old Testament* since the *New Testament* is a Roman phenomenon which raises the question, beyond faith, of whether a man called Jesus existed in history or not. Indeed, "The first set of amalgamated books to be approved as the Hebrew Bible appeared after the fall of Jerusalem to the Roman general Titus in AD 70."[57]

Moreover, given the fact that no historical record has been found showing beyond doubt that even the very name *Jesus Christ* existed prior to the Council of Nicea in 325 AD, his existence is therefore purely a matter of faith. A matter of faith this book is not about to digress into nor challenge, other than to say that Christianity reflects the religious worship of Osiris and his son Horus that once existed in Khem for thousands of years prior to the birth of Jesus Christ. Indeed, according to E. A. Wallis Budge, "from the first to the last Osiris was to the Egyptians the god-man who suffered, and died, and rose again, and reigned eternally in heaven."[58]

In fact, there may even be a Celtic origin for the name Jesus. Of course, Emmanuel is the *Old Testament* name of the person later identified as Christ in the *New Testament*. Nevertheless, the names Hesus and Esus for example were once well-known gods of the Gaulish people. In 1862, a Welsh Druidic revivalist of the 19th century addressed this issue in his work *The Barddas of Iolo Morganwg* by identifying Esus with Jesus, not only on "the strength of the similarity of their names"[59] but on the similarity of Hesus with the Welsh name for Jesus which is Iesu (pronounced, 'yesi').

That aside for the moment, there is the issue of the legend of the Black Madonna, mother of Christ for whom Ast, or to use the Greek form of her name, Isis, the Khemite Queen of Heaven, is the more ancient prototype. Nevertheless, the biblical manifestation of Mary as Isis in the *New Testament* once again receives the whitewashing technique unique to Ralph Ellis when he describes in *Cleopatra To Christ* that there is "epigraphic evidence for Mary's title's direct descent from the Maakhah Tamar queens of Egypt ... [that] ... underlines Mary's Egyptian heritage once more, *undermining any politically correct moves to turn Mary into a negress*. Once again, this analysis demonstrates that the name Mary was not Greek, nor indeed was it Hebrew. In fact, the name 'Mary' is pure Egyptian, and so it should not be so surprising that both Thea Muse Ourania and her daughter Julia Muse Ourania became known as Mary."[60] (Italics added.)

Ralph Ellis of course is correct that the name Mary is 'pure Egyptian.' The name Miriam, the sister of Moses, for example, is derived from Meri-Amun, which means the 'Beloved of Amun.' Thus, Mary means beloved. But above Ellis is stating most emphatically that Mary's "pure Egyptian" name indicates she is not a Negress! Therefore once again it is asked: Egyptians were what?

For the sake of argument, it is indeed appropriate to note at this point the origin of Ast. For the ancients, there was no disputing the ethnicity of Isis. Born of Nut, "the priests of Dendera asserted that the home of Nut was in their city, and in an inscription on their temple they recorded that it was the birthplace ... of Isis, and that it contained the birth-chamber ... wherein Nut brought forth the goddess in the form of a *dark-skinned* child, who she called "Khnemet-ankhet, the lady of love ... on the fourth of the epagomenal days. When Nut saw her child, she exclaimed, "As (... i.e., behold), I have become thy mother," and this was the origin of the name Ast, or Isis."[61] (Emphasis added.)

One must assume by now from Ralph Ellis' contentions that Cleopatra could never have been a woman of colour, as dear Aunty Chrissy had once contended, let alone Mary. Yet several years ago a television documentary announced the finding of the remains of Arsinoe, the sister of Cleopatra, buried in a Turkish grave. Forensic analysis of her skeletal remains indicated that she was of black African ethnicity! According to *Wikipedia* however, "Hilke Thuer examined the old notes and photographs of the now-missing skull, and concluded that it shows signs of an admixture of African and Egyptian ancestry mixed with classical Grecian features – despite the fact that Boas, Gravlee, Bernard and Leonard and others have demonstrated that skull measurements are not a reliable indicator of race. Afrocentrists have accordingly claimed that Cleopatra VII was black, in spite of the facts that:

> The skeleton is not proven to be that of Arsinoe;
> The shape of the skull is no indicator of a person's race;
> Arsinoe was a half-sister to Cleopatra, having a different mother;
> Cleopatra's ancestors were of Greek-Macedonia origin."

Unexplained in Wikipedia's quote above however is why Hilke Thuer's reference to "an admixture of African and Egyptian ancestry mixed with classical Grecian features" emphasizes a distinction between the terms African and Egyptian, not even hinting at whether they are one and the same. Nevertheless, the above facts notwithstanding, there remains uncertainty regarding the possibility that the sisters had a different mother while neither is Cleopatra's Greek-Macedonian origin an indicator that she was not an "admixture of African and Egyptian" ancestry, given that no pharaoh sat on the throne unless married to a princess of Khem. To say nothing of *Black Athena*, the seminal work of Martin Bernal that explores the deep Afro-Asiatic cultural roots found in the classical civilization of ancient Greece.

This primary matriarchal factor of ancient African culture would never have permitted a foreigner, conqueror or no, to sit legitimately on the throne unless his queen was of Khemite blood. So from the very beginning of the Ptolemaic period there would have had to have been a mixing of the Greek-Macedonian with native Nile valley blood if only to keep peace in the land. Unless, of course, it is assumed that 20th and current 21st century racial biases and bigotries were equally prevalent during the Classical Era!

The historical record however does not account for such a conjecture. On the contrary, the evidence demonstrates an effort to integrate the Greek and African religions in the form of a composite god named Sokar-Osiris-Apis "created on purpose by the late Pharaoh Ptolemy I Soter (305-282 BCE after the

Thirty-first Dynasty). The pharaoh had a major problem to solve, he had to reconcile and unify two different cultures mingling in Egypt. Egyptian and Greek.
Thus, the new cult of Serapis was created, combining the ancient Egyptian cult
of the Apis bull with the ancient cults of Zeus, Hades, Asclepius, and Dionysus,
trying to bring them all together into this composite god who represented fertil-
ity and the powers of the underworld."[62]

Indeed, near to the Step Pyramid of Djoser is an amazing and labyrinthine
subterranean temple built in ancient times that contained many sarcophagi of
mummified sacred Apis bulls, alleged by some to date from the Twenty-Sixth
Dynasty (664-525 BCE) up to the Ptolemaic period. *Wikipedia*, on the other
hand, reports that the "most ancient burials found at this site date back to the
reign of Amenhotep III." However, this date too may be an underestimation of
its true age, since there are 24 enormous dark granite sarcophagi located in
these underground catacombs that cannot be moved even with today's modern
technology.

In an essay entitled *Secrets of the Serapeum at Saqqara*, published in the book
Mysteries of the Ancient Past, Antoine Gigal queries the age of the Apis Bull Cult
and wonders why the bulls were deified. As Gigal tells us, the bull Apis contained
the divine manifestation of the god Ptah and later of Osiris. But what makes this
interesting is that he later states that, "the Babylonian god Ea was called Serapsi,
that is to say the King of the Depths."[63] Ea, of course, is another name for Enki,
one of the principle leaders of the Anunnaki of Sumerian lore who Zecharia
Sitchin identifies as the Neter Ptah.

With regard to the age of The Cult of Apis however, "According to Manetho
… it went back to the Second Dynasty,"[64] but Gigal believes that "it is much
older still, because many objects from the earliest times that show the importance of the bull in connection with the heavens had been found, for example
the palette from the predynastic period of Naqada (4000-3000 BCE),"[65] located
near to the gold mines of Nubia.

One vital and pertinent factor, not listed against Afrocentrism in the argument cited above however, concerns the language the Greek-Macedonians spoke
while living in Khem. At a later stage, the symbolic aspects of the native language will be examined in more detail. For the moment however, it is agreed

and understood that initially the then Greek-Macedonians unfamiliar with the language of the country Alexander had liberated required the native Manetho to translate the history of Khem into Greek. However, are we to understand that during the entire span of the following three hundred years they never spoke or read the MeduNeteru, the native symbolic system that underpinned the language of the people, the very Afro-Asiatic language that black African origin deniers need to believe was spoken by a people who were not black African?

That very Afro-Asiatic language however continued to be spoken and written for many centuries after the Greek-Macedonian era up to the time of Justinian, the Roman Emperor who was ultimately responsible for the closure of the temples. Indeed, Robert Temple, author of *The Sirius Mystery*, emphatically declared that, ""I should add that it was the Emperor Justinian (reigned 527-565 AD) who *destroyed* North African civilization, before the Moslems came."[66] (Italics added.)

Ironically, Justinian's edict was a repetition of an event that took place more than 2,000 years earlier in the reign of the enigmatic pharaoh Akhenaten, a mere example of history repeating itself. The former's edict however brought the native knowledge of the sacred writing of Khem to an end until 1822, when its French decipherer Jean-François Champollion cracked the code written on the Rosetta Stone.

Thus, with that resurrection of the ancient script and from perusals through the ancient chronicles of Manetho, Strabo and many others, as well as the examination of relics found in Nubia, and other archaeological and prehistoric findings, the once hidden elements of black African participation in the formation of the Nile valley civilization are seeing the light of day again. Indeed even its presence in the era of the biblical narrative is reemerging from the dark recesses of the muddied waters of our sometimes confusing, ancient past. More importantly however, the hesitant speculations made here so far have at least begun to demonstrate the lengths experts will go to avoid the blindingly obvious.

TWO

THE CHILDREN OF HEAVEN

Let him thank the gods that they have not put in into the heart of the
sons of the Ethiops to covet countries which do not belong to them.

KING OF THE ETHIOPS

W̲ere we to accept the Eurocentric view that the ancient Land of Khem was
not the result of a black African culture, it would mean the overlooking
of a very important discovery, already mentioned in chapter one, concerning the
ancient kingdom of Ta Seti, otherwise known as the "Land of the Bow."

The *Herald Examiner* article that described Keith C. Seele's discovery of the
world's first kingdom in the early 1960s stated that, "new findings suggest that
the ancient Nubians may have reached this stage of political development as long
ago as 3300 B. C., several generations before the earliest documented Egyptian
king."

This finding of course was not without controversy as many Egyptologists
immediately deemed it extremely unlikely. Nevertheless, the same article affirms that certain artefacts like the broken incense burner that had to be pieced
together contained a "depiction of a palace façade, a crowned king sitting on a
throne in a boat, a royal standard before the king and, hovering above the king

the falcon god Horus ... commonly associated with kingship in later Egyptian traditions."

Indeed prior to the establishment of the unified land of Khem, Nubia was the site of a major war that apparently took place in prehistoric times. Thus the Horus connection between Nubia and 'later Egyptian traditions' is a significant and important historical factor since it tends to affirm that Nubia is a primary source of the former's origin.

Known as *The Contendings of Horus And Seth* the story of that battle between the "gods" was found inscribed on the walls of the temple of Edfu. This is the very same inscription that also contained the "single reference" with regard to the construction of the pyramids that Edward E. Malkowski mentioned in chapter one.

Very popular during the 20th Dynasty (1149-1145 BC), this legendary tale was based upon the histories of Osiris, Seth and Horus. Indeed, the ancient African motif expressed in this account of their battle has reverberated down through the millennia even expressing itself in Walt Disney's production of *The Lion King*, an animated film and musical stage production that depicts the classical battle between uncle and nephew.

According to E. A. Wallis Budge, "The great battle between Horus and Typhon [Seth] took place we are told in the IVth Sallier Papyrus, on the 26th day of the month of Thoth."[1] The cause of this conflict however is found in African matriarchal rules that had deprived Seth of both the throne and the succession due to the fact that his brother Osiris had fathered a child by his half-sister Isis. The latter however was a full sister to Seth. Failing to be the husband of his sister Isis, Seth was thus thwarted from producing an heir to the throne of the Black land. Indeed, it was these matrilineal factors that set the stage for Seth's increasingly violent rage against his brother, driving him to devise a plot to murder him by concealing his brother alive in a made-to-measure coffin.

According to Zecharia Sitchin's interpretation of the ancient text, which he quoted from Plutarch, "The occasion for Seth's revenge was the visit to Egypt of "a certain queen of Ethiopia named Aso." In conspiracy with his supporters, Seth held a banquet in her honor... For his scheme Seth had a magnificent chest constructed, large enough to hold Osiris: "This chest he brought into the banqueting room; where, after it had been much admired by all who were present, Seth – as though in jest – promised to give it to any one of them whose body it would fit. Upon this the whole company, one after the other, went into the chest.

""Last of all, Osiris lay himself down in it, upon which the conspirators immediately ran together, clapped the cover upon it, and then fastened it down on the outside with nails, pouring likewise melted lead over it." They then carried the chest in which Osiris was imprisoned to the seashore, and where the Nile flows into the Mediterranean at Tanis sank the chest in the sea."[2]

The coffin of Osiris however was put into the river "upon the 17th day of the month of Athyr, when the sun was in Scorpio, in the 28th year of Osiris's reign..."[3] Moreover, as the late Phillip Coppens described it, "When Osiris was encoffined, he was literally in the hands – in the domain – of Seth, his evil brother, who would continue to grow into the Christian concept of Satan."[4]

Seeking vengeance for the murder of his father, Horus engaged his uncle Seth in major combat, a conflict originally presumed mythological. Indeed, in Egyptology the events and characters in this drama are all considered part of the Osirian mythic complex and, in fact, by the time of Grecian contact with Africa these events were so hoary with age they had become psychological archetypes even for the people of Khem. Nevertheless, as recorded on the walls of the temple of Edfu from an earlier text that has been lost to the mists of a far earlier time, the *real* and historical armies of Horus came up from the south to drive out the enemies of the Black land back into the Red land, the Land of Seth. These loyal armies would eventually become known as the once thought mythological *Shemsu Hor*, or Followers of Horus, also known as the *mesniu*, the metal people, because they received weapons made of iron from a foundry Horus had built in Edfu.

In his book, *The Wars of Gods And Men*, Zecharia Sitchin states that, "The inscription on the temple walls at Edfu, it has been established, was a copy of a text that was known to the Egyptian scribes from earlier sources; but when and by whom the original text had been composed, no one can really tell. Scholars who have studied the inscription have concluded that the accurate geographical and other data in the text indicate (in the words of E. A. Wallis Budge) "that we are not dealing entirely with mythological events; and it is nearly certain that the triumphant progress ascribed to *Hor-Behutet* (Horus of Edfu) is based upon the exploits of some victorious invader who established himself at Edfu in very early times.'"[5]

From the aforementioned inscriptions Sitchin also quotes that Ra joined Horus in Nubia, from there to accompany Horus on his war against "the Enemy." In *Horus, Royal God of Egypt*, S. B. Mercer summed up the scholarly opinions on the subject in one concise statement: "The story of the conflict between Horus and Set represents a historical event."[6]

Indeed, Horus' grandfather joined him in the battle. As the inscription so states, "In the year 363 His Majesty, Ra, the Holy One, the Falcon of the Horizon, the Immortal Who Forever Lives, was in the land of Khenn. He was accompanied by his warriors, for the enemies had conspired against their lord in the district which has been called Ua-Ua since that day."[7]

Ultimately, as the inscriptions indicate the story ends in the overthrow of the Shemsu Seth, the armies of the murderous Seth. Indeed, for a front row seat at this exciting spectacle, I highly recommend readers to review chapter two of Zecharia Sitchin's above-titled book.

In any event, as a consequence of his driving out the enemies of the Black land back into the Red land, the Land of Seth, Horus is victorious and as it happens "the city of Behutet, which was granted to Horus as a prize for his first victory, was the very city of Edfu, which has been dedicated to Horus ever since."[8]

Questioning whether this battle was prehistoric or not, the research of Robert Bauval and Thomas Brophy may have resulted in the decoding of the myth by shedding light on its possible date of occurrence and on the use of the *serekh*, a representation of a rectangular enclosure indicating that the text contained a royal name. In *Imhotep The African – Architect Of The Cosmos* for example, they indicate that:

> even though all of the kings of Egypt from earliest times had the falcon (Horus) symbol over their serekh, there were nonetheless two exceptions, namely King Peribsen and King Khasekhemwy of the 2nd Dynasty – the immediate predecessors of King Netjerykhet/Djoser, who probably was the son

of the latter. Peribsen's serekh had the Seth dog on it, whereas Khasekhemwy had both the Seth dog *and* the Horus falcon. The distinct impression one gets is that some sort of rebellion against the Followers of Horus took place during the 2nd Dynasty by the Followers of Seth, perhaps a much older clan of black-skinned people originally from the Western Desert who had been subdued forcefully and integrated into the Horus clan by the 1st-Dynasty King Narmer.

This rebellion … seems to have been led by Peribsen and to have succeeded – at least for a while. In the reign of his successor, Khasekhemwy, however some sort of truce took place leading to a merger of the gods Horus and Seth into the person of the divine king, as attested on his serekh. This, too, was short-lived, for Khasekhemwy's son/successor, Nejerykhet/Djoser, not only removed the Seth symbol and used only the Horus symbol, but also moved his court to the North at Memphis and chose nearby Saqqara, not Nekhen, for his revolutionary funerary complex.

This historical sequence of events seems to be confirmed by an elaborate historical text inscribed in the temple of Edfu dedicated to the falcon god Horus. This text narrates how the now-deified Imhotep informs King Netjerykhet/Djoser how the god Horus, upon returning to Egypt after a military campaign abroad, finds that his brother Seth has usurped his kingdom. Another inscription of Edfu claims that the plan of the temple was culled from "the book that fell from the sky north of Memphis" and that it was built using a construction manual that was written by Imhotep himself. From all these archaeological and textual clues, we are compelled to think that the Followers of Seth were originally from the Paleolithic culture of the Sahara. After becoming Followers of Horus, these people temporarily reasserted their authority in the 2nd Dynasty, but then lost it again – or were assimilated – in the reign of Netjerykhet/Djoser."[9]

Thus, Bauval and Brophy appear to indicate that this conflict between the Shemsu Hor and the Shemsu Seth occurred in historical times. If this proves true, either this conflict actually occurred during the period of the 2nd Dynasty or the chronology of ancient times needs to be thoroughly reexamined.

In any event, after defeating the Followers of Seth, Horus became the hero of the day. Indeed the word "hero" as such is quite commonplace as is the name of Horus but most people these days are unaware that the origin of the name hero is derived from his name, which of course is the Greek version of the African, or more precisely Nubian, warrior god whose name was Heru.

Probably because of his role in bringing an end to the great battle fought between Horus and Seth, Imhotep of Nekhen, the most ancient capital of the Black land, became known as "The Prince of Peace" or "He who comes in peace," which is the meaning of his name.

As part of the Osirian mythic complex however the "deities" and "divine events" featuring in *The Contendings of Horus and Seth*, though derived from historical figures and events of Africa's past, have with time been transformed into psychological archetypal elements.

From a biblical point of view however, since *The Contendings of Horus and Seth* revolve around the subject of birthright, biblical scholar Gary Greenberg sees in them the struggle of Jacob and Esau, biblical patriarchs who, if this identification proves correct, have thus been transformed directly out of African consciousness into historical characters of the Bible, providing additional proof that the biblical stories are in fact rewritings of African legend and history. Indeed more biblical correlations to African historical events such as the latter observation will unfold as we continue our journey.

Meanwhile, with regard to further investigation of the finds Keith C. Seele discovered in the cemetery at Qustul, it is unfortunately disheartening to know however that the city of Qustul "in Upper Nubia, about thirty kilometers south of Abu Simbel … was totally flooded after the completion of the High Dam."[10]

Thus, a sorry consequence of the building of the Aswan Dam in the 1960s of course is the fact that Ta Seti "is now submerged, lost forever like a mini-Atlantis beneath the artificially created Lake Nasser"[11] where many of its royal temples and tombs will remain until such time as underwater archaeology is advanced or remunerated enough to explore at such depths.

This loss to the lake waters of such an exciting and important discovery is of course very convenient for black African origin detractors, but despite such misfortune for the African continent, "Black Africa …still holds many surprises for us…" as Rene A. Schwaller de Lubicz so astutely stated in *Symbol and the Symbolic*.[12] Indeed, among such surprises was "the metaphysical basis of the customs of the Dogons"[13] that the Dogon priest Ogotommêli revealed to French anthropologist Marcel Griaule during the 1930s because he knew "that the time has come when these things, kept secret until now, must be said."[14]

Indeed, in recent times the very ankh that pharaoh Akhenaten appears to have usurped for himself and his queen alone has resurfaced from the mysterious depths of the less excavated and distant reaches of Africa's most southern regions. Through photographic evidence Michael Tellinger, for example, reveals in *African Temples of the Anunnaki* that there was an inner African influence that guided what would become ancient Khem.

Found on a petroglyph carved into a glacier slab at Dreikopseiland, a remote location in South Africa, that influence is an image that clearly shows an "Egyptian" ankh inscribed within a circle that has radiating beams protruding from it.[15] That this symbol of the ankh represents universal knowledge and eternal life is a self-justifying fact in this case since this carved image is potentially 200,000 years old! Not to mention the fact that the circle may also be a representation of Ra!

Assuaging the controversy in Egyptology surrounding Keith C. Seele's findings, not only does his discovery of the image of the "falcon god Horus" emerge from the ancient land of Ta Seti but a larger than life representation of the ankh encircled by Ra, displayed on a petrified glacier of the hardest rock in southern Africa, now impresses itself not only onto the land but ultimately onto global consciousness.

Before descending to the lower reaches of the continent in our continuing search for sources of biblical material however, another exciting discovery lies just beyond the borders of "Upper Egypt." West of the Nile valley, near to Ta Seti in the region of modern day Nubia, and adjacent to Libya and Sudan is the Egyptian Sahara, an area about the size of France. There, in one of the most arid and desolate places in the world, is found Africa's Stonehenge, an ancient star clock much researched by Robert Bauval and his physicist colleague Thomas Brophy. Discovered on a dried out lake bed named Nabta Playa, this astronomical calendar was originally constructed by a mysterious stargazing people from the Sahara who may have been the ancestors of the "People of Yam" and the "People of Takhebet" that Bauval and Brophy described in *Black Genesis* as being visited in ancient times by Old Kingdom pharaohs.[16]

Incidentally, not lost to the waters of Lake Nasser, Bauval and Brophy reported "the find of another cemetery at Gebel Ramlah, some twenty kilometers from Nabta Playa ... hardly 100 kilometers west of Lower Nubia. This cemetery was dated to the Neolithic period and showed the dominant presence of sub-Saharan or black people alongside Mediterranean type populations."[17]

Moreover, from their research, the above-mentioned star clock indicates the rising of Sirius in 6,100 BC. This date forms a significant calculation in the Sothic Calendar, so-called because the heavenly body Sirius was known to the Greeks by the name of Sothis, though the people of Khem referred to her as Ast, the Isis of the Greeks. Interestingly, as Bauval and Brophy demonstrate in *Imhotep — The African*, the alignments and coordinates of the star clock also foreshadow similar numerical and geometric encodings for the astronomical layout of many of the future temples of Khem.

Originally brought to the attention of the world by Fred Wendorf, professor *emeritus* of Anthropology at Southern Methodist University, this find at Nabta Playa raises the question of how ancient is the concept of the zodiac. According to Bauval and Brophy "there is significant dissent among historians as to the age of the zodiacal signs, with some proposing that they may be much older than we have generally presumed."[18]

Interestingly, in his correlations of Old Kingdom chronology with that of Genesis, the first book of the Bible, which will be further discussed in depth much later, Gary Greenberg observes that "Enoch's life span and date of birth certainly suggest that this patriarch served as a marker for the start of the Sothic cycle, but without more evidence such a conclusion remains only a theory."[19] Nevertheless, such a theory is an interesting one, to say the least, as many have identified the biblical Enoch with Thoth, Khem's Neter of wisdom, justice and writing.

As stated in *The Moses Mystery*, Gary Greenberg nevertheless also believed that the people of Khem lacked "sufficient mathematical and astronomical skills to accurately measure the Sothic cycle."[20] In fairness to him however, this latter comment was made before the discovery of the more ancient African astronomical calendar had been made known to the general public. For the people of Khem the Sothic Calendar was indeed the first of three that clearly had their earlier development at Nabta Playa.

Found in the work of Michael Tellinger, another interesting anomaly includes the Great Pyramid at Giza, for there are indeed other symbolic representations pertinent to Khem far older than those found at Ta Seti and possibly Nabta Playa but before that subject can be explored however Joseph P. Farrell's *The Grid Of The Gods* needs closer examination for its analysis of the ancient numerical encoding of the prime meridian.

Nowadays the fact that the prime meridian is located at Greenwich, London in the United Kingdom is taken for granted. Encircling the entire planet while passing through the north and south poles, the prime meridian of course forms an imaginary line in the shape of a grand circle.

Known as Greenwich Mean Time, or GMT, from this location the Giza Plateau is said to be 30 to 31 degrees east longitude. Farrell's work however demonstrates that this was not always the case as in ancient times the prime meridian itself ran straight through the apex of the Great Pyramid which at that time represented a longitude of 0 degrees.

Moreover, besides this intriguing finding, centographers have inadvertently presented a reason why Giza is located at the exact geometric centre of the earth's landmass! From this location, according to Joseph P. Farrell, a grid system can be formed "based on latitude and longitude positions of ancient sites, using as a prime meridian the line running from the north to the south pole through the apex of the Great Pyramid at Giza."[21]

Indeed, according to Phillip Coppens, "Creating a meridian for ancient Egypt has been a favourite pass-time for many Egypt-enthusiasts. The best-known example is the meridian defined by the Great Pyramid by Livio Catullo Stecchine, which he identified as the "the central meridian of ancient Egypt.""[22] Furthermore, "Stecchini pointed out that the original name that was used by the ancient Egyptians for their country was *Ta-Mera*, "The Land that was Measured". The hieroglyph for the *mer* phonetic used in this name is the picture of the hoe, or tilling instrument, supporting the intended reading of "measured". Mer, of course, is also the name for a pyramid."[23]

Indeed, the 'Land of the Pyramid' is an apposite name, in fact one that reinforces Zecharia Sitchin's speculation concerning the true age of the monument. As he pointed out in chapter one with regard to the two-sided victory tablet of the very first King, Menes, to the right of his head "the artist spelled out the epithet "Nar-Mer" acquired by the king" where "the tablet depicts the most important structure in the newly acquired districts – the pyramid!"[24]

In *Heaven's Mirror*, Graham Hancock drew similar conclusions with regard to the prime meridian, the Earth's axis and the Great Pyramid when he stated in 1998 that "It is worth emphasizing that we do not speak here of compass directions, which orient to the magnetic north pole. 'True north-south' means, very specifically, the *geographical* north and south poles of the planet – the actual points around which its axis spins. The normal way of establishing the direction of true north is through observations of stars lying at or near the 'celestial north pole' (i.e. the point in the northern heavens, presently marked by the 'north star' Polaris, directly in line with the infinitely extended axis of the earth). In addition, sightings of stars in the southern heavens are also used by astronomers to establish an accurate north-south line – for such stars lie due south of the observer as they 'culminate' – i.e. reach their highest altitude – each night at the meridian. The fine accuracy displayed by the Great Pyramid suggests that both northern and southern sightings must have been used in its setting-out. What is certain, moreover, is that sightings of *this precision could only have been undertaken by astronomers*."[25] (Italics added.) Very intriguing to say the least, however the ancient observations of the southern heavens will be reexamined in chapter six with regard to Canopus, the South Pole star.

Following this once 0, but now 31 Degree line, down through the entire continent of Africa however, Michael Tellinger's research fascinatingly demonstrates that that longitudinal line which passes through the apex of the Great Pyramid also runs directly through Great Zimbabwe and then on to southern Africa near to the site of two newly discovered pyramids located near the Transvaal escarpment. Indeed, the remains and ruins scattered across this southern African region imperatively imply the one time existence of more than a million people living there!

In fact, with regard to underestimated population size, the same can be said for the ancient Nile valley. In their investigation of the region outside of the oldest capital of the land of Khem, Bauval and Brophy observed that, "Just beyond Nekhen is the open Western Desert, or Sahara. The vast sandy, dusty area adjacent to Nekhen is filled with debris from the largest Predynastic settlement in Egypt."[26]

Indeed, American archaeologist, space archaeologist and Egyptologist, Sarah Parcak, who is also assistant professor of Anthropology and Director of the Laboratory for Global Observation at the University of Alabama at Birmingham, demonstrated through satellite imaging technology that there were many more cities on either side of the banks of the Nile than previously recognized. This discovery, which has provided a much clearer picture of the population of the Black land, necessitates a revision of the numbers of people that once inhabited the Nile Valley.

Meanwhile in southern Africa, the archaeological remnants found there drew Michael Tellinger's attention to certain Sumerian clay tablets that speak of a people known as the Anunnaki and a place known as the ABZU which Oriental scholars, prior to Zecharia Sitchin, regarded as the Sumerian underworld or as an abyss. Professor Samuel Noah Kramer for example described its ruler, Enki, the lord of wisdom, as he who "dwells in his watery abyss, the Abzu."[27]

Sitchin however radically and insightfully decoded the Sumerian pictographs of this underworld to mean the actual southern hemisphere of our planet making South Africa the physical, not metaphysical or mythological location in the "watery abyss" of the ABZU, a place moreover said to contain legendary amounts of precious gold.

At first reading, the idea Sitchin proposed for why the Anunnaki needed the gold seems quite preposterous and has therefore been challenged by expert exobiologists. Nevertheless, according to Sitchin the Anunnaki required copious amounts of this precious ore in order to scatter it as gold particulates throughout their dying atmosphere for the purpose of protecting life on their home planet Nibiru, a celestial body that allegedly orbits our sun once in every 3,600 earth-years.

When chemtrails that consistently crisscross the skies above the cities of the world on a daily basis are taken into consideration, Sitchin's sensational hypothesis is indeed made rather less outlandish. This ever present phenomena in our skies clearly demonstrates that the militaries of the world are spraying the Earth's atmosphere with silver particulates that contain aluminium, barium and strontium for the alleged purpose of reflecting sunlight back into outer space in order to save, through the process of geo-engineering, our planet Earth from global warming!

Of course, the danger these metals pose for humanity is something else to take seriously but that aside for the moment, Sitchin's proposal is therefore not so preposterous after all.

Consider now the implications that the new information discussed above provides for a black African origin of civilization along the Nile valley. One whose span now covers not only adjacent countries like Nubia or Chad but an entire continent! Indeed, those ancient peoples from the interior of Africa who were to create that civilization had to have travelled at one time in the distant past through "the region of Lower Nubia of today that runs between Abu Simbel and Aswan."[28]

According to Bauval and Brophy "Recent evidence, strongly suggests that "civilization" first entered the Nile Valley in the 450-kilometer strip from the Western Desert (the Sahara). Excavations over the last century … have revealed a wealth of prehistoric artifacts that leave absolutely no doubt that civilization in Egypt took root first in that region and then, a bit later, intertwined with other cultures entering the Nile Valley from the east, the Levant, and the Mediterranean coastline to create the Egyptians of the Dynastic Era."[29]

Moreover, given the advanced knowledge and technology that apparently existed in ancient times, particularly that concerning the astronomical sightings necessary for the precision built Great Pyramid, it becomes evident that Khem and Sumer were in fact legacy civilizations, not therefore civilizations that emerged from the trial and error of some alleged primitive nomadic or newly sedentary peoples. Without doubt, before their decline set in their antecedents were evidently aware of the functional significance and purpose of the cosmic principles that would eventually become identified as the Neteru.

Nevertheless, these legacy civilizations that were evidently at their height from their very beginnings began their slow deterioration with the loss of the scientific knowledge that had been previously bestowed on them by a preexisting civilization, the former civilization that Edward F. Malkowski described in chapter one as "Civilization X," some remnants of which now appear on the plains of southern Africa, destroyed by the Flood.

These revelations bring to mind Joseph P. Farrell's profound hypothesis of *a paleoancient very high civilization of high antiquity*. That is the civilization that preceded Noah's Flood, an event far more detailed in the Sumerian cuneiform than it is in the biblical text. Intriguingly, the kings of Sumer even claimed to know the writings of the kings who lived before the Deluge.

Indeed, with regard to the superior technology that clearly existed prior to the Flood, in *The Temple In Man*, Rene A. Schwaller de Lubicz observes that in the land of Khem, "We are dealing here, not with an evolution of science, but rather, on the contrary, with an immutable basis: for the existence of a language and a form of writing that were already complete from the time of the earliest dynasties of the historical period seems to confirm this. What we see is not the beginnings of research, but *the application of a Knowledge already possessed*."[30] (Italics added.)

This was the global civilization inevitably responsible for the grid that required the prime meridian to pass through the apex of the Great Pyramid. However, long after that traumatic and catastrophic Ice Age calamity had caused amnesia to set in, Sumer, another offspring of that prior civilization, apparently declined into Babylon, while the inchoate degeneration and ensuing demise of Khem gained momentum in the aftermath of Akhenaten's revolution.

From the foregoing, it appears that Plato's recording of Atlantis in the *Timaeus And Critias*, derived indeed from Solon who himself learned of it from the priests of Amun, may well have been Europe's earliest conscious acknowledgement of a preexisting global civilization that for many centuries in the West has been relegated to myth. However, the Flood happened. Just because exegetical analysis of the biblical text has caused many to reject as religious myth or fiction many stories of the Bible, let's not throw the baby out with the bath water.

As the biblical version probably originated in the clay tablets of Sumerian origin, it will be shown that the story of the Flood was a later interpolation into the Bible, as was the Garden of Eden. Nevertheless, as Phillip Coppens observes "In the Theban Recension of the Book of the Dead, there is a flood story, in spell 175. Both Faulkner and Budge have translated this, with Faulkner stating that the Egyptian supreme deity Atum was responsible for the flood, and Budge attributing it to Thoth, the scribe of the gods, acting on the orders of Atum. *"I am going to blot out everything which I have made. This Earth shall enter into the water abyss of Nu by means of a raging flood, and will become even as it was in primeval time."* This meant that the Earth was covered with salt waters."[31]

Either the Hebrews remembered these stories from their ancestral history in the Black land or learned of them from the Babylonians. Either way their inclusion into the pages of the Bible could only have occurred during their captivity on the banks of the rivers of Babylon under the watchful eye of the Persians who at the same time had already conquered and subdued the land of Khem.

Therefore, out of a dubious and potentially manipulated Hebraic version of these events, Genesis 10 states: Now this is the genealogy of the sons of Noah: Shem, Ham and Japheth. And sons were born to them after the flood. Indeed, further on we discover that:

18 … the sons of Noah who went out of the ark were Shem, Ham, and Japheth. And Ham *was* the father of Canaan.

19 These three were the sons of Noah, and from these the whole earth was populated.

20 And Noah began to be a farmer, and he planted a vineyard.

21 Then he drank the wine and was drunk, and became uncovered in his tent.

22 And Ham, the father of Canaan, saw the nakedness of his father, and told his two brothers outside.

23 But Shem and Japheth took a garment, laid it on both their shoulders, and went backward and covered the nakedness of their father. Their faces were turned away, and they did not see their father's nakedness.

24 So Noah awoke from his wine, and knew what his younger son had done to him.

25 Then he said: "Cursed *be* Canaan; a servant of servants he shall be to his brethren."

26 And he said: "Blessed *be* the Lord, the God of Shem, and may Canaan be his servant.

27 "May God enlarge Japheth, and may he dwell in the tents of Shem; and may Canaan be his servant."

According to Verse 24 of the above text, the Bible refers to Ham as the younger son when according to the genealogy (Genesis 18) he is the middle son. Be that as it may, as so pronounced Noah, it appears that servants only indeed shall be the descendants of Ham.

Notwithstanding this inexplicably unjust and rather extraordinary condemnation, Noah was the first drunkard in recorded history, according to the Bible, and since he was drunk out of his mind, how on earth did he know what Ham did before he cursed his grandson Canaan and all his darker skinned descendants? Moreover, are we to believe that if Ham the father of Canaan had thrown a blanket over his naked father while he lay drunk in a tent Black people would have been exonerated from perpetual servitude?

Beyond divine intervention, Noah could only have known what Ham did if Shem and Japheth had told him. But one has to wonder what indeed was wrong with seeing his father's nakedness in the first place? Other than to conclude that the curse on black people was inspired by the racial hatred of the Nile valley culture by its new rulers, in all these thousands of years since those words were written few, if any, have presented a suitable rationale for this otherwise inexplicable curse. There is however an extraordinary one provided by Alan F. Alford, the author of *When the Gods Came Down — The Catastrophic Roots Of Religion Revealed* that will be of interest to examine a little later on in chapter six.

From the foregoing explanation of Babylonian and Persian antipathy toward its captives of unquestionably black African origin however, it may thus be presumed that the root of racism is to be found in this biblical rendition of the story of Noah, a version contrived during the era of the captivity of the so-called Hebrews on the banks of the rivers of Babylon.

However, whatever the case, another consequence of the reality of post flood conditions was that it left the earth's surviving populations in an abject state of devastation having undone all their previous accomplishments, causing anthropologists to assume that early man was a primitive being.

Indeed, there is afoot a British mythology, proffered in the guise of science that presupposes that humans were once primitive and arose from a nomadic hunter gathering way of life to a sedentary means of support that allowed humanity's gradual evolution into farming and subsequent development of civilizations emanating from northern climes of course then later to be disseminated henceforth toward the southern regions.

This concept was the brainchild of an Australian anthropologist once resident in the United Kingdom. Considered "one of the most influential archaeologists of the past century,"[32] V. Gordon Childe, according to the *National Geographic* magazine of June 2011, was a great synthesist who "wove together his colleagues' disconnected facts into overarching intellectual schemes. The most famous of these arose in the 1920s, when he invented the concept of the Neolithic Revolution."[33] The latter theory of course could be better viewed as a psychological tactic and methodology much suited to otherwise imperial pursuits.

Lending support to the modern presumption that civilization only began *after* the flood, it was however the resultant multigenerational amnesia that followed the traumatic deluge that gave rise to the theory that somehow early man was primitive. Detailing such primitive beginnings, Gary Greenberg observed from the works of the Roman historian Plutarch, that, "Osiris had a civilizing influence on what was then a barbarous Egyptian culture. He taught agricultural skills, passed laws to regulate conduct, and instructed Egyptians in the proper manner to worship the gods. After ruling for a while, he decided to travel abroad to spread his teachings. During his absence Isis safeguarded the throne against Set's covetous actions."[34]

Therefore given the foregoing, is it not possible that the barbarous culture that Plutarch describes however was the direct result of the cataclysmic catastrophe that had completely destroyed and eradicated the *paleoancient very high civilization of high antiquity*, a cataclysm so severe it had thrown its inhabitants back into the dark ages of desperation, savagery and cannibalism?

This myth of the Neolithic Revolution and its assumptions of early human life however are now finally being challenged from all sides. Thus given such promising circumstances, the rehabilitation of what is referred to as prehistory raises the thrilling question of the age of the civilization of Khem. How old is it really?

Mainstream Egyptology, of course, acknowledges a date of 3,100 BC, as the beginning of the unified state. However, a crack in the edifice of academic opinion readily appeared during the 1930s when Rene A. Schwaller de Lubicz noticed that erosion on the back of the Sphinx appeared to be caused by torrential rainfall, or precipitation, as the meteorologist would say. Since the last time rain had fallen in that part of Africa far exceeded the accepted and thus conventional date of Khem's beginning, Schwaller de Lubicz' exact and thorough findings were completely ignored.

Nevertheless, in his attempt at decoding the complexities of Schwaller de Lubicz' alchemical work for general public consumption, John Anthony West brought the issue of the age of the Sphinx to the forefront once again, in his 1979 publication of *Serpent In The Sky*. As with Schwaller de Lubicz' case, West's arguments were inevitably challenged by mainstream Egyptology but for his part, not to be deterred, he resolved to solve the matter by seeking the assistance of a professional geologist. As he had no axe to grind regarding the inner sanctum arguments of scholastic Egyptology Robert M. Schoch of Yale University was the one chosen to fit this bill.

After his studied geophysical analysis of the weathering of the Sphinx and its surroundings it became very evident to Schoch that this erosion had to have occurred before the end of the last Pluvial i.e. a torrential down pouring that terminated approximately 8,000 years ago. His professional opinion however stopped short of the 6th millennium BC beyond which he dared not speculate which is not to say the Sphinx is a mere 8,000 years old for it may very well be even older than that.

Not so extraordinary an assertion to make however, if one takes into account Manetho, the Khemite historian of Ptolemaic times who claimed in his *Aegyptiaca* that "the reign of Ptah over the lands of the Nile began 17,900 years before Menes,"[35] the first king of the unified state. That is approximately 23,000 years ago!

Given moreover that on his visit to the Amun priests of the land of Khem circa 500 BC, Herodotus was informed that the "sun had set twice and one half where it now rises" since the beginning of Khemite civilization, software developer and historical researcher Edward F. Malkowski arrived at the even older figure of 39,000 BC.

Of course, such a remarkably early date confirms or at least implies something quite extraordinary. If indeed the ancient priests of Khem had evidence of their country's existence dating back to such a time as Herodotus informs us, then that location of the world also had to have been part of the original *paleo-ancient very high civilization of high antiquity* that existed prior to the catastrophic cosmic event the Bible refers to as the Flood.

For Malkowski, this astonishing conclusion implied knowledge of the precession of the equinoxes which mainstream Egyptologists had a tendency to claim was a discovery of the Greeks, the first, according to them, to understand such a highly dynamic and intricate celestial mechanism. Nevertheless, as Bauval and Brophy pointed out earlier "there is significant dissent among historians as to the age of the zodiacal signs, with some proposing that they may be much older than we have generally presumed."[36]

Indeed, as their art and architecture was dictated by the imagery of the constellations, Schwaller de Lubicz would emphatically disagree that the Nile dwellers lacked an understanding of the Zodiac. Indeed, there is a problem with the accepted idea that the Zodiac was introduced to the Black land from Babylon in Ptolemaic times, since no evidence of its use has been found prior to the arrival of the Greeks. Absence of evidence however is not proof of non-existence.

As Rene A. Schwaller de Lubicz has ably demonstrated the symbolic celestial tradition of the Black land that governed the art of its civilization wholly reflected the consecutive changes of the known Zodiac. Therefore, its alleged non-existence on the banks of the Nile could be attributed to it being sequestered within the esoteric and thus secret, deep structure knowledge taught in the temples. Some researchers for example give the Age of Leo as the time for the construction of the Sphinx.

In *Keeper of Genesis*, Robert Bauval and Graham Hancock for example observe that "Throughout the ancient world the moment of sunrise, and its conjunction with other celestial events, was always considered to be of great importance. At the spring equinox in 10,500 BC ... a particularly spectacular and statistically improbable conjunction took place – a conjunction involving the moment of sunrise, the constellation of Leo and the meridian transit of the three stars of Orion's belt. It is this unique celestial conjunction (which furthermore marks the *beginning* of the 'Age of Leo' and the *beginning* of the upward precessional cycle of the belt stars) that the Great Sphinx and the three Pyramids of Giza appear to model."[37] Intriguing as these findings sound however, in deference to Egyptological convention, both Bauval and Hancock disclaim the idea that the pyramids and the Sphinx were actually built at that time.

These revelations nevertheless suggest that the report of Herodotus has substance, as an unwinding of this precessional clock would actually reveal that Khem is as old as one complete revolution of the celestial star clock, i.e. approximately 26,000 years, plus a half turn, a reasoned implication that formed the basis for Malkowski's radical calculation of 39,000 BC. Indeed, Graham Hancock concluded what he had to say above about the axis of the earth and the grand circle of the prime meridian running through the apex of the Great Pyramid by asking: Is it really so unreasonable to suppose that adepts like these [ancient astronomers] might have known about the obscure phenomenon of precession – and learned how to predict its effect?[38]

Such dates, for the age of the ancient land of Khem of course, appear to stretch back way beyond the limits of acceptable chronology. On the other hand, *as a result of its history being reduced and camouflaged* in biblical text, humanity has been deprived of an important part of its ancient heritage. Indeed, if proved, understanding a society with such longevity may provide an example of sustainability that modern society apparently appears to lack and therefore finds itself deprived of lessons that could be taken from our paleo-ancient past. But is 39,000 BC a reasonable answer to the question: How old is it really?

This too – Malkowski's extremely early date – was also received with incredulity. Given that present day knowledge, based on Darwin's theory of evolution, is covertly implied to be inevitably superior to that of ancient times, according to the standard paradigm or rather that British Myth again, no people advanced enough to sculpt the Sphinx existed at that remote age in time. Moreover, American Egyptologist Mark Lehner further objected on the grounds that there was no archaeological evidence for their existence. Not one pickaxe or stone tool, nor pottery existed to show that they were there. Not one blessed shard.

Raising a disconcerting alarm however, evidence of earlier high level human activity was not too slow in coming forward with the amazing discovery of Göbekli Tepe in southern Turkey that the June 2011 *National Geographic* magazine headlined as *The Birth of Religion*.

A "temple" (of course) dated 10,000 BC had been partially unearthed to reveal an extraordinary Stonehenge-like find, one however built 8,000 years previously but on a much grander scale yet nevertheless constructed in the proposed ancient time frame for the building of the Sphinx.

Though, given the evidence of erosion on some of its stones, even the conventional age of the Salisbury Plain monument is doubted. Although he does not say so in his book *African Temples of the Anunnaki*, Michael Tellinger believes that Stonehenge may have an age of more than a million years!

Unlike those at Stonehenge however, the standing stones of the so-called temple of Göbekli Tepe were exquisitely sculpted in high and bas-relief causing anthropologists to hastily readjust and recalculate humanity's early beginnings.

Thus the chase was on for who built this magnificent structure. Leading the way, in *Göbekli Tepe – Genesis Of The Gods*, Andrew Collins for example seeks to validate the British Myth, bolstering once again its moribund hypothesis by writing about the Swiderian power elite, known as the Hooded Ones, when he references the "European hunting tradition in the Pre-Pottery Neolithic world that existed in the lead-up to the construction of Göbekli Tepe and other religious centers in the south east of Anatolia during the tenth millennium BC."[39] These, he suggests are the people who may be the possible constructors of this newly discovered find.

Be such speculation as it may, though he makes a valid contribution to our knowledge of this unique and interesting site in Turkey, for much of the rest of his work, Collins appears to take a strong Christian fundamentalist approach to the subject in that once again paleo-ancient artefacts are measured according to their validation of what is now considered by us "corrupt" biblical text.

In his quest for verification, Collins does make however the interesting observation that prior to medieval times the Garden of Eden was "considered a paradisiacal realm created by God for the benefit of our First Parents, Adam and Eve"[40] that had "no material presence in the mundane world"[41] and that medieval theologians even went so far as to say, "God had removed it to the vicinity of the Moon."[42]

Nevertheless, Collins still goes in search of a physical paradise on Earth where Anatolian monks "believed that the landscape thereabouts was the actual Garden of Eden"[43] ... a place "not far from the huge inland sea named Lake Van a couple of hundred miles east of Göbekli Tepe."[44]

The Garden of Eden itself however was evidently a late edition to the biblical narrative taken directly from a Sumerian source, probably while the Hebrews were in Babylonian captivity, as "The similarities between the Dilmun epic and the Garden of Eden story found in the Book of Genesis are too similar to be ignored."[45]

In fact, the prototypical Adam and Eve story is also found in the Nile valley. As the rabbi brothers Sabbah indicate, "In the Egyptian notion of creation, there is a reference to Atum, a god who created himself and who fashioned man by dismembering himself. According to Freud, Atum was a distant ancestor of Aten."[46] Indeed, "Aten had fashioned Akhenaten in his own image."[47] Thus, "Akhenaten and Adam were both fashioned by the One God in his own image."[48]

Therefore, according to the Sabbah brothers, "Atum was the first god and Adam was the first man of the creation stories. Eve, the first woman (Isha) is reminiscent of Isis.

"Adam, then, came out of remembrance of the Egyptian god Atum, the god who existed prior to creation, a personification of the celestial deep. And *Isha* (Woman, Eve) came out of remembrance of Isis, with whom Nefertiti was identified."[49]

To corroborate this identification, the brothers Sabbah observe from depictions on temple walls that, "the Ankh appears before Pharaoh's nostrils. This represents the breath of life, the same breath that God (the Elohim Adonay) breathes into Adam's nostrils in the Genesis story."[50] Indeed, as stated earlier, "Akhenaten appears to have usurped" this privilege "for himself and his queen alone," as only "those of royal rank could receive this symbol of life. No ordinary Egyptian had the right to that "divine breath," which was the prerogative of Pharaoh and his family. Akhenaten required his people to worship him as the sacred image of god, Aten."[51]

Thus, not only was Akhenaten described as the first man, more intriguingly the brothers Sabbah refer to an explanation that "posits Akhenaten and Nefertiti as the primordial couple of creation. This last explanation finds its parallel in the Adam and Eve story… Unlike Adam, though, Akhenaten is shown as both male and female. He had proclaimed himself "the father and mother of humanity," a notion which applies allegorically to Adam, and to Abraham (Father of Nations)."[52] Thus, from the foregoing correlations they conclude, "The roots of Genesis seem to have grown in Egyptian soil."[53]

Indeed, alternative Egyptologist and biblical scholar Ralph Ellis also recognizes that "the early sections of the Book of Genesis are wholly unreliable as a historical record and therefore must have been based upon some very ancient myths."[54] Thus Ellis' argument would seem to undermine Andrew Collin's Anatolian Garden of Eden hypothesis.

Having previously advanced the supposition that Solomon was in reality a pharaoh of Egypt, a subject that shall be examined later in this work, Ellis continues to speculate that searching for Eden on the banks of the Euphrates in Sumer, or Anatolia for that matter, as Andrew Collins suggested, was the wrong approach, as it seemed "highly likely that the Genesis story may actually contain elements of Egyptian mythology."[55] There is only one "great river that flows through Eden and then divides off into four branches,"[56] he indicates in *Eden In Egypt* and continues by emphasizing that "there is only one river in the region that conforms with this description."[57] His implication and research leave no doubt that that river is the Nile!

Therefore, if the river Nile flowed through the Garden of Eden, Herodotus was quite right in referring to the Nile valley civilization as the gift of the Nile. This was indeed the true Holy Land. For not only was Khem seeded from Ta Seti and other mysterious depths of Africa but from "about 5,200 years ago, Egypt became the only country in the world to form a central political state whose borders extend from Palestine and the Mediterranean in the north, to Nubia and Aswan in the south."[58]

The original Holy Land therefore included the Black land in the Nile valley and its southwest Asian desert counterpart known as the Red land. Indeed in chapter one, the question was raised as to where exactly was the specific boundary between Asia and Africa, given that the Sumerian record claimed that, "Asia was the domain of Enlil while Africa the domain of Enki."

Though this ancient cartographical issue remains contentious, there is however some indication that the Red land stretched as far as the Euphrates, making all this territory therefore part of the original Land of Khem, the true Land of God. From an African perspective therefore, Palestine was *in* Khem. Indeed in ancient geopolitical terms, that region was already in northeast Africa, the domain of Enki/Ptah.

Thus by extracting the Red land of "northeast Africa" from the original Holy Land and placing it under the political fiction of the Middle East, modern historians regard Khem's military ventures as far as Kadesh, supposedly outside the limits of what they declare to be its boundaries, as constituting imperial action on the part of the armies of Khem, when in fact they were still in their own country.

Moreover, because of the calumny and slander perpetrated and perpetuated by scripture, Khem has been confirmed in some quarters as an empire and a slavocracy. Indeed in *The Moses Legacy – The Evidence Of History* for example, Graham Phillips has a chapter called *Slavery In Egypt*. However, with the exception of the fate of the Hyksos, a tribe of people that will be discussed below and in chapter six, the only evidence of slavery in Egypt comes directly from the Bible. Nevertheless, Phillips seeks secular references and reports, "Historically, the Hyksos were eventually enslaved by the triumphant Egyptians. Under a series of eighteenth-dynasty pharaohs, Egyptian armies repeatedly swept through Canaan, laying the country waste. Tuthmosis III, often referred to as the Napoleon of ancient Egypt, was the most formidable campaigner: he finally crushed the Hyksos in Canaan at the decisive battle of Megiddo somewhere around 1500 BCE. During his reign, thousands of the Hyksos were returned to Egypt in chains. This may be the time referred to in Exodus 1:11, when the Israelites were enslaved:

"Therefore they [the Egyptians] did set over them [the Israelites] taskmasters to afflict them with their burdens.

"Tomb illustrations of the eighteenth dynasty include scenes showing Hyksos slaves making bricks, while taskmasters stand over them, rods in hand. According to Exodus, this is precisely the fate of the Israelites: 'So they were made to work in gangs, with officers set over them, to break their spirit with heavy labour' (Exodus 1:12). 'And they made their lives bitter with hard bondage, in mortar, and in brick' (Exodus 1:15)."[59]

As no major penal system existed in the culture of African societies forced labour therefore was the judicial punishment meted out to its enemies, as the description above so demonstrates.

Be that as it may, Graham Phillips, like the ancient Jewish historian Josephus before him, endeavours to identify the Hebrews as the Hyksos. Referring to their migration from Syria, he reports that, "The first references to the Hyksos in Egyptian records appear shortly after the collapse of the Mari Kingdom. Unlike the previous Semitic traders, these people seem to have been settling in Egypt."[60]

To this, he adds some historical background indicating that, "The Mari Kingdom was invaded by the Babylonians around 1800 BCE, and its capital was taken and destroyed. With the overthrow of their kingdom, the Mari migrated south into Canaan and within a few years had formed themselves into an effective alliance of tribes. By the end of the next century they were powerful enough to threaten Egypt. The Egyptians at the time refer to the Mari as the *Hikau Khasut*, 'rulers of the desert uplands', a term the Greeks later rendered as Hyksos, 'desert princes', the name by which historians still refer to them today. If they represented an historical people, therefore, Jacob and his family would evidently have been a Hyksos tribe."[61]

Why the scattered people of the Mari Kingdom would not have sought revenge on their Babylonian despoilers has not apparently been considered. Be such circumstances as they may however, as stated elsewhere it was Josephus who first equated the Hebrews with the Hyksos and their assault on the Land of Khem. But as Egyptologist Alan Gardiner cast doubt on that assumption by describing their alleged invasion as a more moderate and gradual "infiltration of Palestinians glad to find refuge in a more peaceful and fertile environment,"[62] the Hebrews, as such, are more identifiable as part of the latter people who were infiltrating from Palestine rather than the Hyksos who, as history dictates, were in fact enslaved.

Though such a state can unquestionably be affirmed of Rome which did build its empire on slavery, Khem, on the other hand, was never such. Nevertheless, the battles of Khemite armies as far north as Kadesh give modern historians who speak of imperial pharaohs the misguided notion that Khem extended its alleged "imperial" power into foreign lands but, as these lands were located in the Red land of northeast Africa to begin with, this damaging hypothesis becomes yet an another non-African misconception.

"If we recall the Old Testament,"[63] writes Dinesh D'Souza for example in *America — Imagine A World Without Her* "we see how the victories of Israel over its enemies are considered by the Israelites to be unambiguously good. It's either them or us, and it may as well be us."[64]

D'Souza of course, taking verbatim this text to be truth, is discussing whether conquest is moral or not. That argument aside however, the so-called victories this biblical passage highlights are in fact a flagrant reinterpretation of actual African historical fact.

As the rabbi brothers Sabbah confirm, "the campaign undertaken by Joshua after Moses' death corresponds with the historical conquests of Pharaoh Sety I in Canaan and in Phoenicia after the death of Ramesses I"[65] and as "reported for Joshua, Sety I attacked Kadesh, a former Egyptian fortress north of Galilee *that had been captured* by the Hittites. The city was liberated and once more came under Egyptian domination."[66] (Italics added.)

Thus, these victories were those of the armies of pharaoh Seti I who restored the lands of Khem's northeast African territory from the assaults of Hittite and other Asiatic armies that had taken advantage of this area as a direct result of Akhenaten who, too busy orchestrating the overthrow of the true "Sacred

Science," had ignored the pleas of various dignitaries who in their cuneiform clay tablet script had previously informed him of these troubling and worrisome invasions. Indeed, those supplicant dignitaries were kings who like the rest of the Nile dwelling population regarded pharaoh as God's representative on earth. In fact, as the rabbi brothers Sabbah tellingly point out, "The Amarna Letters show that the Canaanite kings worshiped Pharaoh"[67] in the name of Yahu-Heh, the great god.

Therefore, pharaoh Seti I, the Joshua of the Bible, was not conquering a foreign territory, as D'Souza assumes, but protecting land that already belonged to Khem since it formed its central political state with borders that extended "from Palestine and the Mediterranean in the north, to Nubia and Aswan in the south"[68] more than 2,000 years previous to Seti's campaign.

Thus once again it becomes plain to see that the so-called historical figure portrayed in biblical text as Joshua, who supposedly led "the victories of Israel over its enemies," was none other than the crowned African general, pharaoh Seti I! Thus another fictional figure from the biblical text has therefore found its true historical place in the reconstructed annals of African history.

Indeed the very name Joshua itself is rendered in the biblical text as "Yahu-Shua,"[69] very similar indeed to one of the multiple pharaonic names of Seti I that included the titles Yahu-Heh and Yahu. Thus if that is true, this provides further corroboration that the biblical Joshua was in fact an African warrior!

As to the Amarna Letters mentioned above, these are a reference to the correspondence found in the archives of the city pharaoh Akhenaten built on the banks of the Nile during the tumult that occurred in the 18th Dynasty. This city however will be discussed in more detail later in chapter four.

In the meantime, ancient African affairs, once shrouded and secreted within the pages of the Bible, are now beginning to see the light of day and indeed when combined with the archaeological evidence of Ta Seti, Nabta Playa, and the Great Pyramid at the prime meridian pushing mankind's advanced culture further back in time, one wonders then, how old was the culture and religion of the people of Khem?

With regard to that subject, Gerald Massey in his *The Egyptian Book Of The Dead And The Mysteries Of Amenta* saw in the rituals of the late 19th century

Australian Aborigines a continuation of the ancient Ritual of the Duat that Nile Dwellers followed to the letter to assure the continuance of their souls in the Afterlife. If that is true, then the Nile valley belief system was in existence for more than 40,000 to 50,000 years or even earlier as those dates represent the approximate time of the arrival of the aboriginal people in Australia after the arduous journey that followed their earlier departure from the continent of Africa thousands of years previously (Messrs. Spencer and Gillen).[70]

The works of Gerald Massey of course, especially his identification of Jesus with Horus, were inevitably challenged. According to Christian theologian W. Ward Gasque, Ph.D., as sourced in Wikipedia for example, Gerald Massey's work, "which draws comparisons between the Judeo-Christian religion and the Egyptian religion, is not considered significant in the field of modern Egyptology and is not mentioned in the *Oxford Encyclopedia of Ancient Egypt* or similar reference works of modern Egyptology." It was however mentioned earlier in the century by a prominent British Egyptologist that, "If the parallel between the mythological history of Isis and Horus and the history of Mary and the child be considered, it is difficult to see how they could possibly avoid perceiving in the teaching of Christianity reflections of the best and most spiritual doctrines of the Egyptian religion."[71]

Nevertheless, despite E. A. Wallis Budge's take on the matter, it would appear that Gerald Massey's "not considered significant" contributions have been ignored and downplayed by *the last bastion of prejudice*, modern Egyptology. Indeed the revelation of this outright rejection by mainstream Egyptology of Massey who drew strong African connections between the religion and culture of the Nile valley civilization with Judeo-Christianity, resolves incidentally a personal mystery with regard to the dubious reaction I received in the Department of Egyptology at UCLA in the mid-1970s after proposing to write a paper on *A Comparative Study of Ancient Egyptian & Traditional African Religions*, an issue I elaborated on in more detail in a previous volume: *Voodoo Detective — A True Story*.

To my astonishment I was the only student who had to present a bibliography beforehand as such a topic had clearly not been on the radar of Egyptology at that time either. In any event, the argument I presented in that paper was accepted and received the praise of Professor Callendar. Given however that the latter discipline categorized its subject as belonging to eastern or oriental studies to begin with, its reaction is not surprising but clearly exposes its initial anti-African bias.

Apparently the less prejudiced Gerald Massey was definitely on the right track however, as was E. A. Wallis Budge whose dictionary is much prized by Laird Scranton for its accuracy with regard to African linguistic references whose symbolism supported verification of the Nile valley origin of the Dogon. Indeed, Scranton has shown that the myths the Dogon tell are the same as those of the people of Khem. As stated on the rear of his book, *The Science Of The Dogon*, "The Dogon people of Mali, West Africa, are famous for their unique art and advanced cosmology. The Dogon's creation story described how the one true god, Amma, created all the matter of the universe. Interestingly, the myths that depict his creative efforts bear a striking resemblance to the modern scientific definitions of matter, beginning with the atom and continuing all the way to the vibrating threads of string theory. Furthermore, many of the Dogon words, symbols and rituals used to describe the structure of matter are quite similar to those found in the myths of ancient Egypt and in the daily rituals of Judaism."

Returning to Gerald Massey's reference to the rituals of ancient man however some say that early man, nomadically wandering in the savannahs and on the plains of the African continent more than 50,000 years ago, stumbled upon hallucinogenic mushrooms that grew in cow dung, discovering as a consequence the inner world and multiple dimensions of the psychotropic human mind. A door to the "invisible landscape" as Terence and Dennis McKenna described it had indeed swung open that led to a kind of mind expanding noetic revolution that provides an understandable reason for why cows became so venerated and even deified in the Nile valley in the form of the Neter Hathor.

Since an effigy of a cow has also been found buried beneath Complex Structure A (CSA) of the African Stonehenge in the Nabta Playa, according to Fred Wendorf, one of the site's discoverers, this Neter is most assuredly pre-historic. As Bauval and Brophy have indicated, "We can also note that several megalithic alignments emanating from CSA mark both the rising of Sirius and the Big Dipper – and the ancient Egyptians often identified the former with a

cow and the latter with a bull's thigh. Indeed the possibility of a cultural link between the cow stone at Nabta Playa and the ancient Egyptians was suggested by
Wendorf when he proposed that this strange, sculpted megalith "may have been
the origin of the ancient Egyptians' fascination with working large stones."[72]
Thus, another major contribution to the early formation of the ancient land of
Khem, unearthed in Nubia, may have originated on the primal savannahs and
plains of sub-Saharan Africa.

Indeed the earliest evidence of symbolic expression is found at Blombos
Cave near the tip of South Africa where engraved ochre shell beads, a chimeric
creature – part bison, part woman, among 442 animals and paintings etched
onto cave walls have been found. In addition to this, "Bone harpoon points, found
nowhere else before 45,000 years ago, have been uncovered in the Democratic
Republic of the Congo in sediments nearly twice that old."[73]

According to Chip Walter's article *The First Artists*, published in the *National
Geographic* magazine of January 2015, "Modern human beings have inhabited these
hills and shallow caves off and on for more than 165,000 years."[74] He also makes
the astute observation that "Creating a simple shape that stands for something
else – a symbol, made by one mind, that can be shared with others – is obvious
only after the fact. Even more than the cave art, these first concrete expressions
of consciousness represent a leap from our animal past toward what we are today – a species awash in symbols from the signs that guide your progress down
the highway to the wedding ring on your finger and the icons on your iPhone."[75]

In *Food of the Gods*, for example, Terence McKenna alleges that, "the rise of
language, partnership society, and complex religious ideas may have occurred
not far from the area where humans emerged – the game-filled, mushroom-
dotted grasslands and savannahs of tropical and subtropical Africa. There the
partnership society arose and flourished; there hunter-gatherer culture slowly
gave way to domestication of animals and plants. In this milieu the psilocybin-
containing mushrooms were encountered, consumed, and deified. Language,
poetry, ritual, and thought emerged from the darkness of the hominid mind."[76]

Witness the ancient and exquisite cave art found across Africa, particularly
the rock paintings in the Tassili-n-Ajjer plateau in the western regions of the
Sahara and those of southern Europe. Indeed, Chip Walter claims that, "While

Europe is home to famous examples of Paleolithic art such as the paintings at Chauvet, Lascaux, and Altamira, evidence of modern behavior is far older in Africa and the Middle East."[77]

No doubt, of course, such exposure to psychedelic mushrooms, as suggested above, did occur. But such ideas also presuppose that man is merely a terrestrial being. Yet, is it possible some of us are not? Indeed, while still a student at UCLA, I discovered that one of the meanings of the name Zulu was "The Children Of Heaven." As I thought so at the time, this appeared to be a rather quaint expression, similar to the concept of "The Chosen People" as was used by people of the Jewish faith. A concept designed to mark out a people as somehow special. With that understanding, the curiosity faded and eventually got shelved somewhere in the furthest recesses of my mind from where it had to be quickly retrieved from its hoary cobwebs and dusted off after I learned in more recent times there was more to "The Children Of Heaven" myth than my earlier impression permitted.

Most extraordinarily, the Zulus claim that they *literally* came from heaven! Their shamans, sangomas and sanusis imply that they are the extraterrestrials moderns are so ardently in search of as they once lived on Mars! For that to be possible of course they had to have been there more than 500,000 years ago as that was the time a major celestial catastrophe within our solar system made the once habitable planet Mars uninhabitable. But there they insist they lived.

Absurd as such an idea may appear at first there is more, if not indeed technological proof. Viking satellite evidence debatably shows the remnants of the structural existence of an ancient Bronze Age type civilization on the surface of Mars, particularly in the region of the Sea of Cydonia where the enigmatic Sphinx-like Face and five-sided pyramid have been observed though not interpreted or ratified as such by NASA.

Overriding cautious official skepticism for the moment however, could this have been the home of the Zulus? Indeed, included in their myth are claims that their astronomer-priest class was aware of the pending destruction about to hit their planet and thus searched the heavens for another habitable location and struck upon the Earth.

From Mars they made the "Great Leap" landing on earth and residing where today we find the Sahara Desert which at the time of their arrival was a landscape of lush vegetation and in fact until about 15,000 years ago this densely populated region which also had an inland sea still had the largest number of people anywhere on the planet. Indeed there may well be archaeological proof of their arrival as will be discussed in chapter three. As for Mars, more will be discussed in the Epilogue.

In the meantime however, there in the Sahara location "The Children of Heaven" remained until such time as the desert made its appearance and thus began the Bantu migration throughout Africa towards the major water ways: The Niger, the Congo, the Nile, etc. and the Great Lakes. A migration that continued on into the early 1600s AD when, spearheaded by the Tswana, the Zulu tribes arrived in southern Africa.

So *the paleo-ancient very high civilization of high antiquity* may well have included Zulu visitors from Mars! Indeed, it would not be out of place to mention at this point that, "It was believed by the Egyptians that Ra, too, had come to Earth from the "Planet of Millions of Years" in a Celestial Barge.[78] Perhaps it was his arrival that caused the image of "an Egyptian ankh inscribed within a circle that has radiating beams protruding from it" to be etched, as was discussed earlier, into a 200,000 year old glacier slab at Dreikopseiland.

This of course is high speculation in the realms of prehistory and high antiquity. Yet, if the link along the ancient prime meridian of the Great Pyramid, Great Zimbabwe and the two pyramids of southern Africa was the result of a conscious scientific knowledge possessed by certain members of this global and seemingly interplanetary civilization then there must also be a connection between them and the alleged interplanetary Anunnaki who knew southern Africa as the ABZU.

According to the Sumerians, it was the Anunnaki who allegedly created the Lulu for the specific purpose of creating workers to work in the gold mines they discovered in this region of the world. This name they gave to the people they created translates as, "The Black Headed Ones." In the biblical text of course this creation of mankind is attributed to the Elohim who said: "Let us make man in our image."

Anthropologists have gone to great lengths in describing the Lulu as being people with a shock of black hair, hence their curious name. I think that explanation for such a title however is weak and not well founded. The Anunnaki after all called them *Black headed* not *Black haired*. Indeed, the late Phillip Coppens also "noted that Sumer, as Egypt, has been the subject of "racial discolouration". Sumer has been identified as a Semitic culture, even though the Sumerians referred to themselves as "black heads".[79] It appears therefore that those ancient commentators were describing the very people who are ordinarily associated with the continent of Africa.

Now the gods described in the Bible as the ones who said: "Let us make man, in our own image," these were in fact the Sumerian Anunnaki, the ones the biblical text refers to as the Nephilim, the Sons of God, or the Elohim.

Intriguingly, the rabbi brothers Sabbah see in the Elohim "the many pharaohs, the fathers of Egypt."[80] Indeed Gary Greenberg's take on this same subject is that "In the biblical story, the "Sons of God" would originally have been the sons of the Memphis pharaoh, the god Horus. The "Daughters of Man" would have been the daughters of a Herakleopolitan king, the false Horus – a man. The biblical story suggests that a marriage occurred between members of the Memphis court and the Herakleopolis court, one that led to a dispute over which line of princes – Herakleopolitans or Memphites – would ascend to the throne of Horus. It would have been marriage that gave the Herakleopolitans a veneer of legitimacy to their claim for the Egyptian throne."[81]

Indeed, with respect to the latter country's later history, the rabbi brothers Sabbah further notice that, "the Bible reveals that there were two classes of people who were involved in the Exodus. There were the Yahuds, the priestly class, and there were Children of Israel, the commoners, the "multitudes.""[82] The latter by definition may or may not be the origin of "the real Children of Israel" who can be found living *in the ghettos, inner cities and slums across the four corners of the earth and are the ones suffering today* that the *Gathering Of Christ* organization referred to in its flyer.

Although, the rabbi brothers Sabbah do not equate Moses with Akhenaten, as does Ahmed Osman, they do say that, "Moses was a Yahud by birth, a son of the Elohim, belonging to the Egyptian nobility, probably the son of one of Pharaoh's daughters."[83]

The Yahuds moreover were the residents of Akhetaten, the multiethnic capital of Khem during the Amarna period when Akhenaten waged war on the Neteru, the ancient deities still worshipped by the rest of the population left bereft and abandoned throughout the kingdom. Those latter neglected ones probably are the real Children of Israel, the actual descendants of those who had bequeathed to Khem the esoteric knowledge of the MeduNeteru, the symbolic writing system that the ancient Greeks came to call the sacred writings, or more commonly, the hieroglyphs.

Eventually, the Yahuds, the priests of the new Aten cult, and other residents of Akhetaten would be driven out of Khem, escorted by the armies of generals Horemheb, Seti and Ramesses, each of whom would later become pharaohs.

Unlike Ahmed Osman incidentally, it is not Akhenaten but Ramesses that the rabbi brothers Sabbah see as Moses. In their fascinating book *Secrets of the Exodus*, they came to this identification of the leader of the Exodus after observing that "In the cartouche of Ramesses I, a lion is depicted. Biblically the lion is the symbol of Judah: the Lion of Judah. The tribe of Judah was Moses' army (the Levites), who had the same objective as the leaders of Egypt, the submission of the Canaanite territories."[84] Moreover, they add that in "Hebrew, lion is pronounced "lavi." Moses was the son of Levi, or son of the lion, "Ben-Levi."This symbol of power is found in the royal cartouche of Ramesses I and in the family name of Moses."[85]

Other candidates however have been suggested. Some believe for example that Tuthmose, a son of Amenhotep III is the biblical Moses. In his book, *The Moses Legacy*, Graham Phillips suggests that, "If the Exodus took place during the reign of Amenhotep III, then Prince Tuthmose is the best candidate by far for the historical Moses. If our assumptions are correct, his background uniquely matches Moses' in a number ways: *commander of the army in Ethiopia*; priest at the temple of Ra; and he is disgraced or exiled. Even his name is intriguing: Tuthmose means 'son of [the god] Thoth'. If Tuthmose had abandoned the old gods and decided to drop the god-element Tuth – Thoth – from his name, then he would actually have been called Mose, the original rendering of the name Moses."[86] (Italics added.)

Throughout this text however and obviously more in agreement with Ahmed Osman, the case is being made that Moses and Akhenaten are one and the same person, one biblical myth the other historical entity. Akhenaten, of course, was the son of Amenhotep III whereas the Bible states that Moses was the child of his mother Jochebed and his father Amram.

Given that their names shared the same symbol of power, the lion, the rabbi brothers Sabbah, in an attempt to identify Moses as Ramesses I, demonstrated that "Moses was the son of Levi, or son of the lion, "Ben-Levi,""[87] as indicated above. However, if these identifications prove to be true, how can Amenhotep III, Levi, and Amram all be reconciled as the father of Moses?

With regard to the name Amram however, Osman observed that, "in the God's second cartouche, Aten's name is given as Im-r-n (Imran), which has been translated as "in his name." As Akhenaten regarded Aten to be his divine father, Imran became the name of his father. For this reason, the city of Akhetaten is called Amarna. Contrary to the general belief, the name Amarna does not derive from a Muslim Arab tribe that settled in the area in modern times. No evidence of such event exists, while Amarna is part of the Minya Province, whose population is mostly Christian Copts. The name "Amarna" derived from Aten's name as found in his second cartouche, Im-r-n."[88] Thus, an explanation for the origin of the name Amram has been found a solution. Now one is needed for the name Levi.

Once again, Ahmed Osman proves the ultimate detective when he demonstrates that another "similarity between Akhenaten and Moses is the close relation they both had with the Levite priests. The Bible tells us little about the origins of the Levites who played an important role in the Exodus account. In his book *Moses and Monotheism*, Sigmund Freud suggested that the Levites "were the Egyptian followers of Moses." To support this view, he points out that only among the Levites do Egyptian names occur later. What makes Freud's argument more acceptable is the fact that the name of Meryre, the High Priest of Aten at Amana [sic], is the Hebrew equivalent of the name Merari, who is described in Genesis 46:11 as one of the sons of Levi."[89] Thus it would appear that Amram, the father of Moses was a, or the one and only, Levite High Priest of Amarna.

As will be discussed in chapter three, the Levites belonged to a group known as the Yahuds, the main priesthood of Akhetaten, made up of original native but converted, or better said subverted, African priests of Khem. Ultimately, the Yahu priesthood would eventually become known to the world as the Jews and their banishment would be recorded in the Bible as the Exodus.

Within 40 years of the Exodus, which allegedly occurred around 1330 BC, the land of Judah was created in the southern part of Khemite controlled Canaan but eventually it divided into two after the reign of Solomon in 930 BC making Israel its northern region after which it formed a separate kingdom later known as Judaea.

Whether the Exodus occurred or not is, in any event, a heavily debated issue among scholars but a time around the 1st or 2nd millennium has nevertheless been posited as the major contender for its occurrence. As a commentary in Wikipedia states, "Pharaoh's fear that the Israelites might ally themselves with foreign invaders seems unlikely in the context of the late 2nd millennium, when Canaan was part of *an Egyptian empire* and Egypt faced no enemies in that direction, but does make sense in a 1st millennium context, when Egypt was considerably weaker and faced invasion first from the Persians and later from Seleucid Syria."[90] (Author's italics.)

Disregarding Wikipedia's observations however, the research here of course rules out the 1st millennium for the Exodus in favour of the time of the 18th Dynasty as proposed by Ahmed Osman dated around 1543-1292 of the 2nd millennium BC.

In any event, during the 1st millennium in the fateful year of 586 BC, the Babylonian and Persian armies attacked the territory of Judaea and Israel and brought about its fatal demise along with the exile of its people to the rivers of Babylon.

Under Cambyses II in 525 BC that same attack continued on to the Nile Valley. In geopolitical military terms, since both these regions were under North African protection, those Persian advances can be seen as a forthright and concerted attack against the African nation of Khem. In fact, history shows that the power of the Persian Empire only reached its height with the direct conquest of Khem.

According to Herodotus, and in contrast to how Dinesh D'Souza and other scholars imagined the Khemites as imperial conquerors, "when Cambyses conquered Egypt he wished to cross the Nubian desert but nearly lost his life there. He then sent "*ichthyophagous*" Ethiopians to spy on the King; the latter exposed the plot and through his representatives, lectured Cambyses in the following terms:

"The King of the Ethiops thus advises the king of the Persians – when the Persians can pull a bow of this strength thus easily, then let him come with an army of superior strength against the long-lived Ethiopians – till then let him thank the gods that they have not put it into the heart of the sons of the Ethiops to covet countries which do not belong to them."[91]

Thus, with regard to the sovereign defense of African territory, to the Persians spoke a righteous but unnamed 'non-imperialistic' Ethiopian king. Need the reader still be reminded that 'Ethiop' is a Greek word meaning 'burnt face,' a mere description of an otherwise black person?

Indeed, with regard to imperial invasions, shortly before the beginning of the first millennium BC, the people of Khem were constantly besieged and having to fight off such external attempts at conquest. According to Immanuel Velikovsky, for example, the major event of the reign of Ramses III (circa. 1200 BC) "was the successful opposition to the armies coming from the north. In their sweep of conquest, the northern hordes came to the very gates of Egypt, the greatest and most glorious of kingdoms. In all ages conquerors have made Egypt their goal – Esarhaddon and Assurbanipal the Assyrians, Cambyses the Persian, Alexander the Macedonian, Pompey the Roman, Omar the Arab, Selim the Turk, and Napoleon; and some unidentified leader or group of leaders, before any of these, had armed troops to drink water from the Nile. But Ramses III rose to the occasion. He battled the invaders on land and sea and turned back the tide that threatened to envelop Egypt."[92]

Let us therefore dispose of, once and for all, the oxymoronic concept of an ancient African imperialism!

Nevertheless, regardless of the disputed date of the Exodus and despite the debate over whether it occurred or not, interestingly most scholars, as stated in Wikipedia, accept that the Exodus "is the charter myth of Israel; its message is that the Israelites were delivered from slavery by Yahweh and therefore belong to him through the covenant."

Ironically, as will be seen in chapter three, Yahweh, Yah or Yahu, the name of the God of the Israelites, is one of the divine titles of the god-king Amenhotep III. And, as stated above, and repeated here for emphasis, the rabbi brothers Sabbah pointed out that, "the Canaanite kings worshiped Pharaoh"[93] in the name of Yahu-Heh, the great god, the very Yahweh whose covenant the Israelites still keep. Thus, in no uncertain terms, this is indeed a pledge of allegiance to a divine black African King.

Let not black African origin deniers disparage the truth about the race of the pharaohs of the Nile valley civilization any longer. Ask the police officer who detained me at approximately 10:15 p.m. on Westgate Street in my hometown of Cardiff for an hour more than necessary on that cold and damp Saturday night of 28 February 2015 whether I am black or not. Clearly by today's standards, even if Amenhotep III were as light skinned as me, he would still be considered a black African king.

Nevertheless, to the detriment of the history of black Africa, the baffling obscurity that surrounds the ancient facts revealed so far can as such be traced to the treacherous actions of the original iconoclast, King Akhenaten, the pharaoh who by means of the imposition of his traitorous and insidious patriarchal mono-theistic revolution, chose to initiate the suppression of the true understanding of the black cultural roots of Africa's highly advanced matriarchal civilization.

Three

The god of most monotheistic religions was not the creator god,
not the ultimate god, but a lesser, evil being.

Sun Ra

Today there can hardly be anyone who does not know something about the strange and enigmatic 14th century BC Pharaoh Akhenaten. This was a man who at one fell swoop overturned an ancient African religious tradition and as a consequence changed the course of human history.

Indeed, knowledge of his time is no longer confined to the domain of scholarship. To say nothing of the iconic image of Nefertiti, his queen, we are confronted with his image and history in many television documentaries and moreover ever since the spectacular find of Tutankhamun's burial chamber in the 1920s knowledge of the 18th Dynasty to which Akhenaten belonged is indelibly impressed in modern consciousness.

But what is the significance of this resurrection of Akhenaten for Africa and the world today? Given that humanity currently stands on the precipice of economic collapse and the potential brink of thermonuclear warfare, exacerbated to no little extent by Bernard Lewis' and Samuel Huntington's manufactured "Clash of Civilizations," which is nothing more than a thinly disguised late 20th century revival of the Crusades, the answer to this may be the key to the future success of human evolution on this planet!

The easily accessible and influential scriptural creeds Siegfried Morenz mentioned in chapter one that were distinguished from the Sacred Science of the land of Khem are also referred to as the Abrahamic faiths. From these, the West has taken on the mantle of the Judeo-Christian portion only. Currently used as a kind of Babylonian divide-and-conquer device, the battle lines have now been drawn in the oil-rich sands of Central Asia.

Under the current circumstances, where we are presented with the fact that the majority of the world's governments and their military industrial and intelligence complexes have fallen under the influence of Seth, the Neter for whom death, war and destruction are the favoured attributes, it is crucial to understand certain ancient spiritual truths for in his current incarnation Seth is the ultimate Terrorist let loose.

Turn on your television and instantly evidence of the *Shemsu Seth* is ubiquitous, whether in the form of the Taliban, Al Qaeda, Boko Haram, ISIL, for example, organizations or groups which in some circles are viewed as NATO's legions, to say nothing of the duplicitous nature of the principle countries that nurture and support them.

Having deceitfully abandoned the centuries old nation state principle of Westphalia in favour of regime change, in addition to divesting Western Christianity of its treasured tenets: "Turn the other cheek" and "Love thy enemy," the forces of the Shemsu Seth, in their quest for material gain and desire for ultimate power, as currently manifest in the West, demonstrate a propensity to manipulate the latter religion in the apparent interests of a secreted Babylonian corporate power structure lurking behind all global military industrial and intelligence complexes.

Inspired by ancient Babylonian intentions that undermine in fact the very concepts of freedom and democracy, the misuse of modern technology is driving the early 21st century's populous toward insanity, exacerbating its future prospects as it zaps the optimism of the youth while clouding the vision of the mature with inevitable pessimism resulting from the pursuit of a dangerous and reckless war policy that is leading to thermonuclear World War III, indeed an antiquated geopolitical policy that increasingly gained momentum in the immediate post-9/11 moment, as expressed through the West's 'false flag' invasion of Afghanistan, its despicable 'Shock & Awe' assault on Iraq, NATO's unconscionable devastation of the African nation of Libya, and the not so subtle current New World Order regime change policy targeting Syria at the moment.

The cadre of individuals who recently instigated and orchestrated these on-going wars have been most pertinently identified by American physical economist, Lyndon H. LaRouche, Jr., as *The Children of Satan*, the title of his 2004 book of the same name. As uncovered in chapter two, the very name of Satan in the West, is in fact derived from the name of Seth.

Indeed, though he does not refer to former British Prime Minister Tony Blair and his duplicitous regime change policy jargon, in *Dreaming War*, Gore Vidal has corroborated the former opinion expressed above by also identifying the current day reincarnation of the Shemsu Seth as "the-oil-and-gas Cheney-Bush junta."[1] With an ominous historical presage, delivered in his unique satirical American parlance, Vidal foreshadows his analysis of this critical resurgence of Sethian power with the following historical recollection:

On August 24, 1814, things looked very dark for freedom's land. That was the day the British captured Washington, D.C., and set fire to the Capitol and White House. President Madison took refuge in the nearby Virginia woods, where he waited patiently for the notoriously short attention span of the Brits to kick in, which it did. They moved on and what might have been a Day of Utter Darkness turned out to be something of a bonanza for the D.C. building trades and upmarket realtors.

One hundred and eighty-seven years later - and one year after 9/11, we still don't know by whom we were struck that Tuesday, or for what true purpose. But it … does seem fairly plain to many civil libertarians that 9/11 put paid not only to our fragile Bill of Rights, but also to our once-envied republican system of government which had abruptly taken a mortal blow the previous year, when the Supreme Court did a little dance in 5-4 time and replaced an elected president with the oil-and-gas Cheney-Bush junta."[2]

Moreover, after conjuring up "a nightmare vision of an America incited to vengeance by orchestrated media hype, its citizens reduced to spear-carrying, and the Cheney-Bush junta as the latest, most cynical strategists of American empire-building,"[3] Gore Vidal ponders whether Afghanistan was:

> then turned to rubble in order to avenge the three thousand Americans slaughtered by Osama? Hardly. The junta is convinced that Americans are so simple minded that they can deal with no scenarios more complex than the venerable lone, crazed killer (this time with zombie helpers) who does evil just for the fun of it 'cause he hates us, 'cause we're rich 'n' free 'n' he's not."[4]

Regardless of the reasons why however, "Osama, if it was he and not a nation, simply provided the necessary shock to put in train a war of conquest. But conquest of what? What is there in dismal dry sandy Afghanistan worth conquering?"[5]

What is there, indeed? At this point, for an answer to that pertinent question, Gore Vidal quotes from the hawkish National Security Advisor to President Carter, Zbigniew Brzezinski who reminded us that, "Ever since the continents started interacting politically, some five hundred years ago, Eurasia has been the center of world power."[6] The reason for this is due to the fact that Eurasia is all the territory east of Germany including Russia, the Mideast, China, and parts of India. Thus "Brzezinski acknowledges that Russia and China, bordering oil-rich central Asia, are the two main powers threatening American hegemony in that area."[7]

Therefore, it appears that despite her magnificent revolution America has truly lost her envied "republican system of government" because the foregoing policy is nothing more than an echo of the very same policy utilized by her erstwhile British imperial master and enemy who, as Vidal described above, attempted to re-conquer its American colonies in 1814.

Indeed British fingerprints are everywhere, as Joseph P. Farrell, with reference to the Babylonian inspired three Abrahamic faiths, also reminds us that, "The creation of a Western apocalypse culture simultaneous to the creation of an Islamic apocalypse culture easily lends itself to perpetual manipulations by an elite or elites for political and geopolitical ends."[8] Without doubt, the very target of the Sethian Cheney-Bush junta was the identical aim of British geopolitician, Sir Halford John MacKinder (1861-1947), who among many other things was a one-time director of the London School of Economics.

According to MacKinder, there were "three basic geopolitical realities to the world: (1) a resource-rich *Heartland* comprising central Eurasia and dominated by Russia, and touching upon China... Around this area were (2) an Inner Crescent, comprising Europe, the Arabian Peninsula, the Indian Subcontinent, and the Chinese-Japanese orient, and (3) an Outer or "insular Crescent" comprising the two American continents, sub Saharan Africa, and the vastness of the Indian and Pacific Oceans."[9] This obviously is the very same territory that Zbigniew Brzezinski claims is vital to the strategic interest of the United States government.

Therefore, the United States of America needs to be on guard if it wants to retain its leading position in the turbulent course of human affairs. Those who lost the Revolutionary War still sulk. They have not forgotten 1776, hence, the events of 1814. Geopolitically speaking therefore, modern Israel is a Trojan Horse, a consequential gift of post Sykes/Pico Treaty British Colonial Policy, that may well undermine the United States Constitution and thus bring an end to that country and its stated goal of being a beacon of light since escaping its feudal past.

Thus, the old Babylonian game is still on, only this time in its American phase. Indeed, according to Noam Chomsky, this is what that country's "highly centralized and class-conscious dominant social group"[10] referred to as "Grand Area" planning, a power controlling concept designed to encompass "a region "strategically necessary for world control""[11] that included "at least the Western Hemisphere, the Far East, and the former British Empire..."[12] as well as western and southern Europe and the oil-producing regions of the Middle East."[13]

Thus, if those voices that proclaim that they are fighting a war against terrorism are truly serious then they need to know why one of the first things to puzzle the student about Akhenaten's history is the reason the ancient Nile Dwellers considered him to be a **heretic** and a **criminal**. Furthermore, they need to know why it was felt necessary to eradicate his name from all records only for it to reemerge from obscurity after 20th century archaeologists serendipitously rediscovered him as some sort of Wunderkind, the author of monotheism, an ideology however ascribed to Moses, the alleged author of the Pentateuch, the first five books of the Bible.

According to that biblical text, we are indeed informed that God commandingly spoke to Moses on Mount Sinai telling him: "Thou shalt have no other gods but Me." Or as Exodus 20:3 of the *New King James Bible*, prefers, "You shall have no other gods before Me."

Moreover, in the words of the medieval French-Jewish scholar and commentator on the oral tradition concerning the Pentateuch, Rabbi Shelomoh ben Yishak (1040-1105 AD), known to historians as Rashi reported that, "Before naming the "ten" commandments, the Bible speaks of "the" commandment:

"Yahweh said to Moses: 'Come up to me, on the mountain, and stay here. I will give you the stone tablets, the law and the commandment that I have written for their instruction.'" (Exodus 24:12)"[14]

As it was based on the Aramaic Bible and on written and oral traditions, according to the rabbi brothers Sabbah, the teaching of Rashi "is one of the most important in the Jewish tradition."[15] From a review of such an authoritative source, in their brilliant book *Secrets Of The Exodus* the Sabbah brothers reveal that, "six hundred and thirteen commandments are included in the Ten Commandments," they themselves are contained in the first. Thus the commandment could correspond to the stone tablets of Akhenaten consisting of a single commandment: the name of Aten, or Adonay in the Bible. The commandment given to Moses would then be a transmission of the pharaonic power of the sacred name. It signifies the heritage of the pharaonic monarchy, a heritage that had to be due to Moses and not to Aaron.""[16]

Indeed, in their decoding of the Bible, instead of Joshua it was "Sety" and his father, "Ramesses I" who "accompanied the "dissidents" with the symbols of the monotheistic religion, as well as the name of Akhenaten engraved on a double stone tablet. The first and last word on these tablets (now in the Turin Museum...) form "Ankh Aten," the living Aten or Anokh Aten, Akhenaten's name, in perfect accord with the first Biblical commandment "Anokh Adonay."[17]

Now the fact that written Hebrew did not exist at the time raises the interesting linguistic issue of what language was used indeed to write the Ten Commandments. According to the aforementioned rabbis, the "divine characters"[18] containing this pharaonic legislation had to have been written in the MeduNeteru, the symbolic writing system of the "Afro-Asiatic" language of the people of the Land of Khem. Moreover, the tombstone image of the tablets that the Christian Church has promoted throughout the centuries was therefore more than likely based indeed on the stone cartouche that represents the name of Aten.

Alternatively however, according to the geometrician and lay biblical scholar John Ten, a true interpretation of the name for the tablets written in the original Bible did not describe stone tablets at all but rather a crystalline object made of sapphire with a di-hexagonal shape. This latter interesting fact was really important to him as it revealed "information that doesn't quite match the Christian interpretation of the Torah where Moses is not said to have come down from the mountain with [stone] tablets"[19] with the Ten Commandments on them because what the original text described as being in his hands were in fact sci-fi types of a crystalline structure that were hexagonal in nature.

Interesting as that momentary foray into the possibility of the existence of ancient high technology happens to be, which indeed will be further discussed in chapter seven, shortly after those initial admonitions were delivered, it is further commanded in Exodus 20:4 that, "You shall not make for yourself any carved image, any likeness of *anything* that *is* in heaven above, or that *is* in the earth beneath." And finally in Exodus 20:5 God says, "You shall not bow down to them nor serve them. For I am a jealous God!"

Then quite extraordinarily, and indeed quite surprisingly, in the verse that accompanies Exodus 25:3, this jealous God nevertheless requires a gift of an ornate sanctuary from the followers of Moses. "And this is the offering which you shall take from them: gold, silver, and bronze."

Now for whatever the purpose of these alleged divine commands, it cannot be denied that this curiously covetous and avaricious request is a suspiciously mundane desire for a supposedly ethereal spirit.

Thus, given such an apparent penchant for material things, is it possible that the biblical passage cited above is not a reference to a metaphysical entity at all but a reference to an actual historical figure, a personage of high rank or nobility perhaps? One, indeed, who has a need for richly endowed raw material commodities. If so, and if Moses was a man of flesh and blood, he must have been speaking with an actual historical individual.

In fact, from the dialogue quoted in Exodus 33:20-22 during another discussion that had taken place between the two on a later occasion, it definitely appears that Moses was in the presence of the same or another flesh and blood individual who related that:

"You cannot see My face; for no man shall see Me, and live."
And the Lord said, "Here is a place by Me, and you shall stand on the rock.
"So it shall be, while My glory passes by, that I will put you in the cleft of the rock, and will cover you with My hand, and you shall see My back; But My face shall not be seen."

At this point, it is a reasonable assumption to make that the faithful would regard the questioning of this apparent theophany as sacrilegious and prefer the matter understood in metaphoric terms only or better than that left alone. Nevertheless, here for the first time in history we are confronted with the first explicit legal threat to the sacred doctrines of ancient Africa and its remnant traditions inherited from *the paleoancient very high civilization of high antiquity*.

Therefore, though such numinous sensitivities are respectfully taken into account, this biblical passage requires further scrutiny nonetheless for it describes an inexplicably intimate encounter between Moses and an anonymous person who possesses the power of legislative command.

Evidently, this divine and authoritative entity described as the Lord nevertheless possessed a "face," a "hand" and a "back!" Moreover, Moses is graciously permitted a rear view of this otherwise unknown-by-name "physical" person.

No matter the intimacy and no matter the implications of the nature of this meeting, in the interests of African history there is a need for the identification of these historical personages. Thus who really were these powerful men? Indeed, who were the nobility the ancients regarded as gods on earth in those days?

Curiously the historical record of the same time period makes references to a pharaoh who was wreaking havoc throughout the Nile valley by closing down its many ancient temples and at the same time disbanding the priesthood, while simultaneously banning the worship of the Neteru, the sacred elements of nature, the nature powers, the sacred 'scientific' entities generally misunderstood, misnamed or traduced as pagan gods.

This was the so-called Amarna period when Akhenaten waged war on the Neteru, the ancient deities still worshipped by the rest of the population throughout the kingdom who were now left bereft and abandoned. Indeed by bringing about the destruction of representations of the carved images or likenesses "of *anything* that *is* in heaven above, or that *is* in the earth beneath," as cited above, the reverence that had been bestowed upon these symbols of the Neteru was about to be abolished. Therefore the spiritual element that lay at the foundational heart of the peoples of ancient Africa, the spiritual principles that had previously given them solace for untold thousands of years, was about to be eliminated at one violent and audacious stroke.

This was an extremely radical and alien action to take place on African soil. For this reason it is contended herein that this was the arrogant result of a Babylonian infiltration of such a scale and order of magnitude it rent a fundamental ontological division of cataclysmic proportions that would reverberate throughout time between the "Old World," i.e. everything that had ever happened in pre-history, including activities not known outside of Africa, and the to-be-forged, "New World" of subsequent materialism, death and destruction to come.

The impact of such a catastrophic psychological upheaval on that ancient African spiritual belief system ranks as the second "Cosmic Division" since Atum divided heaven from earth. This was a momentous act for a pharaoh to take, one whose perverse ideology has created serious complications and circumstances for the world ever since.

Indeed, as the bodies of thousands of desperate people drown in the Mediterranean Sea, the current refugee crisis and the racism that it is stirring up on the shores of Europe and at the Channel Tunnel entrance into the United Kingdom is nothing more than the colonial chickens coming home to roost. Euro-American society only has itself to blame for the fact is this is the result of NATO's catastrophic resource war policy and its consequent destruction and destabilization of the populations within Central Asia, the so-called Middle East, and Africa.

From a biblical perspective moreover, the global catastrophic refugee and migrant crisis seen today is nothing less than a continuation of the same Exodus that came as a result of the enforcement of an arrogant and false monotheistic ideology. Indeed, prior to his immolation by the Italian State in the early 17th century, Giordano Bruno recognized the destructive nature of this historical event when he wrote in no uncertain terms of the critical necessity for *The Expulsion Of The Triumphant Beast*.

Throughout the world of course, Moses who led the Exodus is well known from biblical legend whereas Akhenaten, the king who became the first to name himself pharaoh, and who wielded the power to utterly destroy a long established religious system, was the enigmatic but particularly iconoclastic son of king Amenhotep III and Queen Tiye the daughter of Tuya and Yuya, the latter persons well known only among certain specialists or members of the general public who have an interest in the subject.

As luck would have it however, the remains of Queen Tiye's father Yuya, Akhenaten's maternal grandfather, caused quite a stir at the time of their discovery. One enthusiastic Egyptologist even waxed poetic about his appearance, especially since he looked so *unlike the rest of the people* of Khem. His aquiline or hooked "Syrian" nose for example and his staunch dignity were emphasized and his looks even compared to that of a Pope! Strangely contrary to this view however, Wikipedia evidences the fact that some "Egyptologists have suggested that Tiye's father, Yuya, was of Nubian descent due to the features of his mummy and the many different spellings of his name, which might imply it was a non-Egyptian name in origin. Indeed Ahmed Osman's observations also affirm that "eleven different versions of Yuya's name were found in his tomb, on his sarcophagus, the three coffins, and other funerary furniture: Ya, Yaa, Yiya, Yuya, Yayai, Yuyu, Yaya, Yiay, Yia, and Yuy, which makes one wonder what was the name the craftsmen were trying to inscribe?"[20]

With reference to his possible Nubian descent however, unless Nubians are now to be considered Caucasian in appearance, looking at a photograph of the mummy of Yuya, it is staggering to think that anyone, let alone an Egyptologist, would consider him as in any way remotely resembling anything like a black African!

That circumstance notwithstanding, in any event, according to Velikovsky, "It has been repeatedly conjectured that one of Tiy's parents was of Mitannian origin."[21] Thus the question is, which one? If that parent is Yuya, then the origin of his alleged foreign location was the Persia that is modern day Iran, a probability that will be examined in chapter four.

Be that as it may, Mitannian, Syrian or Nubian, Yuya, with more or less unanimous consent, is thought to have been a foreigner of Asiatic origin, which is a quite very interesting observation given that he held such grand titles as *Father of the King* and *Chief of the Charioteers*, among many others. Contrary to what was stated in chapter one, this was a highly remarkable achievement and position to be held by one considered an outsider.

In fact, he was king Amenhotep III's right hand man and father-in-law! As the rabbi Sabbah brothers pointed out in *Secrets of the Exodus*, "At the age of fourteen … Amenhotep III married Teye [sic], the daughter of Yuya, who came from a tiny village called Akhmim in Upper Egypt. After the marriage of his daughter to Amenhotep, Prince Yuya was promoted to the supreme rank of "Father of the God," or father-in-law to the God-King."[22]

Now it just so happens that these fascinating physiognomic descriptions of the Asiatic foreigner and the titles bestowed on him struck Egyptian author Ahmed Osman with the thunderous and booming sound of a resonant African bass drum. Indeed, in *Stranger In The Valley Of The Kings*, Osman reveals, that after intense study of this matter, he was suddenly blessed with such clarity that he instantly recognized that these very same titles that Yuya possessed also belonged to none other than the biblical Joseph! The one made famous as the man with the coat of many colours.

In point of fact, Osman has presented us with the dramatic proposition that the maternal grandfather of Akhenaten was indeed the biblical Joseph. Thus, if Osman's assertions prove true, Yuya's rise to power through the marriage of his daughter to king Amenhotep III is a better explanation of the rise to power of Joseph than the untenable biblical version of him as a mere interpreter of dreams, especially ones with ancient motifs already familiar to the African people of Khem.

Indeed, their ancient folklore recalls that "Imhotep, the man credited with erecting the first pyramid at Saqqara ... went to the Per ankh ... as it was an academic library ... As one of Imhotep's titles is "priest of Thoth amid the House of Life" ... what is intriguing is that the story of his consultation was recorded on the island of Sehel. The hieroglyphic rock inscription is known as the Famine Stela. The narrative relates an episode set in the court of king Zoser, in which Imhotep seeks an explanation for *seven years of famine*, and asks that, "I may enter the Mansion of Life, and unroll the 'Souls of Ra' (sacred books) and lead my action according to them."[23] (Emphasis added.)

According to Osman, it was however Tuthmosis IV, the eighth king of the Eighteenth Dynasty (*c.* 1413-1405 B. C.), "who appointed Joseph as his vizier"[24] and the king who invited Joseph's family to settle in Egypt, offering them land at Goshen. After his death, Joseph and his wife continued to serve Amenhotep III, the next Pharaoh, who broke with Egyptian tradition and, although he married his sister, instead of making her his queen, married and gave the title to Joseph's daughter, Tiye. Thus, Tiye not only replaced the rightful queen of Amenhotep III but, as will be revealed soon, she was destined to usurp the throne of Nefertiti as well.

Interestingly, Osman goes on to say that the "evidence suggests that despite the years he spent in Egypt and the high office he held, Joseph remained aloof from Egyptian religious worship. It seems therefore, a reasonable assumption that by the time Joseph died, Egyptians must have realized that he would not accept the protection of any other gods, only that of his own Yhwh or Yhwe (Jehovah), and what they were trying to write, following their traditions, was the name of this God. The two parts of Yuya's name, Yu and Ya are both short for the name of Yhwe, the Hebrew letter Y (J in English) being in both parts."[25]

As we shall soon see however, another explanation for this conundrum of confusion over his name will have to be found. In the meantime however, following from the logical consequences of his rigorous academic research, Osman also discovered that the true era for the Exodus out of Egypt also coincided with that of the 18th Dynasty. As with the Exodus however, his identification of Yuya with Joseph is not without its challengers. In *The Moses Mystery*, for example Gary Greenberg asserts that, "Joseph, like the other patriarchal leaders, belongs to the realm of myth."[26]

Alternatively, the rabbi brothers Sabbah see for example the same physical and nominal descriptions as those of one of Yuya's sons Ay, a penultimate pharaoh of the 18th Dynasty who will be reviewed later on. Moreover, by declaring that the "priests of Akhet-Aten and the prominent citizens and functionaries formed the people of the Elohim,"[27] they also provide an answer to the question asked earlier, "who were the nobility the ancients regarded as gods on earth in those days?" They were none other than "the children of all the pharaohs of the past, who were seen as the gods of Egypt."[28] The Bible calls them the *Elohim*. Indeed, it is known "From earliest times, perhaps even far back into prehistory, the ancient Egyptians called their royal ancestors the Souls of Nekhen and the Souls of Pe."[29] According to Bauval & Brohpy, "In ancient times, Nekhen was considered the capital of Upper Egypt and Pe the capital of Lower Egypt. Nekhen, however, was probably the older settlement and the original capital of Egypt before the so-called Unification of the Two Kingdoms or Two lands."[30]

On the other hand, Akhet-Aten, the name of the newly created desert "City of Light" or "Horizon of the Sun," where Akhenaten was to proselytize his flock to the new religion was however the capital of Khem's 18th Dynasty for a mere 20 years only.

Equidistant from the old capitals of Memphis and Thebes, cities that were among the suffering victims of his sacrilegious rampage, Pharaoh Akhenaten ruled the whole land safely from Akhetaten, after moving to it in the 5th year of this reign.

Located 250 miles north of Thebes, the city was dedicated to the cult of the power of the sun and was six miles in length and three miles in width. It will eventually be shown however that the inhabitants of those previously mentioned cities described as "suffering victims," those who in fact endured the decimation of their ancient beliefs, were numbered among *the real children of Israel*. These were *"The Children of the God Ra,"* the meaning of their being so named Israel.

On the subject of the more ancient religion however, Siegfried Morenz intriguingly reported that there was a "strict national exclusiveness of the spiritual centre of Egyptian religion,"[31] making the meticulous description of the Asiatic facial features of Yuya given above very interesting indeed. More so since, the 'Per ankh,' "the 'House of Life', which served mainly as a place where sacred writings were compiled... is categorically placed out of bounds to foreigners. 'An Asiatic ... may not enter into ... this House of Life, he may not see it.'"[32]

Though the contrast between Asiatics and "Egyptians" here is emphasized, the question of the latter's ethnic distinction however still remains unanswered. In Morenz' case, as well as for many other Egyptologists, "Egyptian" is a Greek term used as a euphemism that obviates the need to state the ethnicity of the person or people in question while, without reservation or hesitation, the ethnicity of the Asiatic is freely given or otherwise understood.

Nevertheless, there is no getting away from the fact that no outsider would have been taught the esoteric meaning behind the enormous multitude of symbols that composed the entire symbolic lexicon of the enigmatic-for-the-uninitiated MeduNeteru, the so-called hieroglyphs, which also contained the complete scientific knowledge bequeathed from ancient pre-Flood times.

Therefore despite the high position Yuya held he would not have been permitted to enter the 'House of Life' and thus would not be greatly informed of its inner secret, esoteric depths. More importantly, such a strict prohibition would inevitably apply to Yuya's descendants as well.

Indeed, according to the research of Gary Greenberg, Akhenaten, the grandson of Yuya, "apparently came to the throne by accident. The evidence of the time suggests that Amenhotep III intended for one of his other sons to become king and that son went through the rigorous training in religious and administrative skills required of a monarch. But the heir-apparent died prematurely, and Akhenaten, poorly trained in the necessary administrative skills, became the successor."[33]

Though historical clues appear to be lacking at the moment, dare it be put forth for consideration at this time that some nefarious Babylonian scheme nevertheless was behind Akhenaten's succession to the throne.

Whatever the case, as stated in chapter two, there is the suggestion that the unnamed son Greenberg identifies above is Tuthmose who according to Graham Phillips did not die prematurely but disappeared from the pages of history in disgrace or exile. Indeed, for Phillips it is the latter who bears the characteristics of Moses, the Law Giver.

Since, as a consequence of the actions of Moses, the Bible frowns upon idolaters who it must be assumed, by the standard of modern times, could only have been misguided and ignorant irrational primitives as far as their cognitive capacity or noetic development was concerned, some may be wondering therefore if there were any true esoteric depths to be considered. But such misplaced misgivings would be unfounded, as there did indeed exist inner sanctum depths to be plumbed concerning a secret knowledge found at that time only in Khem.

After wading through and brushing away the calumny and slander that the biblical text has wrought upon the True Religion that once existed in ancient black Africa, now known as the "Sacred Science" that preexisted the civilization known as Egypt, those deeper secrets will be outlined shortly for as Rene A. Schwaller de Lubicz noted in chapter two, *Black Africa still holds many surprises for us.*

Thus, long before the American computer technologist and comparative cosmologist Laird Scranton made his groundbreaking and painstaking discoveries in the decoding of the myths and symbols of the Dogon people of Mali and their cross-fertilizing cultural relationship to the MeduNeteru Rene A. Schwaller de Lubicz, who coined the term "Sacred Science," had already peered through the veil that had kept hidden the untranslatable symbolic writings of the people of Khem that the deciphering work and method of the French genius Jean-François Champollion, who fortuitously broke the 'hieroglyphic' code found on the Rosetta Stone, had not been able to translate.

Such grammatical difficulties aside nevertheless, as a consequence of these latter day discoveries, the secret knowledge that lays at the foundation of the MeduNeteru system is finally about to be revealed to the world. But with regard to the secret knowledge found only in the 'House of Life,' there is a problem.

When Schwaller de Lubicz posed the intriguing question, "Who is capable of understanding the themes of the principle of relativity and their ramifications,"[34] he was prying open and exposing the astounding cosmic correlations between the insights of Albert Einstein that underlie the fundamental principles of modern quantum physics and the hidden knowledge of the ancients.

Thus, what was taught in the 'Houses of Life' therefore is no more difficult than understanding the science of modern quantum physics, providing the student undertakes the necessary preparatory studies. Of course the reality is, many are called but few are chosen.

"Even among the great mathematicians, there are few capable of getting to the bottom of this study,"[35] warns Schwaller de Lubicz. "Consider, then, the noble admission of Louis de Broglie, when he says that, after studying Planck's constant for 25 years, he has not yet succeeded in "exhausting" the entire significance of the *quantum* of energy and action. The richness of certain "illuminations" of modern thought is such that it will be exhausted only with difficulty."[36]

And that is the nature of the problem. For as Siegfried Morenz indicated in his *Egyptian Religion*, "The difficulties encountered in translation are as a rule not of a graphical or grammatical nature but stem from the fact that the Egyptians had *a mode of thinking* very different from our own."[37] (Italics added.)

For the modern mind this is a challenge that calls for a radical rethink. To comprehend that ancient way of thinking, *very different from our own*, and indeed the corresponding functional nature of the ancient MeduNeteru, the highly fêted linear left-brain, digitally oriented aspect of modern thinking and its consequential cell-phone zombie apocalypse culture must be temporarily disposed of in favour of right-brain analogical thinking. Thus the ditching of analog in modern times may well prove to have been premature. For the Neter is a verb not a noun.

Rather than a mere fetish of the superstitious mind, the proscribed and prohibited so-called idol of wood or stone, vévé, sign, or symbolic word used to portray an individual Neter is in fact a specific visual and or audial representation of a functional, analogical process in nature, a *Verbe Nature*, as Schwaller de Lubicz identifies it, or a universal physical principle, as American physical economist Lyndon H. LaRouche, Jr. refers to such processes.

Indeed in an effort to understand the underlying principle of such functional operations, Laird Scranton discovered that the people of Khem had a "tendency to use words that sound alike as a way to associate the true meanings of religious concepts"[38] and indeed referenced their use of "wordplay as a fondness for puns and suggests that the priests deliberately used them to disguise references to the innermost secrets of the Egyptian religion."[39] Moreover, he also clarified the fact that this "technique of using multiple meanings serves to disguise the full import of a concept from the uninitiated while at the same time enhancing a broader definition for the initiated."[40]

Correlating a similar function of punning as practiced by the Dogon, he recognized from their mythological symbols that remarkably "whatever source originally composed these myths knew more about the fundamental aspect of science"[41] than he did!

Indeed, science as such is a search for the underlying principles that govern the universe. That is precisely what the MeduNeteru represented for the ancients. Though the magical spells and incantations of the individual Neteru are so despised by Yahwist tradition, they nonetheless represented the underlying functional principles that govern the universe. However, for the purposes of keeping the masses in a malleable and indeed perpetual state of ignorance they have become, as a result of their historical traducement, a suppressed quantum phenomenon.

Be such circumstances as they may, this symbolic concept of the divine Neter nevertheless provided an analogical model of an invisible but functional ontological power that spoke and still speaks directly to right-brain consciousness that the current proponents of linear left-brain digital technology of modern society have removed from the public educational system and therefore the understanding of modern contemporary society.

How could it be otherwise, Gore Vidal pondered, "considering a public educational system that no longer teaches geography in primary schools, much less comparative history or even relevant American history?"[42] Of course, added to that list should be the current shocking state of innumeracy and geometric understanding in modern society.

Moreover, as it should be common knowledge that the original prototype of the Madonna in the West is Ast, or as the Greeks identified her Isis, an ancient African goddess known as the Queen of Heaven, the recent negative reaction to her name on the part of the general public since the modern terrorist group known as ISIS arrived on the scene is also quite shocking. Other than the discontinuance of *classical humanist education* within the public school system of the Western world, no other explanation exists. The general public, clearly influenced by myopic Western mass media propaganda, has no other recourse than to identify the otherwise sacred name of Isis with the *Islamic State In Syria*. To speakers of the Arabic language on the other hand, this particular manifestation of the *Shemsu Seth* is otherwise known as *Da'esh*, which unlike the Greek version of the name Isis has no etymological relationship whatsoever to the Afro-Asiatic 'Ast.'

Thus after 2,000 years or more of reductionism, succeeded by empiricism and positivism, Aristotelian thinking has distanced modern man by light years from the thinking of the ancients. That too is the nature of the problem. Men and women of today do not see as the ancients saw. Hence the difficulties that arose subsequent to Champollion's deciphering of the "hieroglyphs." Ordinary text, for example laundry lists, court cases, and myths etc. were easily understood but certain other symbols of the MeduNeturu, many considered magical, were, like so-called junk DNA, left untranslatable into anything rational or logical for a modern mind bereft of a knowledge of the recently *re*discovered principles of quantum physics to comprehend.

Notwithstanding that situation, given that society now stands on the verge of potential comprehension of the metaphysics of space and the hypergeometrical fabric of space-time it is thus seemingly possible to arrive at the root of the problem in modern thinking, as its source is none other than the thinking of King Amenhotep IV, the iconoclastic pharaoh Akhenaten whose monotheistic ideology was an apparent "alien infiltration" into Africa designed to overthrow the Osirian belief system and to undermine the ancient African mode of thought. In fact, a farcical consequence of empirical Aristotelian reductionist thinking is the moribund philosophy that there is no God!

Despite radical reductionism's fundamental misunderstanding of reality however, Osiris, the African God *par excellence*, was indicative of the inner psychic life of the ancient African mentality. Only an African outsider, a Babylonian influenced Asiatic for example, would conceive of obliterating this African concept, eliminating the inner psychic life of Africa by means of the gradual transformation of its divine elements into the fabricated and historicized characters we now find in the pages of biblical text. A monumental transmutation of a mode of thought that was surely influenced by the man called Moses.

Indeed, the obvious similarities of the biblical and historical figures known as Moses and Akhenaten were the catalyst that inspired Sigmund Freud to write *Moses and Monotheism* in the first place. However even before Freud, it is quite apparent that a connection between the Hebrew religion and that of Akhenaten was being made. For example, in *The Gods of the Egyptians*, E. A. Wallis Budge observes that "Attempts have been made to prove that the Aten worship resembled that of the monotheistic worship of the Hebrews, and to show that Aten is only another form of the name Adon ... but as far as can be seen now the worship of Aten was something like a glorified materialism, which had to be expounded by priests, who performed ceremonies similar to those which belonged to the old Heliopolitan sun-worship, without any connexion whatsoever with the worship of Yahweh."[43]

Though from a symbolic perspective Budge's argument is now outmoded, it does highlight the materialism that was pertinently observed earlier with reference to the verse from Exodus 25:3 that indicated that, "this jealous God requires a gift of an ornate sanctuary from the followers of Moses." Indeed, for Budge, "it is clear that in practice the religion was of a sensuous character, and eminently materialistic."[44]

From Freud's analysis of Moses and Akhenaten of course, it can arguably be concluded that the latter is the creator of monotheism while the former was clearly influenced by Akhenaten's monotheistic revolution. However, the millennia long weight of orthodoxy backing the authenticity of the Bible has led many researchers along a path that of necessity forces them to contort historical fact into biblical narrative. From such an entrenched traditional biblical point of view, it becomes axiomatic that Moses influenced Akhenaten rather than vice versa.

Graham Phillips, the author of *The Moses Legacy*, for example, is one among many who maintain such a supposition and thus draws the conclusion, "That two different cultures in the same place and the same time should both have practiced such a similar religion is surely beyond coincidence. All the more so because the Hebrews and the Atenists are the only peoples on earth for over another millennium known to conceive of monotheism. There would seem little reason to doubt, therefore, that Atenism sprang from the religion of the Israelites as some scholars suspect."[45]

As will be momentarily observed, this is a hypothesis that depends on the catastrophic eruption of a volcano on the island of Thera, modern day Santorini, during the era of the 18th Dynasty that allegedly engendered great fear in pharaoh.

Therefore with such a supposition, Graham Phillips goes on to propose that "If Atenism and the Hebrew religion are related then it appears that, although the Egyptians may have oppressed the Israelite peoples, they had no problem with their religion, certainly not by Akhenaten's time. Why Akhenaten opted to establish Atenism as the state religion of Egypt, though, is something of an enigma. It is possible that if the Israelites had interpreted the cataclysm brought about by the Thera eruption as an act of their god then, perhaps, from Akhenaten's perspective, this was the god to follow."[46]

Undermining the intelligence of the ancients however, the latter supposition is far from credible, given the deep structure knowledge that was hidden within the Sacred Science of the Land of Khem. In any event, even Phillips comes to the conclusion that "we are left with a problem concerning Moses. Although Atenism did not become the state religion of Egypt until Akhenaten's time, it had been a steadily growing sect in the country for around a hundred years. It might only have been a minority cult before Akhenaten's reign, but it existed nevertheless. If it was inspired by the Hebrew religion then it would seem that if Moses existed then he lived before Atenism came into being in the early fifteenth century BCE. Yet, as we have seen, there is much evidence to place the Exodus in the mid-fourteenth century BCE, during Amonhotep's reign. If the Old Testament account of Moses first revealing God to the Israelites in any way reflects historical events, then *there must have been two Moses'*; one who led them to freedom at the time of the Thera eruption about 1360 BCE, and another, earlier Moses, who first revealed God to the Israelites at some point before Atenism made its appearance around a hundred years earlier."[47] (Emphasis added.)

Though extremely interesting, such hypothetical ruminations are a clear indication that Phillips maintains a strong biblical allegiance over historical fact, especially the part where he states that, "although the Egyptians may have oppressed the *Israelite* peoples, they had no problem with *their* religion." (Italics added.)

These interesting speculations nevertheless still left for Phillips "something of an enigma" concerning the establishment of Atenism as the state religion, a conundrum however that has already been resolved in this text as the result of Babylonian infiltration into the land of Khem.

In the meantime however, that two biblical figures are deemed necessary to historically validate the existence of Moses is quite ironic given that a theological controversy that occurred in the Middle Ages was only resolved, as was observed in chapter one, with the creation of two Arks of the Covenant of God!

Nevertheless, this debate on which of the two imposed monotheism onto the land of Khem, is a chicken or the egg sort of argument and moreover, a moot one, if the figure Moses is merely a biblical legend based on an actual resonant echo of a real historical African personage. That indeed is precisely what Egyptian author Ahmed Osman proposes in his, *Moses: Pharaoh of Egypt*.

Although Gary Greenberg sees Moses as a high priest of Akhenaten's cult, contrarily some authors, like French researchers Messod and Roger Sabbah also see Ahkenaten as the prototype for Abraham. Since Abraham and Akhenaton are both alleged to have been idol destroyers, the parallels drawn in *Secrets Of The Exodus* though controversial are very compelling. Ahmed Osman however adamantly proposes that Moses and Ahkenaten are one and the same person, while Immanuel Velikovsky explored historical comparisons with Oedipus, a king of Grecian and Freudian legend making all three resonant echoes of one another that have reverberated throughout time.

Gary Greenberg however soberly reminds us that to "argue that Moses and Akhenaten were theological comrades-in-arms and that the first Hebrews were

Akhenaten's persecuted followers simply because it is theoretically possible does not make it so. Such coincidences provide no solid proof for challenging what almost all biblical scholars believe to be true. We need hard evidence, irrefutable arguments that prove the case."[48]

The argument made herein however is not that the Hebrews were the persecuted followers of Akhenaten but the worshippers of Amun that were outlawed by the heretic pharaoh's actions. These black Africans, these were the so-called Hebrews crying for mercy and salvation now indelibly inscribed in the sacrosanct pages of the Bible.

Nevertheless, with or without solid proof, Greenberg as such has no problem seeing Moses as Akhenaten's high priest but notwithstanding the cautious position he takes, if the identification of Moses and Akhenaten as the same person is true, as Osman contends, it would verify that Moses is an actual African person of part Asiatic heritage rebranded and transformed in the pages of the Bible into a Hebrew.

Accepting this as fact for the moment, given that Moses/Akhenaten essentially made himself the supreme intercessor between the Aten and the rest of humanity, placing the ancient Aten sun disc image above all other Neteru, under such a possibility it can be asked, was he then the God-King who was a jealous god? After all, the success of his extremely egotistical triumph over ancient African tradition made him the "Pope" of the new religion of Amarna. Indeed, Akhenaten made himself the *first ever* Prophet of God.

The Old Testament of the Christian Bible of course is full of prophets such as Isaiah, Jeremiah, Ezekiel and Daniel, among many others. However, as far as history is concerned, the rabbi brothers Sabbah once again assure us that the first prophet of God is not to be found in the assumed biblical lands as "Pharaoh had to hold audience with the many foreign residents in the capital, and made use of translators or interpreters to teach or to converse. Such is the origin of the prophets, guardians of the law, intermediaries between men and the gods, whose language they understand. Indeed, in an Amarnian fresco kept at Cambridge, Akhenaten is depicted accompanied by a dignitary bearing the name of "prophet.""[49]

Putting a different and more ancient spin on Graham Phillips' idea that "Atenism made its appearance around a hundred years" prior to the existence of his theoretical second Moses, the rabbi brothers Sabbah however, reflecting on the origins of the god of that particular era, while at the same time inadvertently providing evidence of the infiltration of Babylonian ideas, pointed out that, "At that time an ancient god, Aten, resurfaced in Egypt. Aten's origin, in all likelihood, goes back to Atum, a primordial Egyptian god of around 2200 BC. This resurgence of Aten was favored by Amenhotep III's in-laws, and most particularly by Teye [sic], Yuya's daughter, the future high queen of Egypt, and Akhenaten's mother. The education she gave her son was influenced by Yuya. And so both Teye [sic] and Yuya played a role in the first stage of the process that led to the rise in power of the religion of Aten after the coronation of Akhenaten."[50]

Referring to Akhenaten by the Greek version of his name however, Siegfried Morenz clarifies the point that "It is quite clear that, even in his early radical phase, Amenophis IV was in no sense an advocate of simple monotheism. On the contrary, what he proposed was precisely a trinitarian formula... The quintessence of his dogma lay in the so-called instructive name which he coined for the god whose cause he propagated. This name is traditionally (no doubt erroneously) rendered as "Aton' (itn); at the time it probably had the form Jāti (i.e., the 'n' was dropped), in accordance with the contemporary pronunciation. The name (surrounded by cartouches) has two parts and runs as follows: 'Re-Harakhti who rejoices in the horizon – in his name: as (m) Shu, who is Jāti ['Aton']. Whether Shu here is simply, as most scholars have assumed, a term for the sun or whether, as seems more probable, it is an allusion (or also is an allusion) to Shu as son (Shu as the son of the primordial god Re - Atum of Heliopolis), thereby raising the god-king Akhanjāti ('Akhnaton') to unity with this father – in either case this is a trinitarian formulation."[51]

Thus, the Holy Trinity of Christianity is apparently far older than its alleged Christian beginnings permit. Indeed it is far older than the time of "Akhanjāti," as the concept of "one in three" was the ancient symbol that represented unity in plurality, a symbol already identified as the ancient topological metaphor much researched by Joseph P. Farrell that will soon be elaborated upon below.

For the moment however, during the days of direct European colonization of the continent of Africa, missionary trained Africans had their own but now contaminated ancient trinitarian religious doctrines regurgitated to them by outsiders who had already ensured the break in the link with Africa's ancient historical past.

Such Amarnian revelations, and in particular the role his mother Tiye and grandfather Yuya played "in the first stage of the process that led to the rise in power of the religion of Aten," may yet resolve the problem of why Akhenaten despised the ritual and cult practices of the exceedingly ancient religious customs of the then Amunian priesthood. Indeed, how is it possible that he believed that the people of Khem were idolaters who worshipped mere wood and stone objects! How is it possible he did not know that those symbolic objects were utilized as votive icons used to identify the hidden esoteric powers and processes of the physical and noetic medium, the spiritual substance of a nonetheless ontological actuality not perceptible however to the five senses?

Apparently, Akhenaten never grew up in the major holy cities of the Black land. As Ahmed Osman, focusing on his mother, observes: "Fearing for her son's life, Tiye kept her baby away from the royal residence at Memphis and Thebes. Akhenaten's absence from the royal residence during his early years can only be explained by the fact that, during this period of his life, he was living at Zarw and Heliopolis. Zarw was the military border city in northern Sinai, surrounded by lakes and an ancient branch of the Nile. It was the capital city of the area known as Goshen in the Bible, where the Israelites were allowed to settle. It is from his behavior and the kind of knowledge he seemed to have acquired at the time of his arrival at Thebes that we have to guess at where Akhenaten most probably passed the greater part of his childhood. His appearance does not suggest that he had any physical training, contrary to the custom among the Eighteenth-Dynasty kings and he is never shown hunting lions or other wild animals. Nor is he depicted smiting an enemy or leading his army in combat."[52]

Tiye's fear for her son's life, as Osman mentioned, is intriguingly reminiscent of Jochebed, the mother of Moses, putting him in a basket and then floating him down the Nile, also out of fear for her son's life. Indeed, it is even similar to the story of Isis who feared for the life of her son and thus hid Horus "from Seth in the papyrus swamps of the Nile delta."[53]

Finding itself in the pages of the Bible moreover, the story of the basket also appears as a conflation of a story told of the birth of Sargon of Akkad. Either way, these stories provide a valid explanation for Akhenaten's lack of esoteric knowledge. Thus, excluded from the inner sanctum, clearly the door to the House of Life had been barred to him.

It is pertinent to recall here that "the 'House of Life', which served mainly as a place where sacred writings were compiled... is categorically placed out of bounds to foreigners. 'An Asiatic ... may not enter into ... this House of Life, he may not see it.'"[54]

As modern political interpretations take no apparent account of the inner psychic life of the ancient African mentality, other than to say it was primitive, only those such as Ogotemmêli, the Dogon priest of Mali, the Bambaras, or other yet to be explored African tribes, come anywhere near to any natural cognitive equivalence of the people that once lived on the banks of the Nile who composed or were the first recipients of the symbolic language they called the MeduNeteru.

Thus here, at this point, *we* finally enter the Temple, the deeper recesses of the African mind. Indeed understanding the symbolic language that was designed to interact with the primordial ocean from which creation occurs, a phenomenon that will be more fully explained below and in chapter five, is paramount to the furtherance of modern microphysics as Rene A. Schwaller de Lubicz observed many years ago.

Moreover, from within this realm we discover what Joseph P. Farrell refers to as *the topological metaphor of the physical medium*. For the people of Khem nevertheless, the symbol they composed to represent the primordial ocean was the all powerful Neter Nun, a name whose individual glyphs were designed to represent the originating noetic and physical medium of creation, a medium filled with electromagnetic vibration. According to Schwaller de Lubicz, this is the medium that came into existence as a direct result of the Primordial Scission.

However, the two nasal consonants of this non-Indo-European word serve only for its pronunciation in English but the Afro-Asiatic symbolic representation of Nun in the MeduNeteru speaks to the mind spiritually, or in less theological terms subliminally, by showing each glyph to be jagged zigzag-like objects specifying water, current and flow, a dynamic symbol used incidentally in modern physics to describe the phenomenon of electromagnetism! What was true then is still true now!

Indeed, archaeological evidence may exist that gives credence to the true age of this symbol. For example, as a result of the discovery of those very same zigzag markings engraved upon a 400,000 year old stone, BBC Breakfast News announced on the morning of December 12, 2014 that the early history of mankind may need to be reset. This symbol of course is the familiar glyph that represents the "N" of the word Nun. As previously discussed in chapter two, this is in fact the scientific symbol that coincides with the approximate age the Zulu's claim to have arrived on earth from Mars sometime prior to 500,000 BC.

Even the King himself, according to the people of Khem, was conceived in the Nun before the creation of heaven and earth. In other words, the "quantum theory" message from the ancients is God the Pharaoh preexisted the creation of the universe and thus intelligent essence preexists and therefore predetermines matter.

The hoary antiquity of this scientific fact clearly indicates that the ancient Nile dwellers were very much aware that Atum, a single entity, the representative of Reality Absolute, the first element to emerge from the Nun, created the physical universe. Therefore, Akhenaten's so-called monotheistic revolution was in fact no such thing. His lack of esoteric knowledge indicates this. This account therefore is surely justified by the fact that after the termination of Amarna rule Akhenaten, as a result of his violation of sacrosanct knowledge, was branded a heretic and a criminal!

Indeed, Atum, the sole principle and representative Neter of the Absolute Unity from which all other Neteru were conceived, is perhaps the most ancient concept of the Supreme Being known to man. Although brought to birth in the material world through the womb of Net, the different aspects of Atum, such as Ptah, Ra, and Amun etc. ultimately gained prominence at different times throughout the history of Khem for symbolic reasons that were designed to represent the cosmic gestation of our constantly growing, anti-entropic physical and spiritual universe.

Nevertheless, according to Zecharia Sitchin, who however provides an alternative origin for the Neteru, "Ptah and the other gods were called, in Egyptian, *Ntr* – "Guardian, Watcher." They had come to Egypt, the Egyptians wrote, from *Ta-Ur*, whose name *Ur* meant "olden" but could have also been the actual place name – a place well known from the Mesopotamian and biblical records: the ancient city of Ur in southern Mesopotamia."[55]

Biblical myth of course also proclaims that Abraham, the founding patriarch of the Hebrew religion, came from Ur of the Chaldees. On the other hand, for Gary Greenberg, he is nevertheless Ra, that is, another divine and therefore sacred element of the African imagination. Whatever the case, Ur, as the "Far/Foreign land," is just as likely to be a memory of *Ta-Ur*, the "olden" land that existed prior to the flood.

From his studied examination of the Sumerian pictograms and Akkadian cuneiform clay tablet writing, Zecharia Sitchin also determined that Ptah was a historical entity, a member of the Anunnaki known as Enki, Lord of the Earth, the one who was made ruler of the continent of Africa hundreds of thousands of years ago. Thus, if the Anunnaki are indeed the biblical Elohim, as well as the Neteru of the land of Khem, and Ptah really is, as Sitchin claims, Enki, there could be something to this since the rabbi brothers Sabbah identified the Elohim as "the children of all the pharaohs of the past, who were seen as the gods of Egypt."[56]

The lack of knowledge on the part of Akhenaten notwithstanding if, as we contend here, he and Moses are the same person, then the foregoing analysis is therefore confronted with a major problem: Who did Moses meet at the rock? Obviously, it could not have been Akhenaten himself. Thus, who was the person, described in Exodus 33:20-22, whose face could not be seen? Who then is the biblical God?

The *New King James Bible* refers to God as the Lord. The earlier Hebrew Bible however prefers Yahweh. Therefore, is Yahweh the Supreme Being? Or is *He* another historical figure to be recovered from the ancient papyri? Once again, the rabbi brothers Sabbah appear to be in a position to provide an answer since Yah or "Yahu is one of the divine names of the god-king Amenhotep III."[57]

Finding the name of Yahu in the *YHW* cartouche on the columns of the Temple of Soleb in Nubia, the rabbi brothers Sabbah observe that, "several elements indicate that the name Yahu designates Amenhotep III."[58] This is interesting because one of the latter's most popular epithets was *Aten-tjehen* which means "the Dazzling Sun disk," a title that "appears in his titulary at Luxor temple, and more frequently, was used as the name for one his palaces as well as the Year 11 royal barge, and denotes a company of men in Amenhotep's army."[59]

In contrast to the aforesaid meaning of the epithet *Aten-tjehen*, Egyptologists identify the Neter *Iah* [*Yah Jah*], from which the name Yahu is derived, not as the sun but as a Moon god who lost prominence as a Moon god by the time of the New Kingdom. This opinion in the latter part of the preceding sentence however is a somewhat strange view to hold, given that Ahmose I whose name had the meaning "Born of Iah" or "son of the moon" is the king who expelled the Hyksos and founded the 18th Dynasty.

Indeed, since the cosmic elements identified as Neteru had been handed down on the continent of Africa through millennia of oral tradition long prior to the civilization that grew on the banks of the Nile, the name *Iah* however may very well be as old as mankind's first ever observation of the moon.

As to the veracity of oral teachings and their ability to maintain accuracy over time, in personal correspondence Laird Scranton stated that "cultures that seem to have done the best job of carrying this tradition forward are the ones who never adopted a system of writing!"

As it pertains to the Dogon of Mali, he said that since they "have no native written language, they also have no ancient texts. *Symbolism and mnemonics*, which are the effective language of their cosmological tradition, seem to have done an excellent job of carrying intact knowledge forward for generations..." (Emphasis added.) Therefore, this would have been the case prior to the introduction of a writing system in the Nile valley from whence the Dogon, as their current knowledge and symbolic understanding indicates, originated.

For Siegfried Morenz, on the other hand, *Iah* is in fact the substance of the moon since "it is possible to explain why different names were given to the substance and the god by the fact that the god originated from a different plane and was associated with the substance only in a secondary way. This may well have been the case with the moon, which as a substance is called *yah* but as a deity is represented mainly by Thoth, who is called the 'messenger' by virtue of an entirely different function he possesses."[60]

Since Iah and *Aten-tjehen*, "the Dazzling Sun Disk," were contrasting epithets attributed to the pharaoh, the name of the god-king Amenhotep III therefore contained elements of both the sun and the moon. Indeed, evidence that could be used to reinforce such a possibility was found on the Sabean Stone, discovered in the Wadi Musa close to the amphitheatre in Edom, a country where Graham Phillips believes the origin of the Hebrew religion is to be sourced, which has inscribed on it "a crescent moon with the sun between its horns. Beneath the sun and moon there is another symbol, an elongated triangle,"[61] the latter triangle, a subject that will be discussed below and in more detail in chapter four.

As noted by Graham Phillips in *The Moses Legacy*, "The archaeologist Crystal Bennett reasoned that the triangle depicted the sacred mountain of Jebel Madhbah and that the sun and moon symbolized the ancient Edomite deity who was worshipped there. As many early civilizations considered the moon to be feminine, because of the perceived link between the menstruation and lunar cycles, and the sun to be masculine, Bennett reasoned that the Edomite god was an androgynous deity, having both male and female attributes."[62]

Of course, unlike the position taken herein, it is the opinion of Phillips that Moses influenced the monotheistic revolt that took place in the Nile valley. Therefore, he queries, "If the cult of the Aten in Egypt was inspired by the Israelite religion, as we have reasoned, then once again we find evidence that God was originally considered both male and female. Although often described in the masculine, the Aten is clearly envisaged as having both male and female characteristics. In addressing the Aten, the 'Hymn to the Aten' refers to the pharaoh Akhenaten as 'your son who came forth from your body': the god is seen as not only siring a child, as would a man, but actually giving birth, as would a woman."[63]

Indeed, as was revealed in chapter two, "Akhenaten is shown as both male and female. He had proclaimed himself "the father and mother of humanity," a notion which applies allegorically to Adam, and to Abraham (Father of Nations)."[64] Moreover, such androgyny also found expression in the behaviour of his father, as according to Immanuel Velikovsky, Amenhotep III was the only pharaoh who "permitted his artist to portray him dressed as a woman."[65]

Representing therefore both the sun and the moon, perhaps Amenhotep III considered himself a dual gender god, for in the ancient philosophy it was believed that the Ka of the deceased could not be perfected in the Afterlife unless its male and female elements were unified in the Akhu, the light body. As was stated in chapter one, the ancients "lived their lives with the intention of perfecting their "light" body's transformation into a "glorified spirit" that had earned the right to live like the greater Neteru, the cosmic elementals such as Osiris, Isis, Nut and Geb, in eternity in the Duat, as described in the *Pyramid Texts* out of which comes *The Book Of The Dead*," or rather more definitively *The Book of the Day of Coming Forth Into The Light*.

Since the Lord is thus Yahweh, the Yahu of the Khemites, from the perspective proposed here this implies that Amenhotep III is the god described in Exodus 33:20-22 who appeared to Moses while he stood on the rock. This would make Amenhotep III the Yahweh who was the jealous god. If true, this was an encounter between biological father and son and therefore begs the question of why he couldn't see his face? Surely he would have known what his father's face looked like.

Indeed, if this is true then Ahmed Osman's *reasonable assumption* concerning the confusion of how to spell the name of Yuya's God at the time Joseph died is null and void. Given that this name is related to that of Yahu, the well-known, at that time, Amenhotep III, some other explanation is necessary to explain that mystery, as only Theban priests still unaware of the new and burgeoning religion of the revivified Aten would have experienced any confusion over the spelling of Yhwh or Yhwe (Jehovah), the God of the newly forming religion of the so-called Hebrews to be. In any event, there remains an alternative possibility that this mysterious historical African personage was not Amenhotep III at all but in fact was the father of Nefertiti and another son of Yuya, Ay.

Indeed, the Divine Father "Ay is the forgotten pharaoh. The discrete sovereign of Egypt, he is above the pharaohs. He is the one "whose face is never seen." Ay was the artisan and sculptor of the Great Exodus. He would impose his seal upon the face of all consequent Western civilization."[66]

During the upheaval caused by Akhenaten's reforms, Ay's role was to rule Khem as if he were pharaoh, that is God on earth. Being part of the Theban elite who ordered the expulsion of the Yahuds to the land of milk and honey perhaps it was his duty to see that all was well with the exiles, hence the story of the biblical visitation of God to Moses.

In corroboration of this possibility, once again the rabbi brothers Sabbah's research is useful here for they uncover the fact that, "During Akhenaten's last ten years, while the pharaoh was cloistered and worshiped within the capital, and during the reigns of Smenkhare and Tutankhamun, Ay was lord of the land, the Divine Father, respected and venerated throughout Egypt."[67]

Thus, if it is true that Ay is the God "whose face is never seen," as they contend, there is therefore every possibility that we have discovered here the identity of the person Moses was in the presence of as described in Exodus 33:20-22.

Moreover, they also point out that, "The face of a powerful person inspires respect and, above all, fear. To stare at Pharaoh without his permission constituted a grave offense."[68]

Ultimately, given that there is an ancient African custom that kings could not be gazed upon, and often times could not be spoken to directly, alternatively this tradition of the people in the Nile valley could be otherwise explained as an expression inherited from their paleoancient African ancestors.

Of course, as was mentioned in chapter two, there is Alan F. Alford's extraordinary theory for why one could not look at the face of God "that will be of interest to examine a little later in chapter six."

In any event, the priests of Yahu, known as the Yahuds were worshippers of the great god Heh, or Yahu-Heh who, as the rabbi brothers Sabbah indicate, "represents the Divine Breath."[69]

Indeed, Yahu-Heh is "the One God represented successively by Amenhotep III, Akhenaten (Aten), Smenkhare, Tutankhamun, and Ay: the Elohim or "individual gods" who are none other than the [African and Afro-Asiatic] pharaohs of Egypt."[70] But if Akhenaten was Afro-Asiatic then so was his biblical counterpart.

Thus, it appears that Akhenaten, who flagrantly misruled the Black and Red lands of Khem from the doomed city of Akhetaten, was the biblical Moses, an Afro-Asiatic king. Indeed, the first to call himself pharaoh!

Four

THE DOOMED CITY OF AKHETATEN

*The Biblical Exodus is a masked narrative of
the actual exodus of the monotheists.*

MESSOD AND ROGER SABBAH

The Old Testament is full of many interesting tales from the ancient past
that have fascinated people for thousands of years. The allegorical stories
of "Noah's Flood" and the "Tower of Babel" for example or the tale of the cities
of "Sodom and Gomorrah for another." With the purpose of discovering those
ancient sites and proving the truth behind these biblical stories, the divine power
imbued in them has sent many an archaeologist or biblical scholar off on a journey to the "Middle East" in search of their physical geographic location. Indeed,
Zecharia Sitchin even advanced a most intriguing and plausible account of his
belief that these ancient cities once stood on a plain at the southern end of the
Dead Sea.

Though the Bible refers to the 'fire and brimstone' that rained down from
heaven, in his *Wars Of Gods And Men*, Sitchin imaginatively described the destruction of "Sodom and Gomorrah" as the result of a nuclear war against these cities, suggesting that they can now be found beneath the waters of the southern
lip of the Dead Sea where radiation, still present in its waters, can be viewed as

possible evidence of that devastating holocaust prosecuted by the Sumerian warrior god Nergal.

After the cataclysmic bombing that destroyed these biblical cities, the Dead Sea flooded onto the plain and submerged them forever. However whether Sitchin's horrendous nuclear warfare scenario occurred during the biblical era or not is, of course, a moot point, given that other scholars refused to look to the east for the events recorded in the Bible and sought a different geographic location toward the south.

Gary Greenberg, for example, explained the reason biblical scholars had previously veered from such a radical turn was due to the fact that "In the morass of conflict, Israel lost touch with its Egyptian roots. By the time modern scholars came to review its history, the long religiously orthodox image of Israel as firmly rooted among Semitic tribes wandering in Canaan and Mesopotamia was fixed in the Western mind. Biblical scholars saw no need to apply to Egypt the scholarly intensity of research reserved for the Semitic world. Israel was Canaanite. Biblical history was assumed true, at least in its outlines. That the biblical scribes and redactors could have committed such a major error in location never entered the biblical mind."[1]

According to some modern scholars nevertheless, those biblical events are in reality only to be found in the myth and actual history of events that took place in the *real* Garden of Eden, that is the ancient land of Khem, or rather the portion situated on the continent of Africa. The rabbi brothers Messod and Roger Sabbah, for example, also appear to be in full accord with this view as they see the biblical fable of "Sodom and Gomorrah" reflected in a city that was constructed on the banks of the Nile during the 18th Dynasty. Occurring in the same location, they also see reflections of the tale of "The Tower of Babel," a matter that will be further discussed later on.

According to biblical text of course, Sodom and Gomorrah "were located in Canaan, in desert regions close to the Dead Sea."[2] However, in that part of the world nevertheless "there exists not a single archeological trace of Sodom and Gomorrah."[3] Using the Aramaic Bible as one of their major sources to argue the case for a southern, and as it happens African, location, they explain that, "The name Gomorrah, in Hebrew, is *Amora*, which means "people of Re" or "people of Pharaoh,"[4] Ra, of course, being the traditional god of the sun to the people of the Land of Khem.

Indeed, at this more southern location on the continent of Africa is a city that was dedicated to an Old Kingdom god named the Aten, the invisible power behind the sun that for Akhenaten represented the exclusive and only god that he wanted his people to worship. Hence the declaration, "Thou shalt have no other gods but Me!"

As mentioned in chapter three, this was the time of a pharaoh "who was wreaking havoc throughout the Nile valley by closing down its many ancient temples" while at the same time disbanding the priesthood and "banning the worship of the Neteru." This rebellious individual was the very egotistical and iconoclastic pharaoh now identified by some as Moses.

While Akhenaten/Moses prayed to his newfound god within the security of his fortified and well-guarded city, the 'Houses of Life,' now under attack throughout the rest of the land, were falling into disrepair and their priesthood into otherwise wretched despair. Thus, as a consequence of "the perversion reigning"[5] in Akhetaten, the ancient theocratic tradition of the temples of Khem was temporarily disrupted.

In point of fact, the newly despised priesthood of Amun had been representative of the long tradition of the scholars of "Sacred Science" whose *raison d'être* was now under threat and therefore on the verge of being abolished over night!

Moreover, as a consequence of this radical action, the rest of the African populous, for whom the biblical text does not identify as the "Children of Israel" but rather tarnishes them as idolaters, were left distraught and shocked at the closure of these ancient temples, their ancient places of worship, work and study.

As a refuge from the rage of the populous and the increasing ire of the entire priesthood of Khem, whose anger could not be abated, Akhenaten built his city on neutral territory, a stretch of desert land alongside the Nile, that had no prior claims of tradition or cult to overturn. Nevertheless, a large police force of fierce warriors known as the Medzay was needed to insure the security of Akhetaten.

This new 'gated' metropolis, though short lived, was considered an amazing architectural feat. In addition to the Temple of the Aten, a major north south highway ran through the city. "Running a great distance to the north, the King's Way passed between the Royal House and the State Palace. This palace, area for area, was the largest secular building known from the ancient world. It had a frontage of 700 meters (2200 feet) facing the King's Way. Between the Royal House and the State Palace an arched viaduct spanned the road, and there, probably, was the Window of Appearance at which the pharaoh used to appear before his subjects and from which he showered royal gifts on his favorites."[6]

Apparently, it is this 'Window of Appearance' which is at the root of the tradition of the Pope appearing on the balcony at St. Peter's Basilica as well as the Queen of England appearing on the balcony of Buckingham Palace.

In fact, more daring than the two previously mentioned dignitaries, Akhenaten and his queen may have appeared on this balcony before their people completely unclothed. In general, "With the exception of Akhnaton, the pharaohs did not leave portraits of themselves in the nude."[7] However, on the bas-reliefs of some of the aristocratic tombs of Akhetaten, "the king generally appears with his queen Nefretete... Frequently Akhnaton is shown in attitudes of great affection toward his wife; and the bodies of the august pair are regularly presented covered only by thin tunics, with the breasts of the queen and her belly exposed for everyone to see. In this there is unmistakable exhibitionism and in the king's exuberant pleasure in seeing himself portrayed thousands of times there is narcissism or self-adoration."[8]

Though available today to the prying eyes of 20th and 21st century voyeurs, that the sacred artwork on the 'aristocratic' tomb walls would ever be seen again was a future probability that never would have entered the minds of the people of ancient Khem. Therefore, be Velikovsky's imposition of modern psychology and incorrect patriarchal moral assessment of the acceptance of nudity in African culture as it may, it was nevertheless once assumed that Akhenaten was a pharaoh who privileged the residents of Akhetaten, at the expense of course of the wider population.

Contrary to this view however, some indication that Akhenaten may have worked the young people of his new city to death has now come to light. For example, a recent *Time Watch* TV programme has furnished new evidence that may contradict the claim that all the residents of Akhetaten were privileged since there were lots of teenage deaths and food was not of a high nutritional quality even though in the Temple of the Aten, which was a half mile in length, there is evidence of at least 1,800 offering tables on display demonstrating the abundance of Akhetaten. As many residents suffered from anemia, in fact there was a 60% anemia rate among children, many of them were clearly not thriving and thus found themselves living in conditions that were much worse than anywhere else in the entire land of Khem.

On the other hand, there is indeed evidence that suggests, "Pharaoh excluded from slavery the tribe of Levi. This tribe, composed of priests and nobles and their families, would have escaped the servitude imposed by the king of Egypt. The Hagadah (the story of the Exodus from Egypt) gives this explanation: "It [the tribe of Levi, the Yahuds] owed its safe standing to the care of the nobles and to ancestral practices, like circumcision and the study of the law."

"Rashi's commentary is just as explicit: "The Midrash [Commentary] still says that the tribe of Levi, to which Moses belonged, was never enslaved by Pharaoh.""[9]

In stark contrast to the treatment received by the Levites, in recent years Barry Kemp, Field Director of the Egypt Exploration Society, has closely examined bodies found in the desert cemeteries of Amarna that indicate a high death rate among teenagers, many showing signs of spina bifida from a hard and heavy workload and poor nutrition. Quoting from the Hebrew Bible, Exodus 1:13-14, which recalls the ill-treatment the Hebrew slaves endured, the rabbi brothers Sabbah indicate that "They worked them unmercifully, and made their lives bitter with hard labor, in mortar and brick; and in all kinds of fieldwork; in all their work the Egyptians used them unmercifully."[10]

Indeed, the building of Akhetaten required copious amounts of limestone that came from distant limestone quarries that belonged to his mother, Queen Tiye. Since it has been speculated that a new disease, plague or virus may have affected the people of Akhetaten, perhaps these recent finds will provide proof that the slavery remembered in the Bible is an echo of the actual hardship and obvious forced labour imposed upon the ordinary residents of Akhetaten.

Thus although Akhenaten did privilege the nobility, at the same time, he abdicated his responsibility to the general welfare of the other residents of his new city and moreover the rest of the people of Khem at large, and just as worse the international political affairs of the day where other regions of his state in the distant Red land, located in what is known today by the political fiction of the "Middle East," became vulnerable to enemy attack.

Indeed, according to Immanuel Velikovsky, as stated in his book *Oedipus And Akhnaton*, Akhenaten "mounted the throne in complete ignorance of the affairs of the state in previous years, and was advised in a letter from a foreign king to find out from his mother about the relations between their states in the time of his father."[11]

As was shown in chapter three, by contrast with the priests of the "Sacred Science," the privileged priests of Akhetaten, "were worshippers of the great god Heh, or Yahu-Heh" which, as the rabbi brothers Sabbah indicate, "represents the Divine Breath, the number five, and the five names of Pharaoh."[12] In the Bible however, Yahu-Heh is known as Yahweh, the Lord, or Jehovah, the One God who was in historical fact represented successively by Amenhotep III, Akhenaten, Smenkhare, Tutankhamun, and Ay.

As factual history indicates, these priests were worshippers of Yahu and thus became known as the Yahuds. During the Amarna period, they were high functionary residents of Akhetaten, the newly multiethnic capital of Khem, whilst Akhenaten waged war on the Neteru still worshipped by the rest of the population left abandoned throughout the kingdom. As for those latter neglected ones, they have become the true Children of Israel, descendants of those otherwise known as the children of the God Ra, a member of the Neteru who like Thoth and Osiris had bequeathed to Khem the knowledge of the MeduNeteru.

Thus, as a consequence of their sacrilegious behaviour the Yahuds, the priests of the new Aten cult, recruited from the priesthood of the nation's temples at large and other residents of Akhetaten, along with the Medzay, would eventually be driven out of Khem, escorted by the armies of generals Seti, Ramesses and Horemheb, all of whom would later become pharaohs.

From their same Aramaic source, the rabbi brothers Sabbah found that Genesis 18:20-22 makes clear that it was Ay who orchestrated the destruction of the new city. Indeed, it is also quite clear that the "corruption of Sodom and Gomorrah is similar to Ay's perception of Akhet-Aten."[13] According to the verses found in the Aramaic Bible "Adon-Ay decided to destroy the two cities because of the perversion reigning there."[14] But although he initially wanted to "destroy the city at first"[15] he "finally compromised in favor of deporting the population to Canaan and dismantling the buildings."[16]

From the foregoing, it might be argued that since "Sodom and Gomorrah" are described, in the above quote, as two cities, one may be dissuaded from the idea that Akhetaten is the correct historical match for the cities of the plain, Nevertheless, in his examination of the stelae from the sixth year of Akhenaten, Ahmed Osman shows that they define "both the city on the east bank and a large area of agricultural land on the bank opposite, apparently with a view to making the new capital self-supporting if it ever came under siege."[17]

Moreover Osman states that, "across the river from Amarna, on the west bank of the Nile, we find the modern city of Mal-Lawi. As Egyptian W becomes V in Hebrew, this name becomes Mal-Levi, which literary [sic] means "the City of Levi." This could only be explained by the fact that the Levites, who held priestly positions with Moses, held the same positions at Amarna, which can also confirm Manetho's Osarseph account, when he includes priests among the followers of the rebel leader."[18] Indeed, the story of Osarseph is considered to be one of the rare instances, if not the only instance, of the biblical story of Moses being corroborated and recorded in the annals of the history of the Nile valley. Thus, it can be concluded from the foregoing that as a single city Akhetaten could also be described as a city of two parts with one city located on either side of the Nile.

As was mentioned above and in chapter two, Seti I, the Joshua of the biblical text, was part of the campaign that sought to exile the Yahuds to the outer regions of northeast Africa in the land known as Palestine. Indeed, according to the research undertaken by the rabbi brothers Sabbah, the "successors of the Aten pharaohs, the Ramessides, honored the alliances of Ay and Ramesses I, distributing the provinces to the south to Judah (Yahuday) and those to the north to Israel (Erev-rav)" and further revealed that "the Judahite priests still remained Egyptian subjects."[19]

If the word Egyptian is read as African, and Israelite as The Children of Ra, then the following gives historical proof to the *Gathering Of Christ* organization's belief that "the real Jews were black" and also corroborates the account of Strabo that Ralph Ellis mentioned in chapter one, "that the Israelites were not simply emigrants who had escaped Egypt, but that they were actually of Egyptian stock themselves." In fact, Gary Greenberg makes the point that, "the very first mention of the name Israel occurs in Egyptian writing; it does not appear again in the historical record for almost four hundred years afterward."[20]

As it happens, Nana Banchie Darkwah also sees correlations between biblical names and cognate meanings found in names of his native Akan language and goes so far as to say that, "the names of the biblical patriarchs are *Akan* names."[21] He also says that modern Jewish people hold "*Akan* and African tribal names."[22] For example, Darkwah identifies Ephraim, one of the sons of Joseph (Yuya), as Afrim. In the Akan language, Afrim is derived from *Fri-mu* a word that signifies "breaking away from a group or seceding,"[23] Of course, if these linguistic comparisons prove true, given the position taken herein this would mean that the even the Akan language of modern day Ghana, like Hebrew and Arabic, had its origin in the newly evolving language of the cosmopolitan city of Akhetaten.

Indeed, the rabbi brothers Sabbah once again provide evidence that corroborates the fact that "The new language of Akhet-Aten was created from the foreign dialects. This new language incensed the Divine Father Ay. He could not tolerate this insult, this heresy to the holy language of ancient Egypt. Ay could not speak or understand the new language. He needed an interpreter in order to be understood in the capital of his own country; Ay needed an interpreter to communicate with Pharaoh and the people of Akhet-Aten. This new language was the beginning of Hebrew."[24]

Even the Arabic language is to be found here. Indeed, the name ""Arab" refers to the many kinds of people from Akhet-Aten, newly converted to monotheism, and called *Erev-rav* in the Bible (Exodus 12:38),"[25] as was stated above. This is quite explosive information, given the conditions that exist today in Palestine, for its means that the actual residents of Akhetaten were in fact what are called today Arabs! Therefore, it is the people of modern day Palestine who are the true descendants of the people of the land of ancient Israel! Adonay, Ay, the Divine Father, granted this land to *them*.

In fact, there is even an Ethiopian element to the language. Indeed, to put it as the rabbi brothers Sabbah described it, "Ay had to negotiate with Pharaoh Smenkhare who spoke Hebrew, the new popular language of Akhet-Aten. The pharaoh also, of course spoke Egyptian. However, an interpreter was indispensable in dealing with the court, since many of the courtiers spoke only their own foreign language and the new language, Hebrew. Thus we find Egyptian words in the Hebrew language. These words come from the Delta to Lower Egypt. Additionally there are words derived from Canaanite, Phoenician, Aramaic, *Babylonian*, and from many roots of the Arabic language. (Italic added.) At the beginning of the last century, the learned linguist Frederic Portal mentions, in his work on the symbols of the Egyptians:

> *"It cannot be denied that intimate relations exist between the Ethiopian and Hebrew languages. Wansleben showed the parallels between five hundred roots that are the same in Ethiopian and Hebrew, independently of the other Semitic languages. This work is printed in the* Dictionnaire Ethiopian de Ludolf *(p. 475 et seq.) ... Hebrew and Ethiopian flow from a common source, proved by philology.*

"This analysis is confirmed by Rashi (Genesis 11:13): "They spoke to each other. One people to another, Egyptian to Ethiopian, Ethiopian to Put, and Put to Canaanite."[26] Indeed, in modern terms, this implies that black Africans spoke to the black Cushitic people of Somalia (Put), and they, in turn, spoke to the Palestinians (the *Erev-rav*, the true residents of Canaan).

The official language of the black African people of Ethiopia is of course Amharic, an Afro-Asiatic language descended from Ge'ez. After Arabic, it is the second-most spoken Semitic language in the world and is the official working language of the Federal Democratic Republic of Ethiopia and is also the working language of government, the military, and has been the language of the Ethiopian Orthodox Tewahedo Church throughout medieval and modern times.

Thus, from an assessment of the foregoing, one can confidently say that the ancient Hebrews spoke a black African language, i.e. a form of Ge'ez that modern Amharic is derived from. Thus, of course a break away group, such as the meaning Darkwah's 'Afrim' conveys, is an apt description for the Israelites, whose actions caused such turmoil in the country, at the time previous to the Exodus. Indeed, as Gary Greenberg points out, "prior to the Exodus Egypt suffered a series of great disasters at the hands of the Hebrew God. Again, allowing for significant amounts of exaggeration in the biblical account, we must still acknowledge that something unpleasant must have happened between the Israelites and the Egyptians. The departure of Israel could not have been without incident. Neither Sethos [Seti I] nor Ramesses II, both militaristic kings who battled continuously in Canaanite territory, would have allowed such a large opposition movement to peacefully depart so that it could later regroup and challenge Egyptian authority.

"At the very least, there must have been some military confrontations between the Exodus group and the Egyptian government. It need not have escalated into a full-scale civil war, but it must have so threatened Egyptian stability that the two sides negotiated some sort of peace treaty granting the rebels safe passage out of the country. This is the historical context behind the story of the confrontation between Moses and the pharaoh, with endless negotiations, broken promises, and series of plagues leading to the Israelites' departure."[27]

As has been described, from that new city the Yahuds went north while their fighting force the Medzay, on the other hand, went south. The latter whose name means the Sons of Ay, were the police force of Akhetaten. Being strategically separated from the Yahuds allowed the dispersal of both monotheistic groups, although for the Medzay the land of milk and honey would be the lush plains of what is now modern day Kenya. The high priest family of this group was called Lebe, a word that some believe closely assimilates to Levi of the Yahuds.

Ultimately, the banishment of the Yahuds, an original native people of Khem, rebranded as Hebrews, would be recorded in the Bible as the Exodus. They would eventually become known to the world as the Jews, the Chosen people. The Medzay, on the other hand, would become known as the Massai, the Elect of God.

"Yah seated on Mount Zion," incants the Jamaican Rastafarian prophet and praise singer Bob Marley in reference to the biblical name for God in the lyric of the reggae song 'Jammin.' The name Yah of course, as has previously been discussed, is indeed one of the five pharaonic names, "one of the divine names of the god-king Amenhotep III,"[28] divine father of the Rebel, Akhenaten.

However, as his initial attempt at conversion of the traditional priesthood to the new religion, Akhenaten's radical rift from traditional African religious practice began with the building of his first temple to the Aten in Karnak. That is "he took the opportunity of restoring or enlarging the temple of Aten which had been built by his father"[29] while "at the same time . . . he worshipped both Amen and Aten, the former in his official position as king, and the latter in his private capacity."[30]

Aten worship, of course, can be traced to the Old Kingdom, but its resurgence gains momentum around the time near to the end of the Middle Kingdom and the rise of the New Kingdom, particularly during the 18th Dynasty, the time of Akhenaten. As Budge indicates the latter's father, "Amen-hetep III, the son of Thothmes IV., held the same views as his father . . . and he was, apparently, urged to give effect to them by his wife Thi, the daughter of Iuaa [Yuya], and Thuaa [Tuya] … [who] appears to have supported the king in his determination to encourage the worship of this god."[31]

Akhenaten's new temple at Thebes however was apparently insufficient to his needs for there at the refurbished temple he was still under the shadow and watchful eye of his father King Amenhotep III, with whom he was co-regent, as some Egyptologists presume. Intriguingly, with regard to the latter situation of co-regency, there is a hint of a cosmic threat that may have been at the turbulent root of global social instability, the result of ominous and traumatic celestial events that took place during the time of the Eighteenth Dynasty, an interesting subject that indeed will be returned to in the Epilogue.

The neglect of the nation as a whole however was sufficient reason to bring about an end to this monotheistic experiment but there was also profound change in ancient traditions and culture being introduced within the confines of this new riverside city. Upturning ancient rules of ascent within traditional African culture, violations of matriarchal principles abounded as well as other forms of licentiousness. Indeed, this disobedience to tradition would mark for the very first time the gradual emergence of patriarchy on African matriarchal soil.

As for the matriarchy, according to Chiekh Anta Diop, "The agrarian and matriarchal character of the Egyptian society of the Pharaohs is amply explained in the myth of Isis and Osiris,"[32] in that they are both gods of corn as is so stated in legends recorded by the likes of Herodotus and Sir James George Frazer. Found among those legends is some confirmation of "the tradition which attributes to women the active role in the discovery of agriculture,"[33] reports the same author from his book *The Cultural Unity Of Black Africa*. As for the honoured position of women in African society, Diop further points out that "it is worthy to note that during the first thousand years before our time, that is to say at a time situated between the Trojan War and Homer, the Southern lands could still be ruled by women."[34]

Indeed Diop also emphasizes the fact that the land of Khem "is one of the African countries where matriarchy was most manifest and most lasting. It has been determined, in fact, by means of astronomical calculations of mathematical precision, that in 4,241 B.C. a calendar was in use in Egypt. That is to say that the Egyptians had acquired enough theoretical and practical scientific knowledge to invent a calendar whose periodicity was 1,461 years. This is the interval of time separating two heliacal risings of Sothis or Sirius; every 1,461 years Sirius and the Sun rise simultaneously in the latitude of Memphis."[35]

Thus the celestial knowledge the people of Khem possessed "would also assume the existence of written astronomical archives, of precise chronology at a period considered as prehistoric. Be that as it may, the myth of Isis and Osiris precedes this time, since it dates from the origin of Egyptian history. From this distant period – and to the end of Egyptian history – marriage between brother and sister existed in the royal family, Isis and Osiris being, at one and the same time, man and wife and brother and sister. During this lengthy period, unique in history, by its duration, Egypt must have known all the refinements of civilization, and must have instructed all the younger peoples of the Mediterranean without its own social structure ceasing to be essentially matriarchal. It is therefore possible to be legitimately surprised that there was no transition from matriarchy to patriarchy."[36] That is, of course, until the time of Akhenaten's treacherous apostasy.

Thus, with the further introduction of "foreign" women into Akhetaten also posing problems, as well as mixing with many non-native peoples from outside of Africa, this was the earliest cosmopolitan gathering known in recorded history, one even beginning to speak a creole or multiple mix of native and foreign languages that developed into its own language.

As the rabbi brothers Sabbah once again point out, "Rashi cites the different languages spoken in Babel (Genesis 11:3), "To each other: one people against the other people, Egyptian to Ethiopian. The Ethiopian to Pout, and Pout to Canaanite" – all languages spoken in Akhet-Aten before the appearance of the common language, the holy language. "A same language: this was the holy language ... they had the advantage of being a single people and of having a single language, and it was thus that they began to commit evil." This language discovered by the archeologists in the Amarna Letters, was called the "Pre-Biblical Hebrew."[37]

This indeed is the point where a connection to the biblical story of "The Tower of Babel," or as Joseph P. Farrell refers to it, *The Tower of Babel Moment*, may well be applicable. For the rabbi brothers Sabbah also highlight once again from a "commentary of Rashi regarding the city of Babel that: "The language was confounded, the people were dispersed from the valley and were spread out across the entire world."[38] This of course was also the fate of the people of Akhetaten. They also reveal that the "story of Babel demonstrates the concerns of the Divine Father Ay in the face of the population of priests who identified themselves with the One God. Each priest presided over his own sphere of influence. This multiplicity of little One Gods, each one seen by his adherents as the very image of Pharaoh, engendered in Ay the fear of seeing himself disposed of his power by the "sons of the Elohim," the Yahuds of Akhet-Aten."[39]

As for the Tower reaching up to heaven, recalling the biblical account of the building of the tower, the brothers continue to narrate that, "In the Temple of Abu Simbel there are engraved the following words: "The master builder constructed a temple whose summit is as high as the heavens. The sun rises for love of it.""[40]

For those who desire further information however, in *Secrets of the Exodus* the rabbi brothers Sabbah have a lot more to say than revealed here about the similarities of the two cities, one a historical fact, the other biblical fable.

Whatever the case, if Akhetaten was distinguished as a cosmopolitan capital, as Egyptology so states, what then was the rest of Khem? Was it homogeneous? Was its excluded population not the indigenous African people, the logical descendants of the two waves of black-skinned peoples who migrated from the interior of Africa into the Nile valley in prehistoric times, who were now the followers of the ancient African God Amun and whose culture and way of life was now under threat?

Clearly the activities of the residents of Akhetaten posed a distinct and noticeable ethnic and cultural difference to the rest of the then existing society of Khem. Indeed, a modern day political sex trial of politician Anwar Ibrahim that took place in Malaysia, and particularly his conviction after the failure of his appeal on 10 February 2015 AD, has struck a deep and resonant chord with regard to ancient Akhetaten. For one of the crimes of "Sodom and Gomorrah" recorded in the Bible is alleged to have been the act of homosexuality. Thus if the city of Akhetaten is the biblical "Sodom and Gomorrah" that puts quite a different spin on the encounter of Moses with the 'Back' of the god while he stood in the cleft of the rock.

Blasphemous implications aside the issue of homosexuality is however clearly a patriarchal concern, a matter I strongly suspect was less, if not ever, suppressed under African matriarchal regimes. Nevertheless, stirring up much controversy and divisiveness on the modern day continent of Africa are American evangelical missionaries such as Brian Brown and Scott Lively, as well as many Afrocentric contributors who claim a monolithic block of heterosexuality for the African Continent and its cultures, stating moreover that there was no mention of homosexuality in Africa prior to European contact and as a result require source proof to the contrary.

In *The Psychological Covert War On Hip Hop* for example, Bro Umar authoritatively, though naively, states that, "homosexuality does not have any roots in Africa."[41] Had this statement been made in Victorian times however, no mention of homosexuality would have been discovered in Europe either as no such word existed in the English language.

At the continuing onset of the British Empire, the word "homosexuality" was coined in the 1880s to define a pathological act. Reinforced as a sin by the King James Version of *Leviticus*, the law of the priest class of Levi, which declares: "You shall not lie with a male as with a woman. It *is* an abomination," it was subsequently used to describe an activity abhorrent to the patriarchal sexual mores of the sexually suppressed upper class Victorians, and then ultimately made illegal. To the relief of women of course, Queen Victoria couldn't see what the female gender could possibly do, so Lesbianism was never legislated against!

Thus it seems that the irrational and sporadic persistence of a homophobia that has existed in one from or another since the fall of the matriarchy is explainable only by the fact that the blurring of sexual lines somehow threatens to undermine the iron fist rule of patriarchy.

Of course, for philosophical and historical reasons homoerotic culture is commonly associated with ancient Greece. Indeed from the observations of Joel D. Wallach, the author of *Epigenetics – The Death Of The Genetic Theory Of Disease Transmission*, according to historians, "Plato is the only recognized authority to have surmised that there were "three sexes (male, female, and hermaphrodite)."[42]

According to Plato, members of the human race were originally joined in pairs, two men, two women, and a man/women [sic] pair. "Zeus cut each pair apart to diminish their power and to teach them to fear the gods. Humans thus spend their time on the earth searching for their other half, with whom they can merge in love.

"The disposition of these people differed,"[43] Plato wrote, "according to the original pairing: those whose sex had been mixed were obsessed by coupling and often became adulterers, whereas people sprung from single-sex pairs were more fitted for the everyday business of the world. In particular men whose bond was with another man were most suited for government and leadership! Thus Plato gave the first interpretation of the origin of homosexual behavior."[44]

Though himself influenced by the homophobic sentiments of his day, according to Immanuel Velikovsky, "in Persia, Babylonia, Judea, and Egypt homosexuality was thought of as contemptible. The story of the population of Sodom who, in violation of the laws of hospitality, wished to work their will on Lot's overnight guests, and the horrible punishment that befell that city and other cities of the plain *bears witness* both to the ancient existence of *the urge* and its indulgence and to the moral attitude of the Hebrew penman and his readers, which may reflect, to an admittedly exaggerated degree, the attitude toward this aberration found in the ancient East."[45] (Italics added.)

Thus, despite the opinion of Afrocentric patriarchalists on the subject or indeed Velikovsky's moralistic take on the matter, same sex activity did exist in ancient times, and as will be demonstrated below, on African soil itself.

It is nevertheless unfortunate that scientific Egyptology began in a sexually repressive Victorian psychological climate, as it was inevitable that the "natural-ness" and "openness" of African sexuality, as expressed in ancient Khem via art and sculpture, to say nothing of the fact that African nudity was a continent wide accepted norm, would be abhorrent to them after 2,000 years or more of European patriarchal indoctrination and seem therefore perverted. Hundreds of wooden phalluses excavated at the temple of Hatshepsut for example have found their way to Canada and a basement in the British Museum, with no further comment.

As Wilhelm Reich asserted in *The Mass Psychology Of Fascism*, "Religiosity that is hostile to sex is the product of patriarchal authoritarian society. The son-father relationship, which we find in every patriarchal religion, is only the inevitable socially determined content of religious experience. The ex-perience itself, however, derives from the patriarchal suppression of sexu-ality. The function that religion comes to serve in the course of time, the bearing obedience toward authority and renunciation, is also only a second-ary function of religion. It can build upon a solid foundation: *the structure of patriarchal man molded by means of sexual suppression*. **It is the negation of the pleasures of the body that serves as the living source of the religious view**, and is the axis of every [patriarchal] religious dogma."[46] (Bold added.) Moreover, Reich counsels and forewarns future generations that: "*Genital shyness* and *pleasure anxiety* remain the energetic core of all anti-sexual patriarchal religions."[47]

Suppressed African erotic art moreover speaks volumes on this subject, to say nothing of the ancient literary description in the Chester Beatty Papyrus I of *The Contendings of Horus and Seth* that were previously mentioned in chapter two.

To resolve the question of the rulership of the Black and Red lands of Khem, these stories of the *Contendings* for the throne, also detail a same sex activity between two brothers, who in other myths are referred to as uncle and nephew. Also found within this account is the cosmological myth that the sun and the moon resulted from such an act.

Highlights of this story's details are pertinently revealed in *The Moses Mystery*, where Gary Greenberg relates that, "As *The Contendings of Horus and Set* unfolds, the gods begin to weary of the continuous arguing between Horus and Set. Re directs the two brothers to share a peaceful meal in the hope of resolving the dispute. Set, with ulterior motives, invites Horus over to his house and Horus accepts. During the night, while Horus is asleep, Set manages to sodomize his rival, which, if proven, would cause the gods to favor Set over Horus. When Horus realizes what has happened he goes to Isis, who first purges her son of Set's semen and then secretly places Horus's semen in Set's food. When the two disputants appear before the council the next day Set brags of his deed, but Horus denies the deed was done. To resolve the issue, the god Thoth called forth semen to see where it resided. As a result, the semen of Horus came out from Set: This caused the gods to believe it is Horus who has sodomized Set. Once again they declare Horus king, but Set continues to assert new claims and propose new challenges."[48]

Indeed, in Seth's aborted attempt to disqualify Horus from rulership, it is more graphically stated in the literal version of *The Contendings of Horus And Seth* that "in the night Seth caused his member to become stiff, and he made it go between the loins of Horus."[49]

As also referenced in chapter two however, that story of course was very "popular during the 20th Dynasty," and thus only dates as far back as 1149-1145 BC. Nevertheless, as E. A. Wallis Budge has demonstrated, there are indeed older references as "it is clear that in the VIth dynasty a belief was current that, after Osiris had been raised from the dead and had entered into heaven, his son, Horus, caused Thoth to bring before him his old enemy Set, so that the murderer of Osiris might see, in a state of glory, the god whom he had killed. When Set appeared the god threw him down, and Thoth lifted Osiris on to his back, and whilst Osiris sat there triumphant the gods mocked Set, and told him to carry one mightier than himself. At first, Osiris appears to have hesitated for Thoth exhorted him to "make his seat upon him," and to "come forth and sit upon him." He further promised that Set should not defile him, and that *he should not commit an act of paederasty upon him*. This passage shows only too plainly that in remote times in Egypt the victors committed nameless acts of abomination on the vanquished, besides frightful mutilations, and evidence is not wanting that such practices were not unknown in the Southern Sûdân a very few years ago. Osiris did as Thoth and Horus arranged he should do, and "made his seat," or seated himself, upon the body of Set in triumph, and was, presumably, ever after called the "seat-maker," As-ar, or As-ari, which the Greeks turned into Osiris. The crudeness and, it may be added, childishness of the story prove that it is very ancient, and it probably existed in Predynastic times. It may be argued that the story was invented to provide an etymology for the name of Osiris, but even if this were the case it is still very ancient, for the text which contains it was cut upon King Teta's tomb under the VIth dynasty, and it is unlikely that it was new at that time."[50] (Italics added.)

As for *Leviticus*, the mere fact that a law in antiquity prohibited such activity implies its ubiquitous expression otherwise, why ban it! Literal proof therefore exists, as the foregoing demonstrates, that same sex activity occurred in greater antiquity, as was the practice of temple "prostitution," both male as well as female, in a time prior to any definition of a European culture expressing itself.

More pertinently, not all the evidence is so ancient. Indeed, as exemplified in more recent pre-colonial times, after the patriarchal missionary interference of Westernized Christianity introduced *Leviticus* to the African people of Uganda in the late 1800s, many pages who were the male lovers of Kabaka (King) Mwanga II of Buganda were executed after they converted to Christianity. According to Wikipedia, "whatever the significance in traditional culture of the "corporal intimacies" that Mwanga desired, those who refused them considered them incompatible with the new religion, for which they were prepared to die as martyrs."[51] Indeed, Kevin Ward noted that, "the immediate cause of the killings was the refusal of the pages to engage in homosexual practices." The king, who by tradition had the power of life and death over his subjects, was angered by this refusal to obey his wishes."[52] Moreover, Marie de Kiewet-Hemphill concludes that, "the immediate pretext, if not the whole cause, was the refusal of the pages to yield to what she calls Mwanga's "unnatural desires.""[53] There are others however of a less homophobic opinion who argue that "these Christians were rebels against the Kabaka, unwitting tools of foreign imperialism."[54] In fact, the 30 October 1886 edition of *The Times* of London, quoting the dictum, "the blood of martyrs is the seed of the Church", stated: "On the success of the Uganda experiment, with its alternation of favourable and adverse circumstances, depends the happiness of the interior of the vast continent for generations. This sentiment developed into a campaign for English intervention in the region."[55] That is, this was indeed a mere excuse for direct colonization. But pray tell, where indeed is the anticipated continent wide happiness?

Thus, as definitively and literally demonstrated in *The Contendings of Horus And Seth*, the sexual mores of the ancients are clearly another example of "a mode of thinking very different from our own," as notably in an African matriarchal context, the act of sodomy in and of itself did not prevent the contender who sodomized another from becoming king.

Thus therefore, there may be more to the sins of Akhetaten/Sodom & Gomorrah than this. However before we further indulge in the salacious 'tabloid press' of that murky historical era, the issue of Akhenaten's queen Nefertiti requires some comment.

Of course, the official Great Royal Wife of Akhenaten was Nefertiti who these days is more predominantly known from the iconic image of her portrayed in the famous and dramatic art deco-like limestone bust currently on display in the Berlin Museum.

Interestingly, in the days that followed the slowly dying bloom of the *Flower Power* and *Free Speech Movement*, days when *Sun Ra & his Galactic Arkestra* pervaded and transformed the musical experience of the California jazz scene in Berkeley and the San Francisco Bay Area, while African American author Ishmael Reed influenced the current literary thinking with *Yellow Back Radio Broke Down* and *Mumbo Jumbo*, a rumour was in full swing that the famous painted limestone bust of Nefertiti was in fact a fake!

Indeed, at the time this intriguing notion was circulating, this idea had a striking appeal, as it did seem a little strange that an African queen, the Great

Royal Wife of Akhenaten, would appear to have such an alabaster complexion, given that she came from the sun-drenched climate of the land of Khem. On the other hand, personally however, I have a niece who is quite dark skinned but her daughter, for all intents and purposes, appears quite blond and white but of course pertinent to this outcome the father of my great niece is also white. Therefore, it is not impossible for Nefertiti to appear as she does in the limestone bust even though her aunt Tiye is quite dark skinned. The question is, of course, who then was Nefertiti's white parent?

As it happens, it has taken a long time to piece together the genealogy of the family of Akhenaten and, in the meantime, as a consequence it had been speculated that Nefertiti was a foreigner. Indeed, several women at the Theban court were from Mitanni and even the mother of Amenhotep III, Mutemwija, was a Mitannian princess.

Thus by ethnic descent, Amenhotep III and his descendants were Afro-Asiatic, assuming of course that the country of Mitanni was in Asia. However, according to Immanuel Velikovsky, "The whereabouts of the kingdom of Mitanni is not positively known. In view of the close contact between the Mitannian and Egyptian royal houses, modern historians usually place Mitanni in northern Syria, in the neighborhood of Carchemish on the Euphrates, though this region, as is well known, was in the domain of Assyria, where Arameans, "Hurrians," and "Hittites" occupied parts of the crowded territory. There is reason to believe that this geographic assignment is incorrect and that Mitanni was in northern Iran, where Herodotus in the fifth century before the present era described the people of Matiene: this Persian satrapy was near Mount Ararat,"[56] adding that "The Kings of that people prayed to and swore by Mitra, Varuna, Indra, and other Indo-Iranian gods."[57]

In any event, in 2009, Henri Stierlin, a Swiss art historian, published a book, *Missing Link in Archaeology*, that indeed made the claim that the Nefertiti bust was a modern fake. Others have suggested that the existing Nefertiti bust was crafted in the 1930s on Hitler's orders, and that the original was lost in World War II, while historian Edrogan Ercivan even went so far as to claim that the German wife of its discoverer was the model for the bust. And indeed both Stierlin and

Ercivan argue that though discovered in 1912 it was not revealed to the public until 1924 because it was a fake.

In more recent times, even British television drew attention to this subject in a 2014 documentary. So there does seem to be a great deal of suspicion associated with this historical artefact. Though the sculptor Thutmose is believed to have crafted this said to be masterpiece in 1345 BC, the question still remains, is the Nefertiti bust really a true image and representation of Mother Africa? She certainly does not resemble any of the Ethiopian queens that have been previously inferred.

Beyond speculation however, there is no proof to indicate that she was a foreign personage? Indeed, according to Velikovsky, Ay was Nefertiti's father who was on her side after Akhenaten made his mother the "King's Mother and Great Royal Wife, Tiy,"[58] and thus "led her camp against his sister and son-in-law."[59]

Ay, like Tiye, was a child of Yuya and Tuya. Thus Nefertiti was native, she, the granddaughter and Akhenaten, the grandson of Yuya of whom it has been determined is the biblical Joseph.

Thus, if the foregoing proves true, it would appear that the limestone bust is in fact not the genuine image of an African queen at all, but a modern Germanic fake.

That dealt with, we return to the even graver sins of Akhetaten/Sodom & Gomorrah, Indeed, if there is any credence whatsoever to Velikovsky's theory that Akhenaten was the historical prototype for the incestuous Oedipus, then the former's relationship with his mother, if not equally, was more offensive to the laws of nature than the homosexuality alleged to have taken place in Akhetaten/Sodom & Gomorrah that supposedly brought about its inevitable demise.

Officially, Nefertiti was the Great Royal Wife but it appears that Akhenaten had "two households, and these are pictured on the bas-reliefs of the banquet and on the lintel"[60] of the tomb of Huya, the superintendent of the Royal Harem of Queen Tiye, at Akhetaten.

Long after her husband Amenhotep III was deceased, the Queen Mother and Great Queen Tiye was often depicted wearing the double plumes. Indeed, the King's Mother and Great Royal Wife, "claimed official status and a privileged position for herself and her child. Tiy was not a weakling, and one of the two women soon had to go, either Tiy or Nefretete."[61]

Indeed, referred to as "the king's daughter of his body,"[62] Velikovsky appears to be arguing that just as Oedipus in the Greek legend had fathered the child Antigone with Jocasta, his mother, so Akhenaten had fathered his daughter Beketaten not with Nefertiti however but with his mother Queen Tiye.

Moreover, Velikovsky further points out that, "The appellation "King's Mother and Great Royal Wife" applied to the dowager queen is usually interpreted to mean that she was queen mother to the reigning monarch and royal wife to the deceased pharaoh, but this explanation does not completely clear up the peculiarity of Tiy's title."[63]

Supposedly Beketaten was a daughter of Tiye for Amenhotep III but as Velikovsky makes clear, "In the twelfth year of Akhnaton's reign Beketaten was a small child, four, five, or at the most six years old. Amenhotep III had been dead for about twelve years; no wonder the little girl was thought to be a daughter of Akhnaton and Nefretete. However, when it was determined that she was not a daughter of Nefretete, but of Tiy, it was concluded that she was the child of Amenhotep III, Tiy's husband."[64]

Be that as it may, whatever the case with Ahketaten, its sacrilegious vices and other forms of licentiousness nevertheless drew the attention and anger of the power elite located at Naamoni as the Massai refer to what is otherwise known by the Greek name of Thebes which in the language of the people of Khem "was called Ne or No ("Residence") or No-Amon ("Residence of Amon," as in the Hebrew text of the book of the Prophet Nahum 3:8)."[65]

Indeed, the "perverted picture of Sodom is encountered in Akhet-Aten's cult of nudity,"[66] according to the rabbi brothers Sabbah who also make further connections with the Black land by stating that as "at Akhet-Aten, the inhabitants of Sodom had the sun cult. The moon was considered by them to be Re's second eye. Sodom, considered in the Bible as "a garden of Adonay in Egypt" could well be the metaphor for Akhet-Aten."[67]

Thus the foregoing description gives some validation to the possibility that Akhetaten is the origin of the biblical city of Sodom that awaited its inevitable destruction, along with Gomorrah, in fire and brimstone.

"For we will destroy this place, because the outcry against them has grown great before the face of the Lord, and the Lord has sent us to destroy it?" Who then indeed were the historical figures the preceding quote from Genesis 19:13 reports were sent by Yahweh to warn Lot? Who were these allegorical nuclear warriors who were sent to put an end to this city's perversions?

Indeed, the men in question who visited Lot were clearly physical, as Genesis 19:16 indicated that, "while he lingered, the men took hold of his hand, his wife's hand, and the hands of his two daughters, the Lord being merciful to him and they brought him out and set him outside the city."

Although Zecharia Sitchin stated in *The Wars Of Gods And Men* that, "Sodom and Gomorrah went up in flames when Ninurta and Nergal unleashed the Doomsday Weapons,"[68] is it not more reasonable to see in these three men mentioned in Genesis 19:13, the generals Seti, Ramesses and Horemheb sent by Ay from No [Thebes] to escort out of the land the troublemaking community that had defied the sacred symbolic and cosmological teachings of the MeduNeteru? In deference to Sitchin however, his nuclear holocaust hypothesis may indeed be representative of a different truth, one that will be examined much later in the Epilogue.

For the moment however, in contrast to the new language that emerged in Akhetaten, according to Scranton, symbolism indeed was "the original language of ancient cosmology."[69] As was shown in chapter three, the "symbolic concept of the divine Neter provides an analogical model of an invisible but functional ontological power that speaks directly to right-brain consciousness that the current proponents of linear left-brain digital technology of modern society have removed from the public educational system and therefore the understanding of modern contemporary society."

Newly discovered powers or natural principles were always accepted and included into the realm of the Neteru, if they proved efficacious. This process is and always has been standard religious practice throughout the whole of Africa. The Yoruba of Nigeria for example, have 1,600 Orisha their equivalent of the Neteru. Indeed, the introduction of Jesus was incorporated into Obatala because they share similar traits. Thus the introduction of a new moral or physical principle causes no problem, but for the ancient people of the land

of Khem to introduce a Neter to the exclusion of all others, that was the greatest anathema.

Clearly, Akhetaten threatened the very existence of the ancient tradition
and culture of the African way of life, a situation that the still existent powerful
Amunian priesthood of Thebes could not tolerate. Thus its complete and utter
destruction of "the Atenist heresy and all those associated with its traditions,"[70]
which took place under the administration of Horemheb, was inevitable.

Though he doesn't mention any group by the name of Yahud, in examining
the consequences of this city's destruction, Gary Greenberg concluded that the
"destruction of the city of Akhetaten must have caused the displacement and possible enslavement of many thousands of people, priests, civil servants, soldiers,
and peasants, who served the heretic pharaoh and administered the wealth of his
temples. We can imagine the wholesale seizure of wealth and property from his
adherents and the disillusionment of many noble families and priests. We can envision extensive house cleaning, with hordes of administrators who traced their
patronage to the disgraced pharaoh being swept from office, and large numbers
of soldiers punished and exiled to – interestingly – Sinai, where Moses received
the Law. It does not take great imagination to envision under Horemheb large
numbers of angry and resentful citizens from all classes suffering humiliation,
persecution, and banishment. They would easily provide a substantial reservoir
of support for anyone who would challenge the source of their discomfort."[71]

It is of interest to note at this point that Horemheb has already been identified as the biblical Aaron (A-Horon), the eldest brother of Moses, the one who
made the Golden Calf. This connection is owed once again to the rabbi brothers
Sabbah who reveal in *Secrets Of The Exodus* that, "The Aaron whom [sic] acts as the
person second-in-command in the Exodus, historically, was General Horemheb,
a son-in-law of the Divine Father Ay and, later, a pharaoh of Egypt."[72] In fact, the
coronation name of Horemheb is "Golden Horus, the powerful bull."[73]

Thus not only was Akhenaten's "proto-Jerusalem" completely and utterly
raised to the ground, the Atentists were forcefully expelled from their central
location in the Black land, as Nefertiti's historical moment also suddenly disappears from the pages of history. Nevertheless, "The drama at Akhet-Aton did
not come to an end with the disappearance or disgrace of Nefretete, and could

scarcely be expected to have done so. The gallery of pictures in the tombs, in the ateliers of the artists, in the ruins of the palaces cease to relate what was taking place in Akhet-Aton. For four or five years after the desertion or disgrace of Nefretete Akhnaton continued to occupy the throne. It is generally agreed that some tragedy occurred in the personal life of the king. It is also agreed that Ay became even more powerful and was directing the fortunes of the state and the palace. And, finally, it is agreed that after a while Tiy was no longer present. Her end is shrouded in mystery because she was not buried like a great queen of a great empire."[74]

Indeed, after Akhenaten died in his 17th year, the city was abandoned and his name hacked from temple walls throughout the land of Khem as he himself had done the same in his rampage against Amun. Nevertheless, according to the biblical text, this historical event has travelled down through the ages as the tragic persecution of the Hebrews by the Egyptians.

The latter myth of course is still reinforced in popular culture to this very day. Ridley Scott's latest venture into biblical history, his new movie version of the Moses myth, *Exodus Gods And Kings* for example, in complete disregard of its Sacred Science, once again imposes modern "Babylonian" political and economic motivations onto the land of Khem, describing it as an imperial empire and slavocracy. One indeed that was brought down to its knees by an ethereal god, ironically represented by a precocious child, an infantile shade of Giordano Bruno's "Triumphant Beast."

When one considers that even in the time of Herodotus, about a thousand years after the events portrayed in this movie, the people of Khem were still described as having "black skins and woolly hair" can it be an accident that black people in this latest extravaganza were not represented in roles of power but were still represented as mere soldiers or servants? Is this an historical repeat in the 21st Century of the early 20th Century's version of the Black & White Minstrel Show?

Clearly, the irreparable damage Akhenaten has wrought to the African personality is still promoted even today by such cinematic endeavours that more so still include a number of significant historical anachronisms. Indeed, the head of the Sphinx, which stood out most significantly in a number of scenes, should have been represented intact with a true African visage since it only lost its nose subsequent to the vandalism perpetrated during the Arab invasion and Napoleon's troops who used it for target practice.

The other anachronism was the pyramid. Once again, prior to the Arab invasion of the land of Khem, the Great Pyramid was clad in its original smooth white limestone casing that shone brightly in the distance and therefore should have been gleaming white if the movie had any intentions of providing any accuracy to Africa's ancient past. It and the Sphinx however appear in the same ruinous state that we witness today.

But, of course, designed for the entertainment of the masses, this is after all only a commercial venture, one however that is also propaganda since, in the interest of the monotheistic viewpoint, it misrepresents Africa and fails to inform or rather continues to misinform modern audiences of the ancient truth.

However the political nuances of today are not applicable to the motivation of the ancients, for not only did the Nile Dwellers think differently, as Siegfried Morenz was astute enough to point out, their motivations were governed by the higher principles of the Sacred Science, the longevity of which stretches back deep into Africa's extremely ancient past.

Thus Akhenaten's outrageous threat to overturn the very existence of the ancient tradition and culture of the African way of life constituted a spark that would initiate a nation-wide rebellion creating a popular uprising that stirred up much political dissent, for the rebel king's actions could not be tolerated. Hence, Akhenaten's flight from No, and his decision to move to a future capital located equidistant from Memphis and No, the traditional centres of Ptah and Amun, respectively. Thus it is from No/Thebes that much dissent would inevitably emanate and it is there that we must look for the three men the Lord sent.

The "Lord" of course is the word used to identify God in *The New King James Version* of the Bible whereas in the Hebrew Bible it is rendered as "Yahweh." It might be appropriate at this point however to mention that one scholar has taken issue over the *concept* of the god that Yahweh is alleged to represent.

From his intense biblical research, geometrician John Ten has drawn the conclusion that the Catholic Church had not appropriately interpreted the Old

Testament's concept of the Hebrew God because the ancient text described God as some kind of equilateral triangle on a throne. Indeed, in his own words which can be heard in his YouTube video lecture, he was "stunned by the fact that He wasn't an old man considering me as a sinner but was some kind of geometry that was described as the throne of God, the point of interaction between human and God."[75]

Examining "various allusions to it in very specific parts of the Bible," he also discovered that it referred to certain "angles that radiated in this tetrahedron," the latter being a 3-D geometric version of a triangle, and gave descriptions of some sort of crystal seas and all sorts of things that made him think of technologies and geometries and physics much more than some kind of guy on a throne.

In fact he began to realize that the Old Testament is ambiguous because it described God not as something that's somewhere in the sky or anything but rather describes *God as an object*.

Indeed, this object is something that Graham Phillips also came across: "Strangely, considering the Judean stance on idolatry, the Old Testament refers to something as "the Lord" that is clearly an object. During the forty years in the wilderness, when the Israelites were away from the Mountain of God, they worshipped in a holy tent known as the tabernacle. It is during a ceremony in the tabernacle that the object is first mentioned:

"And they brought that which Moses commanded before the tabernacle of the congregation: and all the congregation drew near and stood before the Lord. (LEVITICUS 9:5)

"What exactly is being referred to as 'the Lord'? Biblical scholars have long puzzled over what this enigmatic artifact might have been. All we can gather is that Moses had told the congregation to bring it with them. Although on many subsequent occasions the Israelites are described as standing before 'the Lord', we are never told what this representation of God actually is.

"Whatever 'the Lord' was, we can assume that it was placed on the tabernacle altar."[76]

Indeed, John Ten indicates that they had some kind of link or communication with God through this equilateral triangle, or better described 3-D geometric tetrahedron, on a throne, that they called the Ark of the Covenant of God, the box-like object of which will be addressed later.

For the moment however, we return to the issue of the name, not the concept of God, in *The Hebrew Version* of the Bible where, according to the latter source, the Lord is named Yahweh, or alternatively Jehovah, the Tetragrammaton, YHWH, which is derived from the name Yahu, or simply the One God. In that Bible however, according to the rabbi brothers Sabbah "the Tetragram Yahwe ... is read as Adon-Ay, because it is forbidden to pronounce the name of God."[77]

The Lord was none other therefore than Ay (Adon-Ay) the ruling pharaoh of the day who inherited the title Yahu from the God-King Amenhotep III. Therefore this pharaoh, under pressure from the traditional priesthood, was the Lord who sent the emissaries to warn Lot of the fate of Sodom and Gomorrah, herein recognized as Ahketaten, a city now marked for doom.

Therefore, with this aspect of African history clarified, if the foregoing proves to be true, it can be confidently concluded that the worship of Yah, Yahu, Yahweh or Jehovah and the resultant religion of Judaism are all in point of fact the result of an African heresy, the brazen outcome of a Babylonian conspiracy that had successfully infiltrated itself into the most powerful seat of authority in the Land of Khem. This thus explains how the banishment of the Yahuds, original native priesthood of the people of Khem, came thus to be recorded in the Bible as the Exodus.

Thus by the command of the God-King Ay, the incorrigible desecrators of the MeduNeteru and the Sacred Science of the priesthood of Amun, the people of the doomed city of Akhetaten, the 'Sodom and Gomorrah' of the Bible, were to be exiled, or as Rashi commented "dispersed from the valley and . . . spread out across the entire world"[78] not only for their desecration but for the violation of the moral principles once revered within traditional African culture, the Yahuds to Palestine and the Medzay deeper into Africa, along with the many other monotheists who may have been the antecedents of the Falashas, the Lemba, and the Akan or other yet to be identified African tribal groups.

Unlike the biblical legend of the two notorious cities that were utterly and devastatingly destroyed, the controversial riverbank city of Akhetaten on the other hand was left abandoned, dismantled and forgotten and thus erased from memory until its unanticipated, and in some respects inauspicious, rediscovery and excavation in the early 20th century.

Five

The MeduNeteru

*Ancient myths were carefully composed, multi-leveled structures
designed to encode a massive amount of technical information that
could be decoded when science had advanced to a similar state of
development as the society that originally created the myths.*

Joseph P. Farrell with Scott D. de Hart

For more than 3,000 long and arduous years, the black descendants of the people of the Land of Khem have endured the calumny and slander resulting from the biblical commandment abolishing their 'alleged' idol worship, which was never such to begin with but to the contrary was the traditional ancient African religious system that Akhenaten so unceremoniously proposed to destroy through the banning of the principles underlying the symbolic system of the MeduNeteru.

However in this work, that tyrannical legislative dictate has been exposed for what it was and as a result there now exists a necessity for a meticulous and intelligent reexamination of the lost origins of that ancient symbolic writing system once known by the name of the MeduNeteru.

Thus from what previous scholarship has determined, the principle architect of that symbolic writing system was Djehuti [*dhwty*] who was also known to the people of the Land of Khem as the Neter of Wisdom. Although Osiris also "instructed Egyptians in the proper manner to worship the gods," an important factor previously stated in chapter two implying that he too understood and disseminated the underlying principles of the MeduNeteru it is nonetheless Djehuti who is at the head of the philosophy taught in the Houses of Life. Indeed, his power was unlimited in the Underworld and rivalled that of Ra and Osiris.

Known as the scribe of the gods, he was the Neter whom the Greeks called Thoth. Generally depicted as ibis-headed and known as the "Three-times great, great,"Thoth, the moon god, was also the god of justice, writing, and patron of the sciences, and messenger of Ra. Moreover, the Greeks declared him the inventor of astronomy, astrology, the science of numbers, mathematics, geometry, land surveying, medicine, botany, theology, civilized government, the alphabet, reading, writing and oratory. They further claimed he was the true author of every work of every branch of knowledge, human and divine. His feminine counterpart was Seshat, and his wife was Ma'at.

Moreover, according to Wikipedia, "the ancient Egyptians regarded Thoth as One, self-begotten, and self-produced. He was the master of both physical and moral (i.e. divine) law, making proper use of Ma'at. He is credited with making the calculations for the establishment of the heavens, stars, Earth, and everything in them. Compare this to how his feminine counterpart, Ma'at was the force which maintained the Universe. He is said to direct the motions of heavenly bodies. Without his words, the Egyptians believed, the gods would not exist."

Indeed, "The period the Egyptians associated with the reign of Thoth was a time of peace among the gods..."[1] As such, Thoth played many vital and prominent roles in Egyptian mythology, such as maintaining the universe, and being one of the two deities (the other being Ma'at) who stood on either side of Ra's boat. In recognition of his greatness, his chief temple was located in the city of Khmun, later called Hermopolis Magna during the Greco-Roman era.

Though known in the Bible as Enoch, according to Zecharia Sitchin, the Sumerians knew him as Ningishzidda, the "Lord of the Artifact of Life," who "was none other than Thoth, the Egyptian god of magical powers who was appointed guardian of the secret plans of the pyramids of Giza."[2]

Hinting at some form of powerful device in his possession, what the Artefact of Life might have been will be further discussed in chapter seven. For the moment however, with such laurels and accolades to his name, one could draw the conclusion that without Djehuti, there would have been no Sacred Science in the Black land, the land of Khem.

Yet that extremely ancient and very important knowledge was soon to be confronted with a major threat to its existence from the newly appointed pharaoh Akhenaten. Indeed, his catastrophic and violent assault on the traditional orthodoxy is without any known historical precedent. Therefore, what historical explanation is there for his vehement abolition of the Sacred Science? Was this pharaoh's blatant act of ignorance the result of his being denied access to the Inner Temple? Indeed, had he been kept from the secrets of the Mystery Schools?

Of course, these questions concerning his probable exclusion from the inner sanctum were explored in chapter three where it was suggested that "the door to the 'House of Life' had been barred to him" as a consequence of the rule that an "Asiatic ... may not enter into ... this House of Life, he may not see it."

Indeed that chapter also clarified that Akhenaten was, as Ahmed Osman suggested, absent from the royal residence during his early years as "he was living at Zarw" in the Delta region. Moreover, as was mentioned in chapter two, "Akhenaten apparently came to the throne by accident" as Amenhotep III intended for Prince Tuthmose, one of his other sons to become king, as Graham Phillips inferred, but with that son's disgrace and exile or, as Gary Greenberg understands, premature death, the poorly trained Akhenaten became the successor.

However, as can be determined from the foregoing, Akhenaten was evidently unprepared for his role as leader of the people of Khem. Thus it would appear that his barring from the Temple has to have been the case, otherwise how could he not have known that the Neteru, the primary subject taught in the temples, the so-called idols that he sought to suppress, were in fact deep structure symbolic multilevel representations of the functional processes of creation?

As was mentioned in chapter three, "the 'House of Life', which served mainly as a place where sacred writings were compiled... is categorically placed out of bounds to foreigners. 'An Asiatic ... may not enter into ... this House of Life, he may not see it.'"

Moreover, in that very same chapter there was mention of the fact that "no outsider would have been taught the esoteric meaning behind the enormous multitude of symbols that composed the entire symbolic lexicon of the enigmatic-for-the-uninitiated MeduNeteru, the so-called hieroglyphs."

Thus, the Houses of Life Akhenaten sought to close down therefore were in no way similar to the temples, synagogues, cathedrals, churches and mosques of the three Great Yahwist religions of today. Indeed, since modern congregations kneel down to pray when attending their respective places of worship, a natural assumption arises from such rituals that that is what the ancients were doing or may have done upon entering their sacred places, their alleged "polytheistic" temples.

To the contrary however, the ancients referred to their places of worship as Houses of Life and unlike our places of worship however, the 'Per Ankh,' that is the House of Life, was more like a university where the philosophy of the MeduNeteru, that is observation of the physical sciences of the day, was handed down.

This is where students were taught the deep structure esoteric meaning behind the glyphs that Rene A. Schwaller de Lubicz has helped to reveal. Thus, the gods the ancients observed with extreme reverence were indeed the Neteru, the high spiritual principles that analogically represented processes of nature understood to underlie the symbolic writing system of the MeduNeteru.

With regard to the glyphs however, Schwaller de Lubicz indicates in a footnote that the individual glyph that composes the very word *Neter* itself "is clumsily translated as "God," which, in Judeo-Christian deism, has the connotation of an absolute Unity. The Greek "daimon" would be more suitable. But why not simply say "Neter"?[3] Indeed, the "*Neter* ... is principal, but is not used as a word signifying "the principle" in ancient Egypt."[4]

Indeed, the theocratic principles taught in the Temple represented the collective *functional* meaning behind the MeduNeteru. But in addition to teaching the subject of pharaonic theocracy, the temples were also places of work, as are factories in modern times. Hence not only were they academic institutions they also contributed to the economic well-being of the nation.

Until recently, modern scholars had been contented to translate mythological narratives, laundry lists, inventory accounts and court squabbles in their attempts at translation of that once lost script. But in trying to utilize the same translation techniques for the ancient understanding of meta-scientific concepts, which we are now rediscovering in the findings of modern physics, they were completely baffled by the incomprehensibility of much of Khem's philosophical output. Once again from chapter three, we recall that certain "symbols, many considered magical, of the MeduNeturu were, like so-called junk DNA, left untranslatable into anything rational or logical for a modern mind, bereft of a knowledge of the recently *re*discovered principles of quantum physics to comprehend."

Jean-François Champollion's contribution as the key to translation of the MeduNeteru aside, the genius behind their symbolic understanding as will be discussed in chapter seven, is Rene A. Schwaller de Lubicz, the only Egyptologist to have lifted the veil of Isis by making the comparison between the knowledge underlying the work of the ancients with that of quantum physics.

By condemning the Neteru as nothing more than mere stone or wooden objects that only superstitious people could believe in, this audacious iconoclastic heretic priest king had rejected the worship of Amun, either because his family was part of a Babylonian conspiracy against the Sacred Science or solely because "the door to the House of Life had been barred to him," a fact which is evidenced by his ignorance of the sacrosanct nature of that Sacred Science.

That modern scholars can and do suggest that the ancients were primitive in their understanding of nature, projecting this modern belief onto the past is somewhat understandable. But in the case of the traducer Ahkenaton, this can only be seen as an unforgivable calumny inflicted upon the traditional African religion. Thus, this has to be one of the principle and fundamental reasons that on the continent of Africa that pharaoh should be known as a criminal and a heretic.

As Siegfried Morenz made succinctly evident in chapter three, "An Asiatic ... may not enter into ... this House of Life, he may not see it." Since therefore there was a "strict national exclusiveness of the spiritual centre," did the Asiatic part of his African heritage play a role in barring him from the deep structure knowledge of the cosmic myth taught to the priests of Amun? If not, Ahkenaton's otherwise utter lack of understanding of the philosophical and functional basis of the MeduNeteru remains inexplicable.

Remarkably, even after more than 5,000 years the Dogon, a present day African people of the Republic of Mali in central West Africa, indeed still possess this knowledge of which Akhenaton appeared to be bereft.

The maintenance of harmony throughout the kingdom and the cosmos was of course the principle function of Pharaoh. Indeed, one of the primary and major philosophical roles of the traditional kings was to uphold the cosmic principle of Maat, the Neter who held the world in harmonic balance. On a personal level however, Maat is also a cognitive functional power that is put into practice each time an individual makes a fair and just decision. Thus, how was it possible that Akhenaton did not know of Maat's cosmic functionality?

As was just said it was the role of Pharaoh to uphold the principle of Maat. Thus, could it be that his rebellion was merely the expression of his lack of commitment to the traditional belief system or, as has been previously suggested, was there something even more nefarious and sinister behind his intrigue, a counterrevolutionary motive, for example, such as an ideological infiltration spawn no less from the imperial denizens of Babylon?

The fact has already been observed that Akhenaton was not Amenhotep III's primary choice for king. Therefore, as was mentioned in chapter four, there exists the possibility, however remote, that his theocratic misconceptions had been derived from the Asiatic influence of his maternal grandfather Yuya, the biblical Joseph, and his native born mother Tiye, the daughter of Yuya, while he was being raised in Zarw? Thus, a new twist on the history of the land of Khem has come to light. Could it be that Joseph was in fact a spy? Could the interpolation of his biblical tale of woe be in fact a Babylonian cover story for his otherwise covert, espionage activities?

Indeed, in *Financial Vipers of Venice*, Joseph P. Farrell explores a plausible hypothesis that supports a Babylonian root for the modern system of economic exploitation. Spreading like a cancer that invades the healthy and wholesome body of its host before successfully destroying it from within, such an oppressive labyrinthine economic process that lends itself to usury and illiberal exploitation was not in point of fact indigenous to Khem, or any other aspect of traditional African culture for that matter, and thus had to be imposed upon it.

Moreover, Farrell's speculations demonstrate how ancient these methods and this paradigm of intellectual sophistry are and give ground to the hypothesis being made here for the Babylonian infiltration of Khem via the immediate family of Akhenaten.

However, since exploitative parasitic forms of government, representative of the *Shemsu Seth*, though clever and devious, lack creativity, to accomplish this goal, the true religion of Africa therefore had to be distorted. For this reason, the imperially minded outsiders had to plunder pre-existing African concepts of divinity in order for its system of exploitation to survive. Hence the many dissembled stories in the Bible that in fact can be traced to actual historical events that most assuredly took place on African soil.

Nevertheless, to obfuscate this understanding, there seems to be a myth abroad that selfish, egotistical, imperial behaviour is somehow innate to human nature. However, this myth has to be maintained precisely because it is not so. It is simply an inevitable expression of patriarchy. This is why it had become necessary to portray African religion and matriarchal culture as pagan because the ancient spirituality that it supported, represented through the MeduNeteru, was not conducive to imperial aims. Indeed, the materialism, egotism and selfishness that the patriarchal personality represents is in fact alien to an untainted African way of life. It is for this reason that the Nile valley civilization lasted for untold thousands of years.

However, given that the Black land had demonstrated a proven stability that may have existed for 39,000 or even more years, the complete overthrow and egregious destruction of the philosophical traditions of ancient Africa appears, as it happened, to have taken about 1,500 years to accomplish.

Regardless of the current millennia long imperial distortion and obfuscation of humanity's ancient past however, inevitably the truth will out. Thus, despite the promoted erudite arguments for the Greek Classical era origin of philosophy, Gerald Massey, Rene A. Schwaller de Lubicz and George G. M. James, and moreover many Renaissance scholars, early suspected this higher and transcendental knowledge, steeped with ancient wisdom, originated with the ancients. For them, Greece was a mere child of the Land of Khem, if not in fact a colony of Africa on European soil. Martin Bernal, author of *Black Athena*, would surely agree.

Even the discoverer of the *New Astronomy* Johannes Kepler for example, the man who transformed the astronomy of the ancients into astrophysics, once said: "I have plundered the golden vessels of the Egyptians, in order to furnish a sacred tabernacle for my God out of them, far from the borders of Egypt."[5] Indeed, his specific research and foray into the past led him to discover the universal physical principle of gravitation, as American physical economist Lyndon H. LaRouche, Jr. refers to it, and that by means of Kepler's principled method of 'vicarious hypothesis,' i.e. the **functional principle** of physical science.

The unseen force of gravitation is of course an example of what the people of the Black Land referred to as Maat, which as stated earlier, was the Neter or "force which maintained the Universe." Therefore, in his *Riemann For Anti-Dummies*, according to its author Bruce Director, gravitation "reflects a power that contains the physical universe as a conceptually finite oneness, a universe as if contained by a principle of universal gravitation."[6] Indeed, the very principle related to the Neter Maat. But, as mentioned earlier, it is Thoth who is the architect, the one who "is credited with making the calculations for the establishment of the heavens, stars, Earth, and everything in them."

Apparently the control of gravity, as will be further discussed in chapter seven, appears to have been part of the scientific arsenal among the esoteric abilities of the priesthood of the Land of Khem.

Therefore, as was also stated in chapter three, there were "indeed inner sanctum depths to be plumbed concerning a secret knowledge found at that time only in Khem." Since this learning even preceded the introduction of written systems in the Nile valley, the esoteric wisdom is so old it apparently disappears into the hoary depths of prehistory as comparative cosmologist Laird Scranton has deftly shown through his examination of the culture of an African people known as the Dogon.

Who could have suspected the explosive impact that would result from a French anthropological study of a remote African tribe undertaken during the 1930s? For many subsequent decades, of interest only to anthropologists, *Conversations with Ogotemmêli*, written by Marcel Griaule and published in English in 1965, would eventually put the Dogon culture on the map in 1976 after English author Robert Temple published his controversial book, *The Sirius Mystery*.

Carl Sagan, who had previously disparaged the theories of Immanuel Velikovsky, and other big guns indeed, had to be rolled out to dissuade the general public of any veracity to the very idea that a "primitive" African tribe could possess any valid scientific knowledge of binary star systems or know of any stars that cannot be seen with the naked eye. Well they could and they did.

Indeed, according to Scranton, "the Dogon are a living culture whose priests have a clear understanding of their own traditions and practices. Also, these Dogon traditions seem to reflect very early practices found in ancient Egypt. For example, the Egyptian hieroglyphic language is thought to have been an early development in dynastic Egypt, whereas the Dogon have never had a native system of writing. The implication is that any relationship between the Dogon and the Egyptians may have ended before writing was introduced."[7]

To further emphasize and corroborate this ancient connection, Scranton adds that "The Dogon also make use of the same set of calendars as were found in ancient Egypt, but without the Egyptian system of five intercalary days to synchronize them. These intercalary days appeared early in Egyptian culture, so this also seems to affirm an earlier relationship for the Dogon with the ancient Egyptians. As we would expect based on that scenario, Dogon culture also shows numerous resemblances to the predynastic Amazigh tribes that resided in Egypt just prior to the First Dynasty,"[8] circa 3100 BCE.

Thus the Dogon turn out to be the descendants of ancient members of a black African breakaway group who formed part of the original people who, like their Nubian brothers and sisters, and the mysterious "People of Yam" and the "People of Takhebet" who may have hailed from Chad, laid the earliest foundations of the Nile valley civilization. That being so, it has become apparent that a sizeable majority of black African groups have now been formally identified as having been in the Black land at the time of the beginning and the seeding of the civilization of Khem. Indeed, awaiting their retrieval by their modern day descendants for those illustrious ancestors represent and reflect the consciousness and subconsciousness of an ancient African civilization that belongs to those who currently suffer *in the ghettos, inner cities and slums across the four corners of the earth* today.

Thus, the foregoing has shown therefore that within the black African mind the symbols of the MeduNeteru were already psychological concepts long in use before ever they were put to pen or carved in stone in graphic form.

Indeed, as mentioned in chapter two, after ruling for a while Osiris "decided to travel abroad to spread his teachings" while during "his absence Isis safeguarded the throne against Set's covetous actions." Thus, is it possible that the underlying system of the MeduNeteru was one of the subjects Osiris taught beyond the shores of the African continent? Does any evidence at all exist to suggest such a possibility?

Examining "the outwardly similar creation tradition and hieroglyphic language of a little-known Tibetan and Chinese culture called the Na-khi (whose name is sometimes given as Na-xi),"[9] Laird Scranton may have just stumbled upon such a probability. Indeed, he informs us that, "The Dongba language of the Na-khi is the last known surviving hieroglyphic language in the world and is considered to have been a predecessor to the Chinese hieroglyphic language."[10] According to Scranton, it was "the priestly language of the Na-Khi-Dongba people..., which is referred to as the Dongba language in honor of the priests, themselves called *dongbas*, who are credited with having preserved it."[11]

Moreover, "An understanding of the Dongba language is considered by linguists to be of great value when researching the origins of classic Chinese language."[12]

As Scranton further observes, "in ancient Egypt there was a tradition in which the Egyptian hieroglyphic language was understood to have been a gift to Egypt from the mythical gods. In Buddhism, it was understood that Buddha had imparted knowledge to mankind in archaic times. The Dogon also associate eight mythical ancestors with specific civilizing skills and provide specific details about how they were taught. The Na-khi of Tibet credit their Mu ancestors with having brought skills of civilization to mankind."[13]

However, as Scranton is keen to stress, although "there is no evidence to suggest any known historical contact specifically between the Dogon and the Dongba (Joseph Rock does claim that there were African influences on the Na-khi in his book *The Ancient Na Khi Kingdom of Southwest China*), nonetheless the Dongba can be seen in many different ways to be effective Asian counterparts of the African Dogon. Both groups recount a long tradition as a nomadic priest-ly tribe, deeply invested in traditional cosmology and reverence for ancestors. Both preserve a highly stable culture that is based specifically on a cosmology that, to all outward appearances, sustained itself in substantially unchanged form for thousands of years. Both evolved a large body of drawn characters – in many cases, arguably the same characters – relating to the concept of their cosmolo-gies. Both credit honored ancestors/teachers with having introduced civilizing skills to the tribe. And both express their cosmology in distinctly similar terms, often with matching cosmological concepts and symbols."[14]

More daringly, in his book *Ancient Future*, author Wayne B. Chandler high-lights Albert Etienne Terrien de Lacouperie, an outstanding contributor to "the history and origins of the Chinese people and their philosophies,"[15] who goes out on a limb by identifying "a group of families known as the *Bak*, who im-migrated into China carrying with them the beginnings of civilization: a well-defined sociopolitical structure, writing, philosophy, and economic fortification. Culturally, this group was intimately related to the Meso-Sumerians of West Asia. Racially and ethnically, the Bak were descended from the Akkadians and Elamites of Mesopotamia."[16]

Intriguingly the word Bak, as Laird Scranton mentions in his latest work, *Point of Origin*, is the Egyptian name for a "god of letters" who was one of seven wise gods, and it's also an Egyptian word for "hawk."[17] In any event, in this partic-ular work herein however we have identified West Asia as part of the Red land of the land of Khem, as its boundaries stretched as far as the Euphrates. As noted in chapter one, "For whatever the reason that sparked the African migration from the southwestern region of the Sahara nevertheless, a logical consequence of that migration would also be the peopling of the near east. After all is said and done, why surmise that the river Nile was the only goal of these ancient migrants when the rivers of the Fertile Crescent also awaited them."

Indeed, according to certain researchers of the people of West Africa, the Yoruba divination system known as Ifa is at least 20,000 years old. Some schol-ars, such as early twentieth century author Paul Carus, imply that it is the source of China's *I Ching*. "Considering the possible antiquity of Ifa and its geographical point of origin, it is plausible that this Tablet of Destiny, now referred to as the

I Ching, evolved out of the older system of Ifa. If we examine the biblical Table of Nations, we are informed that, "The sons of Ham: [father of the Black race] were Cush, Mizraim (Egypt), Phut, and Canaan. Then Cush begot Nimrod, he became a mighty one on the earth. The beginning of his kingdom was Ba'bel, Erech, and Accad, all of them in the land of Shinar [Mesopotamia]." This is the biblical lineage of the Black race; its dawning rooted in the soil of the African continent, originating from a common point, and eventually spreading to West Asia. There is no denying the cultural and linguistic affinities that show a cultural interconnectedness. There are also those *parallels that pertain to the systems of writing between the cuneiform and Egyptian*. Thus, it is probable in my opinion that the Ifa oracle was taken into West Asia and expounded upon and refined by the Akkadians of Accad thus creating, in time, the Book of Changes, known as the I-Ching. This common point of origin and diverse cultural expression is substantiated by current archaeology. The findings of the UNESCO International Scientific committee states that circa 20,000 B.C.E. most of West to East Africa was an inland sea which began to recede and drain, leaving by 10,000 B.C.E large lakes, streams, rivers, and swamps. The various cultures and people that inhabited this area used these waterways as a mode of travel and cultural exchange, and became known as the "Aquatic civilization.'"[18] (Italics added.)

Though Laird Scranton understandably takes a cautious approach, the factor of direct black African immigration into what is modern day China is not therefore a far-fetched supposition.

Nevertheless Scranton does observe that, "Among Chinese scholars, there is some disagreement about the meaning of the name Na-khi. The first portion of the name, *na*, means "great," but can also mean "black" in the Na-khi language. The Dogon word *na* and the Egyptian word *naa* can also mean "great or large," but neither means "black." Notwithstanding a traditional belief that the Na-khi may have originally been black Africans, this second meaning has been the source of some confusion because of an aspect of the cosmology that associates the concepts of good and evil with the colors white and black respectively. Some researchers wonder why a tribe would knowingly name themselves using a term that means "evil." (Rock does claim that there were African influences on the Na-hki in *Ancient Na Khi Kingdom...*, and the word Na-khi, which Rock defines to mean "black man," is written using a glyph that is a stick figure of a man with a blackened face.)"[19]

Be such interesting facts as they may, with regard to the Dongba language Scranton recognizes that, "Like ancient Egyptian hieroglyphs, the Na-khi pictographic words omit written vowel sounds – a characteristic that we view as a signature of our plan of cosmology – and often include glyphs that are not vocalized. Joseph Francis Charles Rock, author of the two-part *A Na-Khi-English Encyclopedic Dictionary*, and a leading authority on the Na-hki culture and language, describes a rebus-like approach to interpreting these pictograms that agrees with the alternative method we proposed in our symbolic approach to the reading of Egyptian hieroglyphic words.[20] For a deeper understanding of the latter however, the many works of Laird Scranton are highly recommended.

Continuing on with the subject of the language however, "We knew that the Na-khi language, which is traditionally considered to be cosmology based, is thought to have influenced the development of written language in China, and we are also aware of *a number of outward similarities between various individual Chinese and Egyptian glyphs*. Likewise, we knew that the time frame of Chinese cosmology and civic development is understood to have been roughly contemporaneous with that of ancient Egypt and that the oldest myths in China are thought to have originated as soon after the earliest myths of ancient Egypt."[21] (Italics added.)

Thus from the foregoing, is it possible we have followed in the post-flood environmental footsteps of Osiris as he travelled across Asia on his civilizing mission to spread the symbolic language of the MeduNeteru abroad, this indeed in the approximate time frame of the emergence of both the African and Chinese civilizations?

Whatever that case may be, Scranton further observed that "in traditional views of the language of the Na-khi, the term *na* reasonably conveys the notion of "mother" and that the concept of "celebrating" can also be assigned to the term *khi*, or *xi*. Realizing that important cosmological terms of the Dogon, Buddhists, and Egyptians typically carry more than one meaning, it seems significant that a second meaning for the term *na* can also be "strong." We found that this meaning is shared commonly in the languages of the Na-hki, the Dogon, and the Egyptian hieroglyphic language. However, in the language of the Na-hki alone, the word *na* can take on the additional meaning of "black." This is a designation that we proposed was derived in Tibet or China, which is consistent with the tradition- ally accepted belief that *the Na-khi were themselves originally black Africans.*[22] (Italics added.)

Meanwhile back on African soil, even though the Greek term "hieroglyphs" does correctly describe the meaning as "the writings of the gods," substituting it for the term "MeduNeteru" serves only to bring understanding and interest in the subject to an end with the realization that the name merely translates into "sacred writing." Albeit, writings of the Neter Thoth.

The Afro-Asiatic language of Khem however was not an alphabetic script, though by Greek times it had developed such possibilities. By contrast, accord- ing to Rene A. Schwaller de Lubicz, "We express ourselves in a convention- al language, and the dictionary defines and limits the meaning of each word. Therefore, we can understand nothing beyond what the dictionary knows. We write with conventional alphabetic signs that in themselves express only sound; thus our alphabet is merely a mechanical means for composing the words in the dictionary and transmitting thought they encompass. It may be said that the combinations of these letters are almost infinite: true, but the number of words is limited by notions already acquired. Thought can also examine observed phe- nomena and seek the causes. . . . Certainly it can, but as soon as it approaches the metaphysical, it can no longer find in our language and forms of writing the means of expressing itself: abstract ideas, formulated in words for which we lack the concepts, are objectified and lose their significance.

"It follows from these observations that either there exists only a concrete world perceptible to the senses, or *we lack a faculty* that would enable us to grasp the abstract, without having to concretize through the imagination. The process is ingrained in us, in accordance with a mode that always leads toward the quan- titative definition. *This is the inverse of the Egyptian mentality.*"[23] (Italics added.)

From its inception therefore rather than being alphabetic, the language of the MeduNeteru was one with a supremely symbolic grammar, one that spoke directly to the deeper levels of human consciousness and whose elements, as will be closely examined in chapter seven, are multi-leveled and analogical in nature. Indeed, the foregoing justifies what Siegfried Morenz had so eloquently indicated in chapter three that, "the Egyptians had *a mode of thinking* very different from our own."

Thus the symbol, according to Schwaller de Lubicz, "is a sign that one must learn to read, and the symbolic is a form of writing whose laws one must know."[24] The very lessons taught in the Per Ankh, the Mystery Schools known as the 'Houses of Life,' a form of symbolic syntax and esoteric transformational grammar.

After reading through the most prolific works of Joseph P. Farrell for his understanding and interpretation of the MeduNeteru however, one surprisingly learns moreover that the symbolic images were in fact "designed as psychotronic objects"[25] that is objects that "manipulate not only the consciousness of their observer, but also of the physical medium itself!"[26]

Moreover and indeed even more interestingly, Laird Scranton's take on the MeduNeteru infers that "the Egyptian hieroglyphs constitute a designed system of language and that the design demonstrates an intimate familiarity with the processes by which modern scientists believe matter is formed."[27]

Furthermore, in private correspondence concerning Farrell's report on *Hieroglyphs and the Analogical Nature of the Physical Medium*, found on page 276 of *The Grid Of The Gods*, Scranton confided with amazement that he was unaware until that time that the MeduNeteru were in fact executable code!

Indeed, each symbol, as has been indicated, is multileveled and therefore contains multiple meanings where one of them, for example, for the name MeduNeteru itself is ""words of the god"Thoth,"[28] or alternatively "cloth of the gods who weave matter."[29]

The physical medium of course is the spiritual polarized substance the ancients already identified as the Nun, a primordial ocean of electromagnetic waves whooshing about in a morass of chaos, as the Greeks were later to refer to it.

This intriguing multileveled phenomenon of the MeduNeteru however will be examined in more detail later when the works of both Rene A. Schwaller de Lubicz and Laird Scranton are further discussed.

As will also be discussed in chapter seven however, from this spiritual substance creation emerged out of a non-polarized Unity, otherwise known as

Reality Absolute. Indeed, "It is understood that this chaos is thought to precede the existence of time, to predate the formation of the universe, and to serve as a foundation for the processes that evoke matter. In regard to the formation of matter, this undifferentiated chaos is considered to be like water and is understood to be the primordial source of all material things. In accordance with what our cosmological plan would lead us to expect, the forms that emerge from this water-like chaos do so as a consequence of primordial vibrations and make their appearance through what is compared to a phase transition – a process similar to that of ice turning into water, water becoming vapor, or gelatin gelling. In regard to the formation of the universe, this initial state of chaos is thought to have resided inside a cosmogonic egg, similar to what is described in the Dogon tradition as Amma's egg. The egg eventually ruptures, and the unrealized potential that resides within the egg bursts out to create the universe as we know it."[30]

With much justification, author and independent software designer Laird Scranton identifies the above-mentioned Dogon god Amma with the Amun of the Nile valley civilization.

Indeed, from a decoding of the very definition of the name Amun, who is also a manifestation of the Nun, Laird Scranton concludes that, "A literal and most understandable reading of the name of Amen might be, "that which draws or weaves waves into particles in a place hidden from interference.""[31]

Moreover, according to Scranton, the symbols used by the Dogon are identical in function to that of the MeduNeteru. One in particular, "the nummo fish graphically depicts a series of microcosmic events that transpire after an initial act of perception disturbs matter as it exists in its primordial wavelike state. This act of perception disrupts the original perfect order of the wave and initiates a process that effectively reorganizes the wave into what we perceive as particles of matter."[32]

Clearly Akhenaten, or his biblical counterpart Moses, the alleged idol destroyers, had no mental grasp of the depths of the concept 'they' temporarily succeeded in legislating against. Apparently, the ancient priests of the priesthood of Amun therefore were in fact in possession of some powerful Juju or Ganga, or as they themselves would have said Heku knowledge, and thus not surprisingly, shortly after the demise of the Amarna regime, they were to become indeed as powerful as Pharaoh, if not more so. Indeed, as the next chapter will reveal, with the exception of Akhenaten, all kings and pharaohs of the Land of Khem were in fact high priests who presided at the head of an ancient African priesthood.

Six

THE PRIESTHOOD OF AMUN

*Hebrew and Christian theologies have been accepted minus
the necessary knowledge of the origins, the means of applying
the comparative method and checking false assumptions.*

GERALD MASSEY

Between the end of the Middle Kingdom and the start of the New Kingdom the Black land fell to the Hyksos, the Shepherd Kings. Known as the 15th Dynasty, the Hyksos Era of 1650-1550 BC is identified as the Second Intermediate Period that interrupted the long accepted conventional history of the ancient land. From the available epigraphic evidence many scholars have studiously assumed that the arrival of the Hyksos represented an invasion of the country by a foreign enemy.

Of this traumatic historical event however, British Egyptologist and linguist Alan Gardiner states to the contrary that "The invasion of the Delta by a specific new race is out of the question: one must think of an infiltration of Palestinians glad to find refuge in a more peaceful and fertile environment."[1] Thus the Hyksos, although of Canaanite and Asiatic origin, had gradually migrated and therefore integrated into the Delta region over a long span of time and by their rise to power were in fact Bedouin Chieftains already native to Khem.

Under the law of Khem however, they were restricted to the northeast section of the Black land in the area of Avaris, the capital of the Hyksos in the Eastern Delta region. That is the same location the family of Joseph was offered that the Bible calls the land of Goshen. This however was the only region of the Black land where pastoralists were permitted to reside.

The Romano-Jewish scholar Josephus ben Matityahu, generally known as Josephus, who was vehemently opposed to Apion's view that Jews were Egyptians, was one of the earliest historians to equate the Israelite Exodus with the time of the Hyksos who were violently expelled from the Land of Khem by Ahmose I, the founder of the 18th Dynasty.

As has been already discussed, there is much disagreement about when the Exodus occurred or even if it occurred. Nevertheless, from a quote by German Egyptologist Jan Assman, Joseph P. Farrell discovered that the people and the land of Khem, as the Bible symbolizes them, were "rejected, discarded, and abandoned. Egypt is not just a historical context; it is inscribed in the *fundamental semantics of monotheism*. It appears explicitly in the first commandment and implicitly in the second... Egypt's role in the Exodus story is not historical but mythical."[2] (Italics added.)

Thus, patriarchal monotheism was intentionally designed to attack and therefore undermine the ancient black civilization on the banks of the Nile. Indeed, as if this ironical 'blackening' of the reputation of the Land of Khem was not enough, not only is there disagreement on the historicity and date of the Exodus, Gary Greenberg observes that "Despite the lack of solid evidence about the Exodus date, scholars all agree that the monotheistic revolution of Pharaoh Akhenaten and the religious teachings of Moses have no common origin. They always choose dates with an eye toward eliminating any possible contact between these two extraordinary thinkers. Given the unchallenged belief that Israel's roots lie outside of Egypt, we shouldn't be surprised by such an attitude."[3]

According to Ahmed Osman, even Immanuel Velikovsky was party to that group of scholars who attempted to fit history into conformity with biblical narrative. This indeed was the motive behind his entire literary output. Disagreeing with Sigmund Freud's *Moses and Monotheism*, Velikovsky in fact "began to develop a radical catastrophic cosmology to prove that Moses and the Israelite Exodus preceded the time of Akhenaten by about five centuries."[4]

All this historical circumnavigation notwithstanding, in his historical analysis, Ralph Ellis nevertheless maintains the Josephus tradition while Ahmed Osman however locates the Exodus to a time after the Hyksos expulsion.

As far as these Shepherd Kings were concerned however, Osman makes the pertinent observation that "shepherds had been looked upon as an "abomination" to Egyptians since the country's long occupation and rule of the Eastern Delta by the pastoralist Hyksos that preceded the foundation of the Eighteenth Dynasty."[5]

Thus for Osman history definitively demonstrates that the Exodus did indeed occur, although not in the time frame to which Ellis subscribes, but rather as a consequence of Akhenaten's aborted attempt at bringing an end to the priesthood of Amun during the 18th Dynasty.

This blasphemous action would result in the ultimate and actual expulsion of the Yahuds to Palestine, and the Medzay to the upper Nile lands of what is now modern day Kenya.

It is of course the Yahuds that the Bible records for posterity. As has been shown, these were the priests of Akhetaten, the worshippers of Yahu whom the various versions of the Bible refer to as the Lord or Yahweh. Since Yahweh is the Hebrew version of Yahu one has to wonder, who then was the transcendental Spirit, the Supreme Being, that pharaoh represented on earth, before the monotheistic interruption that occurred during the reign of Akhenaten?

In the course of reality's constant comic genesis, the priesthood of the MeduNeteru maintained complete and utter faith in an Absolute Unity that could not be situated in time or space. At the same time however they also acknowledged its varying manifestations. Thus, during the spring equinox when Ra appeared on the horizon in the constellation of Aries for the first time in 26,000 years, this momentous event marked the ascendency of the Neter whose zoological representation was the Ram. Clashing with this new cosmic arrival, the previous 2,000-year era of the Apis Bull, the Golden Calf, the Bull of Taurus, the era of bold megalithic architecture, was now no longer. Thus, from a deep structure analysis of the symbolic syntax of the MeduNeteru, it would appear that as a consequence of his ignorance Akhenaten was fighting against the inevitable cosmic transformation that was taking place during his time.

Contradictorily however, since Moses destroyed the Golden Calf after he descended from Mount Sinai, this act implies he knew something of the cosmic significance of the new era and thus had been exposed to some knowledge of the Sacred Science, the esoteric level of which was well known to the original Amunian priesthood.

Indeed, the prominence and significance of Amun during that particular time period was due to the fact that this Neter of the Hidden One represented the precessional turning tide that brought into existence the zodiacal age of Aries.

The sign of the Ram of course belonged to Amun, the universal God of creation. The arrival of the sun in this sign therefore was the announcement of the prominence of this Neter. Amun of course was the God most offended by the upheaval imposed upon the land by Akhenaten after he moved his power base midway between Memphis and Thebes to a desert location where he built his new capital Akhetaten, the Horizon of Aten, the City of Light, and as we now know, the notorious and infamous site of Sodom and Gomorrah.

In devastating contradistinction to Graham Phillips however, according to the rabbi brothers Sabbah, the origin of the Hebrew language and Judaism began there. Indeed as noted in chapter four, even the word ""Arab" refers to the many kinds of people from Akhet-Aten, newly converted to monotheism, and called *Erev-rav* in the Bible (Exodus 12:38)."[6]

Linguistically speaking, it thus appears that the single language that everyone spoke before the Tower of Babel incident occurred was that of the MeduNeteru. Indeed, since the Hebrew and Arabic languages can be traced to the new language that was forming in Akhetaten, strongly influenced by the Amharic language of the Ethiopians of Kush, the connection between this event and the dispersal of its people and dismantling of the city by Ay is precisely what Joseph P. Farrell refers to as the "Tower of Babel Moment. "[7]

After examining the biblical version of *The Tower of Babel*, in his book *Transhumanism*, Farrell recounts that what "is unusual about this story [is that it] lacks the type of moral sanctions usually given in the Old Testament for Yahweh's ... actions.

"Such sanctions are missing here; rather, what one is left with is that somehow, whatever it is that mankind is doing, it requires action to fragment [t]his [sic] unity and stop the project."[8]

Upon review of some of the concepts implied in the story, Farrell revealingly highlights that "The "unified speech" of mankind might also imply a unified language of science, i.e., a highly unified scientific worldview wherein the major sciences – physics, biology, genetics, and so on – are all viewed and understood with a completeness and unity our current science lacks."[9] This is clearly a reference to the MeduNeteru not to the newly forming language at the root of the upheaval about to take place within the land. Nevertheless, on the subject of language in general, Farrell pertinently observes that "The idea of language also subtly implies the idea of *sound* and this might be connected to the Tower."[10]

The importance of "sound" and the scientific aspects of the MeduNeteru will be discussed later. Veering away however from Farrell's otherwise interesting and erudite analysis of the subject, for our purposes Yahweh, as stated in chapter three, has been identified as Amenhotep III while *The Tower of Babel Moment* actually took place in Akhetaten, the new city built by Akhenaten. The tower itself of course, as will be demonstrated in chapter seven, is the Great Pyramid!

Thus the Hebrew story as presented in the Bible is an anachronistic device required to overshadow and make irrelevant the enormous power of the already long-lived civilization that had existed on the banks of the Nile since time immemorial. No need to dig deeper: The Hebrew people were slaves. The people of Khem were idol worshippers, end of story!

However, how did this distorted perception of African history come about? Once again the rabbi brothers Sabbah come to the rescue by relating that "It was during the Babylonian Exile, a period of total submission to the Persian kings (Cyrus was called the Messiah) that *the Bible was modified*, and that the story of the Exodus was recast to the detriment of the Kingdom of Egypt, which, by then, had also submitted to the Persians."[11] (Italics added.)

Indeed, "The scribes in Babylon could remake the Exodus story only by conserving the authentic framework of a minute part of the truth. It is impossible to determine how long this practice lasted. Rashi confirms in his Commentary on Exodus 12:41, "This is one of the passages of the Torah that was modified for King Ptolemy.""[12]

As Gary Greenberg cleverly noted however in *The Moses Mystery: The African Origins of the Jewish People*, the Hebrew story is quite simply built on shifting sand because, "where a group of people lived in the sixth century B.C. — what language it spoke, and what it believed about its historical roots a thousand years earlier, does not, without independent corroboration, prove where it lived a thousand years earlier, what language it *originally* spoke, and what took place in its formative years."[13]

At this point what Ghanaian author Nana Banchie Darkwah said in chapter one with reference to the "lack of any linguistic problems in the travels of Abraham, Joseph, and Jacob and his family to Ancient Egypt" should be recalled. Moreover, Gary Greenberg continued that, "even if we assume that the Bible is derived from earlier sources yet to be discovered, it still described events that occurred more than a thousand years before its completion, and in those ancient times few people had a strong tradition of historical writing and perspective."[14]

For the foregoing reasons, such precarious origins strengthen the speculative assumption that subsequent to the exile, Yahwist scribes began in earnest to develop a formidable tradition of *disguising their past*. The truth however, as they say, is stranger than fiction for Akhetaten is the birthplace of the Yahwist tradition. The fact is, as has already been said, Hebrew, as well as Arabian history has its origins there, an origin that was later embellished after Akhenaten's rebellion at the base of which was his orchestrated attack on the Sacred Science.

As Joseph P. Farrell so keenly perceived, "The Yahwist religions also carry *the implicit imperative to rewrite human history from the prophetic and apocalyptic point of view*. "Egypt" thus becomes not only the symbol of the "Other" … but also of the rejected past and its cultural systems."[15] (Italics added.)

In terms of the outright desecration of the true Land of God, though Phillip Coppens found the origin of Satan in the name Seth as noted in chapter two, according to the rabbi brothers Sabbah however, "The origin of the word "Satan" probably derived from the root "STN" according to Champollion, the representation of a reed used by the Egyptians to designate the king of Egypt."[16] Not satisfied with the mere denigration of pharaoh however, the biblical scribes from the "ministry of false truth" even cast aspersions on Ra himself. Thus, "The Egyptian God of gods was demonized by the Biblical scribes, in the same way as the pharaoh of Egypt."[17]

Indeed, from here on in historically and psychologically speaking Africa was about to take a back seat as Farrell intriguingly exposes the rise of a powerful bureaucracy, a veritable ministry of false truth that had developed a voracious need to maintain itself because, "the rupture with the past is necessary to *enthrone and empower in perpetuity a new elite*, empowered to perpetually interpret the contradictory nature of the faith *and to steer it toward the apocalyptic future*."[18] (Penultimate italics added.) In fact, according to the radical and bold research conducted by Farrell and his colleague Scott D. de Hart, "The three Great Yahwist religions – Judaism, Christianity, and Islam – are all alchemical techniques of the social engineering of mankind into permanent division."[19] Indeed, witness the barbarous Lewis-Huntington 'Clash of Civilizations' fiasco that projects itself on a daily basis into our otherwise acquiescent living rooms.

Thus from Farrell's perspective, it can be determined that a new anti-black African priesthood had come into existence with the deliberate intention of falsifying the past. But, despite the millennia long careful, meticulous and elaborate perpetration of this fraudulent attempt at disguising the origin of the Hebrew language and the religion of Judaism, the truth is nevertheless gradually resurfacing from the depths of the ancient sands and 'black' soil of Africa.

In his book *The Moses Legacy* for example, the English author Graham Phillips has made some important contributions to the subject of biblical reanalysis. Though he maintains the traditional Middle Eastern perspective, it would nevertheless be remiss of me not to refer to some of his findings, particularly his thoughts on the origin of the Hebrew religion which, contrary to the position held here, he believes may be found in Edom, the land of the Edomites, the descendants of Esau.

As Phillips reminds us, "In the Book of Genesis, the Hebrew nation is said to have descended from Abraham, of which there were two separate peoples: the Israelites, who descended from Abraham's grandson Jacob, and the Edomites, who descended from Abraham's other grandson Esau."[20]

Indeed, Graham Phillips finds archeological evidence for the existence of the Edomites. "Samples of human skeletal remains found in the Samarian mountains of Israel and the Shara mountains of Edom, both dating to around 1700 BCE when the story of Jacob and Esau appears to be set, were sent for DNA tests to Japan in 2000. The tests were conducted at one of the world's leading laboratories in this field at Waseda University in Toyko. ... The results showed that both the Samarian and Edomite remains were closely related, certainly from the same ethnic group. It seems, therefore, that the Edomites and the Israelites were both descendants of a Mari tribe who migrated south from Syria around 1750 BCE. The historical truth behind the biblical story of Jacob and Esau would therefore appear to be that one tribe – the ancient Hebrews – originally settled in the Shara mountains of Edom. Around fifty years later, with the growth of Hyksos power, some moved back to the north and made their home in the Samarian mountains. Jacob, it seems, represents the Hebrews who moved north and Esau represents the Hebrews who stayed in Edom."[21]

Of course in the discussion over *The Contendings of Horus and Seth*, we observed in chapter two that Gary Greenberg saw in them "the struggle of Jacob and Esau, biblical patriarchs who, if this identification is correct, have thus been transformed directly out of African consciousness into historical characters" of the so-called Holy Bible.

Indeed, as Graham Phillips himself states, "no written records have been discovered from this area predating the Nabatean era, apart from a few Hebrew inscriptions that tell us only that, in some way, the God of Israel was being worshipped here. The eradication of the kingdom of Israel might not however, have seen the end of their religion. It seems to have survived in the homeland of Edom until at least the time of the Babylonian exile."[22]

Apparently, the evidence is to be found on Jebel Madbhah, a particular mountain in the land of Edom. Thus, on a natural plateau of that mountain, known as Attuf Ridge, Phillips believes that "we really have discovered the place where Moses found God."[23]

Originally thought to be Nabatean, archaeologist Dr Samuel Colby is convinced that the archeological remains found there represent an example of an "Israelite High Place dating from the Edomite period."[24] Among those remains is a raised platform in a sunken courtyard that Colby believes may be a "shewbread table, on which offerings were laid in Israelite temples."[25]

Thus, it would appear that somewhere in the vicinity of Petra there is an example of the 'offering tables' of Akhetaten. As described in chapter four, "in the Temple of the Aten ... there is evidence of at least 1,800 offering tables on display demonstrating the abundance of Akhetaten." That city is indeed the origin of the shewbread tables, the place where the tradition of the 'cakes or loaves of bread which were always present on a specially dedicated table, in the Temple in Jerusalem,' as Wikipedia quotes from the *King James Version* of the Bible, was initially established.

On the same Attuf Ridge mentioned above, Phillips refers to an occasion when the elders of Israel were invited to "the nether part of the mountain"[26] to see the God of Israel, in a place where he describes the existence of two obelisks. From Exodus 24:1-10 he quotes:

And there was under his feet as it were a paved work of a sapphire stone.

Describing the "two towering obelisks" located at the gateway to the High Place on Jebel Madbhah, Phillips observes that, "The feet of God might even have referred to the obelisks themselves."[27] However, by making this observation, he unknowingly corroborates that this ancient idea is derived from the people of Khem and not some imaginary Hebrews. Indeed, after overlaying a human skeleton onto a detailed layout of the Temple of Amun at Karnak, which in fact is a masterful architectural representation of Cosmic Man, on page 23 of *The Temple In Man*, Rene A. Schwaller de Lubicz demonstrated that the two pylons standing at the entrance to the Temple, in front of which stand two obelisks, are in the position of the human foot.

Thus, since it is an apparent translation of African affairs, the biblical account of events upon which Graham Phillips relies however has to be regarded with some suspicion. Indeed, his statement that the "oldest surviving complete Hebrew Bible dates from the third century CE"[28] and as such has "remained unchanged from before Christian times as a number of its books were found amongst the Dead Sea Scrolls, the relevant texts dating from around 100 BCE,"[29] is somewhat disingenuous since all the pages of the Dead Sea Scrolls have not been made available to the general public as of yet in order to completely validate that claim.

That situation notwithstanding, Phillips, making no connection whatsoever with Akhenaten, expresses the opinion that, "Before the apparent time of Moses there is no evidence that anyone in the world had ever considered worshipping just one god – not even the Israelites. Archaeology has revealed that the early Semites, the nomadic tribes who eventually became the Israelites, had many gods, as demonstrated by the numerous statuettes found in their graves."[30] Of course, Phillips' observations as expressed in the latter sentence could equally be a reflection of the situation that existed at the time of Akhenaten in the Land of Khem. That such a similar situation should be expressed in the region identified herein as 'northeast Africa' should not come as a surprise.

Indeed, Phillips exposes the fact that, "Even the Bible confirms that there was no such thing as the Israelite religion before Moses. Although God is portrayed as speaking directly to a few of Moses' forebears, such as Abraham and Jacob, there is no reference to the worship or acceptance of god by the Israelites as a whole. Even Moses has no idea who this God is when he first confronts him. According to the Old Testament Book of Exodus, Moses first discovers God on the Mountain of God when he speaks to him from a burning bush… From the biblical perspective this is where, when and how the Israelite religion first came into existence."[31]

On the surface, Phillips' argument appears strong accept for the fact that Jacob is Horus, the son of Osiris, and therefore part of an African mythic complex. As Nana Banchie Darkwah observantly mentioned in chapter one, the "lack of any linguistic problems in the travels of Abraham, Joseph, and Jacob and his family to Ancient Egypt simply and clearly reveals that the so-called people of the Bible were of the same racial, ethnic linguistic, and cultural heritage as the Ancient Egyptians to whom they supposedly went."[32] Indeed, it is only by linking the Hebrews to the Mari tribe through the "human skeletal remains found in the Samarian mountains of Israel and the Shara mountains of Edom, both dating to around 1700 BCE" that Phillips is able to display the archaeological offering table found on the Attuf Ridge mentioned above as proof of their existence prior to the construction of Akhetaten.

Nevertheless, with reference to Edom, Phillips tells us that, "The Old Testament authors go to considerable lengths to discredit the Edomites."[33] However, he later retracts that opinion going on to say that, "The Edomites cannot have been so badly thought of at the time of the Exodus, however. Indeed, such hostility between the Israelites and the Edomites would not have permitted Moses and his followers to spend so much time at the Mountain of God *if it is was in Edomite territory.*"[34] (Italics added.)

Whether the Mountain of God is to be found in the territory of Edom however is a matter of conjecture and contention. Indeed, the Edomites themselves are most probably the veritable descendants of the Shemsu Seth who Bauval and Brophy identified in chapter two as deriving from the Paleolithic culture of a much older clan of black-skinned people originally from the Western Desert of the Sahara. The same people who "temporarily reasserted their authority in the 2nd Dynasty, but then lost it again – or were assimilated – in the reign of Netjerykhet/Djoser."[35] Indeed, identifying Esau with the Red land, the Land of Seth, is the fact that he possessed red hair. Incidentally, the source of red hair has been identified as located in North West Africa. Thus, however unwittingly, it would appear that Europeanized Semites have usurped an African identity.

Be that as it may, Graham Phillips does give an intriguingly interesting account of the cause of the division of the Promised Land into Israel and Judah. Thus, "According to the Old Testament, after the reign of Solomon it was not only the Hebrew's kingdom that was split in two but the religion. For much of three centuries, from the time the monarchy divided until the period of the Assyrian invasion, the two Hebrew kingdoms of Judah and Israel were apparently worshipping different gods. According to the Books of Kings and Chronicles Judah stayed faithful to Yahweh, the one Hebrew God, whereas Israel, from the moment it separated from Judah, began worshipping another god."[36]

With some biblical scholars crediting Jezebel as introducing this pagan god to the people of Israel, historical research shows she was in fact the demonized recipient of 'bad press' as the god apparently "seems to have been worshipped by Jeroboam half a century before Jezebel's time."[37]

For example, "The first Book of Kings describes how Jeroboam was the first king to build a temple to this other god. His immediate act on becoming the first King of lesser Israel, around 930 BCE, was to order the making of two effigies of calves."[38]

Indeed, from another biblical quote concerning an event, reported in Kings 22:51-53, that occurred fifty years after Jeroboam, Phillips is able to identify the name of this unknown god:

> And Ahab the son of Omri did evil in the sight of the Lord above all that were before him. And it came to pass, as if it had been a light thing for him to walk in the sins of Jeroboam the son of Nabat . . . and went and served Baal and worshipped him.[39]

Subsequently, we learn from Phillips that it was Josiah who "made plans to exterminate the sect"[40] that promoted and fostered the worship of Baal. Moreover, according to the "prophet Jeremiah, who preached in the years shortly before the Babylonian conquest, by the end of the kingdom of Israel's existence the High Places of Israel had all been dedicated to Baal."[41]

Then, after referring to the two effigies of calves, Graham Phillips quotes a passage from I Kings 12:28-33 which states:

> And he set one in Beth-el, and the other he put in Dan. And he made an house of high places, and made priests of the lowest of the people, which were not of the sons of Levi ...[42]

With regard to this quoted biblical verse, Phillips quite interestingly goes on to say that the "reference in the above passage to the sons of Levi refers to the priests of Solomon's temple in Jerusalem, as the tribe of Levi had become the priestly caste amongst the Hebrews. Jeroboam, we are told, rejected their authority however and established another priesthood. As such, he had severed all ties with the religious practices of Judah. Moreover, the calves would, on the face of it, appear to represent a completely different god from the God of Israel, as Yahweh was proscribed under Hebrew doctrine from being represented by idols or images of any kind." [43]

However, after it becomes clear that the name of Baal, like the name Yahweh is not in fact a name of God but a title, Phillips retracts this latter supposition made about the calves. Nevertheless, there is no getting away from the fact of course that in the end Baal is none other than Yahweh!

With that realization, Phillips intensifies his research by pondering ever deeply on the possible reasons behind the division of the exiled community into Judea and Israel. On this particular issue, Phillips has an interesting take that in fact implicates King Solomon as the cause. Indeed, tensions were so high during that time Ralph Ellis also makes the pertinent observation that Josephus translated the word sovereign in relation to Solomon as *tyrannus,* which of course "means tyrant." [44]

Since this quarrel apparently involved two issues, the one over Baal and the other of Beth-el, Graham Phillips questions whether this issue is merely a dynastic one, or whether there was another reason for the division. Since Solomon required that his new Temple in Jerusalem be regarded as the only 'House of God,' the Israelites were infuriated because they believed that Beth el, the site of Jacob's vision of the ladder, was the true place where God inhabited. Indeed, it was Solomon's insistence that brought about the division within the monarchy as subsequently there was a major "disagreement concerning the royal lineage. Should only the descendants of David be kings of Israel, as Solomon's priests maintained, or should, as the prophet Ahijah proclaimed, Jeroboam and his house of Joseph become the monarchy of Israel?" [44] Thus, "The house of the Lord that Jeroboam is condemning is the Jerusalem Temple, recently built by Solomon. It was to remain the most sacred site in Judah until the time it was destroyed by the Babylonians around 597 BCE." [45]

According to this interpretation, the conclusion is that the division resulted from a dispute over the location of Beth–el, the House of God which tradition had made Mount Horeb, a holy place located on the Sinai peninsular that preceded the existence of the so-called Hebrews. It should also be noted that interestingly the handwork of Yuya is still at play here beyond the borders of the Black land since Jeroboam is described as a faithful supporter of the 'house of Joseph.'

As has been previously stated in chapter one, "From the earliest days of Egyptian dynastic history, Sinai was not a separate country, but an integral part of Egypt. Although it had no military garrison or resident governor, it fell directly under pharaonic control," to say nothing of the fact that it formed part of the greater area known to the ancients as the Red land.

Indeed, according to Laurence Gardner, sometime in March 1904, "Sir W.M. Flinders Petrie and his team stood upon a wind-torn rocky plateau in the Sinai desert."[46] Following in the footsteps of Moses and the Israelites, Petrie stood on the holy mountain of Moses, known today as Serâbit el Khâdim (the Prominence of the Khadim). There, Petrie and his team "found the ruins of an old temple, with inscriptions dating it back to the time of the 4th-dynasty pharaoh Sneferu, who reigned about 2600 BC."[47] Expecting to find some form of Semitic altar stone beneath the soil, what he discovered however was in fact "a vast Egyptian temple . . . clearly of some importance."[48] Unfortunately, many of the "specific artifacts, as portrayed in Petrie's photographs and writings, are no longer there"[49] and moreover have been "strategically concealed from open scrutiny."[50]

According to Gardner however, "The reason why many of *the primary artifacts* were secreted to storage is that Petrie's discovery was viewed with great displeasure at the time, and was reckoned to *contradict the Exodus portrayal of events at the holy mountain*. It was here that Moses was said to have seen the burning bush, where he talked with Jehovah, burned the gold calf, and received the Tables of Testimony. In practice, the Petrie report did not overturn the biblical account in any way; what it challenged was the Church's interpretation of the story and the manner in which it was being taught. Essentially, his discovery contravened the regulations of the Egypt Exploration Fund. The Fund's 1891 founding Memorandum and Articles of Association state that its objectives included the "promotion of surveys and excavations for the purpose of elucidating or illustrating the Old Testament narrative." This, of course, meant the Old Testament as it was traditionally interpreted, not necessarily as it was written."[51] (Italics added.)

As a matter of fact, the ruined temple at Serâbit el Khâdim was located in the place identified in chapter one as Mount Horeb, the place where Jacob saw the ladder. Indeed, the place where he saw the ladder was the first ever reference in the Bible to Beth-el.

As Gary Greenberg acutely observed, "The image of a ladder to heaven has puzzled biblical scholars looking for Semitic antecedents for the concept. Some have tried to identify the ladder to heaven with the Babylonian ziggurats. Speiser, for example, finds it hard to imagine a steady stream of angels going up and down an ordinary ladder, and considers "stairway" a better translation than "ladder." Since the ziggurats had a stairway leading to the top, Speiser concludes, "only such a stairway can account for Jacob's later description of it as a 'gateway to heaven.'"[52]

Nevertheless, as E. A. Wallis Budge, who directed his gaze away from the Semitic regions of Mesopotamia with regard to this matter, most pertinently affirms, "That souls needed a ladder whereby to mount from earth to heaven was a very ancient belief in Egypt."[53] Indeed, Greenberg further assures us that "this was no ordinary ladder. To find its origin we need look no further than the Egyptian Pyramid Texts. Consider this example from the tomb of the Fifth Dynasty pharaoh Unas:

> "Ra setteth upright the ladder for Osiris, and Horus *raiseth up the ladder for his father Osiris, when Osiris goeth to [find] his soul;* one standeth on the one side, and the other standeth on the other, and Unas is betwixt them. Unas standeth up and is Horus, he sitteth down and he is Set." (Emphasis added.)

"Or this from the Pyramid of Pepi I (Sixth Dynasty):

> "Hail to thee, O Ladder of God, Hail to thee, O Ladder of Set. Stand up O Ladder of God, stand up O Ladder of Set, stand up O Ladder of Horus, *whereon Osiris went forth into heaven*."[54] (Emphasis added.)

As the foregoing has made so explicit, "Jacob's ladder dream comes straight out of Egyptian imagery. The Egyptian passages quoted come from funerary rituals. As the Unas passage says, Osiris has to climb the ladder to find his soul. Osiris represents the deceased king, and it is the deceased king who will climb the ladder. The ladder itself consists of the bodies of the gods Horus and Set."[55] Indeed, Gerald Massey adds that, "We see from the Pyramid texts (Pepi I., lines 192, 169, 182, Maspero, *Les Inscrip. Des Pyramids de Sakkarah*) that there were two stages of ascent to the upper paradise, that were represented by two ladders: one is the ladder of Sut [Seth], as the ascent from the land of darkness, the other is the ladder of Horus, reaching to the land of light."[56]

As Greenberg himself confirms, "Jacob's ladder dream comes straight out of Egyptian imagery." Of course! But why speak Greek when you can speak in an African tongue: Jacob's ladder dream comes straight out of African consciousness and imagination. As has been said before, and as E. A. Wallis Budge affirmed, Osiris was the African god *par excellence*.

Thus, "Jacob's dream depicts the same ladder. He even recognizes that he stands at the gate to heaven. In place of the deities, however, Genesis has angels.

"As the gateway to heaven, Jacob renamed the city Bethel, "House of God." Coincidentally, the Egyptians identified heaven with the goddess Hathor, whose name means "House of Horus" (i.e., where the sun lives). Thus, Bethel, as the gateway to heaven and the place where God lives, would be the Hebrew equivalent of the House of Horus, which coincides with Jacob's presence there as a Horus figure."[57]

Given this critical evidence of historical dissembling, is this not verification of the fact that the so-called biblical patriarchs were veritable reflections of very important African figures who came out of the history and mythology of the Land of Khem? The true Land of God!

Indeed, as Gary Greenberg was astute enough to observe "the core elements of patriarchal history derive from Egyptian myths and the family of Osiris."[58] He also proffered that while "the genealogical contradictions in Egyptian myths prevent us from making an exact one-to-one correspondence between Egyptian deities and the Genesis patriarchs, a broadset [sic] of parallels can be established."[59]

Thus, though he himself refers to them as Egyptian in origin, Greenberg's radical reanalysis of the patriarchs identifies them as members of an African pantheon of gods. Indeed, as archetypes drawn from the subconscious of the ancient African mentality. However, is it possible that some of them were in fact flesh and blood beings?

From the available evidence indeed, it appears that the anachronistic patri-archs of the Hebrews are nothing more than mental figments of an active and creative Asiatic imagination. Indeed, archeologists have yet to find definitive proof that Abraham was ever in Ur of the Chaldees and thus, as for everyone else, tradition and spiritual faith is so far the only proof for the basis of such belief not scientific or historical fact. Therefore, the "veritable ministry of false truth" had its work cut out for it, as Akhenaten was not only the historical prototype for Moses, as has been discussed, but for Abraham as well. As indi-cated in chapter three, "Since Abraham and Akhenaton are both alleged to have been idol destroyers" French researchers Messod and Roger Sabbah also saw Ahkenaten as the prototype for Abraham. Indeed, according to the Hebrew Bible, (Exodus 17:4-5), the rabbi brothers Sabbah demonstrate that the Bible scribes composed the name Abraham, "from Ab-Rah-Amun, Father of Rah's and Amun's people."[60]

Since it has been determined that Akhenaten is not only Moses, but also Abraham, then the latter's father must also have his counterpart in the his-tory of the Land of Khem. Logically, if such case can be founded in truth, Terah would have to have been Amenhotep III. What evidence however can be mustered to support such a seeming improbability? Researching the is-sue of the biblical Isaac, Ahmed Osman stumbled upon a lead in this matter after discovering that upon "reexamination of the story of the sacrifice in the Koran, it becomes clear that the name of Abraham's intended victim is never stated directly. The account given in Sura XXXVII: 101-103 of the Koran follows immediately after a narration – which does not appear in the Bible, but is found in the Talmud – of a conflict between Abraham and his father, who worshipped idols. As a consequence, Abraham is thrown on a burning fire, but god saves him and Abraham decides to leave his father's house and land."[61]

Branding his father an idol worshiper, is this conflict not a thinly disguised version of Akhenaten's rejection of the Amun who was worshipped by his father and thus the reason why Akhenaten moved from No to worship the Aten in his new city? Indeed, it is this conflict that begins to unravel the relationship be-tween the historical and biblical figures under discussion.

Thus, is it possible that Terah is in fact Amenhotep III? Given the association of the ram of Amun with the latter, there does appear to be a close approximation with the ibex or wild goat, the animal associated with the name of Terah or Térach, as Abraham's father was also called. Although it may seem that we are grasping at straws here, the ram, generally described as a male sheep, is nevertheless also referred to as a male goat.

In addition to the foregoing, given that Amenhotep III was also known as Nebmaatra, heir of Ra; Son of Ra, the Ra or Rah part of the name Terah could be accounted for by the last three character glyphs of the name Nebmaatra. Thus, Terah may well be the biblical counterpart of the historical Amenhotep III.

What other similarities however potentially exist? According to the Bible, Terah was a son of Nahor, son of Serug and father of the Patriarch Abraham, all descendants of Shem's son Arpachshad. As did Amenhotep III however, Terah also had three sons: Abram, Haran, and Nahor II. His daughter Sarai, by a second wife, was also his daughter-in-law, wife of Abram. Thus, despite the contrived biblical account of Abraham encouraging Sarai to pretend to be his sister before pharaoh, Abram and Sarai were in fact brother and sister! Technically speaking however, she was his half-sister. This situation of course nevertheless unfurls a revealing connection to the matriarchal principles that governed marital circumstances in the Black land.

The name Sarai however is not her name but a title that simply means: 'princess.' Sarai therefore could have been any one of the daughters of Amenhotep III, if he is indeed the prototype for Terah.

How many daughters however did the king of the Land of Khem have? Apparently, six or possibly seven have been identified. These include: Sitamun, Iset, Henuttaneb, Nebetah, Beketaten, Nebetnehat and finally, Kiya. According to Wikipedia, the little known Kiya, was possibly a Mitannian princess. Nebetnehat (the "lady of the sycamore tree"), on the other hand, was the Great Royal Wife of an unidentified pharaoh. Indeed, "she could have been someone relatively close to King Amenhotep III perhaps a daughter or some other female relative."[62]

Since the scribes of 'the veritable ministry of false truth' did everything they could to disguise their origins in the Black land, could the case be made for Nebetnehat being the Sarai in question, given that she was the "Great Royal

Wife of an unidentified pharaoh" who, most probably, was Akhenaten. As will be shown in chapter eight however, Osman, who believes that Abraham was an historical entity, is inclined to think that Sarai married Tuthmosis III, (c. 1490-1436 B. C.), the sixth king of the Eighteenth dynasty.

Nevertheless, was one of Amenhotep III's daughters married to Akhenaten? If so, which one? Indeed, how many wives did Akhenaten have? Besides the famous Nefertiti, four other names are listed under consorts of Akhenaten in Wikipedia and, indeed, among them there is one referred to as an unidentified sister. Known as The Younger Lady, she is however identified as a daughter of Amenhotep III and Queen Tiye and possible mother of Tutankhamun. She, too, would therefore be his sister. Thus as the foregoing hints, a plausible connection is beginning to emerge for the possible identification of Terah's historical counterpart residing in the corridors of the royal house of ancient Thebes.

Concerning the Patriarchs prior to Abraham however, Greenberg observes that, "… the predynastic chronology in Genesis … is derived from the same source as Manetho's chronology of the Egyptian gods, and that both are based on the Theban doctrine of Creation."[63] Moreover, he clarifies that, "Since … the birth-and-death chronology derives from Egyptian chronology and dynastic king lists, the author of Genesis, presumably Moses, must have had close and intimate contact with Egyptian records and libraries."[64]

Of the patriarchs that preceded Abraham therefore, Gary Greenberg points out, that after an exceedingly long life Methuselah, the son of Enoch, died "in 2105 B.C. A period of 969 years coincides well with the estimates of how long the Memphite kingdom lasted, and a date of 2105 falls in the acceptable framework. Just as Eber's birth and death framed the first Theban kingdom, we shall now see that Methuselah's birth and death framed the Memphite kingdom."[65] Thus, Methuselah's life spanned the entire length of the Old Kingdom.

Methuselah lived nine hundred years, according to the lyric of It Ain't Necessarily So from George & Ira Gershwin's Porgy and Bess. Such a musical parody of course serves only to assist in placing this particular patriarch further back into the realm of mythology. However in the chronology of the land of Khem, the birth and death of Methuselah has been shown to form the boundaries of the Old Kingdom and subsequent interregnum, just prior to the beginning of the Middle Kingdom. The acceptable date among Egyptologists for the length of this reign is 955 years while Methuselah lived 969 years according to the Bible.

Methuselah, of course, is among the acclaimed ancestors of the Hebrews who allegedly emerged on the stage of history in the distant past, somewhere in the near east. Nevertheless, according to Greenberg, "The name Hebrew, as a term for the Israelites, is not attested to until late in the first millennium B.C."[66] In fact, of these revered biblical characters, Greenberg puts forward a bold hypothesis for their fictional origin. As he says in his own words: "... I will set forth the exact mythological sources from which most of the patriarchal history is derived."[67] Indeed, Greenberg states that, "It will then become clear that the core elements of patriarchal history derive from Egyptian myths and the family of Osiris."[68]

In fact one in particular of those patriarchs is acclaimed to be the last of the pre-flood patriarchs. Known to the Sumerians as Ziusudra, according to the Bible Noah, whose name meant 'respite,' was the son of Lamech. For Graham Phillips however, "The story of Noah's flood ... appears to have been taken from Babylonian mythology. In the Genesis account, the entire human race is said to descend from Adam and Eve, and nine generations later Noah is born."[69]

Indeed, corroborating Phillips' point of view, Gary Greenberg affirms that the "Mesopotamians also believed in a worldwide flood, and the king lists ... show either nine or ten kings prior to the deluge. Because Noah was the tenth generation in Genesis, scholars generally agree that the Genesis and Mesopotamian flood myths derive from common sources. But *nothing in the Genesis account requires that its flood myth was written down earlier than the Babylonian captivity, in the sixth century B.C.*"[70] (Italics added.)

As Phillip Coppens also pointed out in chapter two, the story of Noah's flood preexisted the biblical text by thousands of years, since a version of it is found in the clay tablets of Sumerian origin. On the other hand, he further observed that it is also contained in spell 175 of the Theban Recension of *The Book of the Dead*. Thus, the questions that need to be answered here are: (a) how old is spell 175; (b) is the Sumerian cuneiform older than *The Book of the Dead*; or, (c) given that there are still unexcavated sections of the Turkish find is there any information concerning Noah's flood to be found in the yet to be unearthed untranslated portion of the Göbekli Tepe script?

Whatever the results could possibly be regarding (c) above however, the rabbi brothers Sabbah typically see the story of Noah's Ark as yet another event that reflects what was going on in Akhetaten.

According to the rabbis' intriguing theory therefore, "The story of Noah's Ark reflects the separation between the monotheistic people living within Akhet-Aten and the rest of polytheistic Egypt. "The earth was corrupt in the eyes of Adon-Ay, and full of violence, Adon-Ay saw how corrupt the world had become, because all the people had perverted their ways (Aramaic Bible, Genesis 6:11).""[71]

Thus they therefore conclude that, "The Noah legend cannot be understood literally. The Ark symbolizes Akhet-Aten, the holy land of the exclusive monotheist inhabitants. The Hebrew word "*tebah*" was translated as "ark" by the Hellenists many centuries ago. That ancient translation was refuted by Fabre d'Olivet. "The Hebrew word never meant vessel in the sense of a ship, as later understood... It is rather the symbolic name given by the Egyptians to their sacred city of Thebes, considered the asylum, the refuge, the home of the gods.""[72]

In fact, according to Alan F. Alford, the author of *When the Gods Came Down — The Catastrophic Roots Of Religion Revealed*, "The Hebrew term for Noah's 'Ark' was *teba*, meaning 'box'. This is odd. Why did the Hebrews call Noah's Ark a 'box', when they had a perfectly good word for a ship? Might it have had something to do with an archaic version of the legend reported by Plutarch – that the Egyptian god Osiris had been shut in a box, and cast into the Nile...?"[73]

Moreover, Alford further observes that, "The term *teba*, however, had a second meaning. Not only did it mean 'box', but also 'to sink'. This is more and more curious. It can hardly be said that Noah's Ark 'sank'; it was merely *lowered gently* on to the top of the mountains of Ararat. Unless... could this word *teba* be a distant echo of the box of Osiris, which really did 'sink' *through the celestial waters when it fell from heaven to Earth?*[74] (Italics added.)

Seeing the origin of religion in the exploded planet theory of Tom Van Flandern, Alan F. Alford quite dramatically sees Noah in fact as a meteorite and thus provides an unusual explanation for why Ham turned black.

Thus, as Alford reiterates, "Genesis informs us that Noah became "a man of the soil' by planting a vineyard. He then got drunk, fell asleep naked, and was seen by one of his sons, Ham. This, for some strange reason, caused Noah to condemn the bloodline of Ham to an eternity of slavery."[75] For Alford, this is a "legend which has always confounded biblical scholars, who have suggested that something important must have occurred between Ham and Noah – something which was excluded from the biblical account."[76] However, according to Alford, "nothing significant has been excluded from the account. All that is required to decode this enigmatic passage is a realisation that *Noah was a meteorite which emitted a tremendously bright and powerful light*. Ham's mistake was to look upon this fiery light, whereas his two brothers Shem and Japheth walked in backwards, to avoid looking upon Noah. It was no coincidence … that the Bible identifies Ham's people as those with black and swarthy complexions. In the eyes of the Hebrew priests, these black and swarthy complexions had originated (mythically speaking) from Ham's face to face encounter with the fallen meteorite."[77]

Obviously, there is a major assumption that the biblical script is referring to white people to begin with but that aside for the moment something should be said about this extraordinary hypothesis. With twenty years of experience at the US Naval Observatory, the late Tom Van Flandern was a prize-winning professional research astronomer whose research had "persuaded him that the asteroid belt originated from the explosion of two parent planets, which once existed between Mars and Jupiter."[78] Thus Alford asks: "is it far-fetched to suggest that Shem and Japheth averted their eyes from Noah's naked body because Noah was a [sic] not a man but a meteorite?

"Lest there be any doubt about this, the Bible attests to the fact that it was extremely dangerous to look upon the face of a god. A classic example is found in the book of Exodus, where Moses met God at Mount Horeb, the site of the 'burning bush'. The text informs us that 'Moses hid his face, for he was afraid to look upon God.'"[79]

Planetary explosions within our Solar System or no, in his description of the period of the flood, "when the world was destroyed, when for forty days and forty nights all was chaos, when neither sun nor moon nor twinkling star appeared, when sea and sky were mingled and all was one wide universal "ocean," on the bosom of which the patriarch floated,"[80] Rev. Alexander Hislop, the author of *The Two Babylons*, identifies the water borne patriarch as none other than Osiris.

Indeed, with regard to the Land of Khem, Hislop states that, "The most learned explorers of Egyptian antiquities, including Sir Gardiner Wilkinson, admit that the story of Noah was mixed up with the story of Osiris. The ship of Isis, and the *coffin* of Osiris, floating on the waters, point distinctly to that remarkable event. There were different periods, in different places in Egypt, when the fate of Osiris was lamented... In the great and solemn festival called "The Disappearance of Osiris," it is evident that it is Noah himself who was then supposed to have been lost. The time when Osiris was "shut up in his coffin," and when that coffin was set afloat on the waters, as stated by Plutarch, agrees exactly with the period when Noah entered the ark. That time was "the 17th day of the month Athyr, when the overflowing of the Nile had ceased, when the nights were growing long and the days decreasing. The month Athyr was the second month after the autumnal equinox, at which time the civil year of the Jews and the patriarchs began. According to this statement, then, Osiris was "shut up in his coffin" on the 17th day of the second month of the patriarchal year. Compare this with the Scriptural account of Noah's entering into the ark, and it will be seen how remarkably they agree (Gen. vii. 11). "In the six hundredth year of Noah's life, in the SECOND MONTH, in THE SEVENTEENTH DAY of the month, were all the fountains of the great deep broken up; in the self-same day entered Noah into the ark." The period, too, that Osiris ... was believed to have been shut up in his coffin, was precisely the same as Noah was confined in the ark, a whole year."[81]

Though amusing to consider at this point, there is only one inescapable conclusion to be drawn from the scholarly revelations concerning this diluvial drama: the sacred saga of 'a black man in a box' is the African source of the story of Noah's ark!

Indeed, consolidating this identification of these two momentous figures, according to the pre-biblical texts found in the writings of the MeduNeteru of the land of Khem, it was Osiris who "discovered the use of the vine. He was the first to drink wine ... taught men to plant the vine, and how to make and preserve wine."[82] Indeed, according to E. A. Wallis Budge, "Osiris was greatly devoted to agriculture,"[83] an attributive aspect that affirms that Osiris, the African God *par excellence*, and the biblical Noah were both one and the same person.

The global catastrophe that occurred at the end of the last Ice Age, otherwise known as Noah's flood, is of course generally considered beyond dispute but for the people of the Land of Khem, 'when sea and sky were mingled and all was one wide universal "ocean,"' "The Nun, which existed before the creation of the world, gave birth to rivers and streams, and most particularly to the Nile. Genesis relates, in the same way, the creation of the primal rivers from the primordial waters.

"The waters eventually lowered, allowing the firm land gradually to appear. This emergence gave birth to the sacred Nile. The primordial mound, the image of the pyramid that contains Pharaoh's Ark (Kheops [i.e. "Khufu"] and his Ark), is found in the biblical story of Noah's Ark."[84]

Nevertheless, the foregoing notwithstanding, according to Zecharia Sitchin, "The Sumerian (*and original*) story of the Deluge has as its "Noah" a "Man of Shuruppak," the seventh city established by the Nefilim..."[85] (Italics added.)

Moreover, Sitchin informs us that, "The Sumerian texts contain the dimensions and other structural instructions for the various decks and compartments in such detail that it is possible to draw the ship.... Ea [Enki/Ptah] also provided Ziusudra [Noah] with a navigator, instructing him to direct the vessel toward the "Mount of Salvation," Mount Ararat; as the highest range in the Near East, its peaks would be the first to emerge from under the waters."[86]

Indeed, landing on the mounts of Ararat in eastern Turkey of course would explain the subsequent emergence of the first post-flood civilization from the receding waters of that catastrophe remembered by the people of Khem as the first time or rather Zep Tepi, known to us now however as Göbekli Tepe. Nevertheless, with all due respect to Sitchin's interpretation of these events however, once again the question comes to mind, is the Sumerian cuneiform older than *The Book of the Dead*?

In other words, which can be considered the source of these flood stories? Given that both Sumer and the Land of Khem were evidently legacy civilizations of the *paleoancient very high civilization of high antiquity* that preceded them both, it is quite possible therefore that there is a conflation of the actual facts of the flood and the mythical traditions of both societies but owing to its world-wide gratis distribution the most influential version of course has been that which is found in the Christian Bible. Nevertheless, as stated earlier, "nothing in the Genesis account requires that its flood myth was written down earlier than the Babylonian captivity, in the sixth century B.C."

Thus, it was while they were in captivity that the Hebrew scribes allotted an extremely long age to Noah as well as to the other patriarchs. For example, we are told that, "Jacob lived in the land of Egypt seventeen years. The days of Jacob, the years of his life, were a hundred forty-seven years" (Genesis 47:28). The 17 years of Jacob's life mentioned here correspond to the 17 years of Akhenaten's reign."[87]

Indeed, "The exaggerations in the longevity of Biblical characters stretch over the entire story. Adam is claimed to have lived for 930 years (Genesis 5:5), Noah 950 years (Genesis 9:29), Terah, Abraham's father, for 205 years (Genesis 11:32), Sarah 127 years (Genesis 23:1), and Moses 120 years (Deuteronomy 34:7). This immoderation allowed the scribes to establish the book of the generations in the Biblical tale, and thus spread the story of Akhenaten and the exodus from Egypt over several hundred years."[88] Once again, we are left to conclude that the foregoing tales, though reflected in the clay tablets of Sumer, have finally found their true origin in African history, as recorded in granite and on papyri in the Nile valley.

Thus, the core biblical patriarchs of the Old Testament are based upon mythological and possibly historical entities of black African origin. As it happens, Gary Greenberg does such an excellent and thorough job in making this case for their 'euphemistic Egyptian' origin it requires no improvement from me. Since I have merely highlighted certain aspects of his argument, I suggest therefore that the reader consult *The Moses Mystery* for his erudite interpretation of this religious enigma. However, unlike Greenberg, I conclude that his hypothetical case is in fact the actual truth.

In contrast to such historical uncertainty about the patriarchs however, according to Wikipedia, the African "High Priests of Amun at Thebes," while not regarded as a Dynasty "were nevertheless of such power and influence that they were effectively the rulers of Upper Egypt from 1080 to c. 943 BC, after which their influence declined."

In support of this view Ralph Ellis states that the "Theban influence and power actually declined because of the debilitating attacks by the Sea People, who were being organized by the pre-Tanite leaders. Eventually, the later generations of Tanite leaders were able to declare themselves to be kings, and to take the throne of Lower Egypt by force and establish the twenty-first dynasty."[89]

Of the Sea People, Greenberg observes that, "At the same time that Israel moved into the central highlands, Canaan experienced several waves of invasion from the powerful Sea Peoples' confederation, chief of which were the Philistines. Led by Greek warrior castes, the Sea Peoples established strong roots in this new territory and on several occasions, most notably during the reigns of Merneptah (c. 1239-1229 B.C.) and Ramesses III (c. 1197-1166 B.C.), they battled fiercely against Egypt itself. The pressures exerted by the Sea Peoples in Canaan and against Egypt may have provided the cover that allowed the Israelites to smoothly cross over the Jordan and easily settle in the central highlands."[90]

As will be discussed in the chapter seven, that smooth crossing of the Jordan however may well have been the result of the assistance of Thoth's "Artifact of Life," the highly technological device previously mentioned in chapter five. Indeed, permitting one further foray into modern political motivation, Ellis sees these invaders as regrouped Hyksos taking revenge on Egypt because of their expulsion. However, though the invasion of the Sea People is an historical fact, his and Wikipedia's view of this as the reason for the decline of the Amunian priesthood may not necessarily be an accurate assessment.

During the year 2000 for example, the French underwater archaeologist Franck Goddio discovered several submerged ruined cities beneath the Mediterranean Sea, including a temple dedicated to Amun in the lost city of Thonis.

According to Egyptologists this was a very important city where kings were crowned and made legitimate and where great sacred rites were performed. The god in his ceremonial boat for example was brought in procession from the temple of Amun to his shrine in Canopus when the mysteries of Osiris were celebrated during the month of Khoiak.

Indeed, ancient Canopus was one of the other submerged cities Goddio discovered beneath the waves of the Mediterranean coastline. However, besides this sunken city, there was in fact another city of the same name in the land of Khem, both indeed dedicated to the star of the same name, the one in the north, the other in the south.

With regards to this star, "Velikovsky stated that Canopus was the second brightest star in the sky, but unlike Sirius, its position was more peculiar: *"Canopus is positioned south from Sirius, almost on a straight line drawn from it to the South Celestial Pole and closer to it."*[91]

As Phillip Coppens stated in *The Canopus Revelation – Stargate of the Gods and the Ark of Osiris*, "Canopus formed the axis around which the Southern canopy revolved. Its closest association in the sky is to the constellation Argo, "the Ship: – the largest constellation in the sky, so large in fact that it is now subdivided into "sub-constellations". Furthermore, Canopus occupies a significant place in the sky, to the South of the region occupied by Sirius and Orion. Though set apart from them, in mythology it is linked to these stars."[92]

Indeed, Canopus could be considered the Star of Africa or at least of the southern hemisphere, since it cannot be seen above the 36th parallel. In fact, "There is a band across Northern Africa and the Middle East, stretching from the Canary Islands to Sumer, and beyond to India, in which there was a specific star lore surrounding Canopus."[93]

Moreover, this star also assisted in the layout of the sacred land of Khem itself for "Not only are there six degrees of latitude between Rhodes, the northern limit of Canopus and the Gizeh Plateau, there are a further – precise – six degrees between the Great Pyramid and the Southern boundary of Egypt, Elephantine, the First Cataract – Canopus of the South."[94]

Indeed, there is another special connection concerning the Neter that governs this southern boundary city and the origin of Jacob's ladder, as "The building of the "ladder of ascension" was also linked with the Egyptian god Khnemu, the god of Canopus of the South. In the pyramid texts, he is specifically associated with the act of the King ascending to the sky. He makes both the barque to sail in, and the ladder on which the king ascends to the sky."[95]

Phillip Coppens also believes that the star Canopus is in fact the true celestial representation of Osiris and not Orion, which if true, legitimizes its title as *The Star of Africa*. Indeed, in Egyptian mythology, the constellation "Argo was identified as the Ship of the Dead, with the Egyptian deity Osiris on board. Whereas in Greek myth the ship is controlled by Canopus, the Egyptian ship of the dead is controlled by Osiris. As such, there seems a clear connection between Osiris and the star Canopus …"[96] These facts, if corroborated, makes the purpose of the procession of the ceremonial boat of Amun to Canopus, mentioned above, a reunification with Osiris, the African god *par excellence*.

However on a more secular and mundane level, the temple city of Amun at Thonis was also a great commercial port. Indeed, it was a major import-export harbour for more than a thousand years before the Greeks arrived on the scene and began to call it Heracleion. Indeed, like Tiger Bay, in the South Wales seaport town where I was born, "Canopus was labelled a 'city of sin'. Harbour towns seem to have a very specific aura over them that has not changed in thousands of years."[97]

Thus the power of that weakened African priesthood, though still stumbling from Ahkenaten's assault, did not decline as has been presumed but gradually moved from Thebes to a new centre of power on the Mediterranean coast, still however located in the Black land.

As was shown elsewhere Upper and Lower Egypt were Egyptological synonyms for the Black land and the Red land. Thus with the exception of the Sahara and the Sinai Peninsular, the Red land of the desert is of course considered external to Africa, according to modern day maps. Though still within the boundaries of the Unified Land of Khem, so-called Lower Egypt however was external to the continent known as Africa today as it formed part of the Red land. Hence Thonis, though located in the far north, was not however in the Red land, conventionally described as Lower Egypt, but still in the Black land, a region Egyptological convention would normally describe as "Upper Egypt!"

Situated on the edge of what was once the Canopic Branch of the Nile, Thonis however would eventually become known as a sister to the Greco-Egyptian city of Naucratis and only became superseded by Alexandria after the

Temple of Amun sank into the Sea of the Greeks, the Mediterranean, as a result of liquefaction and subsidence around 200 or so BC.

Nevertheless with regard to its earlier history, Thonis had its beginnings in the 12th Century BC and "by the time Herihor was proclaimed as the first ruling High Priest of Amun in 1080 BC – in the 19th Year of Ramesses XI – the Amun priesthood exercised an effective stranglehold on Egypt's economy. The Amun priests owned two-thirds of all the temple lands in Egypt and 90 percent of *her ships* plus many other resources."[98] (Italics added.)

As if mummies containing cocaine residue in them were not enough, Egyptologists have been loath to admit that the ancient land of Khem ever possessed a navy that navigated the high seas. Yet, the description of such a navy belonging to Solomon in the Bible is a dead give away for its existence.

On the high seas or no, the Amun priests were as powerful as Pharaoh, if not more so. For example, "One of the sons of the High Priest Pinedjem I would eventually assume the throne and rule Egypt for almost half a decade as pharaoh Psusennes I, while the Theban High Priest Psusennes III would take the throne as king Psusennes II, the final ruler of the 21st Dynasty."[99] As Ralph Ellis revealed in *Solomon – Falcon of Sheba*, these High Priest Kings would have been among members of what he refers to as the pre-Tanite rulers.

As the last king of the Twenty-first dynasty, the High Priest King Psusennes II ruled the land from his capital in This, the Greek Tanis, in the Delta region. Also known in Greek as Dzann and in the Bible as Zoan, Psusennes of course, is the Greek derivation of his name, which in the MeduNeteru is: PA SEBA KHA EN NUIT, the meaning of which Ellis translates as "The Star Appearing in the City." As the MeduNeteru are multi-leveled symbols however an alternative version of his name results as "Image of the transformations of Re."

Ruling between 957-943 BC, PA SEBA KHA EN NUIT was according to Wikipedia, "both king at Tanis and the High Priest in Thebes at the same time meaning he did not resign his office as High Priest of Amun during his reign."[100]

Meanwhile, through painstaking research Ralph Ellis has drawn the conclusion that Sheshonq I of the Black land, the biblical Shishak, is none other than Solomon, that the Solomon of the Bible is in fact the son of PA SEBA KHA EN NUIT. Ellis moreover observes that, "the first thing to note about this monarch is that his fabled wealth again outstrips the capabilities of a purely indigenous Israelite monarch:

"So King Solomon exceeded all the kings of the earth for riches and for wisdom.

"In the days of King Solomon, gold was as common as bronze, and silver as lead, and bronze and lead and iron were abundant as the grass of the fields and the reeds of the desert ... and god gave unto him glory, and riches, and wisdom, and grace in such abundance that there was none like unto him among his predecessors...

"At their first reading, these statements might be taken as pure Biblical propaganda, as it seems impossible that an Israelite king could aspire to such wealth. How could the king of a minor province like Judaea-Israel exceed the riches of the great civilisations of Persia and Egypt? While these matters may seem unanswerable in pure biblical terms, the texts continue unabashed:

"And King Solomon made a navy of ships in Eziongeber, which is beside Eloth, on the shore of the Red Sea, in the land of Edom." [101]

Thus Ellis concludes that "It would appear that King Solomon not only had a substantial royal court, untold wealth, a fabulous palace, a richly adorned temple and a large number of wives and concubines; it seems he had a navy, too. Josephus then continues to add that this navy went on an expedition, looking for trade."[102]

Though biblically accredited to Solomon, not only did this navy belong to a king of the people of the Land of Khem, it is more than likely "therefore, that the campaign lists, which were inscribed in the Temple of Karnak by Sheshonq I (King Solomon], were mainly listing the military campaigns of his father, Psusennes II, the High Priest in Thebes. It was for this reason that King Solomon had dominion over so many towns and villages in Israel that he could afford to give some away to Hirom of Tyre as payment for the timbers of cedar."[103]

Like his father, PA SEBA KHA EN NUIT, all pharaohs were high priests but this important Priest King who presides at the head of an African priesthood is all but unknown to the general public, outside of academia. However is there a possibility that the general public knows him by another name?

This is where the remarkable findings of Ralph Ellis come into play. Corroborating the earlier statement concerning the lack of evidence for the existence of the patriarch Abraham in Ur of the Chaldees, Palestine or anywhere else in the so-called Middle East, Ellis highlights the fact that "one of the major problems with the archeological evidence in this area, and era, is the complete lack of evidence for any of these Israelite monarchs. Here are the most famous, influential and powerful monarchs in all of Judaic history, and not one inscription has been found bearing their name – now this is a situation that just has to be considered peculiar. Suddenly, the Egyptian solution has some distinct benefits, for it solves this little puzzle completely. In fact, there are many inscriptions of King David, and even one or two that have been recorded from excavations in the Levant; it's just that the name mentioned on these artifacts is Psusennes II."[104]

Recalling the Star of David, Ralph Ellis searches for such a star in the name of the Priest King showing that the individual symbolic glyphs used to form SEBA in the MeduNeteru stand for a star. In fact, Ellis translates the full name as "My Star is in His City," given that PA SEBA means "my star." Moreover, Ellis demonstrated that there is another set of glyphs that also carry the meaning of star. Those glyphs spell DUAT, which is described in the Pyramid Texts of the MeduNeteru as a star in a circle and is in fact the symbol of the realm of the Afterlife.

As an interesting aside related to the Chinese-African connection made in chapter five, Laird Scranton has discovered a very far-reaching connection between ancient China and its Taoist religion and the Sacred Science of the people of Khem. In his view, the very word "Dao" itself, "correlates in one sense to an Egyptian word *uat*, meaning "way, road, path." This word is written with two glyphs. The first is a glyph, pronounced *ua*, that we associate symbolically with the concept of distance but could also convey the notion of a journey or a road. In fact, Budge actually assigns the meaning of "way, road" to this glyph in his "List of Hieroglyphic Characters." The second is the hemisphere glyph, which we associate with the concept of mass or matter in our cosmologies. Taken together and interpreted symbolically, they convey the meaning the "way, path, or road of matter" – the very subject that we believe is explicitly addressed by the seven Dogon stages of creation. These are the stages of creation that also end up defining the Dogon Second World of matter, which we equate to the Egyptian underworld, and which is referred to in Egypt as the Tuat, or Duat. For both the Dogon and the Egyptians, this world is symbolized by the figure of a star (a concept defined by the Egyptian word *tua*) inscribed by a circle. The suggestion is that the term Dao in China derives from the same original cosmological concept as the terms *uat*, *tua*, Tuat, and Duat in Egypt."[105] Thus, it would appear that Duke Ellington was apparently onto something when he wrote the lyric: "*It Don't Mean A Thing, If It Ain't Got That Swing, Duat, tua, Duat, tua. Duat, Tuat!*"

Returning once again to less musically historical references and thus to the name of the last king of the Twenty-first dynasty, if PA DUAT replaces PA SEBA, one ultimately discovers the etymological basis and origin for the modern name of David.

Of this ruler, Gary Greenberg reveals that, "Under King David, a fusion of ideals seems to have taken place. On the one hand, he established the orthodox Atenist view as the central religion of ancient Israel. On the other, however, he (and Solomon after him) seems to have encouraged all the other factions to worship in their own way, as long as they recognized the fundamental supremacy of the Atentist priesthood. Much of the subsequent Israelite writing about this time revolves around these religious feuds and schisms."[106]

Eureka and voilà! There it is plain to see that it was in David's legally restricted interest to promote the Atentist cult since it had been expelled from the Black land as a result of a compromise to bring an end to the attack on Amun, as this rebellious sector of people who originated in the Black land were now being used as a military buffer zone between the Nile valley and the Hittite and other Asiatic invaders of northeast Africa.

Thus we discover, as a consequence of the geostrategic acumen of an ancient African king, another historical figure of African history, a High Priest of

Amun no less, has now been extracted and rescued from the pages of the Bible, resurrected into the MeduNeteru, the cornerstone of the Sacred Science, and thus reconstituted into the annals of African history. Indeed, PA SEBA KHA EN NUIT, the King David of the biblical text, was a pharaoh whose god was Amun!

King David, High Priest of Amun, was a black African King!

Seven

———

SACRED SCIENCE

Today we know something that people in the nineteenth
century thought was no longer to be dreaded: we know
that all our knowledge must be revised.

RENE A. SCHWALLER DE LUBICZ

Without doubt, the consummate author on the subject of the Sacred Science and the peerless decipherer of the symbolic grammar that underlies the MeduNeteru system of the ancient black African priesthood of Khem is Rene A. Schwaller de Lubicz, the alchemical scholar from the French region of Alsace-Lorraine.

Of his accomplishments, Edward F. Malkowski said that, "Schwaller proved categorically ... that dynastic Egypt possessed mathematics far superior to that of the Pythagorean Greeks, whom they preceded by more than fifteen hundred years, as well as that of the Europeans, an additional fifteen hundred years later."[1]

No wonder Johannes Kepler decided to plunder *the golden vessels of the Egyptians* in order to arrive at his unique solution to the laws of gravitation. Indeed, of their exceptional stance, Malkowski further demonstrated that "Egyptian culture represented a magnificent worldview in which science, religion, philosophy, and art were all part of a single discipline based on man's innate and intuitive knowledge of nature and creation. Despite the fact that traditional Egyptology generally rejects Schwaller's ideas, they have never been refuted since their publication more than fifty years ago."[2]

Including *The Temple in Man*, *Symbol and the Symbolic*, *Esoterism & Symbol*, *Sacred Science – The King Of Pharaonic Theocracy*, *The Egyptian Miracle* and his massive two-volume opus, *The Temple of Man*, as well as many other well-researched works, the complex authoritative magnum opus of this author is certainly not fodder for the casual reader only interested in the category of light entertainment. However, as a result of his intense scrutiny on the subject of Sacred Science committed students of his work can expect to discover the importance of the existence of the eternal Present Moment and the secret it holds.

From his intensive fifteen-year study and meticulous measurement of the monuments situated throughout the ancient Black land, Schwaller de Lubicz was able to determine, and prove what Gerald Massey once said of the High Priests and the entire priesthood of Khem: They were "the greatest realists that ever lived."[3]

Over an extreme length of time, they had held a fundamental point of view about reality that differed in principal from that of modern post-Mosaic times. As was first mentioned by Siegfried Morenz in chapter one, "the Egyptians had a mode of thinking very different from our own." Indeed, for many millennia, those ancient Africans maintained a "Faith in an origin that cannot be situated in time and space."[4] For them, that extra-dimensional location of the eternal Present Moment remained far beyond such mere sense perceptual confines, a transcendental factor that further informed them that this "is reality absolute, not to be grasped by our intelligence. This cannot be regarded as a mystery: it is the eternal Present Moment, indivisible Unity."[5]

Thus, for Schwaller de Lubicz, this was the primary understanding of the people of the land of Khem that the incomprehensible "eternal Present Moment" was undoubtedly the source of the physical medium they identified as Nun.

For the High Priests Nun was the powerful source from which the universe was created and moreover the fundamental understanding of these realists led them, without any measure of hyperbole, to conclude that the power that lies in that omnipresent moment is of such enormous magnitude it could illuminate the entire universe.

In fact, Nun is the source for modern day gateway technologies that can and do manipulate the physical medium. Indeed, as the "geometry of local celestial space is a determinant in the energy output of fusion reactions"[6] that facilitates such physical medium manipulation, Nun is also therefore the source of the intense power of a thermonuclear explosion, the source of Indra's thousand suns, as theoretical physicist Julius Robert Oppenheimer, who, if rumours of the Nazi explosion of an atomic weapon on Russian soldiers during the early phase of World War II prove untrue, witnessed the first atomic blast of modern times, instantly recognized in its shimmering iridescent cloud a terrifyingly similar but ancient phenomenon presciently described in the pages of sacred Sanskrit texts of the *Bhagavad Gita* found in Hindu India's *Mahabharata*.

Quoting the words of Richard Hoagland in his book *Babylon's Banskters*, Farrell amazingly reports that: "When we look at the stars, at the sky at night, we're not seeing chained and imprisoned H-bombs, we're seeing *portals* to another dimension. And the portals are glowing windows through which we can peer and glimpse the fragments of a physics from another side. What is stunning is when you take that metaphor, and you go back and you read the actual Egyptian descriptions in the hieroglyphs for Sirius, the brightest star in the sky, the description is (that) Sirius is a doorway. Now what did they know? What did they know?"[7]

Apparently, the ancients knew that stars were not mere rotating balls of plasma but portals of access to hyper-dimensional torsion energies. Indeed, as with the physics of the very large, Farrell convincingly demonstrates that "particles, as rotating masses, and whose behavior when measured as a statistical aggregate, are *portals* that "gate" a hyper-dimensional reality into our own world."[8] Thus, the ancient adage ascribed to Hermes Trismegistus: As above, so below.

Of course, Sirius is the brightest star when viewed however from the continent of Europe. From North Africa, on the other hand, Canopus, the Star of Africa, is considered by some the brightest star. Indeed, "Canopus is a white binary star in the oars of the ship Argo. It is, according to the Hipparcos satellite, 340 light years (96 parsecs) from Earth. Before Hipparcos, distance measurements for the star varied widely, up to as much as 1200 light years; had the latter been correct, Canopus would have been one of the most powerful stars in our galaxy. As is, it is still at least 30,000 times brighter than the sun and the most powerful star within 700 light years or thereabouts. It is much more luminous, intrinsically, than the sole star that appears brighter than it from Earth; Sirius is a mere 22 times more luminous than our sun, and depends on being much closer to us to beat its rival. In fact, for a large fraction of stars in the local stellar neighbourhood, Canopus is the "brightest star in the sky".[9] Moreover, as Phillip Coppens stated in chapter six, this star and not Orion, as is generally assumed, is the true celestial representative of Osiris.

As for contemporary comprehension of the phenomenon of gateway technologies, Schwaller de Lubicz sees the 'materialistic' rise of modern-day scientific power, based on its understanding of fundamental matter, as belonging to the 'false religion.' Therefore, he asks: "Is this not the "false temple," the false "religion," which is based, not on the Spirit, but on perishable matter and the science of its destruction?[10]

According to the American neurosurgeon, Dr. Eben Alexander whose extraordinary otherworldly experience will be reviewed much later, "The ascendance of the scientific method based solely in the physical realm over the past four hundred years presents a major problem: we have lost touch with the deep mystery at the center of existence – our consciousness. It was (under different names and expressed through different world-views) something known well and held close by pre-modern religions, but it was lost to our secular Western culture as we became increasingly enamored with the power of modern science and technology."[11]

Indeed, Schwaller de Lubicz emphasizes the point that understanding the ancient way of scientific investigation requires a spiritual comprehension, a pure science, not suited to the materialistically inclined, and therefore warns of the dangers of mechanistic science and the rise of scientific power by declaring that, "This brutal evolution, which will place science in the hands of a very restricted elite, will create a new aristocracy in power after the proletarian endeavors and the emergence of a governing "technocratic" class, which are both, however, doomed to failure,"[12] for "where political power may influence people's consciousness through force, more tragically he warns that scientific power "will influence spiritual destiny, not through force, but through conviction. *Then the masses will no longer have any choice but to believe what only a small group of men will understand.* Believe and obey: this is already the case now, but obviously it will soon grow worse."[13]

Prophetic words indeed, when the origin of the promoted scientific fallacies of Global Warming, for one example, is taken into consideration. And moreover, when given the degree to which the rich oligarchical one percent have entrenched themselves above the remaining 99 percent of the world's population since the 2008 economic meltdown.

And this, the 'brutal evolution' that Schwaller de Lubicz referred to, of course, is of a similar nature to the very method that has been used since biblical times and throughout the Medieval era that only began to be challenged in the period after Johannes Gutenberg invented the printing press: the Bible understood only by a few and translated by a priesthood for an otherwise uninformed and thus malleable congregation. The sheep led by the wolf. Is it not ironic that the ancients portrayed Seth as a jackal?

Indeed the effects of long term cosmic cycles and their causes or even the fundamental principles (Neteru) that underlie photosynthesis are still unknown, still a mystery, but despite this fact a magnesium atom surrounded by nitrogen atoms showered by sunlight radiation 'somehow' transforms carbon into oxygen and creates the biosphere. Therefore it is the radiation of the sun, a manifestation of Atum, "the god who existed prior to creation, a personification of the celestial deep,"[14] that is responsible for climate change. Mankind is not a pollutant. Indeed, reality demonstrates that human beings are in fact semi-divine co-creators!

As Fritjof Capra has determined, in atomic physics "the scientist cannot play the role of a detached objective observer, but becomes involved in the world he observes to the extent that he influences the properties of the observed objects. John Wheeler sees this involvement of the observer as the most important feature of quantum theory and he has therefore suggested replacing the word "observer" by the word "participator."[15] Indeed, given that there appears to be a connection between subatomic quantum events and the subconscious of human observers, the microcosmic and hypergeometric fundaments of the Nun are not a force to be played with.

Therefore, this is a realm where modern Western physicists need to tread carefully. As Robert Lawlor, the translator of *Symbol and the Symbolic*, says: "Modern science, particularly subatomic physics, has, as Schwaller de Lubicz points out, expanded its knowledge of matter to the point where Nature must be considered suprarational (as being beyond the limits of rational methods and formulae). These new discoveries and ideas, he emphasizes, demand a new and as yet unfound vocabulary, as well as a radically different approach to education and knowledge itself. This view places Schwaller de Lucbicz at variance with some contemporary writers such as Fritjof Capra who, in *The Tao of Physics*, contends that we can with our present scientific methods move directly into a science with spiritual dimensions. Schwaller de Lubicz *denies this possibility*, emphasizing that the achievement of a sacred science requires a transformation of mind which would considerably alter our relationship to knowledge and its expression. It is here that understanding of the hieroglyphic intelligence of the Ancients may assist contemporary thought in surpassing the intellectual impasse presently incurred by our rational perception and methodologies."[16] (Emphasis added.)

Therefore, in order to understand the power at the core of quantum action an understanding of the ancient African MeduNeteru has become essential for modern physicists. Thus, a foray into the ancient way of "thinking very different from our own" has now become crucial.

Representing the unformed universe, the Neter whose symbolic glyphs the people of Khem composed and designed to represent this function of the quantum realm was named, as had been previously stated, Nun, an image that stood for a primordial ocean filled with waves of electromagnetic vibration. As mentioned in chapter three however, *the two nasal consonants of this non-Indo-European word serve only for its pronunciation in English but the Afro-Asiatic symbolic representation of Nun in the MeduNeteru speaks to the mind spiritually, or in less theological terms subliminally, by showing each glyph to be jagged zigzag-like objects specifying water, current and flow, a dynamic symbol used incidentally in modern physics to describe the phenomenon of electromagnetism!*

Ideographically speaking however, according to Laird Scranton who has made a major contribution in this area, even "the glyphs of the word *khem*"[17] express "the notion of god, not only in distinctly scientific terms, but also in terms that are entirely consonant with traditional religious views. God is defined as the unknown source of creation or, from a scientific perspective, the unknown primordial source of massless waves."[18]

Whereas, the Khemite word for God is in fact Neter, the glyph used for its representation is the symbol of a flag at the end of an upright pole usually placed after the description of the name of any given Neter. As a matter of fact, these Neteru, which were representations of the so-called idols that the heretic and criminal Moses/Akhenaten had sought to suppress, were in fact manifestations of fundamental powers, or better said, divine functional entities of creation.

With regard to the origin of these powers, Scranton further indicated that, "the use of a neter flag implies a relationship to the mother goddess Neith, or Net, who is credited with having woven matter."[19] Nun nevertheless is of course the ultimate manifestation of "the extra-dimensional location" known as Reality Absolute and therefore even the metaphysical womb of Net emerges from that source.

As Reality Absolute, the non-polarized essence of Nun is however incomprehensible to our intelligence. Yet and still through an internal act of primordial consciousness, this irrational source undergoes a polarization that manifests itself nevertheless in spiritual substance, the yin and the yang polar opposites of the Nile valley civilization.

Pursuing the origin of this concept to a paleoancient civilization, Joseph P. Farrell refers to the initial function that occurred in the eternal Present Moment as the "topological metaphor of the physical medium," the exact same phenomenon that Rene A. Schwaller de Lubicz called the Primordial Scission, a functioning concept that lies at the foundation of a philosophy that was bequeathed to the founders of the Black land from the former civilization that existed before the Flood, and that, given the research of Michael Tellinger, in all likelihood may have formed part of southern Africa.

Thus it can be inferred from such speculative sources that the Neteru are a paleoancient symbolic invention designed to represent a fundamental understanding of the natural functioning powers that govern the creation of the Cosmos. Given such understanding therefore, the Sacred Science is in fact a science of genesis.

As Michael Tellinger points out in *African Temples of the Anunnaki,* "southern Africa did not escape the attention of the ancient gods. It is, however, very clear that the relationship those gods had with the ABZU (southern Africa) was quite different from their activities in other parts of the planet. It is very sad that we will never know the full extent of what existed at the most impressive ruins in southern Africa when they were first discovered by the colonialists from the north. The destruction and plundering that took place at these ruins will never be fully realized."[20]

Indeed, "THE RUIN WE call the Hexagon is one of the most important Johan Heine has discovered and measured. The structure and the alignments suggest an advanced knowledge of the cosmos, geometry, and particle physics. It is molded around the structure of a star tetrahedron, which is referred to by leading scientists as the fundamental structure of all matter in the universe."[21]

In his chapter, *Lost Cities - Vanished Civilizations,* Tellinger makes references to the many stone circles, of which there are more than 100,000, strewn across the landscape, most without entrances and mostly only visible from an aerial perspective. Of one in particular, he highlights certain concentric circles around the main structure indicating the knowledge of resonant cavities and the generation of energy from sound and frequency.[22]

Although Michael Tellinger makes allusions to the existence of high technology within the South African finds, he does not however reinforce this idea with concrete facts or details, apart from photographic evidence, which is somewhat disappointing though it does not take anything away from his otherwise interesting analysis. I however do not want to be found wanting in this area and thus feel the need to uncover as much pertinent information about mankind's paleo-ancient scientific past as is available, some of which actually occurs in the Bible where references to the Ark, the object in it, and the force of God it allegedly represents can be found.

Indeed, a technological device of this sort could go a long way to explain the megalithic anomalies located across the planet but particularly with regard to the movement of the gigantic granite sarcophagi in the subterranean temple at Sakkara located in the Serapeum discussed in chapter one, for example, or the huge 70 ton granite blocks that contain the King's Chamber in the Great Pyramid where the dimensions of the Ark are also found.

As was discussed in chapter four, God is described as an object. As such, the Hebrews referred to this object as the glory of the Lord. Intrigued by this epithet, Graham Phillips asks: "What exactly is the glory of the Lord? In later Christian times the term 'glory of the lord' came to be associated with the invisible presence of God: the holy spirit that inspired the pure in heart. However, this notion of an invisible God appears to have been more of a Greek concept. There are only three references in the Bible to God being invisible and they are all in the New Testament:

"Who is the image of the invisible God. (Colossians 1:15)

"Him who is invisible. (Hebrews 11:27)

"The King eternal, immortal, invisible. (1 Timothy 1:17)

"All three are by St Paul who seems to have been a Greek convert to Christianity."[23]

Since the somewhat vague provenance of the apostle has been introduced at this point, it should be noted that evidence exists that does not conclude St Paul was a Greek at all but a Roman citizen, though born in Tarsus. Indeed, this issue is discussed in the last paragraphs of Joseph P. Farrell's 2014 book the *Thrice Great Hermetica And The Janus Age*.

In discussion with Dr. Scott D. de Hart, with whom he often co-writes, the subject soon turned to their "mutual frustrations and difficulties with the person of St. Paul as depicted in the canonical books of the New Testament," [when de Hart suddenly interjected] "I think St. Paul is Flavius Josephus!"[24] This startling revelation however comes as no surprise, as Ralph Ellis had already drawn that conclusion in 1998 in the *Evangelist*, chapter eight of *Jesus, Last Of The Pharaohs*. Indeed, if Jesus is truly the last of the pharaohs as Ellis purports then his father in heaven is most assuredly Osiris.

In that remarkable work, Ellis had made several pages of comparisons between the life of Josephus and that of Saul before asking: "So, who was this second 'Saul', the man whose life followed that of the biblical Saul so closely? Was it someone very obscure who has never been studied in depth before? Have I stumbled upon an ancient manuscript that has never before been translated? Not so. In fact, 'Saul' was none other than Josephus, the first century Jewish historian whose works I have been using all through the early sections of this book."[25]

Moreover, Ellis is able to show that the much-quoted author of *The Jewish War* had "managed to control his true position of Jewish traitor and quisling for the Romans into a glorious victory for himself. Like his alter ego Saul, Josephus was a man who could change sides twice in the conflict and brazenly profess that perfidy was a virtue."[26]

This surprising piece of detective work ultimately led Ellis to ask, "Is it not amazing that this similarity between the life of Josephus and that of Saul has not been commented on before?"[27]

Amazing indeed, but this digression into the dubious origin of fabricators of the past has led us of course away from the foregoing topic that was raised earlier concerning "the glory of the Lord" or more pertinently, the "Artifact of Life," the object in the Ark of the Covenant. Indeed, Graham Phillips relates that, "the Leviticus account goes on to describe exactly what is seen:

"And there came a fire out from before the Lord, and consumed upon the altar the burnt offerings . . . (LEVITICUS 9:24)

"So the glory of the Lord, which is like fire, literally comes out of whatever it is that is described as the 'the Lord'. Some biblical commentators, following Israeli historian Martin Buber's influential *Moses* published in 1956, have suggested that this is the Ark of the Covenant. However, this seems unlikely for two reasons. The ark is mentioned almost two hundred times in the Bible, so why not mention it here? More importantly, the first time this glory of the Lord is seen the ark has not yet been made."[28]

Indeed, geometrician John Ten had also realized that the Ark of the Covenant, this box-like object, was supposed to have been built at the foot of Mount Sinai after Moses crossed the Red Sea which confused him because, having read the Bible about the crossing of the Red Sea, it said: ""By day the Lord went ahead of them."[29] They are going toward the Red Sea fleeing from Egypt:

> "By day the LORD went ahead of them in a pillar of cloud to guide them on their way and by night in a pillar of fire to give them light, so that they could travel by day or night… Neither the pillar of cloud by day nor the pillar of fire by night left its place in front of the people."[30]

Though bordering on the seemingly miraculous, this biblical text, as John Ten sees it, "is describing Moses following this vortex of cloud and at night it would light up, this vortex of fire, through the desert going toward the Red Sea, but the description of the same vorticular action and the same description of the cloud pillar is given when it is describing the Ark of the Covenant."[31]

From this account John Ten drew the dramatic conclusion that maybe the "Artifact of Life" and the Ark of the Covenant are two different objects and thus "maybe the word of God that was not allowed to be discussed was the part about *the source of the energy of the Ark* not the box. The box was built afterward to put that energy source in it so that they could travel through 40 years in the desert."[32] Indeed, it appears that, "Moses is following something, a power source, something that is creating a *vortex in space* as he is coming out of Egypt."[33] (Italics added.)

Moreover, John Ten further surmises from the biblical facts that, "Moses was son of Pharaoh for 40 years and initiated in the highest level of initiation of the Egyptians before he realized he was Hebrew and left with the tribes of Israel. So, if there was a power source [and] if the pyramids of Egypt were not just built to bury pharaohs, which I believe they were not built to do that at all, [but] were actually shielding devices or resonating cavities, resonating space-time in a very specific geometric structure,"[34] then they were now missing this important technological device.

Indeed, in *The Grid of the Gods*, Joseph P. Farrell remarked that, "I myself have suggested that at least the Great Pyramid was a complex sort of phase conjugate howitzer manipulating longitudinal waves in the physical medium itself."[35]

Given what has been mentioned herein with regard to access to the Houses of Life however, it is debatable that Moses, or rather his historical counterpart Akhenaten, came anywhere near to the highest levels of initiation particularly since it was Moses who "cut the umbilical cord which connected his people and his religious ideas to their cultural and natural context."[36] Of course, that situation would not have applied to those members of his priesthood that may have been recruited from the traditional Amunian temples.

Indeed, given the hi-tech abilities of the aforementioned unusual device, John Ten began to think that this object is not a Hebrew object at all. "Maybe this object actually got taken out of Egypt by Moses when he left with the Israelis and that might be a reason why after the king of Egypt, the pharaoh of Egypt, allowed Moses to leave, all of sudden realized he was taking off with the power source and changes his mind and went after him."[37]

Despite John Ten's apparent acknowledgement of the biblical version of events, what is being discussed nevertheless is the fact that the object inside the Ark of the Covenant was some sort of space-time manipulation device, leaving open the intriguing question: what is the connection between the Ark of the Covenant and the Great Pyramid?

In answer to this, the geometric genius of John Ten comes into full swing. After taking the 'dimensioning' of the Ark of the Covenant, as given in the Bible, which is quite precise, and the 'dimensioning' of the inside of the sarcophagus in the Great Pyramid of Giza, he discovered that it was a perfect match!

That is, "if you have the Ark of the Covenant built you will be able to lower that box into the sarcophagus of the Great Pyramid of Giza and it will fit perfectly on the side and perfectly on the length so that you can lower it with the poles, and put the poles which are telescopic in the ark."[38]

Moreover, John Ten realized that "the inside volume inside of the sarcophagus is exactly half of the outside volume of that sarcophagus. Exactly, I mean very highly precisely. And if you take the dimensions of the Ark then you get exactly half the volume of the inside of the sarcophagus. Then if you take the dimension of the inside of the Ark you get exactly half of the outside dimension of the Ark. So you get perfect octaves of cavity, of resonance cavity inside the sarcophagus."[39]

Thus quite extraordinarily, somewhere around 1330 BC, a 'high tech' device is being operated as some form of gravitational generator utilized to part the Red Sea. But was that the first time such a phenomenon was described in history? Indeed it was not. Referencing William Kelly Simpson's and Raymond O. Faulkner's *The Literature of Ancient Egypt*, published in 1973, John Ten began to have a better picture of what was going on.

"I started to study ancient Egyptian texts to see if there was any evidence of that. And I found plenty but one thing that struck me is that there is a story about a king of Egypt, a pharaoh that is on a lake with his wife and she loses a very precious, beautiful bracelet in the lake and the pharaoh's wife is quite distraught and the pharaoh wants to do something about it and so the story goes to say they called the high priests of Egypt and they come and they open the waters of the lake to find the bracelet and give it back to the queen. And I thought, sounds like these guys, hundreds of years before Moses, were doing things similar to opening the Red Sea."[40]

For John Ten, this was an example of controlled gravitation. Now imagine that you have "the power of gravitation under your control, you could do things like stopping the force of water and opening channels. You could push things around. So I started to think about it but when I read Exodus and the crossing of the Red Sea I saw no evidence. It just contends that Moses went to the front of the sea raised his staff, opened his arms and the thing opened. I'm like wow that's some serious staff you've got going. And then I came across something that was much more descriptive that is typically lost by the scholars."[41]

Here, John Ten is referring to what is stated in the Book of Joshua. Thus, "having gone through the desert:

> Moses is now gone, he is dead and Joshua is in charge of the Israelis and they arrive upon the Jordan, which is a large river especially when it is running at flood level and they mention . . . that it is running at flood level and they need to cross the river and they do not know how to do it. At the time there was no bridge. So they are in a conundrum and Joshua is instructed to take the Ark and put all the high priests [around it] and then walk the Ark into the Jordan and start the parting of the Jordan. And in this case, it is quite descriptive,

quite amazing. It says "And the priests came out of the river carrying the Ark of the Covenant of the LORD. No sooner had they set their feet on the dry ground … than the waters of the Jordan returned to their place and ran at flood stage as before." (Joshua 4:18)

So here it is quite very, very direct about using the Ark to actually stop the force of the water of the Jordan to let the tribes of Israel go through and then as soon as they got out of there the gravitational field or whatever you want to call it allowed the water to start running again."[42]

From this graphic and explicit description of what occurred at the River Jordan, John Ten drew the interesting conclusion that "One thing that is really omitted is the paragraph shortly after paragraph 23: "For the LORD your God dried up the Jordan before you until you had crossed over…" Remember, the LORD is the Tetragrammaton described as the Ark of the Covenant. "The LORD your God did to the Jordan just what he had done to the Red Sea when he dried it up before us until we had crossed over."[43] (Joshua 4:23)

Indeed, another author was not only struck by the strange activity that took place at the Jordan but also at what happened shortly thereafter. According to Zecharia Sitchin, "The crossing itself, under the leadership of Joshua, entailed the miraculous backing up of the Jordan's waters, under the influence of the Holy Ark *and its contents.* It was then, "when Joshua was by Jericho, that he raised his eyes and lo and behold, there stood a man opposite him and his drawn sword in his hand; and Joshua went unto him and said unto him: 'Art thou with us or with our enemies?' and he said: 'Neither; a captain of the host of the Lord am I.' And Joshua fell on his face to the ground and bowed, and said unto him: 'What sayeth my lord unto his servant?' and the captain of the host of Yahweh said unto Joshua: 'Remove thy shoe off thy foot, for the place where thou standeth is re-stricted.' (Italics added.)

"Then the captain of the troops of Yahweh divulged to him the Lord's plan for the conquest of Jericho. Do not attempt to storm its walls by force, he said. Instead, carry the Ark of the Covenant around its walls seven times. And on the seventh day the priests sounded the trumpets, and the people let out a great cry, as they were commanded. "And the walls of Jericho came tumbling down.""[44]

Indeed, in the foregoing paragraphs and especially the information previously presented by John Ten, it says that the reason the Red Sea was opened up and crossed is because of the object — later placed in the Ark of the Covenant — that was used to do it.

According to John Ten, "The reason why this is typically omitted is because all scholars believe that the Ark box was built after the crossing of the Red Sea, at the foot of Mount Sinai but the source of power of that Ark box might have come right out of Egypt and it might have been the power source of a technology much more advanced than anything we can dream of today!"[45]

Clearly, as Rene A. Schwaller de Lubicz said in chapter two, "Black Africa ... still holds many surprises for us," as even the glyphs that form the MeduNeteru, being multi-leveled and analogical in nature themselves, are also representations of a power source that can form "a collection of specific functions ... designed ... to manipulate not only the consciousness of their observer, but the physical medium itself,"[46] and therefore are similar, if not identical in function to Kepler's concept of "vicarious hypothesis," or to what Bernhard Riemann and Albert Einstein referred to as a *tensor*, that is a multifunctional factor of physical science.

This indeed is the kind of 'inner sanctum' knowledge that Akhenaten would have been denied. Banished in his youth to the northeast region of the Delta, the science of genesis would have remained out of his reach though clearly, if John Ten's hypothesis is any indication, his High Priests had access to the power source taken from the Great Pyramid with which they were absconding.

Nevertheless, whoever the captain of the host who delivered the plan of attack was, the Lord, Yahweh, at the time of course was Yahu, the divine pharaoh. Thus this scenario implies that Ay was assisting Seti, the biblical Joshua, who was accompanying and safeguarding the recently exiled Yahuds in the liberation of Khem's northeast African territory of Canaan. Under this interpretation however, the use of the 'stolen' gravity-controlling device appears to be condoned by the pharaoh. Therefore, given this explanation, and despite Cecil B. de Mille's magnificent animated recreation of that alleged event, the parting of the Red Sea may indeed have occurred but the exciting story of it swallowing up Pharaoh's armies has to have been an interpolated biblical myth, a complete and utter fiction.

That point aside for the moment, is there however any evidence for the existence in ancient times of a "power source of a technology much more advanced than anything we can dream of today?" Despite Carl Sagan's inference of the possibility that the Dogon incorporated the binary star system of Sirius into their mythology after hearing about it from scientifically inclined visiting Belgian missionaries who allegedly possessed the latest scientific knowledge of their European day, and despite his decrying of their otherwise detailed scientific technological comprehension, within the extraordinary Dogon myth lies another so-called modern scientific concept: the singularity, a black hole represented in the form of their traditional granary.

In image form, on page 57 of *The Science of the Dogon*, Laird Scranton reproduces a comparison between the event horizon of a black hole and the Dogon granary, rendered in the form of Amma's Egg, Amma being the Dogon equivalent of Amun, the shape of which is identical to a diagram produced in Stephen Hawking's, *A Brief History of Time*. As Scranton observed, "The diagram provided by Hawking to describe the event horizon that is formed by the path of the light rays that are unable to leave a black hole is in most respects the very image of the Dogon stone representing Amma's egg."[47] Of course, this example of the singularity is the Dogon version of the power of the Nun.

Since their mnemonic prowess shows signs of an ability to transfer and maintain scientific facts in detailed form from ancient times, the importance of such knowledge and technology implies that it must have existed at such a remote time. Otherwise, why go to such extraordinary millennia long efforts to remember it at all?

Indeed, the present day Dogon are proof of a black African group having left the Nile valley for their current location in Mali prior to dynastic times, but although Robert Temple, in *The Sirius Mystery*, makes a brave attempt at validating the connection between the Dogon and the Nile valley culture by tracing their journey through the North African territory of the Garamantes, the people in the region of Libya from whom he proposes they gained their astronomical knowledge, it seems nevertheless that their journey was made even prior to the arrival of the Garamantes. As Laird Scranton has previously pointed out, the Dogon left the Nile valley before the invention and introduction of the symbolic writing system of the MeduNeteru and also prior to the addition of the five intercalary days that were added to the calendar.

As has been previously explained, two waves of black-skinned people entered the Nile valley in prehistoric times or, if the analysis of Robert Bauval & Thomas Brophy proves correct, at least at the approximate beginning of the Dynastic era. In any event, the research of Keith C. Seele already proves the existence of Nubian kings that predated the dynastic era and thus, as was mentioned in chapter one, "we now find two Nubian Dynasties, thousands of years apart, forming bookends that enclose the entire conventional history, as maintained by mainstream Egyptology, of ancient Egypt."

Thus, although Robert Temple errs in the origin of their stargazing knowledge when he states: "So here is some more light on how the Dogon and related Negro tribes of the Upper Niger came to possess their amazing information,"[48] he goes on to say, "It is a tale of thousands of years, and the drama was enacted across thousands of miles, which only seems suitable considering the nature of the message they were to carry into a much different world – the global village of late twentieth-century culture. According to the Dogon, 'the shaper of the world' visited the earth and returned to the Sirius system, having given men culture. Now that our race has set foot on another heavenly body and we are looking outward to our solar system, we are prepared to give serious consideration to any neighbours who might be within a few light years of us and have solar systems of their own which they inhabit and where they pursue their lives with the same desire to know, to learn, to understand, and above all to build a genuine ethical civilization, that motivates the best of us. For if they are not so motivated it is doubtful that they will have survived their own technologies. In love one can live, but without love there is no world that will not poison itself. One must assume that any creatures living at Sirius will have come to terms with a wholesome and vital ethic. If Sirius is indeed the home of a 'shaper of the world', then it may encourage us, too, to become shapers of worlds."[49] These latter comments by Robert Temple are incidentally somewhat reminiscent of the Zulu interplanetary claim, mentioned in chapter two, that they originated on Mars.

Be that as it may, as a result of the research conducted by John Ten, we know the power associated with the Ark of the Covenant existed prior to its use at the

Red Sea and the Jordan, as it was used centuries before to open a lake in order to retrieve a precious bracelet. Thus, since the Dogon have retained a recollection of the power of such a device, it would appear that it existed even before the Dogon left their Nile valley cradle to end up settling near the cliffs of the Bandiagara escarpment in modern day Mali.

Furthermore, this use of such a device implies the control of some form of an artificial singularity. This in fact is precisely what John Ten has inferred. "From my previous studies and from my physics concepts, I have come to conclude that for instance the black sun or the black crystal described in other civilizations may have been given by the sun god to humans as a very advanced technology like a little sun in a box, a singularity created artificially inside a stone or a crystal that contains *plasma dynamics spinning at high angular velocity generating a torque in space-time producing gravitational effects and energy effects.*

"If that is true, then you would expect that on the top and the bottom of that structure you would see vortices appear, columns of clouds, or columns of light, appear because of the high velocity of the space-time angular momentum along the side of that object. At the north and south of that object large vortices would be produced.

"There, if you want references, in Numbers 14:13 (it is stated) 'that you go before them in a pillar of cloud by day and a pillar of fire by night.' It is called the cloud above the tabernacle and it describes that vortex cloud above the tabernacle. There are chapters where the sons of Aaron get struck by the Ark of the Covenant and die and Moses is called into the tabernacle and instructed to never let anybody go in there without permission because the vortex of the Ark of the Covenant, if it is not dealt with appropriately, can kill. There are all sorts of things like that that happen in the Bible that are striking."[50]

At this point, what John Ten had said in chapter three with regard to the alleged 'stone' tablets that Moses brought down from the mountain should be recalled. According to him, "the original Bible did not describe stone tablets at all but rather crystalline objects made of sapphire with a di-hexagonal shape (and moreover) what the original text described as being in his hands were in fact sci-fi types of a crystalline structure that were hexagonal in nature."[51]

Indeed, many other such scientific anomalies have been left on the mountain at Sinai for posterity to ponder. As was stated in chapter one, "Sir W. M. Flinders Petrie made a monumental discovery" on the mountain of God. According to Laurence Gardner, what he found was "the alchemical workshop of Akhenaten and the generations of pharaohs before him."[52]

Interestingly, among the many items found at the temple at Serâbit el Khâdim, "the discovery of a metallurgist's crucible and a considerable amount of pure white powder concealed beneath carefully laid flagstones,"[53] baffled their explorers. Gardner reports on how "Egyptologists began to argue over why a crucible would have been necessary in a temple, while at the same time debating a mysterious substance called *mfkzt* (sometimes pronounced "mufkuzt"), which had dozens of mentions in the Serâbit wall and stelae inscriptions."[54]

As mentioned in chapter one, Laurence Gardiner had asked "why would there have been such an important Egyptian temple hundreds of miles away from the pharaonic centers, across the Red Sea gulfs at the top of a desolate mountain?" Indeed, in that same chapter, it was also concluded that, "this temple facility was clearly placed out of reach of the common people, like any modern military base." Clearly, such "top secret" goings on at this so-called "temple" facility necessitated such security restrictions.

It was on that same mount indeed that "a mysterious white substance was discovered and according to Exodus 16:15 "When the children of Israel saw it, they said to one another, It is *manna*, for they wist not what it was, And Moses said unto them, This is the bread which the Lord hath given you to eat.""[55] This divine *manna* of course was the 'mufkuzt' over which the aforementioned baffled explorers had debated.

Moreover, in *The Antiquities of the Jews*, "as compiled by the Jewish historian Flavius Josephus in the 1st century AD, Josephus explains that the manna was first identified when it lay upon the ground and "the people knew not what it was, and thought it snowed." He continues, "So divine and wonderful a food was this… Now the Hebrews call this food *manna*; for the particle man, in our language, is the asking of a question: What is this?"[56]

As Laurence Gardner demonstrates, by virtue of its unknown origin, "The sweet-tasting white substance which appeared around the mountain in the mornings and which Moses referred to as "bread" was, therefore, called *Manna* (What is this?)...The same question also appears in the Egyptian *Book of the Dead* – the oldest complete book in the world. Alternatively, known as the *Papyrus of Ani* (a royal scribe), this 18th-dynasty scroll from Thebes (acquired by the British Museum in 1888) is extensively illustrated and around 76 feet (over 23 m) in length. In this ancient ritualistic work the "bread of the presence" is called "schefa food," and the pharaoh seeking the terminal enlightenment of the Afterlife asks, at every stage of his journey, the repetitive question. "What is it?"

"Other *Books of the Dead* (though fragmented and incomplete) date back to the 3rd millennium BC, and it is clear from the Serâbit reliefs that the Egyptian kings were ingesting the white *manna* of gold from around 2180 BC. However, only the metallurgical adepts of the mystery schools ... knew the secret of its manufacture. These adepts were operational priests, and the High Priest of Memphis held the title of Great Artificer."[57] Intriguingly, as mentioned in chapter six, this latter title might well indeed refer to the "Artifact of Life," the highly technological device that Thoth possessed.

However the matter, "In old Mesopotamia the exotic white powder of gold and platinum group metals was called *shem-an-na*. In ancient Egypt it was *mfkzt*. Either way it was "highward fire-stone." Today it is recognized as a high-spin, single-atom substance for which the scientifically coined term is ORME (Orbitally Rearranged Monatomic Element)."[58] Incidentally, besides the necessity for the protection of the atmosphere of Nibiru, according to Zecharia Sitchin, the immortalizing properties found in powdered gold was one of the principal reasons the Anunnaki originally came to earth to mine for gold in southern Africa.

In his *Lost Secrets Of The Sacred Ark*, according to Laurence Gardner, besides life extension ORME has many 'high tech' properties including superconductivity and the anti-gravity power of levitation. For a deeper analysis of these subjects however it is recommended that the reader examine his chapters on this issue.

According to the Nile valley dwellers however, who were privy to such deep structure, esoteric knowledge, one of the primary functioning powers to emerge out of the singularity they referred to as Nun was Atum, the Sun God or Fire God, the self-generated creator of the physical universe. Indeed, Atum was the One, the first known and identified God in post flood recorded history.

Since the modern scientific interpretation of polarized cosmic microwave background radiation represents the oldest light in the universe, most assuredly its existence represents an allusion to the Neter Atum, who alone emerged from the Nun. Thus, if we entertain some Aristotelian reductionist thinking, the ultimate depth into this abyss we can go is found in the as yet unproven theory of gravitational waves. Indeed, the 1979 Inflationary Theory of theoretical physicist Alan H. Guth covers the trillionths of a second after the Big Bang, but the instance just prior to that latter event nevertheless still remains a mystery. Indeed, according to such critical theoretical considerations it took 380,000 years before atoms were able to congeal. Unfortunately, Guth's theory lacked the ability to predict how inflation stopped and thus the search for evidence of gravitational waves continues, as dishearteningly, the search for their signal turned out to be the result of cosmic dust. Thus, Nun still remains a measure that is yet to be fathomed.

As a mystical representation of that primary power however, born out of the eternal Present Moment, the symbolic metaphor that the natural creative imagination of the early African mentality specifically utilized for its demonstration was of a most basic human biological act. As the ultimate representation of virility, Atum accomplished this creative feat through the excitation of his metaphysical phallus.

Thus for the earliest description known to humankind of the creation of the universe, natural human male masturbation was the preferred symbolic metaphor. Indeed according to this understanding, that transcendental orgasmic ejaculation gave birth to the universe in an explosive climax of matter resulting in the separation of earth from heaven. For its Victorian discoverers however, such an explicit symbolic concept from Africa's natural approach to sexuality was far too graphic and shocking for the polite but hypocritical tastes of that day. A barrage of missionaries would have to be sent to put the lid on that! Metaphorically speaking however, to the sexually suppressed a violent Big Bang Theory of course is a far more preferable and non-biologically descriptive linguistic device!

The foregoing however raises the issue of the scientific extent of the ancient knowledge of biology. Indeed, this is precisely the case that Zecharia Sitchin affirms in his *Earth Chronicles* series of books, a matter also discussed in the works of Laird Scranton and Joseph P. Farrell.

According to Sitchin, ancient biological science is in fact attributed to Enki, the Ptah of the people of Khem, while Scranton reveals that, "the references within the [Dogon] myth to the idea of the word being woven into the cloth represent the chromosomes of DNA, which are the genetic words that are woven in the fabric of each cell."[59] Moreover, Scranton observes that the Dogon concept of Amma's Egg not only contained all the seeds of the forthcoming universe but also the seeds of human biological conception.

Indeed, as observed in chapter five, the potential origin of the *I Ching* may be found in the Ifa system of divination that travelled out of Africa through Mesopotamia and on to China. This subject is raised here because encoded within the mathematical structure of the Chinese divination system there is definitive scientific proof of the existence of biological knowledge in ancient times.

It was Gottfried Leibniz of course who was the first to make a connection between the western binary system, which he developed, and the eastern numerical system underlying the *I Ching* as conceived by one of "the great masters of Sung Confucianism, Shao Yung,"[60] whose "mathematical exactitude led him to work out a different *I Ching* table, in which he arranges the hexagrams in a natural system."[61]

This was an extraordinary synchronicity, as Sinologist Hellmut Wilhelm observed. However, in the interests of brevity and thus without going into the intricacies of his system, Shao Yung's schema "led to one of the most extraordinary episodes in the history of the human mind, and to this day it has never been satisfactorily cleared up. More than six hundred years after its origin, Shao's diagram fell in the hands of Leibniz through the agency of Jesuit missionaries, and he recognized in it a system that had previously sprung from his own mathematical genius. To facilitate the solution of certain mathematical problems, Leibniz had thought out the so-called binary, or dyadic, numeral system, which makes use of two numbers only, instead of ten, but otherwise follows the same principle as the decimal system."[62] A further interesting observation concerning this matter was that, "For a long time Leibniz had been trying to validate spiritual truths in mathematical terms, thus making them, as he thought, irrefutable. It is easy to imagine the enthusiasm aroused in him by the discovery of this correspondence."[63]

Indeed, this remarkable discovery would eventually lead to a direct correspondence between the "I Ching World Code and the DNA Life Code" and its connection to the organization of DNA as described by Crick and Watson in the mid twentieth century, lending credence therefore to evidence supporting the biological sophistication that existed in ancient times. Without going into detail and thus distracting the reader from the main purpose of this book, for those who want to see for themselves, Martin Schonberger's *The I Ching & the Genetic Code – The Hidden Key To Life* and Katya Walter's *Tao Of Chaos – DNA & The I Ching* are two highly recommended works.

For his contribution to this subject, in *Genes, Giants, Monsters And Men*, Joseph P. Farrell speaks of biological chimeras such as the "Sirrush" carved on the Ishtar Gate of Babylon, or of "alchemosexuality" in his and Dr. Scott D. de Hart's *Transhumanism* which ultimately imply an ancient understanding of genetic modification.

With regard to the latter, taking pride of place in the legends of the Land of Khem is the miraculous conception of Hor (Heru), or Horus as the Greeks named him. In fact, it is stated that Isis conceived her son Hor subsequent to the murder of her husband Osiris. Despite all mythological evidence to the contrary however, as will be shown in chapter eight the people of Khem had "no doctrine of a physical resurrection of the dead."[64] Thus, for Hor to be conceived after the death of his father there is only one way that that could have transpired, if this is not a myth. For such a miraculous event to have occurred at all however, like quantum theory, a deep knowledge of biology and genetic modification, as it is known today, had to have been available to the scholars of the ancients.

For a more intense examination of ancient biology however it is highly recommended that the works of the aforementioned authors on this subject also be consulted.

In scientific terms nevertheless, the ancient cosmological conception of the separation of heaven and earth or, as Schwaller de Lubicz described it, the

"Primordial Scission" whence One becomes Two, represented in fact the actual separation of matter from space, or as a modern quantum physicist would describe the phenomenon: a virtual particle emerges from and illuminates the void, just as the electron indeed emerges from the vacuum! The latter particle of course is a photon, a particle of light and since Atum was the ancient Sun God this Neter represented therefore the principle of Light.

As we shall soon see this quantum reaction indeed implies the necessity for perception, a factor that infers the preexistence of an intelligent mind. Indeed, as was stated in chapter five, "from a decoding of the very definition of the name Amun, who is also a manifestation of the Nun, Laird Scranton concludes that, "A literal and most understandable reading of the name of Amen might be, "that which draws or weaves waves into particles in a place hidden from interference.""[65]

As Schwaller de Lubicz pointed out, the discovery that most disturbs "the complacency of the "mechanistic" scientists is the "principle of the *quantum of action*, since the study of light shows the *simultaneous existence of two contradictory states*: the *granular* character in the *continuity* of a wave; that is, the photon, that looks like an isolated quantity, appearing in a continuous function of the wave – the discontinuous within the continuous. It is this simultaneity – that "cerebral" intelligence cannot grasp, but the existence of which is shown by experiment – that brings about what the physicist Werner Heisenberg calls the "Uncertainly Principle," which I translate here, psychologically, as the "Present Moment."[66]

Thus it can be safely assumed that the aforesaid knowledge discussed herein underlies the reason why the ancient inner sanctum astronomer-priest-scientists of Khem undertook the 2,000-year long construction of the magnificent Temple of Amun at Karnak. The stupendous undertaking of this symbolic masterpiece in stone, still standing in present day Luxor after approximately 4,000 years, also qualifies as being equivalent to putting a man on the moon as Welsh engineer Peter James remarked in chapter one with regard to the construction of the Great Pyramid.

By means of the methods of sacred geometry and therefore by means of its harmonic proportions, this grand holy structure, for multiple centuries the largest temple known to man, was designed to represent Comic Man and furthermore was a symbolic representation of the Virgin Birth. No historic physical mother necessary. This is *creatio ex nihilo*. Precisely what 20th century modern physicists saw when sub-atomic particles appeared seemingly out of nowhere, and what 21st century physicists find difficult to accept: that the ancients could have known this without electron microscopes. Such an argument represents a resonant echo of the one proposed by Carl Sagan concerning the Dogon's alleged inability to view remote macroscopic objects. Given that they did not have a 200-inch Hale telescope or some such other modern device at their disposal, the feat was thus deemed impossible. But they did have exact knowledge of binary star activity thus clearly there are other means of viewing the large and for that matter the small than those of modern-day technology.

In *The Cosmic Serpent − DNA and the Origins of Knowledge*, Switzerland based anthropologist Jeremy Narby, for example, has demonstrated that other means of seeing the invisible world had been available to so-called primitive people who had ingested *Ayahuasca*, a natural herbal hallucinogen of the indigenous peoples of Peru that facilitates glimpses into the subatomic realms of even the double helix. Though not hallucinogenic, the continent of Africa has its own visionary root, a source of healing power known as *Iboga* that also permits remarkable journeys into the realm of the invisible, to say nothing of its pharmacological ability to cure heroin addiction.

As emphasized in chapter two however, both Khem and Sumer were not civilizations that emerged from the trial and error of some alleged primitive nomadic or newly sedentary peoples but were in fact declining civilizations. Possibly the result of a second attempt, since the people of the Nile valley always referred to a more distant time called Zep Tepi which may well refer to the structures at Göbekli Tepe which were constructed about 12,000 years ago. Indeed, "the ancient megalithic site of Gobekli Tepe in Turkey ... is thought to date to a period around 10,500 BCE, about seven thousand years before the rise of the Egyptian civilization."[67]

With regard to this idea however, Laird Scranton has already indicated that such a possibility may be true. In the summer of 2010 for example, he states in his own words that he:

made an effort to acquire some understanding of the symbolism of that site. Turning to words and language as a likely point of reference, I learned that there are upward of twenty-five definitions in the Turkish language for the word *tepe* and that at least a dozen of these can be found under a similar pronunciation in the Egyptian hieroglyphic dictionary. I also noticed that many of the animal images that are carved in relief on the megalithic stones of Gobekli Tepe portray animals that have symbolic significance within our plan of cosmology. However, I was perhaps most intrigued with the images of animals that, in my experience, play no obvious cosmological role. Realizing that commonalities of language do seem to exist between modern Turkey and ancient Egypt despite their obvious separation in time by several thousands of years, I decided to look for linguistic clues to the symbolic role played by these animals and so turned to Egyptian dictionary word entries, hoping a symbolic reading of the names of these animals would offer me some new insight. What I discovered was that each Egyptian animal name was pronounced like an important term of cosmology.

The first implication of this discovery was that it provided me with a rationale by which to possibly explain the images on the megaliths. The Gobekli Tepe site dates to a time long before the first surviving evidence of any organized system of writing, which does not appear until around 3000 BCE. Gobekli Tepe is located in the same region in which the earliest historical evidence of cultivated grains are found, along with – somewhat later – the earliest known examples of metallurgy. Each of these practices constitutes an instructed skill associated with the Dogon civilizing plan. The megalithic stones at Gobekli Tepe offer perhaps the earliest example of skilled stone masonry, which is yet another of the civilizing skills associated with the Dogon plan.

If we accept the view of the Dogon priests that civilizing concepts, tagged to their system of cosmology, were deliberately taught to humanity in ancient times, then the concurrence of these same skills in the vicinity of Gobekli Tepe could suggest that a much earlier attempt at civilizing instruction had been made. I knew that this possibility was supported by the documented belief in ancient Egypt in a mythical First Time, which was referred to as Zep Tepi. If our supposition were true, then the animal images found on the Gobekli Tepe megaliths could represent a very early type of protowriting, set down mnemonically in the images of animals..."[68]

Of course, Göbekli Tepe was not evidence of the original paleoancient civilization that Joseph P. Farrell referred to but, as Scranton reveals in the above analysis, was the first attempt at civilization in the Post Flood era. In any event, these legacy civilizations of Khem and Sumer were at their height from their very beginnings and only began their slow and clearly inevitable deterioration with the loss of the scientific knowledge and philosophy that had been previously bestowed on them by a preexisting civilization, some remnants of which appear on the plains of southern Africa as potential evidence of its existence before being destroyed by the Flood.

Of course in Western tradition, with regard to the realm of philosophy and science, much has been attributed to classical Greece. Many before me nevertheless have tackled this issue and in my opinion quite successfully. As such I do not wish to burden the reader with a repetition of these arguments but merely to highlight some of their aspects.

As far back as 1954 for example the African-American author George G. M. James made a brave attempt at unraveling the knowledge that Greece "inherited" from the Black land in his book *Stolen Legacy*. Part of James' well-articulated argument revolves around the Memphite Theology carved onto the Shabaka stone that was mentioned in chapter one with reference to *The Nubian Pharaohs, Black Kings on the Nile*. On this stone is found a text that describes the creation of the universe by means of the word. Basically, the origin of St. John's "In the beginning was the word..." as recorded in the Bible.

For the Shabaka Stone, the Neter that created the universe with his word was one of the Neteru named Ptah, a representation of Mind, while the other was Atum, who was activated by the word of Ptah. As the ancients said: *Through the uniting of the heart and tongue of Ptah creation occurs.*

As discussed earlier with reference to the electron emerging from the vacuum, such a reaction requires the perception of an intelligent mind. For mankind's earliest philosophers Ptah was that mind, Atum, the reactionary material response in the form of light.

Given that no vowels were used in the MeduNeteru, the original glyphs for Atum of course only included the consonants TM, and thus any of the five vowels could theoretically speaking be used to assist in the spelling of this name of the power of the creator of the physical universe. Indeed, since George G. M. James is making the point that the structure of the atom was already known thousands of years prior to the so-called discoveries of Leucippus and Democritus, he deliberately spelled the name of Atum as Atom.

Indeed, George G. M. James regards the Memphite Theology as the source of modern scientific knowledge by asserting that Atom "together with the Eight Created Gods composed the Ennead or Godhead of nine: a very striking similarity with modern science which teaches that there are nine major planets."[69] A condensed synopsis of the cosmology and philosophy of the ancient land of Khem that he expressed in *Stolen Legacy* reveals that:

> Atom (Atum) the Egyptian sun God who is the Logos of Heracleitus, the Demiurge of Plato, and the Unmoved Mover of Aristotle creates eight other Gods by projecting them from His own body, thus producing nine Gods of the Ennead. This is identical with the Nebular Hypothesis of Laplace, in which the original Sun creates the nine major planets of modern scientific belief.

Schwaller de Lubicz would no doubt agree with George G. M. James that the Greeks were in fact "the children of 'Egypt.'" As the cover sleeve of his book states: In "*Sacred Science: The King of Pharaonic Theocracy*, the author demonstrates how the thought of the Egyptian sages was altered by the Greek philosophers in their approach to basic metaphysical problems. This was *the beginning of purely rational thinking and the origin of the great deviation toward materialism from the predominantly spiritual aims of ancient times*. The exclusively rational mentality of our age is oriented toward the acquisition of technological data and its utilitarian application, and this unbridled search for new invention hones man's egotism, leading him to destruction. Opposed in the extreme is the pharaonic mentality based on a knowledge of causes and their genesis." (Italics added.)

Atum, being the Neter of the Sun God or Fire God, was therefore symbolic not only of the microcosmic atom but representative of the macrocosm in which He embodied the sun at the heart of our Solar System. As above, so below!

Nevertheless, it was the voice of Ptah who proclaimed: *Let there be light!* And the essence of voice of course is vibration. Throwing a pebble into a pond for example vibrates its surface sending rippling waves that radiate out in concentric circles from its point of entry. This two-dimensional phenomenon however contrasts with what occurs when a sound or musical tone is produced. Describing a three-dimensional process, the opening words of St John's Gospel, "In the beginning was the word..." are in fact a reflection of the knowledge the ancients inscribed on the Shabaka stone which indicated their comprehension of the fact that the "word" is a sound that "spreads in spheres...,"[70] as Rene Schwaller de Lubicz so demonstrated in *The Temple of Man*. By this he meant that the people of the land of Khem understood that sound expands into volume, concentric spheres of varying densities, that determine the vertical axis (the earth has one, e.g.) and the two dimensions of the horizontal plane.

This is the fundamental hypergeometric description of the Virgin Birth of the universe, the manifestation of Atum from Nun, that provides the source for Plato's geometric solids, the most basic and stable of which is the tetrahedron. Indeed, even the human soul is described in spherical terms in the Kabbalah, as will be discussed in chapter eight.

Though one often sees in print that ancient Greek mathematical skill is derived from Babylon, many others make the same claim for the land of Khem. Among the ancients who corroborate this view, "Clement claimed that Plato became the disciple of an Egyptian priest Sechnuphis of Heliopolis. When Strabo toured Egypt in the first century BC, he was shown the places where Plato and the Greek mathematician Eudoxos had supposedly lived and studied. It was the Egyptian knowledge, particularly the "knowledge of Thoth", which he incorporated as the cornerstone of his Platonic Academy which he founded in Athens in 387 BC."[71]

Lest the reader think that the foregoing has nothing whatsoever to do with the Bible, the following should be of great interest. Indeed, as delivered in his YouTube video lecture, John Ten came to the conclusion, after intense biblical research, that the Catholic Church had not appropriately interpreted the Old Testament's concept of the Hebrew God at all. Indeed, from the research he discovered, it described God in such a way that it peeked his interest as a geometrician. For instead of some guy on the throne waiting for him to screw up, there was some kind of equilateral triangle seated on a throne.

Thus, it had to do with geometry. In his own words he said: "I was stunned by the fact that he wasn't an old man considering me as a sinner but was some kind of geometry that was described as the throne of God, the point of interaction between human and God… I was kind of surprised. That's not what I had remembered and I continued to study it and realized that the Old Testament is ambiguous because [it] described God not as something that's somewhere in the sky or anything. It described God as an object. It describes that they had some kind of link or communication with God through an object that they called the Ark of the Covenant of God."[72]

From the many descriptions and illustrations of the Ark, John Ten drew the conclusion that it was a capacitor since it was "a box which had gold on the outside and gold on the inside and wood in the middle."[73] Immediately, he realized that it has got to be a capacitor and indeed, if you were to make a box like that you can generator large capacitance.

Since they can hold energy, capacitors are like batteries but the difference between them is that "a capacitor can discharge extremely rapidly where a battery cannot."[74] Therefore, capacitors are used in all sorts of electronics today. But basically they are an apparatus of electrical plates that create a container for energy. Intriguingly, the large Ark capacitor "was described as having a sphere or something in the middle of it that was very radiant."[75] He observed that they described how they had to shield themselves from it and they had to wear very specific clothing to go in (the Ark room) and that if they didn't they would come out of there with a sunburn. Basically like burnt into their face and so on.

After considering that they are calling this object the Ark of the Covenant of God, John Ten wondered, what then does God mean? Thumbing through the preface of his Bible, he serendipitously stumbled on the answer, stating that, "It says ... that the name Yahweh, the divine name Yahweh, YHWH is currently ... viewed in Greek terminology as the Tetragrammaton,"[76] going on to say:

> Now for a guy like me when you are reading one of the most sacred books on the planet, I guess, and the person is describing God, and the translation is Tetragrammaton, ok, I'm starting to have ideas. I was stunned. Imagine that! Every time you read the word God in the Bible you could translate [it as] Tetragrammaton. So you could replace all the Gods and Lords in the Bible [with] Tetragrammaton. Then you get a completely different reading. Ok. It's like, Oh my Tetragrammaton!
>
> And so I looked at the etymology of this and I thought well the word Tetragrammaton is typically, if you look at the root word, the tetra refers to four, the four faces of a **tetrahedron**. Typically the translation is then done as tetra for four, grammaton for grammar and grammar or letters are interchangeable and so it is the four letters of God: Yahweh, YHWH. But grammaton was what was intriguing me.
>
> So I [dug] a little deeper and I found that actually the word grammaton has a deeper root than grammar in which it refers to the weight of an object. And that is where the word gravity and gram (came out of). So all of a sudden you could have a different interpretation of this as tetrahedron gravitation, right, something along those lines. I know that might sound, you know, a long leap but this was where I started and I was really keen on continuing my research because it was promising. They were talking about tetrahedrons or a triangle on the seat of God and they were describing tetragrammaton as the *force* of God. I was getting you know inspired to say the least.[77]

Thus, an equilateral triangle, as a representation of the three-dimensional tetrahedron mentioned in chapter four, sits on the throne of God whose name YHWH, in the form of the tetragrammaton, represents the *force* of God.

Indeed, among those pre-Euclidean Platonic solids is also found the twelve-sided dodecahedron. In fact, as a result of spherical action all five of those basic and fundamental geometric forms are created from the vibrations of the physical medium. Moreover, the vibratory pattern that forms the dodecahedron also causes and thus influences the double helix pathways that guide the strands that determine the shape of the DNA molecule.

Where the five Platonic solids are concerned however, there is no argument that Plato derived his concept from the works of Pythagoras who in turn obtained them from the system of Spherics that evolved out of the Sacred Science of the people of Khem.

One of the modern scholars to revive this ancient understanding of the metaphysics of space was the prince of mathematics Carl Friedrich Gauss. After he published *The Fundamental Theorem of Algebra* in 1799 he developed a hypergeometric matrix for the description of the "real" universe, a new mathematical concept that conforms to something he called "the Complex Domain."

According to Gauss, the Complex Domain is a hypergeometric phenomenon that "combines the notion of the seen object with the notion of the effect on its motion (the orbit of Mars for example) generated by the unseen but efficiently manifested principle."[78] Thus, he provides a geometrical formulation of how our single but multidimensional universe actually functions.

Thus with his Complex Domain, Gauss determined a mathematical interpretation of the Nun out of which the physical world is projected. In other words, it is a mathematical representation of the invisible world, the Spiritual realm or unseen world, where unseen objects, otherwise not available to the five senses, are defined by the noetic power of the human mind as objects of thought, hidden principles, of which there are potentially an infinite number. This indeed is a modern interpretation of what the ancient people of the land of Khem referred to as Neteru.

Thus, after stating that "universal physical principles and their relationship to objects of sense perception arise in the mind as thought objects,"[79] *the true subject* of physical science, Kepler follower Bernhard Riemann, in his 1854 *Habilitation Dissertation On The Hypotheses That Lie At The Foundation Of Geometry,* described a similar functional process. His original concept of Geistessmassen or Dirichlet's principle, later described as "thought-objects," is therefore another classical example of the function of the MeduNeteru, for as Joseph P. Farrell has demonstrated, "a hieroglyph is much more than a *symbol* of the physical medium, *it is an actual operation and manifestation of it*."[80] Indeed, Laird Scranton has most emphatically demonstrated that "the basic structure of the Egyptian language ... conforms in nearly every respect to ... string theory, quantum theory, and atomic theory."[81]

On a much more metaphysical level however, Bernhard Riemann in fact refers to the soul as a compact thought-object, a subject that will be broached a little later in chapter eight. Of course, it is from the hidden powers within the Nun that Plato derived his notion of powers. However, the concept of powers, as German philosopher Gottfried Leibniz demonstrated, is a concept derived from the African conception of Neteru that the ancient Greeks identified in the unseen, but very real and knowable mental and physical forces that determine activity in the physical world. Indeed, according to Bruce Director, the primary author of the acclaimed series *Riemann for Anti-Dummies*, Plato directly establishes the Grecian debt to Egypt in the *Theaetetus* and the *Timeaus* through recognition of the fact that the "power which creates a square or a cube is an action in the universe, an action knowable to the mind, but not reducible to the sense-certainty numbers of the visible domain."[82]

These forces or principles moreover are also considered to be *intentions*, examples of the very same powers that Plato and other pre-Euclidian Classical Greeks referred to as 'dynamis' (pronounced 'doonamis'). However the priest instructors of Khem had their own name for these "powers." They were none other than the Neteru.

Thus many, if not all, of the representations in image form found in the MeduNeteru were indeed what some modern arithmeticians and geometricians describe as thought objects or processes, or universal physical principles. That is, manifestations as such of the actual intentions of ATUM. Indeed, quoting Serge Sauneron from his book *The Priests of Ancient Egypt*, Laird Scranton highlights the fact that the MeduNeteru are "a resonant echo of the vital energy that brought the universe to life."[83]

Of course, Atum is the ancient name for God. However, it is often remarked that Laplace once said he had no use for such a 'hypothesis' and thus modern mechanistic science maintains that God is a mere projection of mankind's infantile need for a father figure. Needed for proof of such a patriarchal hypothesis however, atheistic, empirical, positivist and reductionist research is itself a futile study in search of the most fundamental material piece of matter situated at the root of physical reality. Such puerile research is devoid of any knowledge of quantum activity which validates the ancient understanding of the Virgin Birth, the photon of light, the electron, the Atum, which appears out of nowhere after the contemplation of Ptah whose transcendental mental act is at the foundation of creation.

Of course, the High Priests of the Nile Valley were well aware of this fact and thus maintained their faith in that origin of Reality Absolute throughout the entire lifetime of the great civilization of the land of Khem. Unfortunately for mankind, out of the patriarchal belief system that was foisted onto that matriarchal civilization however came the permanent division of mankind, as a direct result of philosophical monotheism. Indeed, that is the very purpose of the divisive mechanism of monotheism.

Like the mechanistic science that Laplace represented, a natural corollary of that patriarchal belief system is also atheism. Thus, the atheist argument against the Supreme Being, which refers to God as He or Him, imposing on Him a human personality (the old man with the white beard) against which they argue when they declare that "He" does not exist, is easily winnable. Of course, they win the argument but it is *their* fantasy that does not exist for "He" indeed is not 'a personality' but 'The Personality' of which our own individual personalities are but infinitesimal reflections.

Of necessity, the Supreme Being did not make of us robotic automatons, as some, if not all, mechanistic transhumanists believe, but rather as co-creators with the power of 'free will,' a force that allows us the possibility of deviating from the perfect model that the Supreme Power represents. By such means however, the power of choice opens up the door to the potential path of evil allowing free reign to the rampages of the Shemsu Seth.

As a traumatic consequence of Akhenaten's ill-fated suppression of the metaphoric power of the Neteru, the West has become, as Rene A. Schwaller de

Lubicz poignantly disclosed, distressingly "ignorant of that serenity of which all of ancient Egypt bears the imprint.

"The tombs of the leaders of this people are consecrated to their profession of faith in the survival of the soul. For these men, to die is the certitude of living again. Terrestrial life is merely a passage; the mortal body is a temporary temple for the living soul."[84]

As was said in ancient times, *through the uniting of the heart and tongue of Ptah creation occurs and both Ptah and His creation Atum are the embodiment of Life Energy.*

"The West labels this attitude of Wisdom a state of science that is "still mystical." But the Egyptian technique and their symbolic attest to a realistic sense and to faculties of reasoning, contradicting the view held that this epoch is "a primitive, mystical" age."[85]

Western misinterpretation of eternal truth aside, the root of such misunderstanding can nevertheless be traced. To the advantage of the alien patriarchal and oligarchical powers he knowingly or unwittingly represented, it was the vital understanding of that ancient wisdom that Akhenaten's edicts of "Thou Shalt Not!" were designed to suppress.

This meant the total destruction of the Sacred Science. Though pronounced through the commanding mythological voice of the God of the biblical Moses, the effect of those decrees, which deprived humanity of essential and crucial knowledge concerning the Afterlife, efficiently and inevitably held back the progress of physical science until the early reinvigorating soulful stirrings of quantum theory, which validated the necessity for a cognitive observer, re-emerged in modern times.

Eight

———————

THE DUAT

*There is a single universe characterized by a tendency to
create higher states of organization and existence.*

BRUCE DIRECTOR

Over time the knowledge of the Sacred Science eventually deteriorated and
gradually degenerated into mere religion. This however was not entirely
due to the natural processes of decay but rather to a malignant attrition caused
by the introduction of alien Babylonian ideas, most particularly those enforced
during Akhenaten's sacrilegious rebellion.

Indeed as observed in chapter six, Joseph P. Farrell, after focusing on the
falsifying role of the 'veritable ministry of false truth,' came to an academically
revolutionary conclusion that the Yahwist religions "carry the implicit imperative
to rewrite human history from the prophetic and apocalyptic point of view."[1]

Thus, as a consequence of its negative portrayal in the biblical text, the Land
of Khem became "not only the symbol of the "Other" ... but also of the rejected
past and its cultural systems."[2] Indeed, included in this degradation was the rel-
egation of the Sacred Science to a mere cult of idolatry, a misguided denigration
that would ultimately set the West on a different path to the rest of humanity.

Indeed, given that Laird Scranton discovered a connection to the ancient African concept of the Duat (Tuat) and the Chinese concept of the Dao (Tao) it is therefore not surprising that, as Terence McKenna perceived, "We in the West are the inheritors of a very different understanding of the world. Loss of connection to the Tao has meant that the psychological development of Western civilization has been markedly different from the East's. In the West there has been a steady focus on the ego and on the god of the ego – the monotheistic ideal."[3] Moreover, McKenna draws attention to the point that "Monotheism exhibits what is essentially *a pathological personality pattern* projected onto the ideal of God: the pattern of the paranoid possessive, power-obsessed male ego."[4] (Emphasis added.)

Indeed, isn't the foregoing psychological analysis the most explicit description of the patriarchy that has dominated the Judeo-Christian religion if not indeed the entire Yahwist tradition with its built-in divisionism for the past three thousand years?

Prior to Akhenaten's insane and devastating onslaught however, the pre-biblical sanity provided by the Osirian mythic complex of African consciousness had remained in place and at its height for extensive millennia. Indeed, as E. A. Wallis Budge commented in chapter one, "In the divinity and immortality of the god-man Osiris lay the strength of the power with which he appealed to the minds and hopes of the Egyptians for *thousands of years*" and moreover we were informed that "both these conceptions of Osiris are of *purely African origin* ... [from a time] ... long before the Dynastic Period in Egypt." (Italics added.)

As evidenced from the intricate and sometimes exquisite artwork painted on the walls of Nile valley tombs, those ancient Africans clearly believed that life and its most exceptional faculty, consciousness, indeed continued beyond its current physical expression. Such devoted artistic pronouncements notwithstanding however, was this merely a puerile expression of a superstitious, primitive mentality that modern scientific man with his mechanistic technology has finally and inevitably disposed of or, to put it another way, is there really such a thing as immortality?

Regarding the concept of heaven as a metaphysical matter of faith only, the West's critical exegetical analysis of it however has completely succeeded in discrediting its reality. Nevertheless, with respect to the ontological validity of things spiritual, according to the late Phillip Coppens, "The presence of consciousness as a vital ingredient to the universe, separate from the body (non-local) is what quantum physics has been trying to make Mankind aware of for several decades."[5] Indeed, it has become imperative to ask what was so appealing about the Afterlife that the ancients would provide such a detailed and vivid description of the so-called underworld, the metaphysical realm they named the Duat?

Remarkably, Laird Scranton sees in this detailed ancient concept of the Afterlife "the Dogon Second World of matter, which we equate to the Egyptian underworld, and which is referred to in Egypt as the Tuat, or Duat."[6] Indeed, given quantum theory's insistence on the coalescence of physics with psychology, could the ancient concept of the underworld be a euphemism for what modern psychology refers to as the subconscious? Indeed, did the latter psychological concept predate Freud's discovery of it by thousands of years?

Regarded as the vessel that contains primordial matter in its wavelike state, the Neter Nun for the people of Khem was recognized as the singularity, the source of everything and therefore the location of the Duat. Thus life, having been lived as a consequence of that source, retains the possibility of returning to it in a more evolved "higher state of organization" within the wavelike substance of the Nun, more evolved, of course, only for those who had lived an ethically exemplary life.

According to modern empirical secularists, atheists and other skeptics however, the argument for immortality of course is null and void for in their view there is no ontological actuality to such a concept as divinity for the empiricists have convinced themselves of the misguided fact that a deceased human being is nothing more than a slab of meat. This because they believe that consciousness is a mere epiphenomenon of the biochemical activity of the brain and thus are further convinced of the alleged fact that states: "when you're dead, you're done!" Such radical reductionist thinking however aside, neither they nor spiritual believers for that matter, despite the many legends that claim Osiris, Jesus and Lazarus returned from the dead, can apparently be sure of that conclusion for as the common adage goes: "no one has come back to tell us!"

As indicated that conclusion of course is only apparent, as throughout the 20th and now 21st centuries a growing abundance of literature on near death experience has made a sudden and dramatic resurgence. The author of *The Canopus Revelation – Stargate of the Gods and the Ark of Osiris* for example believed that during the long period between 30,000 and 3,000 BC the African ancestors of the people of Khem monitored near death experiences for the purpose of interpreting them. Indeed, it is the opinion of Phillip Coppens that "this collective knowledge of the "soul" was then written down in what we call *The Book of the Dead*."[7]

Remarkably, such modern NDE accounts in fact also reflect a story recorded in Book Five of Plato's *Republic* that Socrates once told. This was the story of "Er, the son of Armenius, a Pamphylian by birth. He was slain in battle, and ten days afterward, when the bodies of the dead were taken up already in a state of corruption, his body was found unaffected by decay, and carried away home to be buried. And on the twelfth day, as he was lying on the funeral pile, he returned to life and told them what he had seen in the other world."[8]

Indeed, the present day experience of American neurosurgeon, Dr. Eben Alexander showed him that "the death of the body and the brain are not the end of consciousness, that human experience continues beyond the grave. More important, it continues under the gaze of a God who loves and cares about each one of us and about where the universe itself and all the beings within it are ultimately going."[9]

Since these words come from the exacting hand of a neurosurgeon perhaps we who all have a stake in this claim should now take note. Moreover, given that he claims that life "continues under the gaze of a God who loves and cares about each one of us," one wonders whether Eban Alexander was in fact in the divine presence of the Neter Osiris?

Although referred to in general as the 'Lord of the Dead,' for the people of the Land of Khem however, Osiris (Wsjr, Asar), often depicted as green in colour, was known as the ""Lord of Love," "He Who is Permanently Benign and Youthful" and the "Lord of Silence.""[10] Thus, one wonders whether the Islamic poet Rumi was inspired by this verdant vision of Osiris when he wrote the words "Love is forever green, without spring, without autumn."[11]

Be that as it may, whether Dr. Alexander visited the Duat or not is as such open to question. Nevertheless immediately after making such an assertion, he claimed in his own words that, "The place I went was real. Real in a way that makes the life we're living here and now completely dreamlike by comparison. This doesn't mean I don't value the life I'm living now, however. In fact, I value it more than I ever did before. I do so because I now see it in its true context."[12]

Thus, given their profound knowledge of that "true context" and given their quantum theory understanding of the causes of genesis, in addition to their interpretation of the MeduNeteru as symbolic images designed as psychotronic objects that "manipulate not only the consciousness of their observer, but also of the physical medium itself,"[13] as Joseph P. Farrell proposed in chapter seven, and this all combined with the archetypes found in the myth of Osiris, it would not be a step to far to say that those ancient Africans also had an acute knowledge of the inner world of the psyche. Indeed, particularly with regard to the "divine" concepts of the Ba and the Ka, archetypal spiritual elements that preceded Freudian and Jungian understanding of the subconscious and its psychological archetypes by millennia, which may even be, as psychotronic objects, at the root of why some people believe in angels.

Indeed, as mentioned in chapter one, *when you enter the realm of Osiris you enter the realm of African consciousness and witness the mythological archetypes of the African mind.* In point of fact, as was stated previously, Osiris was the African God *par excellence.* In fact, He is the first God in recorded history that was killed, resurrected, and granted eternal life.

Moreover, in the rites and legends of the people of Khem Osiris became, and perhaps still is, the divine judge every living soul faces after death. Being the ruler of the underworld, as the Duat is considered in mainstream Egyptology, The "Hidden Place," or rather the "first floor level" of Amenta as Gerald Massey described it, must therefore be the location of the Hall of Judgment, so eloquently described in *The Book of the Day of Coming Forth Into The Light*, where every soul has to confess its sins.

In the tradition of the people of the land of Khem however, prior to entry into the Osirian 'kingdom' that exists within and beyond the light, the recitation of a series of confessions had to be recited in order to allow deceased supplicants an entrance into life eternal. This test included the *42 Negative Confessions* deemed necessary for entry into the Duat, the paradise the Greeks later referred as the Elysian Fields.

Scrolls of papyri bound in the wrappings of ancient mummies were in fact extracts containing these confessions, MeduNeteru inscriptions that also included the necessary rules, regulations and directions for safe passage that their Arab discoverers however referred to as pages from *The Book Of The Dead*. To the ancient Africans on the other hand, as has already been mentioned, these were pages from *The Book of the Day of Coming Forth Into The Light*. Indeed, as is stated in so many modern anecdotal cases, the majority of near death experiencers eventually see a light in the darkness that exudes a sense of warmth and love.

As has been stated before, Laird Scranton puts a great deal of faith in E. A. Wallis Budge's *An Egyptian Hieroglyphic Dictionary* because of its closer affinity to its African roots which he observed in his comparison of glyphs from the ancient MeduNeteru with the symbols current day Dogon people continue to use to describe similar phenomena. By a similar comparative juxtaposition, a related situation also occurs between Budge's translation of the *42 Negative Confessions* and that of Gary Greenberg.

Knowing that multiple interpretations can be deduced from the glyphs of the MeduNeteru which, in any event, are analogical symbols that contain a complex deep and surface structure, it is not surprising that discrepancies would occur as a consequence of the esoteric transformational grammar underlying various authors' deep structure interpretations of these confessions. That said however, there does not appear to be a complete one-to-one surface structure comparison between the two versions provided by Greenberg and Budge.

With regard to *Negative Confession 21* for example, Greenberg proposes, "I have not committed fornication, and I have not committed sodomy,"[14] whereas Budge interprets this particular confession as, "I have not stolen the offerings of the spirits."[15] In fact, Greenbergs' translation of this confession is not found in any of Budge's translations. Moreover, Budge refers to a second form of the 'Negative Confessions' as well "in which the deceased addressed a series of Two and Forty gods by their names, one after the other, and asserted before each, that he had not committed a certain sin."[16] *Negative Confession 21* in this series states, "Hail, Heri-seru, coming forth from Nehatu, I have made no man to be afraid."[17]

With reference to these 'Negative Confessions,' many of which incidentally are the source of the biblical Commandments given to Moses, while Budge states that this "series of statements was made by the deceased when he entered the Hall of Osiris, i.e., before his heart had braved the ordeal of being weighed in the Balance,"[18] more interestingly with regard to the subject of this book he identifies this "gate-keeper" process with African traditions.

The modern Africans in question were the Calabar tribes-people of the Cross River State of coastal southeastern Nigeria. Indeed, an interesting aside concerning the latter identified people is that it was a Calabar merchant seaman, Henry Bassi, who was responsible for providing Wales with the extraordinary voice that belongs to his famous daughter Dame Shirley Bassey who was born in Tiger Bay's Bute Street in 1937.

Long before Ms. Bassey's birth however, at the time E. A. Wallis Budge made his comparison with her father's people, they were still performing a similar ritual, which substituted the weighing of the heart with the drinking of *Mbiam*, a drink made of filth and blood. In fact, Budge said, "The Egyptian acted exactly as does the modern African. The former made his declaration of innocence of a series of offences, and his heart was weighed by the gods to test the truth of his words; the latter makes his declaration of innocence, and the action of the Juju drink tests the truth of his words."[19]

In contrast to the view of African traditional religion and thus that of the ancient Nile Dweller, Dr. Eben Alexander explains that: "The view of human consciousness held by most scientists today is that it is composed of digital information – data, that is, of essentially the same kind used by computers. Though some bits of this data – seeing a spectacular sunset, hearing a beautiful symphony for the first time, even falling in love – may feel more profound or special to us than the countless other bits of information created and stored in our brains, this is really just an illusion. All bits are, in fact, qualitatively the same. Our brains model outside reality by taking the information that comes in through our senses and transforming it into a rich digital tapestry. But our perceptions are just a model – not reality itself. An *illusion*..."[20]

Indeed, like the shadows on the wall of Plato's cave, our sense perceptions are illusory figments projected nevertheless by an efficient unseen but *very real force*. Thus, despite what Aristotle has to say, the invisible is nevertheless knowable to the human mind. Modern man on the other hand has lost sight of this fact because of his love affair with mechanical technology. As Wilhelm Reich observes, "All the notions man has developed about himself are consistently derived from the machine that he has created. The construction of machines and the use of machines have imbued man with the belief that he is progressing and developing himself to something "higher," in and through the machine. But he also invested the machine with an animal-like appearance and mechanics. The train engine has eyes to see with and legs to run with, mouth to consume coal with and discharge openings for slag, levers, and other devices for making sounds. In this way the product of mechanistic technology became the extension of man himself. In fact, machines do constitute a tremendous extension of man's biologic organization. They make him capable of mastering nature to a far greater degree than his hands alone had enabled him. They give him mastery over time and space. Thus, the machine became a part of man himself, a loved and highly esteemed part. He dreams about how these machines make his life easier and will give him a great capacity for enjoyment. The enjoyment of life with the help of the machine has always been his dream. And in *reality? The machine became, is, and will continue to be his most dangerous destroyer, if he does not differentiate himself from it.*"[21]

Thus, it is now obvious that human society has reached a critical stage in its evolution. Indeed, in order to progress we are now required to look backwards and become reacquainted with our long suppressed pre-mechanistic noetic powers. As Schwaller de Lubicz pointed out in chapter seven, "our present scientific methods" must "move directly into a science with spiritual dimensions" because "the achievement of a sacred science requires a transformation of mind which would considerably alter our relationship to knowledge and its expression." Indeed, the realm of quantum interaction requires that the West reacquaints itself with the Dogon Second World of matter, or what the people of the Black land referred to as the Duat.

Like everything else in the universe of course, the so-called metaphysical realm of the Duat, the underworld to which recently deceased supplicants desire entrance would have to exist in or beyond the vibratory and hypergeometrical domain of the Nun, which from his unique mathematical bent of mind Carl Friedrich Gauss referred to as the Complex Domain, Bernhard Riemann the geometry of metaphysical space, Joseph P. Farrell the **not digital** but analogical underpinnings of the physical medium, Werner Heisenberg the uncertainty principle, and finally what Rene A. Schwaller de Lubicz referred to as the Absolute Reality, the Eternal Present Moment.

These ratifying deductions of the truth of the nature of our single but multidimensional universe by physical scientists of the 18th, 19th, 20th and now 21st centuries is quite sobering and brings to mind the pertinent biblical statement of eternal fact: *In my Father's house there are many mansions there. If it were not true, I would not have told you so.*

With firsthand knowledge at his disposal no less, Eben Alexander declares that he felt like "a citizen of a universe staggering in its vastness and complexity, and ruled entirely by love,"[22] describing moreover that "The entire length and height of the physical universe is as nothing to the spiritual realm from which it has risen – the realm of consciousness (which some might refer to as "the life force")."[23] Indeed, this is an interesting observation since the ancients claimed that *both Ptah and his creation Atum are the embodiment of Life Energy.*

Coming from such a credible source as neurosurgeon Eben Alexander, *one who has come back to tell us*, it appears that his brief sojourn in the Duat was an example of a well understood phenomenon known in the past, as is evidenced from "The oldest surviving treatise on the Kabbalah … called *The Zohar* ("The Book of Splendour"), written about 1275 by the Spanish Jew Moses of Leon. According to *The Zohar*, Kabbalism taught that **the soul could ascend temporarily into heaven during life on earth**. This was done by practising a form of mediation through which the different parts of the mind were understood, brought under control of the will and balanced one against another. In this way the soul could elevate itself into the realm of *Kavod* – 'glory'."[24] (Bold type added.)

According to Graham Phillips, "The Kabbalists view the soul as a series of spheres or *sefiroth*, one successively around the other like the layers of an onion. The outermost sphere was *Kether*, the realm of God, and the innermost was

Malkuth, the physical body. Between these were the eight spheres, which each corresponded with an aspect of the human mind. By moving the will progressively outwards through these spheres, one could join directly with the divine spark."[25]

Describing that very house of "many mansions" mentioned above, the artwork on the inside walls of Nile valley tombs, as mentioned previously, represented as such veritable pictures of life as it had been lived on earth, with depictions of labourers in the fields or the hunting of birds near the riverbank. Such descriptions led many Egyptologists to suggest that the vision of heaven that the people of Khem believed in was logically inspired by their daily life on earth. Thus from an empirical perspective: a logical projection of the desire for their earthly pleasures to continue after death.

From the neurosurgeon's description of his visit to the Duat however this view may well be undermined, opening the door for another reality to be surmised for while in his coma with no functional access to the neocortex of his brain Dr. Eben Alexander found himself in a very dark place for some period of time before something gradually appeared in that darkness:

> Turning slowly, it radiated fine filaments of white-gold light, and as it did so the darkness around me began to splinter and break apart.
>
> Then I heard a new sound: a *living* sound, like the richest, most complex, most beautiful piece of music you've ever heard. Growing in volume as pure white light descended, it obliterated the monotonous mechanical pounding that, seemingly for eons, had been my only company up until then.
>
> The light got closer and closer, spinning around and around and generating those filaments of pure white light that I now saw were tinged, here and there, with hints of gold.
>
> Then, at the very center of the light, something else appeared. I focused my awareness, hard, trying to figure out what it was.
>
> An opening. I was no longer looking *at* the slowly spinning light at all, but *through* it.
>
> The moment I understood this, I began to move up. Fast. There was a whooshing sound, and in a flash I went through the opening and found myself in a completely new world. The strangest, most beautiful world I'd ever seen.

Brilliant, vibrant, ecstatic, stunning ... I could heap on one adjective after another to describe what this world looked and felt like, but they'd all fall short. I felt like I was being born. Not reborn, or born again. Just ... born.

Below me *there was countryside. It was green, lush, and earthlike. It was earth* ... but at the same time it wasn't. It was like when your parents take you back to a place where you spent some years as a very young child. You don't know the place. Or at least you think you don't. But as you look around, something pulls at you, and you realize that a part of yourself – a part way, deep down, – does remember the place after all, and is rejoicing at being back there again.

I was flying, passing over *trees and fields, streams and waterfalls*, and here and there, people. There were children, too, laughing and playing. The people sang and danced around in circles, and sometimes I'd see a dog, running and jumping among them, as full of joy as the people were. They wore simple yet beautiful clothes, and it seemed to me that the colors of these clothes had the same kind of living warmth as the trees and the flowers that bloomed and blossomed in the countryside around them.

A beautiful, incredible dream world ...

Except it wasn't a dream. Though I didn't know where I was or even *what* I was, I was absolutely sure of one thing: this place I'd suddenly found myself in was completely real."[26] (Emphasis added.)

From the detailed picture so vividly described in the foregoing, it appears that Eben Alexander travelled through a portal. Like Alice falling down the rabbit hole, he apparently traversed what theoretical physicists call a wormhole, a gateway between our current physical existence and the hypergeometrical domain that exists beyond it. Therefore, he tore a hole in, and thus bridged, the widely separated regions of space-time.

In *The Elegant Universe* however, Brian Greene asks whether wormholes exist or not and whether it is possible to tear the fabric of space-time but disappointingly he responds by merely saying that: "No one knows."[27] Interestingly, however, the crux of the idea is that one can travel through such a gateway as, hypothetically, "the wormhole creates a new region of space . . ."[28] and in doing so ". . . creates new space and therefore blazes new spatial territory."[29]

Neil M.C. Sinclair

A wormhole or gateway, hypothetical or no, of course is nevertheless a portal and as Richard Hoagland said in chapter seven, "When we look at stars . . . we're seeing portals to another dimension."

Notwithstanding the foregoing, given that this American neurosurgeon, who apparently did bridge the Great Divide, was convinced he *really* flew over a beautiful landscape the ancient tomb wall paintings of farming and hunting activity in the countryside they depict may well indeed be indications of a true reflection of the life to come that the people of Khem expected to experience in the Afterlife, not the one just lived as the empiricists contend.

This evidently well-entrenched and persistent belief of a *real* place may very well be a remnant genetic memory from a time when human beings first gained access to the other world after the ingestion of hallucinogenic mushrooms whilst living on the plains and savannahs of ancient Africa more than 50,000 or perhaps more years ago.

Whatever the case, since quantum action requires an intelligent, conscious observer that observer within each of us would of necessity have to be the soul. Indeed, what the influential German mathematician Bernhard Riemann has to say in his *Habilitation Dissertation* about the soul will soon be reviewed in depth as promised but suffice for the moment to understand how Riemann explains the role of thought, a fundamental essence of soul:

> With each simple act of thought something enduring, substantial enters into our soul. This substantial thing appears to us indeed as a unity. However, it appears, in so far as it is the expression of a spatial and temporal extension, to contain an inner manifoldness. Hence, I call this a thought-object. [30]

Thus for Bernhard Riemann thought has an inner structure, a hypergeometric manifold which he describes as some form of Gestalt. Indeed, this idea has an ancient provenance, as in the *Timaeus And Critias* Plato reports that, "The material of the soul is mixed and given the appropriate mathematical structure." [31]

As will be shown, Riemann's analysis of the imperishable, thus immortal and enduring, quality of thought-objects is quite intriguing and indeed supportive of the ancient's concept of the immortality of the Ka and the subsequently evolved

Ba. For the ancients, the former was a kind of shadow body, an electromagnetic essence that is similar in shape to the physical form, while the Ba, which has the body shape of a bird, indicating volatility and flight, combined with a human head, in fact comes into existence only when a person dies.

Indeed, "the Ba was never considered to be one of the constituent parts of a human composite, the "spiritual" element in man or the "soul" of man, but was considered to represent the man himself, the totality of his physical and psychic capacities,"[32] so stated Louis V. Zabkar in the introduction of his book, *Study of the Ba Concept in Ancient Egyptian Texts*. More specifically, he proclaims that the "Ba is the personification of the vital forces, physical as well as psychic, of the deceased, his alter ego, one of the modes of being in which and as which he continues to live after death,"[33] and moreover signifies "either the manifestation of the power of a being or a being whose power is manifest."[34]

Whether this is a mere theoretical analysis of the soul on the part of Zabkar or whether he believes what is stated in *The Pyramid Texts* or not is uncertain. Nevertheless, the intricate psycho-geometry of the soul as just described will be probed a little later on. For the moment however, at this point a return to the biblical text is necessary because many of the so-called patriarchs it speaks of are in fact reinterpretations of *thought-objects* derived from *mythological archetypes first conceived in the soul of the African mind*.

Therefore, the question is asked: Do you believe in God, the Creator of the world and all in it, and in resurrection and in immortality? If you do, whether you know it or not, your mind has already accepted an ancient African philosophy referred to by Egyptologists as the Osirian mythic complex.

Indeed, as part of that so-called mythology, the deities featured in *The Contendings of Horus and Seth* for example are derived entities that came directly out of African consciousness, as previously mentioned in chapter four. Moreover, with regard to the belief system of the people of Khem, E. A. Wallis Budge indicated to a Victorian world audience that:

> two fundamental, indigenous beliefs stand out in it clearly, namely, the belief in
> God, the Creator of the world and all in it, and the belief in a resurrection and
> in immortality. The student who views the Egyptian Religion from the lofty

standpoint of spiritual Christianity only may say that it was gross polytheism or pantheism, that *Egyptian rites were cruel, bloodthirsty, and savage*, that the legends of the gods are childish, and are the outcome of debased minds and imaginations, that the story of the resurrection of Osiris is a farrago of nonsense in which absurd magical ceremonies play an impossible part, and that heaven of the Egyptian was only an imagination of a people who always remained half savage. Nothing, however, can alter the fact that beneath such rites, and legends, and beliefs there lay the wonderful religious and moral conceptions ... and *the unchanging, persistent beliefs in the resurrection of the righteous and in immortality*. It seems to be a mistake to estimate the Egyptian Religion from the standpoint of the highly civilized Asiatic, eastern or western, or European, for it is an African product, and can only be rightly appreciated and understood when considered in connection with what we know of modern African religion."[35] (Italics added.)

At a time when the Nun and the MeduNeteru were yet to be completely decoded and understood, Budge, of course, was attempting to enlighten a sophisticated Victorian and Edwardian public much inflated with the strain of imperial superiority that interpreted ancient African scientific terms as mere magical tricks. It was not known at that time, that the MeduNeteru were "connected much more directly to the physical medium than just by being products of it, by dint of the fact that the medium ... is analogical in nature, that is, that everything produced within it by a process of repeated differentiations still retains some signature of its original archetype, especially in terms of any overlapping *functions* shared between any of the psychotronic objects – if we may use that term as magical talismans or objects to manipulate not only the consciousness of their observer, but also of the physical medium itself."[36]

Here indeed is an exciting example of Heisenberg's quantum interaction taking place on the level of human understanding. As discussed in chapter seven, "the study of light shows the *simultaneous existence of two contradictory states:* the *granular* character in the *continuity* of a wave; ... It is this simultaneity – that "cerebral" intelligence cannot grasp, but the existence of which is shown by experiment – that brings about what the physicist Werner Heisenberg calls the

"Uncertainly Principle,'" which Rene A. Schwaller de Lubicz translated as the "Present Moment."[37]

Thus the entities found in the so-called myths, and in particular the Osirian mythic complex, were in fact representations of psychotronic objects that connect the seen with the unseen, Riemann's thought-objects. Thus, that is the method defining therefore how the syntax of symbols of the MeduNeteru should be understood and interpreted.

As Gary Greenberg said in chapter six "the core elements of patriarchal history derive from Egyptian myths and the family of Osiris."[38] Indeed as stated in chapter two, from the stories recited in *The Contendings of Horus and Seth,* he also observed that as they revolved around birthright he saw reflected in them the struggle of Jacob and Esau, two biblical patriarchs who have been transformed from Horus and Seth into historical, though fictional, characters of the Bible. As described in chapter two, this is the Horus and Seth who fought that great battle on African soil in the land of *Ta-Khenn*, Nubia.

Moreover, in the aftermath of Akhenaten's heresy, Greenberg most pertinently noted that, "Since Osiris could no longer be openly worshiped, the images associated with his body were transferred to Jacob and his family."[39]

Therefore, the sacred entity who emerged directly out of African consciousness that was Osiris was made profane and subsequently transformed into a sacred biblical but faux historical figure. Ever since the human representative of the Supreme Being has been represented by Jacob. Thus, Jacob, as one of the results of Akhenaten's edicts, replaced Osiris!

Incidentally, Cain and Abel may well be reflections of the other struggle that took place between Osiris and his brother Seth where the latter slew the former as Cain slew Abel. With the exception of Phillip Coppens who observed that "in a Cain and Abel parallel, Osiris was the good brother, Seth the murderer,"[40] and the rabbi brothers Sabbah who state "Seth appears in the Bible as Cain, Adam's son who murdered his brother Abel,"[41] to my knowledge, this issue has never been discussed or written about but I believe it begs further examination.

Nevertheless, given the preceding remarks, surely this marks the earliest result of the first attack on the ancient African belief system and its Sacred Science, providing thus more proof that the biblical stories are rewritings of

African legend and history. Indeed, Jacob is not the sacred historical figure the biblical text would have us believe.

Rather Jacob represents in fact the de-transfiguration of the Neter Osiris, a now defiled and desecrated but still divine entity taken directly out of ancient African consciousness.

Thus in myth Jacob replaced Osiris. However, if on the other hand Jacob *was* historical, as Ahmed Osman contends, who then was his physical African counterpart? The question is therefore, who then was the father of Yuya, the actual historical counterpart of Joseph? Unfortunately, though he hailed from the 'Upper Egyptian' town of Akhmim, such investigation will have to continue on, as according to Wikipedia, "His origins remain unclear."[42]

In contrast to what has been discussed with regard to Jacob however, his grandfather, the patriarch Abraham, the Father of the people of Ra and Amun is in fact, according to Ahmed Osman, another reflection of the historical Akhenaton, as the rabbi brothers Sabbah also concede. While for Gary Greenberg, on the other hand, he *is* Ra! That is, another divine and therefore sacred element of the ancient African imagination.

In discussing the issues expressed in *The Contendings of Horus and Seth*, Gary Greenberg reveals that, "There are several intriguing parallels between the story of Abram and the story of Re. In the Egyptian story Re supports the claim of Set while the other gods support the claim of Horus; in Genesis Abram supports the claim of Ishmael but God favors Isaac. In both stories we find the Set supporter on the ground laughing. In both cases the laughter results from an implied sexual act, in Abram's case with Sarai and in Re's with Hathor. In both stories, each leader falls to the floor almost immediately after declaring a preference for the older brother's claim."[43]

Maintaining his historical perspective however, Ahmed Osman emphatically infers that "Isaac was to be looked upon as Abraham's true heir. It was through him that the glory of the Hebrew tribe would be fulfilled and Israel would be born, of his seed that kings would rule *from the Nile to the Euphrates*."[44] Interestingly, the latter sentence seemingly appears to represent or rather confirms in fact a greater extension of the Red land as far as modern day Iraq. (Italics added.)

Be that cartographical issue as it may, controversially, Osman questions whether Isaac was in fact Abraham's biological son, as the following elaborates: "Abram and Sarai made their initial journey down to Egypt at the time, more than a century after the end of the Hyksos rule, when Tuthmosis III (*c.* 1490-1436 B. C.), the sixth king of the Eighteenth dynasty, was on the throne. It was he who married Sarai and fathered Isaac, the son born to her after the couple returned to Canaan. On the death of Isaac, the elder of his twin sons, Esau, sold his birthright – the title as a prince of Egypt – cheaply to the younger one, Jacob, from whom it passed to his son, Joseph. It was Tuthmosis IV (*c.* 1413-1405 B. C.), the eighth king of the Eighteenth Dynasty, in residence at Thebes and ruling over the precise area – from the Nile to the Euphrates – referred to in the promise to Abraham about his seed, who appointed Joseph as his vizier after he had been sold into slavery in Egypt and had successfully interpreted the king's dreams. The king invited Joseph's family to settle in Egypt and offered them land at Goshen in the eastern delta, remote from the court, a frontier region which, as Alan Gardiner has put it, was already used to 'an infiltration by Palestinians glad to find refuge in a more peaceful and fertile environment'. Joseph and his wife continued to serve Amenhotep III, the next Pharaoh, who broke with Egyptian tradition and, although he married his sister, instead of making her his queen, married and gave the title to Joseph's daughter, Tiye. He also gave her Zaru, the former Avaris of the Hyksos, dominating the land of Goshen where her Israelite ancestors were allowed to settle, as her own city."[45]

Since it is being contended here that the patriarchs are not historical figures but recreations of archetypes derived from African mentality as expressed in the Osirian mythic complex, there is much therefore to unravel here, particularly in the conflation between biblical myth and historical fact.

On one hand, the evidence shows that Tuthmosis III is indeed fact and, moreover, Osman's interpretation certainly brings a measure of legitimacy to the historicity of the biblical Isaac. On the other however, Abram may well be historical or alternatively a psychotronic device. Nevertheless, should Osman's historical position be accepted then remarkably Tiye would be the granddaughter of Isaac and great granddaughter of Sarai and Tuthmosis III.

Indeed, as was mentioned in chapter three, "if Osman's assertions prove true, Yuya's rise to power through the marriage of his daughter to king Amenhotep III is a better explanation of the rise to power of Joseph than the untenable biblical version of him as a mere interpreter of dreams, especially ones with ancient motifs already familiar to the people of Khem." Now we are presented with a further and quite clear reason for the biblical Joseph's high position in African society in that his daughter was in fact the great grand-daughter of Tuthmosis III.

These facts of course do not invalidate the possibility that the biblical Abraham, as an historical personage, is not conflated with aspects of the Neter Ra. Nevertheless, Abraham, Isaac and Jacob are more than likely all Neteru. Indeed, as Gary Greenberg emphatically stated in chapter six, "the core elements of patriarchal history derive from Egyptian myths and the family of Osiris."[46]

Thus we are not only dealing with an ancient mythic African family, but with the psychotronic comprehension of the functional aspects of quantum reality, where the ancient concepts of the Ba and the Ka were understood to be active and manipulatable psychological symbols that have the ability to journey to "The Land of the Hidden One," through the "first floor level" of the "Hidden Dwelling" and other multiple dimensions of the Duat. They are of course the intangible yet psychologically substantial things that Bernhard Riemann described as "thought-objects" that contain an imperishable inner manifoldness of spatial and temporal extension.

Before examination of Riemann's psycho-geometric concept of the soul and its immortality however, at this time it should now be pointed out that the in-fantile notion that it revivifies the deceased physical body it once governed is not what the ancients meant by the everlasting life of the Ba.

According to the alleged 'insignificant' opinion of Gerald Massey, "The Egyptians had no doctrine of a physical resurrection of the dead. Though they retained the mummy as *a type of personality*, it was a changed and glorified form of the earthly body, the mummy that had attained its feet in the resurrection."[47] As things stand, "The resurrection of the dead in mummy form may look at first sight as if the old dead corpse had risen from the sepulchre. But the risen is not the dead mummy, it is a type of personality in the shape of the mummy."[48] Thus,

"There is no possible question of a corporeal resurrection...[49] and therefore it is entirely false to represent the Egyptians as making the mummy and preserving it for the return of the soul into the old earthly body. That is but a shadow of the true idea cast backwards by Christianity"[50] for indeed the fact is "the earthly mummy was left on the earth outside the gates of Amenta."[51]

Thus, with that explanation we are now in a more correct position for a scientific description of the immortality of the Ba, as expressed by the founder of Riemannian geometry. As a caveat, it is suggested that the reader read the following slowly for Riemann assures us that:

> The soul is a compact thought-object bound together in the most intimate and most manifold way. It constantly grows by the introduction of new thought-objects and upon this rests its further development. Once formed the thought-objects are *imperishable*, their blending indissoluble. Only the relative strength of their unions is changed by the addition of new thought-objects.
>
> Thought-objects require no material carrier for their continued existence and exert no lasting effect upon the world of phenomena. Thus they stand in no relation to any part of matter and consequently have no position in space. On the other hand, all beginning, generation or formation of new thought-objects and all unification of the same requires a material carrier. Hence, all thinking comes to pass at a determined place.
>
> Thought is a process within ponderable matter. Our external experience, the facts of our external perception, which must find their explanation in the processes within ponderable or gravitating matter, are: (1) universal gravitation; (2) the universal laws of motion.
>
> Something lasting underlies each act of thought, something which however is manifested only under the specific occasion of memory as such, without exerting any enduring influence upon phenomena. Therefore, with each act of thought, something lasting enters our soul, something which exerts no enduring influence upon phenomena. On the other hand, our external experiences about ponderable matter can be explained, if it is assumed that *a homogenous substance fills the whole of infinite space* and constantly flows into ponderable matter and vanishes."[52] (Italic added.)

Thus, according to Bernhard Riemann, the soul composed of thought-objects is *imperishable* and intimately connected to the whole of infinite space. It was Riemann, of course, who provided the hypergeometrical mathematical structure that inspired Albert Einstein to formulate the Theory of Relativity, the *sine qua non* of quantum theory.

Indeed, this is quantum interaction *par excellence*. In fact, "Einstein's protégé, American physicist David Bohm, felt that quantum theory suggested the existence of **a deeper reality** than the one presented by our senses. He dubbed the *implicate order* an undivided holistic realm that is beyond concepts like space-time, matter, or energy. In the implicate order everything is fully enfolded or entangled with everything else. By contrast, the *explicate order* world of ordinary observations and common sense, emerge, or unfold, out of the implicate order."[53] (Bold added.)

Indeed, as did the influential Bernhard Riemann, did not the black African priest/scientists of Khem have a concept of a homogenous substance that "fills the whole of infinite space?" Most assuredly, they did. This is the physical medium that they precisely identified as the Nun, the source of the creation of all things and the unquestionably inevitable ontological location of the Afterlife: the realm of the Duat.

Epilogue
A Cosmic Revelation

The Babylon system is a vampire, falling empire,
Sucking the blood of the sufferers.

BOB MARLEY

When the white man came, he had the Bible and we had the
land. He taught us to pray with our eyes closed. When we
opened them, he had the land and we had the Bible.

OLD AFRICAN SAYING

Although Greece was initially believed to be the cradle of Western civilization, Western society now takes pride in finding its roots among the practices of the people of the Nile valley. With the discovery of the forgotten civilization of Sumer however, Egyptology soon began expanding the idea of the West's origin to include a de-Africanized Nile valley culture.

Despite such efforts however, and in spite of its allegiance to a Judeo-Christian theology, the cultural traditions of Western society are, in any event, not in fact a reflection of the peoples of the Land of Khem by any means and therefore are not derived from African culture but rather are a continuation of the inhumane economic cultural practices of Asiatic Babylon, a patriarchal society that employed exploitative methods that at the time did not exist in the ancient African land of Khem.

Therefore bringing an end to the longevity of such a harmonic matriarchal civilization, as did exist on African soil, proved to be an enormous and indeed historically multi-generational task. The ceaseless incursions of the Asiatic armies and the battles fought against them particularly by Ramses III for example, demonstrated to the Babylon inspired despoilers that the Land of Khem was not to be won by military force. To overcome this civilization, it would have to be eroded from within. Thus as the research of Joseph P. Farrell affirms, to expedite the take over of the sacred civilization the Sacred Science had to be undermined in order to make way for the exploitative system that Babylon had engendered and which moreover flourishes to this very day in its ubiquitous manifestation of neo-liberal economic regimes of privatization and deregulation that, despite the pure mendacity of corporate media mass brainwashing, to the contrary are in fact wrecking havoc throughout the world.

As stated in the Preface, "The starvation we witness in Africa on a daily basis is the consequence of an ongoing historical exploitation." Indeed, citing the Famine in India as a different historical colonial example according to Nick Dearden of Global Justice, who appeared on the March 3, 2015 edition of *Going Underground* with Afshin Rattansi, the UK has a long history of enforcing free market economic policy conditions.

As to the current situation in Africa however, it has been observed that despite the philanthropy of the likes of those such as Bill Gates, there is chronic and ubiquitous malnutrition even though there is an abundance of food, most of which however is exported to the global market, because the neo-liberal economic free market system fails to deliver within the continent itself. Ironically, as discussed in chapter four, on a micro-economic scale, this was the state of affairs in ancient Akhetaten.

Indeed, Bill Gates and his ilk are pioneering promoters of intensification farming methods which, knowingly or unwittingly, are designed to benefit GM Food conglomerates, particularly at the expense of the wider African populous.

Thus, it would appear that systemic exploitation is intrinsic to the monotheistic tradition and thus the incidental State Terrorist killing of unarmed descendants of the people of Khem currently living *in the ghettos, inner cities and slums across the four corners of the earth*, or their incarceration in the West's prison industrial complex is not an accident.

Although the worldwide multiethnic 'Black Lives Do Matter' reaction to such atrocities is a positive reassurance that humanity does care, one nevertheless has to understand the true nature of the dangerous and psychotic mentality behind Patriarchalism and the inevitable exploitative imperial consequences that of necessity it engenders.

Under such patriarchal regimes, it manifests as a genocidal policy, especially for those victims who are 'fifty shades' of non-white. Though based on biblical text, the origin of its current manifestation however is to be found in the deeper recesses of Anglo-American parliamentary history.

Instilling the idea that "the ideal relationship was between a father and his son to indicate the "mutuall trust and Confidence" which was always necessary to the State,"[1] in *Patriarcha* (composed in the late 1620s), parliamentarian Sir Robert Filmer used "genealogy as a way to legitimize kingship, by tracing the throne's origins back to the original fatherly rule of Adam."[2] Moreover, Filmer argued that the king *is* the father; the relationship is not one of similarity, but of identity, the right of fathers having been passed down genealogically since Adam."[3] Of course, the State that Filmer is referring to *is* the Babylonian State!

As mentioned in chapter four, Wilhelm Reich asserted in *The Mass Psychology Of Fascism* that, "The son-father relationship, which we find in every patriarchal religion, is only the inevitable socially determined content of religious experience." Thus, this socially determined relationship is based on Filmer's interpretation of the Bible, which is a falsification of African history and a text that, as contended here, is in fact a reinterpretation of that history. Indeed, as was demonstrated in chapter two, it would even appear that Akhenaten is the prototype for the biblical Adam.

Throughout this text however, the guiding hand of the scribes who manufactured the current version of the Holy Bible has been exposed. Moreover,
the sacred unmentionable name of God, the Jehovah of the Bible, has also been
uncovered and identified as Yahu along with its associated derivations of YHWH,
and the Tetragrammaton. Indeed, the rabbi brothers Sabbah demonstrate that
"The Tetragram (that contains the Hebraic name) Yahwe is composed of the root
Yahu, Pharaoh's name, and of *Heh*, the divine breath,"[4] the very same Yahu who is
also the Jah so revered in the Rastafarian religion.

Indeed, this name has been etymologically traced back to one of the five
names in the pharaonic titles of the Afro-Asiatic king Amenhotep III, and of the
subsequent members of his dynasty, Akhenaten, Smenkhare, Tutankhamun and
Ay, historical entities who originated and lived in Africa, like many other figures
of note, for more than a 1,000 years before the Bible texts upon whose history
they are based were compiled. Moreover, some of the major biblical patriarchs
have also been traced to Africa's holiest family as recorded in the Osirian Mythic
complex and other sources found written in the MeduNeteru.

Indeed, culled from the very depths of African consciousness, some of the
African historical and mythological personages who have undergone a biblical
metamorphosis into legendary Hebrew characters of the Holy Bible are noted
below for reference:

Yahweh (YHWH)	=	Yahu, Amenhotep III
Adam	=	Atum, Aten, Akhenaten
Eve	=	Nefertiti, Isis
Cain	=	Seth
Abel	=	Osiris
Noah	=	Osiris
Abraham	=	(Father of the peoples of) Ra & Amun. Also Akhenaten
Jacob	=	Horus, Ra & Osiris
Esau	=	Seth
Moses	=	Akhenaten
Aaron	=	Horemheb

Joshua	=	Sety I
Joseph	=	Yuya
Sarai	=	Hathor, Nebetnehat
David	=	Pa-Seba-Ka-En-Nuit (Psusennes II)
Solomon	=	Pharaoh Sheshonq I (Shishak)

As highlighted in the list above therefore, some of the major characters of the biblical text have clearly been extracted from historical aspects of African history. If it is not long enough however to convince the reader, it is nevertheless the beginning of a process of revelation designed to spur curiosity for others to seek out further valid comparisons.

Indeed, as described in chapters one and two, the struggle between Jacob and Esau had been identified with the battle between Horus and Seth that occurred in ancient and possibly prehistoric times. Fortunately for humanity however, Horus was the victor and saviour of the age, in essence the warrior Messiah, the prototype for Jesus Christ and the avatar of the One who is yet to come.

In any event, I have done my level best to make the case. Besides, with regard to the "out of Africa" position diligently presented in this work, the rabbi brothers Sabbah have successfully demonstrated that "The similarities between the bible, the oral tradition, the commentaries of the sages, and Egyptian history, *testify to the existence of a first Hebrew Torah*, now lost. It revealed the history of the Yahuds. The Yahuds, so as not to lose the memory of their past, wrote down in their sacred book the tale of the exodus from Egypt **as they had lived it** in the latter days of Akhet-Aten. Modified from century to century, depending on the dominant kings and gods, the Torah became progressively a Mesopotamian history of the Hebrews."[5] (Italics and bold added.)

Nevertheless, the rewriting of Khemite history by the 'ministry of false truth' had not gone unnoticed even in ancient times, for there were indeed those who complained about this practice: "How can you say, 'We are sages and the Torah of Yahwe is with us?' Yes, but the false pen of the scribes had made a lie of it.'"[6] (Jeremiah 8:8). Or as *The New King James Version* of the Bible translates this verse: "How can you say, 'We *are* wise and the law of the Lord *is* with us?' Look, the false pen of the scribe certainly works falsehood."

Indeed, as even the infuriated prophet Jeremiah implied, it is now clear that "The original Torah was the history of ancient Egypt, reported by the Yahuds."[7]

Therefore, the truth of this radical reinterpretation of the Holy Bible, as presented in this work, can nevertheless only by undermined if the information gathered herein out of the history of the land of Khem is categorically proved false. That task of course is for the reader to decide.

In the meantime, it must be presumed that an alien infiltration and imposition of monotheism had been perpetrated on African soil by means of an ancient Babylonian conspiracy ultimately designed to replace the Sacred Science of an otherwise stable society. That indeed was the chosen methodology for the destruction of the Holy Land, the true "Land of God."

Remove one of the primary fundamental building blocks of the ancient civilization and its calculated eventual collapse would be inevitable. Indeed, this was the purpose for the imposition of monotheism in the first place, as it was a well thought out tool for the undermining of the long-lived Land of Khem.

Thus, in the form of a divisive theological instrument that still generates dissension in the world to this very day, monotheistic patriarchal sophistry was to be the malevolent esoteric Babylonian tool for the destruction of such a successful theocratic society as that that existed in ancient times on the banks of the river Nile.

Indeed, is it really a coincidence that the holy name of Isis, the Queen of Heaven, the mother of Africa, the Madonna and the prototype for the biblical Mary, has recently been denigrated as a result of its acronymic use by another battalion of monotheistic persuasion, the barbarous military cult currently rampaging across the Fertile Crescent?

As most Muslims are inherently peaceful however and "thus don't receive much mainstream news coverage,"[8] the *Nexus Magazine* of February and March 2015 proposed the pertinent question of who exactly is "actively funding (creating) extreme versions of Islam?"[9] According to Duncan M. Roads, its editor, "the most extreme forms of Islam, including Wahhabism, have *massive* funding behind them. Qatar, the United Arab Emirates and Saudi Arabia actively fund, train and promote this extreme version of Islam. They pour *billions* of dollars into mosques that preach *their* form of extremism. They fund and train the "preachers as well as those who become suicide bombers. They, *along with their allies* in the intelligence communities of the UK, USA, France and Israel, created ISIS and Al Qaeda specifically to conduct extreme acts to put on TV, so that we in the West support the USA in its resource wars."[10] (Penultimate italics added.) Indeed, as discussed in chapter three, the British origin of that resource war policy was traced to Sir Halford John MacKinder.

As a consequence of its centuries long power and influence over the common masses however, the plutocracy, the group the millenarian youth movement calls the one percent, wallows in its sociopathic hubris. But for how long do they think *We The People*, and particularly those Bob Marley identifies as the 'black survivors' on his album *Survival* who are *suffering on this earth in the ghettos, inner cities and slums across the four corners of the earth*, will continue to sleepwalk through history? Indeed, for how much longer will Mother Earth's youth bear this oppressive yolk? How long before the sun rises in the West, as was prophesized in 1974 by African-American jazz musician Doug Carn when he composed *Western Sunrise* for his album *Adams Apple?*

As Joseph P. Farrell and Scott D. de Hart stated in chapter six, "The three Great Yahwist religions – Judaism, Christianity, and Islam - are all alchemical techniques of the social engineering of mankind into permanent division." Or alternatively, as one of the foremost essayists of the USA Gore Vidal prefers: into 'perpetual war for perpetual peace.'

In fact, such divisiveness is undoubtedly at the root of racism as well as sexism. However, the scourge of racial discrimination can hardly be considered genetic but it does have, like sexism, an ancient pedigree in patriarchal monotheism. In essence, anti-African bias will never desist so long as Westerners, *whatever their ethnic origin*, continue to subscribe to and follow the ambiguous and false morality embedded in *their* monotheism.

Indeed, the intrinsic mendacity of Western culture and civilization has wrought untold psychological damage to the descendants of the progenitors of the Nile valley civilization, the 'black survivors' of ancient Africa. Indisputably, the global situation has only gotten worse with 'black on black' killing (which doesn't mean 'white on white' killing has ceased), unscrupulous drug dispensing and, with no little assistance from the so-called intelligence services of our 'secret governments,' other corrosive activities that have infiltrated modern day ghettos where the majority of black people apparently live, in spite of the Civil Rights, Black and Proud, and Consciousness Raising movements of the 1960s. In point of fact, racism has become ever more intensified, insidious and endemic and will continue to be so as long as patriarchal monotheism remains the basic tenet that underlies the psychological ethos of Western civilization.

Of course, the current talk in the political circles of the West is not about the chronic failure of patriarchal monotheism and its 'free trade liberal economic monetary system' but instead of multiculturalism. Somehow it appears the 'Other' has failed to adjust to prominent Western values, British values no less.

British values? What be those, one wonders. Indeed, is it not a curious fact that in British soap opera type historical genre dramas such as *Upstairs Downstairs* and the internationally successful *Downton Abbey* for example, there is no mention or attempt made to explain the source of the aristocracy's inordinate wealth, their elevated position is merely taken for granted. The appearance is given that the upper classes somehow inherited a kind of divine status. Nevertheless, the murky source of that opulent lifestyle had a most definite insidious and very corrupt origin in an abhorrent industry that made possible the stately homes of the so-called British aristocracy.

In *Britain's Forgotten Slave Owners*, a two-part BBC documentary aired during the month of July 2015, its narrator, Nigerian born David Olusoga, has finally and once and for all clarified the source of their affluence and equally as important, exposed the racist origin of current anti-black opinion, rampant at home and abroad, as being founded on the argument British slave owners used in their effort to counter the abolition of their inhumane industry.

To the credit and the shame of the British parliamentary system however the slave owners lost the argument for the diabolical continuance of their murderous and abysmal trade as it was forever abolished in 1834, at least in legal terms, only however as a consequence of a compromise that compensated them with a shocking bailout of the equivalent of £80 billion in today's money. Though that latter financial rescue package, the resources of which indeed funded the Industrial Revolution and thus the future prosperity of Britain, faded from the memory of the general public and thus history, the anti-black African arguments and the incorrigible racist opinions that were provoked during the parliamentary debate in support of the slave owner's dastardly cause have nevertheless continued to thrive unabated.

Since the latter widespread sentiments have been persistently held so dear in the hearts of certain elements within British society, these, I would say, are what are meant by British values. Inevitably however, the maintenance of said false ideas has consequences, as the truth of the matter concerning those core British values is of course found in the fact that the more the 'Other' attempts to integrate into these so-called 'higher cultural values' the worse the 'Other' gets treated.

Moreover, there is no getting away from the fact that English as a consequence of the policy of British Free Trade, a trade indeed that was bolstered by the lucrative but immoral earnings from its legalized though nevertheless homicidal slave trading activity, has become the global lingua franca. However, for Africans who have given up their native tongue and their names both in the time of slavery and colonization and indeed in this era of rampant consumerism, it is time to reclaim their languages because it was their ancient tongue, the MeduNeteru, the very language modern quantum physics is currently in need of, that spawned the earliest civilization upon which the modern world is based.

In the meantime, is this materialistic and institutionalized form of monotheism, particularly the sophisticated form that culminated out of the British imperial paradigm, "not the "false temple," that Rene A. Schwaller de Lubicz was referring to in chapter seven? Is this not the "false religion, which is based, not on the Spirit, but on perishable matter and the science of its destruction?" Indeed, with regard to the current social dilemma it has generated, is this monotheistic patriarchal ideology not in fact the true foundational source of Western culture?

In contradistinction to any form of cultural expression that emerged on the African continent however, "For all the successes of Western civilization, the world has paid a dear price in terms of the most crucial component of existence – our human spirit."[11] As has been shown in previous chapters, Dr. Eben Alexander arrived at that foreboding conclusion after returning from the sojourn his Ka had made in the Duat, during the near death experience that the separation of his consciousness from the neocortex of his brain had made possible.

Furthermore, Eben Alexander reflects on the fact that "The shadow side of high technology – modern warfare and thoughtless homicide and suicide, urban blight, ecological mayhem, cataclysmic climate change, polarization of economic resources – is bad enough. Much worse, our focus on exponential progress in science and technology has left many of us relatively bereft in the realm of meaning and joy, and of knowing how our lives fit into the grand scheme of existence for all eternity."[12]

While emphasizing the fact that in "the West there has been a steady focus on the ego and on the god of the ego – the monotheistic ideal,"[13] as has been previously stated, Terence McKenna in his book *Food Of The Gods*, also astutely recognized that "Monotheism exhibits what is essentially *a pathological personality pattern* projected onto the ideal of God: the pattern of the paranoid possessive, power-obsessed male ego?"[14] (Emphasis added.)

The foregoing indeed exemplifies pure patriarchy. In point of fact, a true interpretation of history would show that it was this *pathological personality pattern* that was foisted upon the true Sacred Science of the Nile valley civilization by patriarchal monotheism for the sole purpose of exploiting its spiritual contribution to humanity and claiming the sacredness of the "Land of God" as its own, in a megalomaniacal quest for the future totalitarian enslavement and degradation of the entire human race. A more remarkable sophistry cannot be found in the annals of human history.

Of course, the Triumphant Beast of imperial power will not give up its position because the Truth is told but, as the ancient lesson teaches, it can be undermined as its tool monotheism itself undermined the Sacred Science. Therefore, valid historical truth must be used to undermine the so-called moral authority of a Western hegemony, which is currently using Palestine as an experimental laboratory for modern Israel to foster the 'cold blooded' and 'eighteen month year old baby burning' profit motive of the arms industry by sacrificing the lives of the people of Palestine for the sole purpose of increasing the stock market price in the arms trade.

As it happens, 2015 marks the 70th anniversary of the defeat of Nazi Germany and the liberation of the European Jews from Auschwitz by the Russians. Certain mass media commentators have concluded that it should not be forgotten so that it never happens again. Indeed! Coincidentally, this same year however is approximately the 100th anniversary of the genocide in the Congo, which ironically has apparently been completely forgotten. So it must be true: what is not remembered does repeat itself.

Indeed, as mentioned in the Preface, at the beginning of the 20th century, Belgium's King Leopold "killed as many as 15 millions in the Congo during the first and forgotten holocaust of the 20th century."

Therefore, given that it does not currently rate high in public consciousness, it would not be inappropriate for W. E. Burghardt Du Bois, an early 20th century Pan Africanist and African American scholar, to shed a little more light on this subject. For example, we learn therefore that:

A newspaper correspondent who had received world-wide publicity because of his travels in Africa was hired by the shrewd and unscrupulous Leopold II of Belgium to establish an international country in central Africa "to peacefully conquer and subdue it, to remold it in harmony with modern ideas into national States, within whose limits the European merchant shall go hand in hand with the dark African trader, and justice and law and order shall prevail, and murder and lawlessness and the cruel barter of slaves shall be overcome.

Thus arose the Congo Free State, and by balancing the secret designs of German, French, and British against each other, this state became the worst center of African exploitation and started the partition of Africa among European powers. ... The products of Africa began to be shared and distributed around the world. The dependence of civilized life upon products from the ends of the world tied the everyday citizen more and more firmly to the exploitation of each colonial area; tea and coffee, diamonds and gold ... rare metals valuable lumber, fruit, sugar. All these things and a hundred others became necessary to modern life, and modern life thus was built around colonial ownership and exploitation.

The cost of this exploitation was enormous. The colonial system caused ten times more deaths than actual war. ...

One of the worst things that happened was the complete and deliberate breaking-down of cultural patterns among the suppressed peoples. "Europe was staggered at the Leopoldian atrocities, and they were terrible indeed; but what we, who were behind the scenes, felt most keenly was the fact that the real catastrophe in the Congo was desolation and murder in the larger sense. The invasion of family life, the ruthless destruction of every social barrier, the shattering of every tribal law, the introduction of criminal practices which struck the chiefs of the people dumb with horror – in a word, a veritable avalanche of filth and immorality overwhelmed the Congo tribes."[15]

Without doubt, the foregoing is a condemning indictment of Western interference in African affairs indeed. In fact, "Leopold II was the founder and sole owner of the Congo Free State, a private project undertaken on his own behalf. He used Henry Morton Stanley to help him lay claim to the Congo"[16] and thus the King of Belgium, as history bears witness to, and as also recorded in Wikipedia, "ran the Congo using the mercenary *Force Publique* for his personal gain… Leopold extracted a fortune from the Congo, initially by the collection of ivory, and after a rise in the price of rubber in the 1890s, by forced labour from the natives to harvest and process rubber. **His regime was responsible for the deaths of an estimated 2 to 15 million Congolese**."[17] (Bold type added.)

Yes indeed, this is the forgotten holocaust, the one that had it been remembered may have prevented the second from occurring in the very heart of Europe itself. Clearly, if the theory Arthur Koestler proposed in *The Thirteenth Tribe*, as referred to in chapter one, proves true, then Europeans mistakenly killed six million Europeans who were descendants of people who converted to the Judaic religion but did not ethnically originate from the East, inflicting on the continent of Europe the same atrocities normally reserved for the darker-hued suppressed and colonized populations of the world.

Moreover, were it not for the historically racist omission of the covert atrocities perpetrated on the dark man who, as circumstances would unfortunately have it, has been made invisible for the better part of the last 3,000 years, perhaps the Holocaust of the European Jews would never have happened. Ultimately, this was a consequence of patriarchy *par excellence*, the *paranoid possessive, pathological personality pattern of the power-obsessed male ego*, expressed at the problematic core of monotheism.

However, in contrast to the fore-described Yahwist perspective, in the Brian Browne Walker version of *The I Ching*, hexagram number 25, *Wu Wang* of the Chinese Taoist philosophy, expresses the pertinent, sage wisdom that when the ego is exercised, "it takes us out of the present ... we miss the guidance of the Creative in the present moment."[18] Precisely! No better description can be found for the cause of the megalomania and patriarchal conceit that was expressed in the personality of Akhenaten and which also reincarnated in King Leopold II approximately 2,500 years later.

As was mentioned in chapter one, Schwaller de Lubicz placed great emphasis on "the importance of the existence of the eternal Present Moment and the secret it holds." However, in stark contrast to Akhenaten's Babylonian monotheism, the impulse of continuous creation, from whence the science of genesis was obtained and that the 'Houses of Life' taught to the initiates in ancient times, is the transcendental phenomenon at the beating heart of the Sacred Science.

Indeed the constant belief in the power of the eternal Present Moment held by the sages of Khemite civilization maintained the integrity, stability and sustainability that made their civilization last for millennia, the importance of which is demonstrated by the fact that it is only there, in that solemn and consecrated moment expressing the first act of Atum who divided earth from heaven, that the Primordial Scission takes place. This is the alchemical point where the topological metaphor of the physical medium divides one into two, and, as discussed in chapter seven, the singularity, the gateway or portal of access to hyperdimensional torsion energies.

In previous chapters however, some of the reasons for why Akhenaten rejected the core message of the True Religion have already been discussed. Predominant among them for example, the question of what historical explanation is there for his vehement abolition of the Sacred Science? Was this blatant act of ignorance the result of his being denied access to the Inner Temple, or was there an even more sinister motive? Indeed, even the issue of the infiltration of alien ideas had been considered. And so on.

To take on the establishment in the way that Akhenaten did however cannot be explained solely by the mere political and imperial issues of the day alone. Something far more profound must have lain at the basis of his intriguing actions.

Indeed, something much more sinister and destabilizing to the human soul had to have occurred. Could that ominous something have been a cataclysmic cosmic event?

Was there thus the remote possibility that some terrifying cosmic influences were at the source of his outrageous emboldening? When all is said and done, even in his time astronomical stargazing was exceedingly ancient. After all, via intense observation of the nighttime sky the entire art and culture of this ancient civilization had been determined by the motifs of the changing constellations that resulted from the continuous precession of the equinoxes. Thus, needless to say, by the time of the Eighteenth Dynasty stargazing was an ancient practice that may well have even preceded the time of Nabta Playa.

Therefore, the question must be asked, could celestial events have played a part in his motives? Indeed, according to Immanuel Velikovsky, "The Talmud and other ancient rabbinical sources tell of great disturbances in the solar movement at the time of the Exodus and the Passage of the Sea and the Lawgiving."[19]

Referring to the emergence of the important scientific doctrines of the nineteenth century, according to Gary Greenberg, the then-prevailing theory of Catastrophism had been soundly challenged. "This doctrine held that major changes in the earth's structure were due to cataclysmic events, earthquakes, tidal waves, and crashing comets – a theory scientifically consistent with biblical Creation. But with the march of the theory of evolution, Catastrophism quickly fell by the wayside."[20]

Be that Darwinian influenced perspective as it may however, in a definitive way, cosmic events have most assuredly played a significant role with regard to human history. Moreover, Velikovsky precisely broaches the subject by asking: "Was the cosmic catastrophe that terminated a world age in the days of the fall of the Middle Kingdom and of the Exodus one of these occasions...?"[21] Indeed, far from being science fiction or modern scientific fantasies, cosmic and interplanetary activity between Sirius, Mars and Earth, to say nothing of the Sumerian's planet Nibiru, are in fact recorded in ancient documents.

With regard to such interplanetary activity, as part of his research of biblical scripture, Zecharia Sitchin identified Enoch as Thoth, the Neter who introduced the MeduNeteru to the people of Khem, the latter deity known to the Sumerians as Ningishzidda, whom they believed was one of the Anunnaki, referred to in the Bible as the Nephilim and or Elohim making them all one and the same entities.

As a result of Zecharia Sitchin's exceptional decoding of the pictographic and cuneiform writings of the Sumerian civilization, these entities have been described as extraterrestrials and accepted as such in the alternative community though, given the billions upon billions of dollars NASA has spent on trying to find proof of life in outer space, surprisingly not by the establishment in official academia.

Nevertheless, in chapter seven Robert Temple revealed the Dogon belief in the 'Shaper of the World' arriving on Earth from Sirius to instruct them in creating civilization. Moreover, in chapter five Laird Scranton observed that many cultures entertain the notion that their civilization was created by mysterious ancestors and other spiritual or celestial beings. Furthermore, Zecharia Sitchin uncovered the evidence that indicates that the journey the Anunnaki made from Nibiru required a way station along the way to Earth, identifying that refuelling and resting stop as Mars. Of course, the role of Mars arose earlier in this text when mention of the Zulu belief that they came from that planet was discussed.

Bizarre as the Zulu claim may at first appear, it is nevertheless not beyond the realm of possibility for though you would not have seen or heard it on the nightly news of October 15, 2015, if you turned on your computer on that day you would have learned that "'Blips' in the light of a distant star seen by the Kepler Space Telescope could be our first sight of extraterrestrial life..." Indeed, "Alien-hunters ... think that the object might be a 'power station' built to harvest energy from a nearby stars [sic]" and that "it might be an alien 'mega-structure' – a huge power station' orbiting in space, harvesting energy from its parent star." Moreover, this strange new object may just be "one of the tell-tale signs of a massively advanced alien civilization" existing out there in deep space.

More pertinent to our discussion however, it was also announced on that same day that "the most conclusive proof yet of intelligent life on Mars" was the discovery of what appears to be an intricately carved gigantic statue of Buddha serenely seated on the Martian landscape showing the "face and head turned to its right, with breasts and a plump stomach, [and] shoulders."

Thus, from the foregoing extraordinary material, it is beginning to appear that we are only now just rediscovering what others seemed very much aware of in our ancient past. Indeed, as is well known, every culture regards Mars as a planet of war but we moderns presumed nevertheless that ancient primitives had merely cast their earthly squabbles and conflicts onto the celestial landscape of a heavenly domain. But...

Some of the stories in the Bible may reflect a genetic memory of far more ancient times than the life of civilization on Earth. We noted in chapter four that in the story of Sodom and Gomorrah there was a conflation of biblical and historical facts. For us, the version from the Land of Khem was preferred over that of Zechariah Sitchin whose Sumerian nuclear warriors Nergal and Ninurta were rejected in favour of Horemheb, Ramesses and Seti. However the notion of Sitchin's nuclear scenario was nevertheless derived from the ancient Sumerian and Akkadian cuneiform writings that may ultimately reflect a remembrance of far more ancient times, of traumatic events that may have actually occurred on a different planet.

In *Death on Mars,* for example, rocket scientist John E. Brandenburg, Ph.D., made "a thorough study of the Bible in the Ancient Greek, the original language of the New Testament ... and ... found that the Bible actually strongly implied life and intelligence elsewhere in the Cosmos"[22] supplying as an example the time when Jesus "tells his disciples to "go into the world and preach the gospel to every creature,""[23] highlighting the fact that this text "does not imply in the Greek that these creatures are necessarily human."[24] Indeed, this very "verse was interpreted by Saint Francis of Assisi that he should preach even to animals of the forest. But most profoundly, the word translated as "world" in the verse in the King James Bible is actually the Greek word "kosmos", the same Greek word invented by the Greek Philosopher Pythagoras to describe the entire universe. Thus Jesus had told his disciples to go out into the entire universe to preach to whoever would listen."[25]

Thus, it appears that the question of extraterrestrial life was already answered millennia ago, as the New Testament had recognized that someone is definitely out there! Therefore, we are entitled to ask is there any substance to the Zulu account of their origins on Mars?

Corroborating Zechariah Sitchin's account of a nuclear catastrophe being the potential cause of the destruction of Sodom and Gomorrah, Brandenburg shows that based on "the widespread evidence for a geologically long period of Earthlike condition on Mars and evidence for life on Mars, the author (Brandenburg) concludes that the civilization was indigenous to Mars and perished during some catastrophe that collapsed Mars's climate system. Evidence that this catastrophe may have been a nuclear holocaust is also present, suggesting that the Mars civilization reached high levels of technology, though it's (sic) overall appearance is of a primitive Bronze Age civilization. This latter conflict between evidence for nuclear weapon technology and yet primitive civilization of the other, means that hostile technological agencies extrinsic to Mars may be implicated in the Red Planet's demise."[26]

Moreover, from a technological point of view, it is indeed possible to "calculate the energy release of the hypothetical nuclear explosions."[27] According to Brandenburg indeed, the "resulting yield is approximately a billion megatons. Such an energy release would be a planetary scale catastrophe and would have wiped (out) almost all life present on Mars."[28]

Quite ominously and unnervingly, John E. Brandenburg proposes that "The massive size and apparent deployment from space of the weapons meant they were most likely not Martian in origin."[29] Indeed, "their construction and employment seemed all too clear. Somebody wanted to destroy all life on Mars permanently and created weapons in space and dropped them from space to do this. The pattern was clear; the two centers of archeology on Mars had been targeted by massive nuclear weapons. Their size was only slightly smaller than the Burj Khalifa tower in Dubai... Mars had been murdered by some other intelligent entity."[30]

Unlike Robert Temple's extraterrestrial scenario of benign entities in the Sirius system, as expressed in chapters five and seven, according to Brandenburg however "death by natural causes"[31] on Mars "is no longer a viable hypothesis. Sadly, the simplest hypothesis now appears that these catastrophic events were connected and that some space power arrived and decided to wipe out the apparently primitive indigenous civilization on Mars and render the planet uninhabitable."[32]

Unless the Zulu concept of time is at fault however, this evidence contradicts their mythic claim to have lived on Mars 500,000 years ago since the planetary civilization there had been destroyed approximately 250 million years ago! On the other hand, Zecharia Sitchin claims that the Sumerian record indicates that the Anunnaki arrived on Earth after journeying from Nibiru 400,000 or more years ago while the Dogon say the Nommo came from Sirius to cultivate civilization on Earth in a similar time frame. With regard to the Zulus, the archaeological evidence on the surface of Mars, though officially suppressed, nevertheless shows two centres of technology based in the Cydonia and Galaxia regions, the two areas that show evidence of nuclear destruction. The question is, were they there before or after that nuclear holocaust?

The foregoing is important to the research conducted herein because of John E. Brandenburg's proposed Cydonian Hypothesis which in essence confirms for him that "apparent eroded archeology exists from a dead indigenous civilization on Mars at several sites consistent with a long-lived and evolved biosphere on Mars in the past, as on Earth."[33]

Thus, what does NASA know that we are not being told? Has it already discovered proof of hostile extraterrestrial activity and thus are suppressing this knowledge out of fear of or for the general public's reaction? Without official answers from the establishment to the contrary at our disposal, it would appear humanity's recollection of divine beings, recalling their high technology as a reflection of divine powers, may be indeed a celestially dramatic remembrance of the arrival of ancestors from the upper reaches of outer space who were in fact fleeing from some natural or intelligently contrived form of celestial cataclysm.

Therefore, it can be concluded from Zecharia Sitchin's analysis that our concept of God has been undermined because who we had thought of as the Supreme Being and his angels turn out to be our misrepresentation of the extraterrestrial Anunnaki. That being so, as the people of Sumer regarded them as gods, who was God to the Anunnaki? How or to who did they worship or were they devoid of such a need? Sitchin however never proposed nor answered such a question, but from the inevitable enigma such a situation raises it would appear that the highly technological civilization created on the banks of the Tigris and Euphrates by the earthly survivors of the utterly destroyed *paleoancient very high civilization of high antiquity* was indeed counterbalanced by what we refer to as the religion of the Nile valley civilization. The higher spiritual entities of the Sacred Science were possibly the Khemite Yin to the Sumerian Yang.

With regard to cosmic catastrophes of course, in 1950 when Immanuel Velikovsky revived the already discredited theory of catastrophism by proposing such a literal scenario in his book *Worlds In Collision*, the entire scientific establishment came out in vehement opposition to this extremely radical idea.

Revisiting this subject however in his 2012 publication of *The Velikovsky Heresies*, Laird Scranton pertinently reminds us that, "The magnetic fields of the planets play a large role in Velikovsky's theoretic scenario of the cosmic interactions of Earth, the moon, Venus, and Mars. According to Velikovsky's scenario, Venus made its approach to Earth around 1500 BCE, after which Mars is said to have made recurring near passes of Earth, the most significant of which is said to have happened around 750 BCE. Just as the eruption of Thera on the island of Santorini is associated by traditional historians with the end of the Minoan Empire, Velikovsky also associates these planetary interludes with the major transitions of ancient Egypt."[34]

Thus with the seemingly improbable close approach of Venus established during 1500 BCE, it appears that a major cosmic disturbance in our planet's magnetic field did take place at the time of or just prior to the Eighteenth Dynasty, the era of Akhenaten's heresy! Indeed and in fact, could it not have been the causal factor of the tremendously violent volcanic eruption that took place on the island of Thera around 1500 BC? For certain, the latter eruption has indeed been cited as a possible factor behind the ten plagues that affected the Nile valley just prior to the Exodus.

Most intriguingly, in both *Act of God* and *The Moses Legacy*, Graham Phillips dramatically indicates such possible scenarios. For example, in *Act of God*, he observes that "It is not only Akhenaten's new religion which suggests that something very unusual had occurred just prior to his reign, but the behaviour of his father Amonhotep III. A year or two before Akhenaten comes to the throne, Amonhotep does something very strange for someone so completely devoted to the god Amun-Re; he erects literally hundreds of statues to another diety [sic] – the goddess Sekhmet. No other deity of ancient Egypt is represented by so many large-scale statues – and nearly all of them were erected by order of Amonhotep III. These statues of Sekhmet are a clear indication that, despite the apparent stability and wealth of the country, something was wrong, as Sekhmet was the goddess of devastation."[35]

Indeed, agreeing with Graham Phillips, Gary Greenberg states that, "Under Amenhotep III, over seven hundred statues were erected of the goddess Sekhmet, the Egyptian goddess of pestilence, possibly providing evidence of the presence of plague in this time."[36]

Meanwhile, in *The Moses Legacy*, Phillips observes that according to "the Exodus account, when the pharaoh refuses to let the Israelites leave Egypt, God punishes the Egyptians by a series of what the Bible calls plagues, including darkness over the land, fiery hailstorms, the Nile turning to blood. Such events may have been the result of a natural catastrophe: the gigantic volcanic eruption on the island of Thera that occurred around the time the story is set. Within a day of the Thera eruption a fallout cloud of volcanic debris would have drifted high over Egypt, the skies would have darkened and pellet-sized volcanic debris fallen like hail. As well as the grey pumice ash the volcano blasted skywards, Thera released iron oxide that would have stained the water of the Nile red."[37] Moreover, in regard to the aforementioned volcanic fallout, Immanuel Velikovsky affirms that, "We are also informed by Midrashic and Talmudic sources that the stones which fell on Egypt were hot."[38]

In addition, according to Laird Scranton "Significant changes in the global climate occurred around 750 BCE (the time Velikovsky claims Mars made a close approach to Earth), as evidenced in archeological finds, tree rings, and ice rings, and by known mass migrations. Likewise, there is evidence of major undefined geomagnetic events both at 1500 BCE and 750 BCE that caused great fluctuations in the magnetic field of Earth and that are associated by modern scientists with the same historical transitions claimed by Velikovsky. Because of the irregularities in the time frame of these occurrences, scientists believe that they may have been precipitated by an unknown agent."[39]

As mentioned in chapter two moreover, certain kings "claimed to know the writings of the kings who lived before the Deluge." Therefore, given that the ancients were aware of *the paleoancient very high civilization of high antiquity* that had also been destroyed by an as yet-to-be defined cosmic event that induced the Flood that occurred at the end of the last Ice Age, these planetary fly-bys must have been quite unnerving and menacing, providing a possible reason for the potential upheaval and destabilization of the entire social fabric of the time and the subsequent historical amnesia of which forebodingly we are all genetically traumatised victims.

The significance however of the latter date of 750 BCE is of course that it precedes the Persian invasion of the Land of Khem. Indeed, in the Postscript to *Journeys to the Mythical Past*, Zecharia Sitchin surmises that the "inevitable conclusion … must be, from at least 610 B.C. through probably 560 BC, the Anunnaki gods were methodically leaving planet Earth"[40] and that the specific date of 586 BC is indicated by the pointer on the ancient Greek computer-like Antikythera mechanism.

Indeed, it is not unreasonable to presume from Sitchin's intriguing research that that period in history gave the green light for the violent martial activity that occurred shortly thereafter. Therefore, is it not possible that the unexplained departure of the Anunnaki gods is the reason why Babylonian led Persian armies began their attack on the Land of Khem?

Perhaps this conundrum actually represents an historical instance of 'while the cat's away, the mice will play,' but whatever the case, that Persian invasion inevitably marked the decisive and final blow to the black people of the Nile valley who alone had raised to the heights of spiritual excellence humanity's greatest and first ever successful civilization since the Flood.

Of great cosmological and historical importance, these two fateful dates of 1500 and 750 BCE therefore tragically mark the fatal beginnings of anti-black African racism, if not indeed the overwhelming and devastating decline of *the real children of Israel now found in the ghettos, inner cities and slums across the four corners of the earth … the ones suffering on this earth today.*

Notes for Preface

1. Bauval, Robert & Brophy, Thomas: *Imhotep, The African, Architect Of The Cosmos*, Disinformation Books, An Imprint of Red Wheel / Weuiser LLC, San Francisco, 2013, p. 181.
2. Diop, Chiekh Anta: *Civilization Or Barbarism*, Lawrence Hill Books, New York, 1991. p. xiii.
3. Farrell, Joseph & de Hart, Scott D.: *Yahweh The Two-Faced God: Theology, Terrorism & Topology*, Periprometheus Press, 2011, p. 27.

Notes for Chapter One

1. Scranton, Laird: *Sacred Symbols Of The Dogon*, Inner Traditions, Rochester, Vermont, 2007, p. 205.
2. Ibid., p. 204.
3. Budge, E. A. Wallis: *The Gods of the Egyptians*, Vol II, Dover Publications, Inc., 180 Varick, Street, NY, 1969 originally published 1904, p. 9.
4. Farrell, Joseph: *Financial Vipers of Venice*, Feral House, Port Townsend, WA, 2010, p, 67.
5. Mac Ritchie, David: *Ancient And Modern Britons*, First published by Kegan Paul, Trench & Co., London, 1884, rear cover.
6. Morenz, Siegried: *Egyptian Religion*, W. Kolhammer GmbH., 1960. English translation by Cornell Univ., Press 1973, p. 47.
7. Ibid., p. 47.
8. Ibid., p. 51.
9. Darkwah, Nana Banchie: *The Africans Who Wrote The Bible — Ancient Secrets Africa and Christianity Have Never Told*, Aduana Publishing Book, White Plains, 2003, p. vii.
10. Greenberg, Gary: *The Moses Mystery — The African Origins of the Jewish People*, Carol Publishing Group, Secaucus, NJ, 1996, p. 46.
11. Bernal, Martin: *Black Athena*, Rutgers University Press, 1991, p. 47.

12. Koestler, Arthur: *The Thirteenth Tribe*, Popular Library, a unit of CBS Publications, the Consumer Publishing Division of CBS, Inc., by arrangement with Random House, Inc., 1978, pp. 13-14.
13. Ibid., p. 24.
14. Ibid., p. 18.
15. Scranton, Laird: *China's Cosmological Prehistory*, Inner Traditions, Rochester, Vermont, 2014, p. 13.
16. Darkwah, Nana Banchie: *The Africans Who Wrote The Bible — Ancient Secrets Africa and Christianity Have Never Told*, Aduana Publishing Book, White Plains, 2003, p. vi.
17. Ellis, Ralph: *Solomon – Falcon Of Sheba*, Edfu Books, Cheshire, 2002, p. 3.
18. Diop, Cheikh Anta: *The African Origin of Civilization: Myth or Reality*. Paris: Presence Africaine, 1955 and 1967. Translated and edited by Lawrence Hill & Co., Publisher, Inc., 1974, p. 2.
19. Ibid., p. 1.
20. Du Bois, W. E. Burghardt: *The World And Africa*, International Publishers, New York, 1946; 1947; 1965; & 1978, p. 34.
21. Diop, Chiekh Anta: *Civilization Or Barbarism*, Lawrence Hill Books, New York, 1991. P. 66.
22. Bauval, Robert & Brophy, Thomas: *Imhotep, The African, Architect Of The Cosmos*, Disinformation Books, An Imprint of Red Wheel/Weuiser LLC, San Francisco, 2013, p. 189.
23. Ellis, Ralph: *Solomon – Falcon Of Sheba*, Edfu Books, Cheshire, 2002, p. 81.
24. Sitchin, Zecharia: *The Wars Of Gods And Men*, Bear & Company, Santa Fe, NM, 1985, p. 32.
25. Diop, Chiekh Anta: *The Cultural Unity Of Black Africa*, Third World Press, Chicago, Il. 1959. English edition 1963, p. 56.
26. Osman, Ahmed: *The Lost City Of The Exodus*, Bear & Company, Rochester, Vermont, 2014, p. 146.
27. Diop, Cheikh Anta: *The African Origin of Civilization: Myth or Reality*. Paris: Presence Africaine, 1955 and 1967. Translated and edited by Lawrence Hill & Co., Publisher, Inc., 1974, p. 7.

28. Sitchin, Zecharia: *The Wars Of Gods And Men*, Bear & Company, Santa Fe, NM, 1985, p. 35.

29. Ibid., p. 36.

30. Osman, Ahmed: *The Lost City Of The Exodus*, Bear & Company, Rochester, Vermont, 2014, p. 146.

31. Ellis, Ralph: *Thoth – Architect Of The Universe*, Edfu Books, Cheshire, 1997, pp. 4-5.

32. Sitchin, Zecharia: *The Wars Of Gods And Men*, Bear & Company, Santa Fe, NM, 1985, p. 137.

33. Malkowski, Edward F: *Return Of The Golden Age*, Inner Traditions, Rochester, Vermont, 2014, pp. 136-137.

34. Gardiner, Laurence: *Lost Secrets of The Sacred Ark*, Element, Hammersmith, London, 2003, p. 17.

35. Ibid., p. 4.

36. Ibid., p. 7.

37. Malkowski, Edward F.: *The Spiritual Technology of Ancient Egypt*, Inner Traditions, Rochester, Vermont, 2007, p. 206.

38. Gardiner, Laurence: *Lost Secrets of The Sacred Ark*, Element, Hammersmith, London, 2003, pp. 61-62.

39. Sitchin, Zecharia: *The Wars Of Gods And Men*, Bear & Company, Santa Fe, NM, 1985, p. 46.

40. Farrell, Joseph: *Babylon's Banksters*, Feral House, Port Townsend, WA, 2010, pp. 165-166.

41. Ibid., p. 167.

42. Ibid., p. 167.

43. Ibid., pp. 167-168.

44. Ibid., p. 168.

45. Ibid., p. 169.

46. Gardiner, Laurence: *Lost Secrets of The Sacred Ark*, Element, Hammersmith, London, 2003, p. 77-78.

47. Ibid., p. 78.

48. Sitchin, Zecharia: *The Wars Of Gods And Men*, Bear & Company, Santa Fe, NM, 1985, p. 28.

49. Sinclair, Neil M. C.: *The Tiger Bay Story*, Butetown History & Arts, Cardiff, 1993, 90.

50. Creighton, Scott: *The Secret Chamber of Osiris*, Bear & Company, Rochester, Vermont, 2015, p. 86.

51. Ibid., p. 86.

52. Sitchin, Zecharia: *The Wars Of Gods And Men*, Bear & Company, Santa Fe, NM, 1985, p. 129.

53. Ellis, Ralph: *Scota – Egyptian Queen Of The Scots*, Edfu Books, Cheshire, 2006, p. 89.

54. Massey, Gerald: *The Egyptian Book of the Dead And The Mysteries of Amenta*, T Fisher Unwin, London, 1907, p. 21.

55. Morenz, Siegried: *Egyptian Religion*, W. Kolhammer GmbH., 1960. English translation by Cornell Univ., Press 1973, p. 4.

56. Mbiti, John S.: *African Religions and Philosophy*, U.S.A.: Anchor Books, 1970, p. 87.

57. Gardiner, Laurence: *Lost Secrets of The Sacred Ark*, Element, Hammersmith, London, 2003, p. 64.

58. Budge, E. A. Wallis: *The Gods of the Egyptians*, Vol II, Dover Publications, Inc., 180 Varick, Street, NY, 1969 originally published 1904, p. 126.

59. Wikipedia: Hesus.

60. Ellis, Ralph: **Cleopatra To Christ**, Edfu Books, Cheshire, 2006, p. 98.

61. Budge, E. A. Wallis: *The Gods of the Egyptians*, Vol II, Dover Publications, Inc., 180 Varick, Street, NY, 1969 originally published 1904, p. 108.

62. Hancock, Graham: *Mysteries of the Ancient Past*, Bear & Company, Rochester, Vermont, 2012m p 218.

63. Ibid., p 216.

64. Ibid., p 218.

65. Ibid., p 218.

66. Temple, Robert: *The Sirius Mystery*, Random House, London, 1998, p. 265.

Notes for Chapter Two

1. Budge, E. A. Wallis: *The Gods of the Egyptians*, Vol II, Dover Publications, Inc., 180 Varick, Street, NY, 1969 originally published 1904, p. 126.

2. Sitchin, Zecharia: *The Wars Of Gods And Men*, Bear & Company, Santa Fe, NM, 1985, pp. 41-52.
3. Budge, E. A. Wallis: *The Gods of the Egyptians*, Vol II, Dover Publications, Inc., 180 Varick, Street, NY, 1969 originally published 1904, p. 188.
4. Coppens, Phillip: *The Canopus Revelation – Stargate of the Gods and the Ark of Osiris*, Frontier Publishing, Enkhuizen, the Netherlands, 2004, p. 87.
5. Sitchin, Zecharia: *The Wars Of Gods And Men*, Bear & Company, Santa Fe, NM, 1985, p. 32
6. Ibid., p. 45.
7. Ibid., p. 25.
8. Ibid., p. 28.
9. Bauval, Robert & Brophy, Thomas: *Imhotep, The African, Architect Of The Cosmos*, Disinformation Books, An Imprint of Red Wheel/Weuiser LLC, San Francisco, 2013, pp. 192-193.
10. Ibid., p. 198.
11. Ibid., p. 198.
12. Schwaller de Lubicz, Rene A.: *Symbol and the Symbolic*, first published 1949; Autumn Press, Brookline, MA., 1978, p. 39.
13. Ibid., p. 39.
14. Ibid., p. 39.
15. Tellinger, Michael: *African Temples Of The Anunnaki – The Lost Technologies of the Gold Mines of Enki,* Bear & Company, Rochester, Vermont, 2009, p. 16.
16. Bauval, Robert & Brophy, Thomas: *Imhotep, The African, Architect Of The Cosmos*, Disinformation Books, An Imprint of Red Wheel/Weuiser LLC, San Francisco, 2013, p. 161.
17. Ibid., p. 189.
18. Bauval, Robert & Brophy, Thomas: *Black Genesis*, Bear & Company, Rochester, Vermont, 2011, pp. 135-136.
19. Greenberg, Gary: *The Moses Mystery – The African Origins of the Jewish People*, Carol Publishing Group, Secaucus, NJ, 1996, p. 67.
20. Ibid., pp. 66-67.
21. Farrell, Joseph & de Hart, Scott D.: *The Grid Of The Gods*, Adventures Unlimited Press, Kempton, Illinois, 2011, p. xii.

22. Coppens, Phillip: *The Canopus Revelation – Stargate of the Gods and the Ark of Osiris*, Frontier Publishing, Enkhuizen, the Netherlands, 2004, p. 141.
23. Ibid., p. 141
24. Sitchin, Zecharia: *The Wars Of Gods And Men*, Bear & Company, Santa Fe, NM, 1985, pp. 136-137.
25. Hancock, Graham: *Heaven's Mirror*, Penguin Books, London, 1998, p. 55.
26. Bauval, Robert & Brophy, Thomas: *Imhotep, The African, Architect Of The Cosmos*, Disinformation Books, An Imprint of Red Wheel/Weuiser LLC, San Francisco, 2013, p. 191.
27. Kramer, Samuel Noah: *The Sumerians – Their History, Culture, And Character*, The University Press of Chicago, 1963, p 160.
28. Bauval, Robert & Brophy, Thomas: *Imhotep, The African, Architect Of The Cosmos*, Disinformation Books, An Imprint of Red Wheel/Weuiser LLC, San Francisco, 2013, p. 188.
29. Ibid., p. 188.
30. Schwaller de Lubicz, Rene A.: *The Temple In Man*, first published 1949; Autumn Press, Brookline, MA., 1977, p. 20.
31. Coppens, Phillip: *The Canopus Revelation – Stargate of the Gods and the Ark of Osiris*, Frontier Publishing, Enkhuizen, the Netherlands, 2004, p. 23.
32. National Geographic: *The First Artists*, June 2011, p. 49.
33. Ibid., p. 49.
34. Greenberg, Gary: *The Moses Mystery – The African African Origins of the Jewish People*, Carol Publishing Group, Secaucus, NJ, 1996, p. 215.
35. Sitchin, Zecharia: *The Wars Of Gods And Men*, Bear & Company, Santa Fe, NM, 1985, p. 126.
36. Bauval, Robert & Brophy, Thomas: *Black Genesis*, Bear & Company, Rochester, Vermont, 2011, pp. 135-136.
37. Bauval, Robert & Hancock, Graham: *Keeper Of Genesis*, Reed Consumer Books Ltd, London, 1996, p. 78.
38. Hancock, Graham: *Heaven's Mirror*, Penguin Books, London, 1998, p. 55.
39. Collins, Andrew: *Göbekli Tepe – Genesis of the Gods*, Bear & Company, Rochester, Vermont, 2014, p. 219.

40. Ibid., p. 226.

41. Ibid., p. 226.

42. Ibid., p. 226.

43. Ibid., p. 225.

44. Ibid., p. 225.

43. Phillips, Graham: *The Moses Legacy*, Sidgwick & Jackson, London, 2002, p. 34.

44. Ibid., p. 34.

45. Sabbah, Messod and Roger: *Secrets Of The Exodus – Did the Pharaohs Write The Bible?* London. Thorsons, An Imprint Of HarperCollins*Publishers*, 2000, p. 60.

46. Ibid., p. 58.

47. Ibid., p. 58.

48. Ibid., p. 60.

49. Ibid., p. 56.

50. Ibid., pp. 56-57.

51. Ibid., pp. 58.

52. Ibid., pp. 60.

53. Ellis, Ralph: *Eden In Egypt*, Edfu Books, Cheshire, 2004, p. xi.

54. Ibid., p. xi.

55. Ibid., p. xi.

56. Ibid., p. xi.

57. Osman, Ahmed: *The Lost City Of The Exodus*, Bear & Company, Rochester, Vermont, 2014, p. 144.

58. Phillips, Graham: *The Moses Legacy*, Sidgwick & Jackson, London, 2002, p. 77.

59. Ibid., p. 74.

62. Ibid., p. 74.

63. Gardiner, Alan: *Egypt of the Pharaohs*, Oxford, England: The Clarendon Press, 1961, pp. 145-157.

64. D'Souza, Dinesh: *America - Imagine A World Without Her*, Regnery Publishing, Washington, D.C., 2014, p. 19.

65. Ibid., p. 19.

66. Sabbah, Messod and Roger: *Secrets Of The Exodus – Did the Pharaohs Write The Bible?* London. Thorsons, An Imprint Of HarperCollins*Publishers*, 2000, p. 164.

67. Ibid., p. 164.

68. Ibid., p. 261.

69. Osman, Ahmed: *The Lost City Of The Exodus*, Bear & Company, Rochester, Vermont, 2014, p. 144.

70. Sabbah, Messod and Roger: *Secrets Of The Exodus – Did the Pharaohs Write The Bible?* London. Thorsons, An Imprint Of HarperCollins*Publishers*, 2000, p. 163.

71. Massey, Gerald: *The Egyptian Book of the Dead And The Mysteries of Amenta*, T Fisher Unwin, London, 1907, p. 123.

72. Budge, E. A. Wallis: *The Gods of the Egyptians*, Vol II, Dover Publications, Inc., 180 Varick, Street, NY, 1969 originally published 1904, p. 220.

73. Bauval, Robert & Brophy, Thomas: *Black Genesis*, Bear & Company, Rochester, Vermont, 2011, pp. 136.

74. National Geographic: *The First Artists*, June 2011, p. 41.

75. Ibid., p. 39.

76. Ibid., pp. 40-41.

77. McKenna, Terence: *Food of the Gods*: A Bantam Book, 1992, p 74.

78. Ibid., p. 45.

79. Sitchin, Zecharia: *The Wars Of Gods And Men*, Bear & Company, Santa Fe, NM, 1985, p. 38.

80. Coppens, Phillip: *The Canopus Revelation – Stargate of the Gods and the Ark of Osiris*, Frontier Publishing, Enkhuizen, the Netherlands, 2004, p. 156.

81. Sabbah, Messod and Roger: *Secrets Of The Exodus – Did the Pharaohs Write The Bible?* London. Thorsons, An Imprint Of HarperCollins*Publishers*, 2000, p. 77.

82. Greenberg, Gary: *The Moses Mystery – The African African Origins of the Jewish People*, Carol Publishing Group, Secaucus, NJ, 1996, p. 109.

83. Sabbah, Messod and Roger: *Secrets Of The Exodus – Did the Pharaohs Write The Bible?* London. Thorsons, An Imprint Of HarperCollins*Publishers*, 2000, p. 47.

84. Ibid., p. 140.

85. Ibid., p. 145.

86. Ibid., p. 145.

87. Phillips, Graham: *The Moses Legacy*, Sidgwick & Jackson, London, 2002, p. 112.

88. Sabbah, Messod and Roger: *Secrets Of The Exodus – Did the Pharaohs Write The Bible?* London. Thorsons, An Imprint Of HarperCollins*Publishers*, 2000, p. 145.

89. Osman, Ahmed: *The Lost City Of The Exodus*, Bear & Company, Rochester, Vermont, 2014, pp. 104-105.

90. Ibid., p. 105.

91. Wikipedia reference: Soggin 1998, p. 128-129.

92. Diop, Chiekh Anta: *The Cultural Unity Of Black Africa*, Third World Press, Chicago, Il. 1959. English edition 1963, p. 57.

93. Velikovsky, Immanuel: *Peoples Of The Sea*, Doubleday & Company, Inc. Garden City, New York. 1977, p. 4.

92. Sabbah, Messod and Roger: *Secrets Of The Exodus – Did the Pharaohs Write The Bible?* London. Thorsons, An Imprint Of HarperCollins*Publishers*, 2000, p. 261.

Notes for Chapter Three

1. Vidal, Gore: *Dreaming War*, Thunder's Mouth Press, New York, 2002, p. 12.

2. Ibid., pp. 11-12.

3. Ibid., rear of book.

4. Ibid., p. 16.

5. Ibid., p. 17.

6. Ibid., p. 18.

7. Ibid., p. 18.

8. Farrell, Joseph & de Hart, Scott D.: *Yahweh The Two-Faced God: Theology, Terrorism & Topology*, Periprometheus Press, 2011, p. 80.

9. Ibid., pp. 82-83.

10. Chomsky, Noam, *The Chomsky Reader*, Pantheon House, a division of Random House, New York, 1987, p. 317.

11. Ibid., p. 317.

12. Ibid., p. 317.

13. Ibid., p. 317.

14. Sabbah, Messod and Roger: *Secrets Of The Exodus — Did the Pharaohs Write The Bible?* London. Thorsons, An Imprint Of HarperCollins*Publishers*, 2000, p. 144.

15. Ibid., p. 32.

16. Ibid., pp. 144-145.

17. Ibid., p. 144.

18. Ibid., p. 145.

19. Ten, John: *Tetragrammaton*, YouTube video.

20. Osman, Ahmed: *The Lost City Of The Exodus*, Bear & Company, Rochester, Vermont, 2014, p. 83.

21. Ibid., p. 98.

22. Sabbah, Messod and Roger: *Secrets Of The Exodus — Did the Pharaohs Write The Bible?* London. Thorsons, An Imprint Of HarperCollins*Publishers*, 2000, p. 42.

23. Coppens, Phillip: *The Canopus Revelation — Stargate of the Gods and the Ark of Osiris*, Frontier Publishing, Enkhuizen, the Netherlands, 2004, p. 119.

24. Osman, Ahmed: *Stranger In The Valley of the Kings*, Paladin, London, 1987, p. 131.

25. Osman, Ahmed: *The Lost City Of The Exodus*, Bear & Company, Rochester, Vermont, 2014, p. 84.

26. Greenberg, Gary: *The Moses Mystery — The African African Origins of the Jewish People*, Carol Publishing Group, Secaucus, NJ, 1996, p. 121.

27. Sabbah, Messod and Roger: *Secrets Of The Exodus — Did the Pharaohs Write The Bible?* London. Thorsons, An Imprint Of HarperCollins*Publishers*, 2000, p. 75.

28. Ibid., p. 75.

29. Bauval, Robert & Brophy, Thomas: *Imhotep, The African, Architect Of The Cosmos*, Disinformation Books, An Imprint of Red Wheel/Weuiser LLC, San Francisco, 2013, p. 186.

30. Ibid., p. 186.

31. Morenz, Siegried: *Egyptian Religion*, W. Kolhammer GmbH., 1960. English translation by Cornell Univ., Press 1973, p. 53.

32. Ibid., p. 53.

33. Greenberg, Gary: *The Moses Mystery – The African African Origins of the Jewish People*, Carol Publishing Group, Secaucus, NJ, 1996, p. 148.

34. Schwaller de Lubicz, Rene A.: *Symbol and the Symbolic*, first published 1949; Autumn Press, Brookline, MA., 1978. p. 24.

35. Ibid., p. 24.

36. Ibid., p. 24.

37. Morenz, Siegried: *Egyptian Religion*, W. Kolhammer GmbH., 1960. English translation by Cornell Univ., Press 1973, p. 1.

38. Scranton, Laird: *The Science Of The Dogon*, Inner Traditions, Rochester, Vermont, 2002, p. 83.

39. Ibid., p. 84.

40. Ibid., p. 85.

41. Ibid., p. 16.

42. Vidal, Gore: *DreamingWar*, Thunder's Mouth Press, New York, 2002, p. 58.

43. Budge, E. A. Wallis: *The Gods of the Egyptians*, Vol II, Dover Publications, Inc., 180 Varick, Street, NY, 1969 originally published 1904, pp. 73-74.

44. Ibid., p. 80.

45. Phillips, Graham: *The Moses Legacy*, Sidgwick & Jackson, London, 2002, pp. 119-120.

46. Ibid., p. 120.

47. Ibid., p. 120.

48. Greenberg, Gary: *The Moses Mystery – The African African Origins of the Jewish People*, Carol Publishing Group, Secaucus, NJ, 1996, p. 21.

49. Sabbah, Messod and Roger: *Secrets Of The Exodus – Did the PharaohsWrite The Bible?* London. Thorsons, An Imprint Of HarperCollins*Publishers*, 2000, p. 79.

50. Ibid., p. 43.

51. Morenz, Siegried: *Egyptian Religion*, W. Kolhammer GmbH., 1960. English translation by Cornell Univ., Press 1973, p. 147.

52. Osman, Ahmed: *The Lost City Of The Exodus*, Bear & Company, Rochester, Vermont, 2014, p. 97.

53. Sitchin, Zecharia: *The Wars Of Gods And Men*, Bear & Company, Santa Fe, NM, 1985, pp. 42.

54. Morenz, Siegried: *Egyptian Religion*, W. Kolhammer GmbH., 1960. English translation by Cornell Univ., Press 1973, p. 53.

55. Sitchin, Zecharia: *The Wars Of Gods And Men*, Bear & Company, Santa Fe, NM, 1985, pp. 38.

56. Sabbah, Messod and Roger: *Secrets Of The Exodus – Did the Pharaohs Write The Bible?* London. Thorsons, An Imprint Of HarperCollins*Publishers*, 2000, p. 75.

57. Ibid., p. 263.

58. Ibid., p. 262.

59. Wikipedia reference: David O'Connor & Eric Cline, pp. 2 & 14.

60. Morenz, Siegried: *Egyptian Religion*, W. Kolhammer GmbH., 1960. English translation by Cornell Univ., Press 1973, p. 30.

61. Phillips, Graham: *The Moses Legacy*, Sidgwick & Jackson, London, 2002, p. 246.

62. Ibid., pp. 246- 247.

63. Ibid., p. 250.

64. Sabbah, Messod and Roger: *Secrets Of The Exodus – Did the Pharaohs Write The Bible?* London. Thorsons, An Imprint Of HarperCollins*Publishers*, 2000, p. 58.

65. Velikovsky, Immanuel: *Oedipus And Akhenaton – Myth and History*, Doubleday & Company, Inc. Garden City, New York, 1960, p. 49.

66. Sabbah, Messod and Roger: *Secrets Of The Exodus – Did the Pharaohs Write The Bible?* London. Thorsons, An Imprint Of HarperCollins*Publishers*, 2000, p. 40.

67. Ibid., p. 40.

68. Ibid., p. 120.

69. Ibid., p. 195.

70. Ibid., p. 264.

Notes for Chapter Four

1.   Greenberg, Gary: *The Moses Mystery – The African African Origins of the Jewish People*, Carol Publishing Group, Secaucus, NJ, 1996, p. 19.

2. Sabbah, Messod and Roger: *Secrets Of The Exodus – Did the Pharaohs Write The Bible?* London. Thorsons, An Imprint Of HarperCollins*Publishers*, 2000, p. 70.

3. Ibid., p. 70.

4. Ibid., p. 71.

5. Ibid., p. 70.

6. Velikovsky, Immanuel: *Oedipus And Akhenaton – Myth and History*, Doubleday & Company, Inc. Garden City, New York, 1960, p. 74.

7. Ibid., p. 79.

8. Ibid., 78.

9. Sabbah, Messod and Roger: *Secrets Of The Exodus – Did the Pharaohs Write The Bible?* London. Thorsons, An Imprint Of HarperCollins*Publishers*, 2000, p. 256.

10. Ibid., p. 256.

11. Velikovsky, Immanuel: *Oedipus And Akhenaton – Myth and History*, Doubleday & Company, Inc. Garden City, New York, 1960, p. 92.

12. Sabbah, Messod and Roger: *Secrets Of The Exodus – Did the Pharaohs Write The Bible?* London. Thorsons, An Imprint Of HarperCollins*Publishers*, 2000, p. 195.

13. Ibid., p. 71.

14. Ibid., p. 70.

15. Ibid., p. 71.

16. Ibid., p. 71.

17. Osman, Ahmed: *The Lost City Of The Exodus*, Bear & Company, Rochester, Vermont, 2014, p. 101.

18. Ibid., pp. 104-105.

19. Ibid., p. 166.

20. Greenberg, Gary: *The Moses Mystery – The African African Origins of the Jewish People*, Carol Publishing Group, Secaucus, NJ, 1996, p. 15.

21. Darkwah, Nana Banchie: *The Africans Who Wrote The Bible – Ancient Secrets Africa and Christianity Have Never Told*, Aduana Publishing Book, White Plains, 2003, p. 33.

22. Ibid., p. 27.

23. Ibid., p. 27.

24. Sabbah, Messod and Roger: *Secrets Of The Exodus – Did the Pharaohs Write The Bible?* London. Thorsons, An Imprint Of HarperCollins*Publishers*, 2000, p. 79.
25. Ibid., p. 280.
26. Ibid., pp. 79-80.
27. Greenberg, Gary: *The Moses Mystery – The African African Origins of the Jewish People*, Carol Publishing Group, Secaucus, NJ, 1996, p. 168.
28. Sabbah, Messod and Roger: *Secrets Of The Exodus – Did the Pharaohs Write The Bible?* London. Thorsons, An Imprint Of HarperCollins*Publishers*, 2000, p. 263.
29. Budge, E. A. Wallis: *The Gods of the Egyptians*, Vol II, Dover Publications, Inc., 180 Varick, Street, NY, 1969 originally published 1904, p. 71.
30. Ibid., p. 71.
31. Ibid.,, pp. 69-70.
32. Diop, Chiekh Anta: *The Cultural Unity Of Black Africa*, Third World Press, Chicago, Il. 1959. English edition 1963, p.p. 58-59.
33. Ibid., p. 60.
34. Ibid., p. 56.
35. Ibid., p. 58.
36. Ibid., p. 58.
37. Sabbah, Messod and Roger: *Secrets Of The Exodus – Did the Pharaohs Write The Bible?* London. Thorsons, An Imprint Of HarperCollins*Publishers*, 2000, p. 84.
38. Ibid., p. 169.
39. Ibid., p. 85.
40. Ibid., p. 83.
41. Griff, Professor: *The Psychological Covert War On Hip Hop*, Heir To The Shah, Atlanta, GA. 2011, p. 228.
42. Wallach, Joel D., Lan, Ma, & Schrauzer, Gerhard N., *Epigenetics,* SelectBooks, Inc., New York, 2014, p. 354.
43. Ibid., p. 354.
44. Ibid., p. 354.
45. Velikovsky, Immanuel: *Oedipus And Akhenaton – Myth and History*, Doubleday & Company, Inc. Garden City, New York, 1960, p. 49.

46. Reich, Wilhelm: *The Mass Psychology Of Fascism*, Mary Boyd Higgins as Trustee of the Wilhelm Reich Infant Trust Fund, 1970. Originally published in 1946, pp. 151-152.

47. Ibid., p. 151.

48. Greenberg, Gary: *The Moses Mystery – The African African Origins of the Jewish People*, Carol Publishing Group, Secaucus, NJ, 1996, pp. 234-235.

49. Sitchin, Zecharia: *The Wars Of Gods And Men*, Bear & Company, Santa Fe, NM, 1985, p. 44.

50. Budge, E. A. Wallis: *Osiris & The Egyptian Resurrection*, Dover Publications, NY 1973. Originally published 1911, pp. 26-27.

51. Wikipedia: *Ugandan Martyrs*.

52. Ibid.

53. Ibid.

54. Ibid.

55. Ibid.

56. Velikovsky, Immanuel: *Oedipus And Akhenaton – Myth and History*, Doubleday & Company, Inc. Garden City, New York, 1960, pp. 98-99. x

57. Ibid., p. 99.

58. Ibid., p. 86.

59. Ibid., p. 106.

60. Ibid., p. 103.

61. Ibid., p. 103.

62. Ibid., p. 93.

63. Ibid., pp. 86-87.

64. Ibid., p. 90.

65. Ibid., p. 37.

66. Sabbah, Messod and Roger: *Secrets Of The Exodus – Did the Pharaohs Write The Bible?* London. Thorsons, An Imprint Of HarperCollins*Publishers*, 2000, p. 71.

67. Ibid., p. 71.

68. Sitchin, Zecharia: *The Wars Of Gods And Men*, Bear & Company, Santa Fe, NM, 1985, p. 309.

69. Scranton, Laird: *China's Cosmological Prehistory*, Inner Traditions, Rochester, Vermont, 2014, p. 33.

70. Greenberg, Gary: *The Moses Mystery – The African African Origins of the Jewish People*, Carol Publishing Group, Secaucus, NJ, 1996, pp. 164.

71. Ibid., pp. 164-165.

72. Sabbah, Messod and Roger: *Secrets Of The Exodus – Did the Pharaohs Write The Bible?* London. Thorsons, An Imprint Of HarperCollins*Publishers*, 2000, p. 127.

73. Ibid., p. 128.

74. Velikovsky, Immanuel: *Oedipus And Akhenaton – Myth and History*, Doubleday & Company, Inc. Garden City, New York, 1960, p. 106.

75. Ten John: *Tetragrammaton*, You Tube.

76. Phillips, Graham: *The Moses Legacy*, Sidgwick & Jackson, London, 2002, pp. 264-265.

77. Sabbah, Messod and Roger: *Secrets Of The Exodus – Did the Pharaohs Write The Bible?* London. Thorsons, An Imprint Of HarperCollins*Publishers*, 2000, p. 247.

78. Ibid., p. 169.

Notes for Chapter Five

1. Sitchin, Zecharia: *The Wars Of Gods And Men*, Bear & Company, Santa Fe, NM, 1985, p. 148.

2. Ibid., p. 267.

3. Schwaller de Lubicz, Rene A.: *Symbol and the Symbolic*, first published 1949; Autumn Press, Brookline, MA., 1978, p. 59.

4. Ibid., p. 59.

5. Schwaller de Lubicz, Rene A.: *Sacred Science – The King of Pharaonic Theocracy*, Inner Traditions International, Ltd., New York, 1961 (May 15. 1618), p. 30.

6. Director, Bruce: personal communication.

7. Scranton, Laird: *China's Cosmological Prehistory*, Inner Traditions, Rochester, Vermont, 2014, pp. 12-13.

8. Ibid., 13.

9. Scranton, Laird: *China's Cosmological Prehistory*, Inner Traditions, Rochester, Vermont, 2014, p. 1.

10. Ibid., p. 2.
11. Ibid., pp. 150-151.
12. Ibid., p. 150.
13. Ibid., p. 15.
14. Ibid., p. 151.
15. Chandler, Wayne B: *Ancient Future*, Black Classic Press, 1999, p. 86.
16. Ibid., p. 88.
17. Scranton, Laird: *Point of Origin*, Inner Traditions, Rochester, Vermont, 2015, p. 67.
18. Chandler, Wayne B: *Ancient Future*, Black Classic Press, 1999, p. 221.
19. Scranton, Laird: *The Cosmological Origins of Myth and Symbol*, Inner Traditions, Rochester, Vermont, 2010, pp. 151-152.
20. Ibid., p. 134.
21. Ibid., p. 152.
22. Ibid., p. 44.
23. Schwaller de Lubicz, Rene A.: *The Temple In Man*, first published 1949; Autumn Press, Brookline, MA., 1977, pp. 17-18.
24. Schwaller de Lubicz, Rene A.: *Symbol and the Symbolic*, first published 1949; Autumn Press, Brookline, MA., 1978, p. 27.
25. Farrell, Joseph & de Hart, Scott D.: *The Grid Of The Gods*, Adventures Unlimited Press, Kempton, Illinois, 2011, p. 277.
26. Ibid., p. 277.
27. Scranton, Laird: *Sacred Symbols Of The Dogon*, Inner Traditions, Rochester, Vermont, 2007, p. 208.
28. Scranton, Laird: *The Cosmological Origins of Myth and Symbol*, Inner Traditions, Rochester, Vermont, 2010, p. 105.
29. Ibid., p. 106.
30. Scranton, Laird: *China's Cosmological Prehistory*, Inner Traditions, Rochester, Vermont, 2014, pp. 153-154.
31. Scranton, Laird: *The Science Of The Dogon*, Inner Traditions, Rochester, Vermont, 2002, p. 109.
32. Scranton, Laird: *China's Cosmological Prehistory*, Inner Traditions, Rochester, Vermont, 2014, p. 136.

Notes for Chapter Six

1. Gardiner, Alan: *Egypt of the Pharaohs*, Oxford, England: The Clarendon Press, 1961, pp. 156-157.
2. Farrell, Joseph & de Hart, Scott D.: *Yahweh The Two-Faced God: Theology, Terrorism & Topology*, Periprometheus Press, 2011, p. 39.
3. Greenberg, Gary: *The African Origins of the Jewish People*, Carol Publishing Group, Secaucus, NJ, 1996, p. 123.
4. Osman, Ahmed: *The Lost City Of The Exodus*, Bear & Company, Rochester, Vermont, 2014, p. 54.
5. Osman, Ahmed: *The Lost City Of The Exodus*, Bear & Company, Rochester, Vermont, 2014, p. 18.
6. Sabbah, Messod and Roger: *Secrets Of The Exodus – Did the Pharaohs Write The Bible?* London. Thorsons, An Imprint Of HarperCollins*Publishers*, 2000, p. 280.
7. Farrell, Joseph & de Hart, Scott D.: *Transhumanism*, Feral House, Port Townsend, WA, 2011., p. 19.
8. Ibid., 21.
9. Ibid., p. 21.
10. Ibid., p. 21.
11. Sabbah, Messod and Roger: *Secrets Of The Exodus – Did the Pharaohs Write The Bible?* London. Thorsons, An Imprint Of HarperCollins*Publishers*, 2000, p. 31.
12. Ibid., p. 31.
13. Greenberg, Gary: *The African Origins of the Jewish People*, Carol Publishing Group, Secaucus, NJ, 1996, p. 3.
14. Ibid., p. 3.
15. Farrell, Joseph & de Hart, Scott D.: *Yahweh The Two-Faced God: Theology, Terrorism & Topology*, Periprometheus Press, 2011, p. 48.
16. Sabbah, Messod and Roger: *Secrets Of The Exodus – Did the Pharaohs Write The Bible?* London. Thorsons, An Imprint Of HarperCollins*Publishers*, 2000, p. 257.
17. Ibid., p. 257.
18. Farrell, Joseph & de Hart, Scott D.: *Yahweh The Two-Faced God: Theology, Terrorism & Topology*, Periprometheus Press, 2011, p. 48.

19. Farrell, Joseph & de Hart, Scott D.: *Transhumanism*, Feral House, Port Townsend, WA, 2011, p. 71.

20. Phillips, Graham: *The Moses Legacy*, Sidgwick & Jackson, London, 2002, p. 173 .

21. Ibid., p. 174.

22. Phillips, Graham: *The Moses Legacy*, Sidgwick & Jackson, London, 2002, pp. 138-139.

23. Ibid., p. 203.

24. Ibid., p. 203.

25. Ibid., p. 204.

26. Ibid., p. 211.

27. Ibid., p. 212.

28. Ibid., p. 202.

29. Ibid., p. 202.

30. Ibid., p. 2.

31. Ibid., p. 2.

32. Darkwah, Nana Banchie: *The Africans Who Wrote The Bible — Ancient Secrets Africa and Christianity Have Never Told*, Aduana Publishing Book, White Plains, 2003, p. vii.

33. Phillips, Graham: *The Moses Legacy*, Sidgwick & Jackson, London, 2002, p. 180.

34. Ibid., p. 181.

35. Bauval, Robert & Brophy, Thomas: *Imhotep, The African, Architect Of The Cosmos*, Disinformation Books, An Imprint of Red Wheel / Weuiser LLC, San Francisco, 2013, p. 193.

36. Phillips, Graham: *The Moses Legacy*, Sidgwick & Jackson, London, 2002, p. 131.

37. Ibid., p. 137.

38. Ibid., p. 131.

39. Ibid., p. 133.

40. Ibid., p. 135.

41. Ibid., p. 135.

42. Ibid., p. 131.

43. Ibid., p. 133.

44. Ellis, Ralph: *Solomon — Falcon Of Sheba*, Edfu Books, Cheshire, 2002, p. 177.

45. Phillips, Graham: *The Moses Legacy*, Sidgwick & Jackson, London, 2002, p. 149.
46. Gardiner, Laurence: *Lost Secrets of The Sacred Ark*, Element, Hammersmith, London, 2003, p. 3.
47. Ibid., p. 4.
48. Ibid., p. 4.
49. Ibid., p. 4.
50. Ibid., p. 5.
51. Ibid., p. 5.
52. Greenberg, Gary: *The African Origins of the Jewish People*, Carol Publishing Group, Secaucus, NJ, 1996, pp. 232-233.
53. Budge, E. A. Wallis: *The Gods of the Egyptians*, Vol II, Dover Publications, Inc., 180 Varick, Street, NY, 1969 originally published 1904, p. 92.
54. Greenberg, Gary: *The African Origins of the Jewish People*, Carol Publishing Group, Secaucus, NJ, 1996, pp. 232-233.
55. Ibid., pp. 232-233.
56. Massey, Gerald: *The Egyptian Book of the Dead And The Mysteries of Amenta*, T Fisher Unwin, London, 1907, p. 43.
57. Greenberg, Gary: *The African Origins of the Jewish People*, Carol Publishing Group, Secaucus, NJ, 1996, pp. 232-233.
58. Ibid., p. 218.
59. Ibid., p. 218.
60. Sabbah, Messod and Roger: *Secrets Of The Exodus – Did the Pharaohs Write The Bible?* London. Thorsons, An Imprint Of HarperCollins*Publishers*, 2000, p. 128.
61. Osman, Ahmed: *Stranger In The Valley of the Kings*, Paladin, London, 1987, p. 163.
62. Wikepedia: Amenhotep III.
63. Greenberg, Gary: *The African Origins of the Jewish People*, Carol Publishing Group, Secaucus, NJ, 1996, p. 283.
64. Ibid., p. 121.
65. Ibid., p. 92.
66. Ibid., p. 16.
67. Ibid., p. 18.

68. Ibid., p. 218.

69. Phillips, Graham: *The Moses Legacy*, Sidgwick & Jackson, London, 2002, p. 36.

70. Greenberg, Gary: *The African Origins of the Jewish People*, Carol Publishing Group, Secaucus, NJ, 1996, p. 66.

71. Sabbah, Messod and Roger: *Secrets Of The Exodus — Did the Pharaohs Write The Bible?* London. Thorsons, An Imprint Of HarperCollins*Publishers*, 2000, p. 78.

72. Ibid., p. 78.

73. Alford, Alan F.: *When the Gods Came Down — The Catastrophic Roots of Religion Revealed.* Hodder & Stoughton, London. 2000, p. 240.

74. Ibid., pp. 240-241.

75. Ibid., p. 316.

76. Ibid., p. 243.

77. Ibid., p. 343.

78. Ibid., p. 367.

79. Ibid., p. 244.

80. Hislop, Rev. Alexander: *The Two Babylons*, A&B Publishers Group, Brooklyn, New York, undated, p. 136.

81. Ibid., pp. 136-137.

82. Budge, E. A. Wallis: *Osiris & The Egyptian Resurrection*, Dover Publications, NY 1973. Originally published 1911, Vol. I, p. 10.

83. Ibid., Vol I., p 10.

84. Sabbah, Messod and Roger: *Secrets Of The Exodus — Did the Pharaohs Write The Bible?* London. Thorsons, An Imprint Of HarperCollins*Publishers*, 2000, p. 53.

85. Sitchin, Zecharia: Sitchin, Zecharia: *The 12th Planet*, Bear & Company, Santa Fe, NM, 1976., Bear & Company, Santa Fe, NM, 1976, p. 334.

86. Sitchin, Zecharia: *The Stairway To Heaven*, Bear & Company, Santa Fe, NM, 1980, p. 106.

87. Sabbah, Messod and Roger: *Secrets Of The Exodus — Did the Pharaohs Write The Bible?* London. Thorsons, An Imprint Of HarperCollins*Publishers*, 2000, p. 104.

88. Ibid., p. 104.

89. Ellis, Ralph: *Solomon – Falcon Of Sheba*, Edfu Books, Cheshire, 2002, p. 144.

90. Greenberg, Gary: *The African Origins of the Jewish People*, Carol Publishing Group, Secaucus, NJ, 1996, p. 280.

91. Coppens, Phillip: *The Canopus Revelation – Stargate of the Gods and the Ark of Osiris*, Frontier Publishing, Enkhuizen, the Netherlands, 2004, p. 41.

92. Ibid., p. 17.

93. Ibid., p. 65.

94. Ibid., p. 144.

95. Ibid., p. 132.

96. Ibid., p. 19.

97. Ibid., p. 36.

98. Clayton, Peter, *Chronicle of the Pharaohs*, Thames & Hudson Ltd., 1994. p.175

99. Wikipedia: *Amun*.

100. Ibid.

101. Ellis, Ralph: *Solomon – Falcon Of Sheba*, Edfu Books, Cheshire, 2002, pp. 167-168.

102. Ibid., p. 168.

103. Ibid., p. 177.

104. Ibid., pp. 87-88.

105. Scranton, Laird: *China's Cosmological Prehistory*, Inner Traditions, Rochester, Vermont, 2014, p. 79.

106. Greenberg, Gary: *The African Origins of the Jewish People*, Carol Publishing Group, Secaucus, NJ, 1996, p. 281.

Notes for Chapter Seven

1. Malkowski, Edward F: *The Spiritual Technology of Ancient Egypt*, Inner Traditions, Rochester, Vermont, 2007, p. 188.

2. Ibid., p. 188.

3. Massey, Gerald: *The Egyptian Book of the Dead And The Mysteries of Amenta*, T Fisher Unwin, London, 1907, p. 112.

4. Schwaller de Lubicz, Rene A.: *The Egyptian Miracle*, first published by Flammation, Paris 1963; Inner Traditions International, Ltd., New York, 1985, p. 11.

5. Ibid., p. 11.

6. Farrell, Joseph & de Hart, Scott D.: *The Grid Of The Gods*, Adventures Unlimited Press, Kempton, Illinois, 2011, p. 24.

7. Farrell, Joseph: *Babylon's Banksters*, Feral House, Port Townsend, WA., 2010, p. 19.

8. Ibid., 211.

9. Coppens, Phillip: *The Canopus Revelation – Stargate of the Gods and the Ark of Osiris*, Frontier Publishing, Enkhuizen, the Netherlands, 2004, p. 16.

10. Schwaller de Lubicz, Rene A.: *Symbol and the Symbolic*, first published 1949; Autumn Press, Brookline, MA., 1978, p. 25.

11. Alexander, Dr. Eben: *Proof of Heaven*, Simon & Schuster, US, 2012, p. 152.

12. Schwaller de Lubicz, Rene A.: *Symbol and the Symbolic*, first published 1949; Autumn Press, Brookline, MA., 1978, p. 24.

13. Ibid., p. 25.

14. Sabbah, Messod and Roger: *Secrets Of The Exodus – Did the Pharaohs Write The Bible?* London. Thorsons, An Imprint Of HarperCollins*Publishers*, 2000, p. 60.

15. Capra, Fritjof: *The Tao of Physics*, a Bantam book / published by arrangement with Shambhala Publications, Inc., 1976, p. 127.

16. Schwaller de Lubicz, Rene A.: *Symbol and the Symbolic*, first published 1949; Autumn Press, Brookline, MA., 1978, pp. 9-10.

17. Scranton, Laird: *Sacred Symbols Of The Dogon*, Inner Traditions, Rochester, Vermont, 2007, p. 204.

18. Ibid,, p. 204.

19. Scranton, Laird: *China's Cosmological Prehistory*, Inner Traditions, Rochester, Vermont, 2014, p. 98.

20. Tellinger, Michael: *African Temples Of The Anunnaki – The Lost Technologies of the Gold Mines of Enki*, Bear & Company, Rochester, Vermont, 2009., p. 31.

21. Ibid., p. 74.

22. Ibid., p. 86.
23. Phillips, Graham: *The Moses Legacy*, Sidgwick & Jackson, London, 2002, pp. 286-289.
24. Farrell, Joseph: *Thrice Great Hermetic and the Janus Age*, Adventures Unlimited Press, Kempton, Illinois, 2014, p. 330.
25. Ibid., p. 222.
26. Ellis, Ralph: *Jesus, Last Of The Pharoahs*, Edfu Books, Cheshire, 1998, p. 223.
27. Ibid., p. 222.
28. Phillips, Graham: *The Moses Legacy*, Sidgwick & Jackson, London, 2002, p. 270.
29. Ten John: *Tetragrammaton*, YouTube.
30. Ibid.
31. Ibid.
32. Ibid.
33. Ibid.
34. Ibid.
35. Farrell, Joseph & deHart, Scott D.: *The Grid Of The Gods*, Adventures Unlimited Press, Kempton, Illinois, 2011, p. 323.
36. Farrell, Joseph & de Hart, Scott D.: *Yahweh The Two-Faced God: Theology, Terrorism & Topology*, Periprometheus Press, 2011, p. 39.
37. Ten John: *Tetragrammaton*, YouTube.
38. Ibid.
39. Ibid.
40. Ibid.
41. Ibid.
42. Ibid.
43. Ibid.
44. Sitchin, Zecharia: *The Wars Of Gods And Men*, Bear & Company, Santa Fe, NM, 1985, p. 191.
45. Ten John: *Tetragrammaton*, YouTube.
46. Farrell, Joseph & deHart, Scott D.: *The Grid Of The Gods*, Adventures Unlimited Press, Kempton, Illinois, 2011, p. 277.

47. Scranton, Laird: *The Science Of The Dogon*, Inner Traditions, Rochester, Vermont, 2002, p. 56.

48. Temple, Robert: *The Sirius Mystery*, Random House, London, 1998, p. 265.

49. Ibid., p. 265.

50. Ten John: *Tetragrammaton*, YouTube.

51. Ibid.

52. Gardiner, Laurence: *Lost Secrets of The Sacred Ark*, Element, Hammersmith, London, 2003, p. 17.

53. Ibid., p. 8.

54. Ibid., pp. 8-9.

55. Ibid., p. 24.

56. Ibid., p. 24.

57. Ibid.. pp.24-25.

58. Ibid., p. 159.

59. Scranton, Laird: *The Science Of The Dogon*, Inner Traditions, Rochester, Vermont, 2002, pp. 50-51.

60. Wilhelm, Hellmut: *Change – Eight Lectures on the I Ching*, Bollingen Foundation, New York, 1960, p. 89.

61. Ibid., p. 89.

62. Ibid. p. 90.

63. Ibid. p. 91.

64. Massey, Gerald: *The Egyptian Book of the Dead And The Mysteries of Amenta*, T Fisher Unwin, London, 1907, p. 57.

65. Scranton, Laird: *The Science Of The Dogon*, Inner Traditions, Rochester, Vermont, 2002, p. 109.

66. Schwaller de Lubicz, Rene A.: *Symbol and the Symbolic*, first published 1949; Autumn Press, Brookline, MA., 1978, pp. 32-33.

67. Scranton, Laird: *China's Cosmological Prehistory*, Inner Traditions, Rochester, Vermont, 2014, pp. 117-118.

68. Ibid., pp. 117-119.

69. James, George G. M.: *Stolen Legacy*, Julian Richardson Associates, *Publishers*, San Francisco. 1954, p. 146.

70. Schwaller de Lubicz, Rene A.: *The Temple of Man*, first published 1957; Inner Traditions International, Rochester, Vermont, 1998, p. 104.

71. Coppens, Phillip: *The Canopus Revelation – Stargate of the Gods and the Ark of Osiris*, Frontier Publishing, Enkhuizen, the Netherlands, 2004, p. 45.

72. Ten John: *Tetragrammaton*, YouTube.

73. Ibid.

74. Ibid.

75. Ibid.

76. Ibid.

77. Ibid.

78. Director, Bruce: Paraphrastic summation derived from the entirety of *Riemann for Anti-Dummies*.

79. Riemann, Bernhard: *Habilitation Dissertation On The Hypotheses That Lie At The Foundation Of Geometry*. 1854.

80. Farrell, Joseph & de Hart, Scott D.: *The Grid Of The Gods*, Adventures Unlimited Press, Kempton, Illinois, 2011, p. 276-277.

81. Scranton, Laird: *Sacred Symbols Of The Dogon*, Inner Traditions, Rochester, Vermont, 2007, p. 208.

82. Director, Bruce: *Greece Child of Egypt*, Pt 1 at http://www.wlym.com/pedagogicals/greece1.html, p. 2.

83. Scranton, Laird: *The Science Of The Dogon*, Inner Traditions, Rochester, Vermont, 2002, p. 84.

84. Schwaller de Lubicz, Rene A.: *Symbol and the Symbolic*, first published 1949; Autumn Press, Brookline, MA., 1978, p. 87.

85. Ibid., p. 87.

Notes for Chapter Eight

1. Farrell, Joseph & de Hart, Scott D.: *Yahweh The Two-Faced God: Theology, Terrorism & Topology*, Periprometheus Press, 2011, p. 48.

2. Ibid., p. 48.

3. McKenna, Terence: *Food of the Gods*: A Bantam Book, 1992, p. 62.

4. Ibid., p. 62.

5. Coppens, Phillip: *The Canopus Revelation – Stargate of the Gods and the Ark of Osiris*, Frontier Publishing, Enkhuizen, the Netherlands, 2004, p. 148.

6. Scranton, Laird: *China's Cosmological Prehistory*, Inner Traditions, Rochester, Vermont, 2014, p. 79.

7. Coppens, Phillip: *The Canopus Revelation – Stargate of the Gods and the Ark of Osiris*, Frontier Publishing, Enkhuizen, the Netherlands, 2004, p. 149.

8. Plato, *The Portable Plato – The Republic*: Viking Press, Inc. Ltd., 1948, p, 687.

9. Alexander, Dr. Eben: *Proof of Heaven*, Simon & Schuster, US, 2012, p. 9.

10. Wikipedia.

11. Rumi: *Rumi's Little Book of Life*, Hampton Roads Publications Company, Inc., Charlottesville, VA, 2012, p . 123.

12. Alexander, Dr. Eben: *Proof of Heaven*, Simon & Schuster, US, 2012, p. 9.

13. Farrell, Joseph & deHart, Scott D.: *The Grid Of The Gods*, Adventures Unlimited Press, Kempton, Illinois, 2011, p. 277.

14. Greenberg, Gary: *The African Origins of the Jewish People*, Carol Publishing Group, Secaucus, NJ, 1996, p. 154.

15. Budge, E. A. Wallis: *Osiris & The Egyptian Resurrection*, Dover Publications, NY 1973. Originally published 1911, p. 338.

16. Ibid., p. 340.

17. Ibid., p. 341.

18. Ibid., p. 339.

19. bid., p. 340.

20. Alexander, Dr. Eben: *Proof of Heaven*, Simon & Schuster, US, 2012, p. 80.

21. Reich, Wilhelm: *The Mass Psychology Of Fascism*, Mary Boyd Higgins as Trustee of the Wilhelm Reich Infant Trust Fund, 1970. Originally published in 1946, pp. 334-445.

22. Alexander, Dr. Eben: *Proof of Heaven*, Simon & Schuster, US, 2012, p. 95.

23. Ibid., p. 156.

24. Phillips, Graham: *The Moses Legacy*, Sidgwick & Jackson, London, 2002, p. 252.

25. Ibid., p. 252.

26. Alexander, Dr. Eben: *Proof of Heaven*, Simon & Schuster, US, 2012, pp. 38-39.

27. Greene, Brian: *The Elegant Universe*, Vintage 2000, Great Britain, 1999, p. 265.

28. Ibid., p. 265.

29. Ibid., p. 265.

30. Riemann, Bernhard: *Habilitation Dissertation On The Hypotheses That Lie At The Foundation Of Geometry*, 1854. H. Weber, ed. (New York: Dover Publications reprint edition, 1953), p. ?

31. Plato, *Timaeus And Critias*: Penguin Books Ltd, Harmondsworth, Middlesex, England, 1965, p. 46.

32. Zabkar, Louis V.: *Study of the Ba Concept in Ancient Egyptian Texts*. London: The Univ., of Chicago Press, 1968, p. 3.

33. Ibid., p. 162.

34. Ibid., pp. 161-162.

35. Budge, E. A. Wallis: *Osiris & The Egyptian Resurrection*, Dover Publications, NY 1973. Originally published 1911, pp. 348-349.

36. Farrell, Joseph & deHart, Scott D.: *The Grid Of The Gods*, Adventures Unlimited Press, Kempton, Illinois, 2011, p. 277.

37. Schwaller de Lubicz, Rene A.: *Symbol and the Symbolic*, first published 1949; Autumn Press, Brookline, MA., 1978, pp. 32-33.

38. Greenberg, Gary: *The African Origins of the Jewish People*, Carol Publishing Group, Secaucus, NJ, 1996, p. 218.

39. Ibid., p. 271.

40. Coppens, Phillip: *The Canopus Revelation – Stargate of the Gods and the Ark of Osiris*, Frontier Publishing, Enkhuizen, the Netherlands, 2004, p. 87.

41. Sabbah, Messod and Roger: *Secrets Of The Exodus – Did the Pharaohs Write The Bible?* London. Thorsons, An Imprint Of HarperCollinsPublishers, 2000, p. 65.

42. Wikipedia: *Yuya*.

43. Greenberg, Gary: *The African Origins of the Jewish People*, Carol Publishing Group, Secaucus, NJ, 1996, p. 251.

44. Osman, Ahmed: *Stranger In The Valley of the Kings*, Paladin, London, 1987, p. 41.

45. Ibid., p. 131.

46. Greenberg, Gary: *The African Origins of the Jewish People*, Carol Publishing Group, Secaucus, NJ, 1996, p. 218.

47. Massey, Gerald: *The Egyptian Book of the Dead And The Mysteries of Amenta*, T Fisher Unwin, London, 1907, p. 57.

48. Ibid., p. 55.

49. Ibid., p. 57.

50. Ibid., p. 58.

51. Ibid., p. 56.

52. Riemann, Bernhard: *Habilitation Dissertation On The Hypotheses That Lie At The Foundation Of Geometry*, 1854. H. Weber, ed. (New York: Dover Publications reprint edition, 1953), p. ?

53. Radin, Dean: *Entangled Minds*, Paraview, New York, 2006, p. 254.

Notes for Epilogue – A Cosmic Relevation

1. Wikipedia: *Patriarchalism*.

2. Ibid.

3. Ibid.

4. Sabbah, Messod and Roger: *Secrets Of The Exodus – Did the Pharaohs Write The Bible?* London. Thorsons, An Imprint Of HarperCollins*Publishers*, 2000, p. 263.

5. Ibid., p. 179.

6. Ibid., p. 179.

7. Ibid., p. 179.

8. Nexus Magazine: *Editorial*, February & March 2015.

9. Ibid.

10. Ibid.

11. Alexander, Dr. Eben: *Proof of Heaven*, Simon & Schuster, US, 2012, p. 152.

12. Ibid., p. 152.

13. McKenna, Terence: *Food of the Gods*: A Bantam Book, 1992, p. 62.

14. Ibid., p. 62.

15. Du Bois, W. E. Burghardt: *The World And Africa*, International Publishers, New York, 1946; 1947; 1965; & 1978, pp. 35-36.

16. Wikipedia: *Leopold II*.

17. Ibid.

18. Walker, Brian Browne: *The I Ching or Book Of Changes*, St Martin's Press, New York, 1992, p. 53.

19. Velikovsky, Immanuel: *Worlds in Collision*, Pocket Books, New York, 1950, p. 128.

20. Greenberg, Gary: *The African Origins of the Jewish People*, Carol Publishing Group, Secaucus, NJ, 1996, p. 30.

21. Velikovsky, Immanuel: *Worlds in Collision*, Pocket Books, New York, 1950, p. 128.

22. Brandenburg, Jphn E.: *Death On Mars*, Adventures Unlimited Press, Kempton, Ill., 2013, p. 39.

23. Ibid., p. 39.

24. Ibid., p. 39.

25. Ibid., p. 39.

26. Ibid., p. 234.

27. Ibid., p. 254.

28. Ibid., p. 254.

29. Ibid., p. 254.

30. Ibid., pp. 254-255.

31. Ibid., p. 292.

32. Ibid., p. 292.

33. Ibid., p. 291.

34. Scranton, Laird: *The Velikovsky Heresies*, Bear & Company, Rochester, Vermont, 2012, p. 94.

35. Phillips, Graham: *Act of God*, Sidgwick & Jackson, London, 1998, p. 235.

36. Greenberg, Gary: *The African Origins of the Jewish People*, Carol Publishing Group, Secaucus, NJ, 1996, p. 196.

37. Phillips, Graham: *Act of God*, Sidgwick & Jackson, London, 1998, p. 19.

38. Velikovsky, Immanuel: *Worlds in Collision*, Pocket Books, New York, 1950, p. 67.

39. Scranton, Laird: *The Velikovsky Heresies*, Bear & Company, Rochester, Vermont, 2012, p. 130.

40. Sitchin, Zecharia: *Journeys to the Mythical Past*, Bear & Company, Rochester, Vermont, 2007, p. 214.

Bibliography

Alexander, Dr. Eben: **Proof of Heaven**, Simon & Schuster, US, 2012.

Alford, Alan F.: **When the Gods Came Down – The Catastrophic Roots of Religion Revealed**. Hodder & Stoughton, London. 2000.

Bernal, Martin: **Black Athena**, Rutgers University Press, 1991.

Bauval, Robert & Brophy, Thomas: **Black Genesis**, Bear & Company, Rochester, Vermont, 2011.

Bauval, Robert & Brophy, Thomas: **Imhotep, The African, Architect Of The Cosmos**, Disinformation Books, An Imprint of Red Wheel/Weuiser LLC, San Francisco, 2013.

Bauval, Robert & Hancock, Graham: **Keeper Of Genesis**, Reed Consumer Books Ltd, London, 1996.

Bonnet, Charles & Valbellte, Doninique: **The Nubian Pharaohs – Black Kings on the Nile**, The American Press in Cairo, New York.

Brandenburg, John E.: **Death On Mars**, Adventures Unlimited Press, Kempton, Illinois. 2015.

Budge, E. A. Wallis: **The Gods of the Egyptians or Studies in Egyptian Mythology, Vol. II**, Dover Publications, Inc., 180 Varick, Street, NY, 1969 originally published 1904.

Budge, E. A. Wallis: **Osiris & The Egyptian Resurrection**, Dover Publications, NY 1973. Originally published 1911.

Capra, Fritjof: **The Tao of Physics**, a Bantam book / published by arrangement with Shambhala Publications, Inc., 1976.

Carus, Paul: **Chinese Thought**, New York: Open Court Press, 1907.

Chandler, Wayne B: **Ancient Future**, Black Classic Press, 1999.

Chomsky, Noam, **The Chomsky Reader**, Pantheon House, a division of Random House, New York, 1987.

Clayton, Peter: **Chronicle of the Pharaohs**, Thames & Hudson Ltd., 1994.

Collins, Andrew: **Göbekli Tepe – Genesis of the Gods**, Bear & Company, Rochester, Vermont, 2014.

Coppens, Phillip: **The Canopus Revelation – Stargate of the Gods and the Ark of Osiris**, Frontier Publishing, Enkhuizen, the Netherlands, 2004.

Creighton, Scott: **The Secret Chamber of Osiris**, Bear & Company, Rochester, Vermont, 2015.

Darkwah, Nana Banchie: **The Africans Who Wrote The Bible – Ancient Secrets Africa and Christianity Have Never Told**, Aduana Publishing Book, White Plains, 2003.

Diop, Cheikh Anta: **The African Origin of Civilization: Myth or Reality.** Paris: Presence Africaine, 1955 and 1967. Translated and edited by Lawrence Hill & Co., Publisher, Inc., 1974.

Diop, Chiekh Anta: **The Cultural Unity Of Black Africa**, Third World Press, Chicago, Il. 1959. English edition 1963.

Diop, Chiekh Anta: **Civilization Or Barbarism**, Lawrence Hill Books, New York, 1991.

Director, Bruce: **Riemann for Anti-Dummies**, www.wlym.com/antidummies/parts1(-69).html.

D'Souza, Dinesh: **America - Imagine A World Without Her**, Regnery Publishing, Washington, D.C., 2014.

Du Bois, W. E. Burghardt: **The World And Africa**, International Publishers, New York, 1946; 1947; 1965; & 1978.

Ellis, Ralph: **Thoth – Architect Of The Universe**, Edfu Books, Cheshire, 1997.

Ellis, Ralph: **Jesus, Last Of The Pharoahs**, Edfu Books, Cheshire, 1998.

Ellis, Ralph: **Solomon – Falcon Of Sheba**, Edfu Books, Cheshire, 2002.

Ellis, Ralph: **Eden In Egypt**, Edfu Books, Cheshire, 2004.

Ellis, Ralph: **Scota – Egyptian Queen Of The Scots**, Edfu Books, Cheshire, 2006.

Farrell, Joseph: **Babylon's Banksters**, Feral House, Port Townsend, WA, 2010.

Farrell, Joseph: **Financial Vipers of Venice**, Feral House, Port Townsend, WA, 2010.

Farrell, Joseph & de Hart, Scott D.: **The Grid Of The Gods**, Adventures Unlimited Press, Kempton, Illinois, 2011.

Farrell, Joseph & de Hart, Scott D.: **Yahweh The Two-Faced God: Theology, Terrorism & Topology**, Periprometheus Press, 2011.

Farrell, Joseph & de Hart, Scott D.: **Transhumanism**, Feral House, Port Townsend, WA, 2011.

Farrell, Joseph: **Thrice Great Hermetica and the Janus Age,** Adventures Unlimited Press, Kempton, Illinois, 2014.

Gardiner, Alan: **Egypt of the Pharaohs**, Oxford, England: The Clarendon Press, 1961.

Gardiner, Laurence: **Lost Secrets of The Sacred Ark**, Element, Hammersmith, London, 2003.

Greenberg, Gary: **The Moses Mystery - The African Origins of the Jewish People**, Carol Publishing Group, Secaucus, NJ, 1996.

Greenberg, Joseph: **Languages of Africa**, The Hague: Indiana University, 1966.

Greene, Brian: **The Elegant Universe**, Vintage 2000, Great Britain, 1999.

Griff, Professor: **The Psychological Covert War On Hip Hop**, Heir To The Shah, Atlanta, GA. 2011.

Hancock, Graham: **Heaven's Mirror**, Penguin Books, London, 1998.

Hancock, Graham: **Mysteries of the Ancient Past**, Bear & Company, Rochester, Vermont, 2012.

Herald Examiner: **Ancient Nubia: Where Kings Began**, Los Angeles, 7 March, 1979.

Hislop, Rev. Alexander: **The Two Babylons**, A&B Publishers Group, Brooklyn, New York, undated.

James, George G. M.: **Stolen Legacy**, Julian Richardson Associates, *Publishers*, San Francisco. 1954.

Koestler, Arthur: **The Thirteenth Tribe**, Popular Library, a unit of CBS Publications, the Consumer Publishing Division of CBS, Inc., by arrangement with Random House, Inc., 1978.

Kramer, Samuel Noah: **The Sumerians – Their History, Culture, And Character**, The University Press of Chicago, 1963.

LaRouche, Lyndon H.: **The Children of Satan**, Lyndon LaRouche PAC, Leesburg, VA, 2004.

Mac Ritchie, David: **Ancient And Modern Britons**, First published by Kegan Paul, Trench & Co., London, 1884.

Malkowski, Edward F: **The Spiritual Technology of Ancient Egypt**, Inner Traditions, Rochester, Vermont, 2007.

Malkowski, Edward F: **Ancient Egypt 39,000 BCE**, Bear & Company, Rochester, Vermont, 2010.

Malkowski, Edward F: **Return Of The Golden Age**, Inner Traditions, Rochester, Vermont, 2014.

Massey, Gerald: **The Egyptian Book of the Dead And The Mysteries of Amenta**, T Fisher Unwin, London, 1907.

Mbiti, John S.: **African Religions and Philosophy**, U.S.A.: Anchor Books, 1970.

McKenna, Dennis & Terence: **The Invisible Landscape**: First published in 1975 by Seabury Press.

McKenna, Terence: **Food of the Gods**: A Bantam Book, 1992.

Morenz, Siegried: **Egyptian Religion**, W. Kolhammer GmbH., 1960. English translation by Cornell Univ., Press 1973.

Narby, Jeremy: **The Cosmic Serpent – DNA and the Origins of Knowledge**, Orion Books Ltd., London. 1998.

National Geographic: **The Black Pharaohs**, February 2008.

National Geographic: **The Birth of Religion**, June 2011.

National Geographic: **The First Artists**, June 2015.

Nexus Magazine: **Editorial**, February & March 2015.

O'Connor, David; Cline, Eric: **Amenhotep III: Perspectives on His Reign**: University of Michigan Press, 1998.

Osman, Ahmed: **Stranger In The Valley of the Kings**, Paladin, London, 1987.

Osman, Ahmed: **The Lost City Of The Exodus**, Bear & Company, Rochester, Vermont, 2014.

Phillips, Graham: **Act of God**, Sidgwick & Jackson, London, 1998.

Phillips, Graham: **The Moses Legacy**, Sidgwick & Jackson, London, 2002.

Plato: **The Portable Plato – The Republic**: Viking Press, Inc. Ltd., 1948.

Plato: **Timaeus And Critias**. Penguin Books Ltd, Harmondsworth, Middlesex, England, 1965.

Radin, Dean: **Entangled Minds**, Paraview, New York, 2006.

Ravalec, Mallendi & Paicheler: **Iboga – The Visionary Roof African Shamanism**: Park Street Press, Rochester, Vermont, 2004.

Reich, Wilhelm: **The Mass Psychology Of Fascism**, Mary Boyd Higgins as Trustee of the Wilhelm Reich Infant Trust Fund, 1970. Originally published in 1946.

Riemann, Bernhard: **Habilitation Dissertation On The Hypotheses That Lie At The Foundation Of Geometry**, 1854. H. Weber, ed. (New York: Dover Publications reprint edition, 1953),

Riemann, Bernhard: **Matter of Mind**, ref: Larouche Pac Video Archive.

Rumi: **Rumi's Little Book of Life**, Hampton Roads Publications Company, Inc., Charlottesville, VA, 2012,

Sabbah, Messod and Roger: **Secrets Of The Exodus – Did the Pharaohs Write The Bible?** London. Thorsons, An Imprint Of HarperCollins*Publishers*, 2000.

Schoch, Robert M.: **Forgotten Civilization**, Inner Traditions Rochester, Vermont, 2012.

Schonberger, Martin: **The I Ching & the Genetic Code – The Hidden Key To Life**, ASI Publishers Inc., 1979. Originally published 1973, O. W. Barth Berlag, Muchen.

Schwaller de Lubicz, Rene A.: **Sacred Science – The King of Pharaonic Theocracy**, Inner Traditions International, Ltd., New York, 1961.

Schwaller de Lubicz, Rene A.: **The Temple In Man**, first published 1949; Autumn Press, Brookline, MA., 1977.

Schwaller de Lubicz, Rene A.: **Symbol and the Symbolic**, first published 1949; Autumn Press, Brookline, MA, 1978.

Schwaller de Lubicz, Rene A.: **The Egyptian Miracle**, first published by Flammation, Paris 1963; Inner Traditions International, Ltd., New York, 1985.

Schwaller de Lubicz, Rene A.: **The Temple of Man**, first published 1957; Inner Traditions International, Rochester, Vermont, 1998.

Scranton, Laird: **The Science Of The Dogon**, Inner Traditions, Rochester, Vermont, 2002.

Scranton, Laird: **Sacred Symbols Of The Dogon**, Inner Traditions, Rochester, Vermont, 2007.

Scranton, Laird: **The Cosmological Origins of Myth and Symbol**, Inner Traditions, Rochester, Vermont, 2010.

Scranton, Laird: **The Velikovsky Heresies**, Bear & Company, Rochester, Vermont, 2012.

Scranton, Laird: **China's Cosmological Prehistory**, Inner Traditions, Rochester, Vermont, 2014.

Scranton, Laird: **Point of Origin**, Inner Traditions, Rochester, Vermont, 2015.

Sinclair, Neil M. C.: **The Tiger Bay Story**, Butetown History & Arts, Cardiff, 1993.

Sitchin, Zecharia: **The 12th Planet**, Bear & Company, Santa Fe, NM, 1976.

Sitchin, Zecharia: **The Stairway To Heaven**, Bear & Company, Santa Fe, NM, 1980.

Sitchin, Zecharia: **The Wars Of Gods And Men**, Bear & Company, Santa Fe, NM, 1985.

Sitchin, Zecharia: **Journeys to the Mythical Past**, Bear & Company, Rochester, Vermont, 2007.

Soggin, John: (1998 [tr. 1999]), **An Introduction to the History of Israel and Judah**, SCM Press.

Tellinger, Michael: **African Temples Of The Anunnaki – The Lost Technologies of the Gold Mines of Enki,** Bear & Company, Rochester, Vermont, 2009.

Temple, Robert: **The Sirius Mystery**, Random House, London, 1998.

Velikovsky, Immanuel: **Worlds in Collision**, Pocket Books, New York. 1950.

Velikovsky, Immanuel: **Oedipus And Akhenaton – Myth and History**, Doubleday & Company, Inc. Garden City, New York. 1960.

Velikovsky, Immanuel: **Peoples Of The Sea**, Doubleday & Company, Inc. Garden City, New York. 1977.

Vidal, Gore: **Perpetual War for Perpetual Peace**, Thunder's Mouth Press, New York, 2002.

Vidal, Gore: **Dreaming War**, Thunder's Mouth Press, New York, 2002.

Walker, Brian Browne: **The I Ching or Book Of Changes**, St Martin's Press, New York, 1992.

Walter, Katya: **Tao Of Chaos – DNA & The I Ching**, Element Books, Great Britain 1996.

Wallach, Joel D., Lan, Ma, & Schrauzer, Gerhard N., **Epigenetics**, SelectBooks, Inc., New York, 2014.

West, John Anthony: **Serpent In The Sky**, Harper & Row Publishers, New York, 1979.

Wilhelm, Hellmut: **Change – Eight Lectures on the I Ching**, Bollingen Foundation, New York, 1960.

Zabkar, Louis V.: **Study of the Ba Concept in Ancient Egyptian Texts**. London: The Univ., of Chicago Press, 1968.

www.ingramcontent.com/pod-product-compliance
Lightning Source LLC
Chambersburg PA
CBHW071329280526
45787CB00001B/44